D0025132

SOUTHERN HUNTING IN BLACK AND WHITE

SOUTHERN HUNTING IN BLACK AND WHITE

NATURE, HISTORY, AND RITUAL

IN A CAROLINA COMMUNITY

Stuart A. Marks

For Helen,

All your hardwork has finally paid
off. Hope you enjoy the final product!

Love,

[signature]
1991

PRINCETON UNIVERSITY PRESS   PRINCETON, NEW JERSEY

Copyright © 1991 by Princeton University Press
Published by Princeton University Press, 41 William Street,
Princeton, New Jersey 08540
In the United Kingdom: Princeton University Press, Oxford

All Rights Reserved

Library of Congress Cataloging-in-Publication Data
Marks, Stuart A., 1939–
Southern hunting in black and white : nature, history, and ritual
in a Carolina community / Stuart A. Marks.
p.   cm.
Includes bibliographical references and index.
ISBN 0-691-09452-7 (cloth : acid free paper)
ISBN 0-691-02851-6 (paper : acid free paper)
1. Hunting—North Carolina. 2. Hunting—Social aspects—North
Carolina. 3. Hunting—North Carolina—Longitudinal studies.
4. Social classes—North Carolina. 5. North Carolina—Social life
and customs. 6. Social status—North Carolina. 7. North Carolina—
Race relations.   I. Title.
SK113.M37   1991
306.4'83—dc20   90-44683

Sources of Epigraphs: The interview with William Faulkner that begins chapter 1
is reprinted from *Faulkner in the University*, ed. F. Gwynn and J. Blotner,
The University Press of Virginia, 1959
The quote by Dickson D. Bruce, Jr., that begins chapter 2 is reprinted with
permission of *The Mississippi Quarterly*, where it appeared in vol. 30, p. 281
The quote by John B. Burnham that begins chapter 3 is reprinted from
North American Review 226 (September 1928):300
The passage from William Faulkner's *Big Woods* that begins chapter 6
is reprinted with permission of Random House

This book has been composed in Linotron Times Roman

Princeton University Press books are printed on acid-free paper,
and meet the guidelines for permanence and durability of the
Committee on Production Guidelines for Book Longevity
of the Council on Library Resources

Printed in the United States of America by Princeton University Press,
Princeton, New Jersey

10   9   8   7   6   5   4   3   2   1
10   9   8   7   6   5   4   3   2   1
(Pbk.)

Contents

PART TWO: ON INTERPRETING THE PRESENT

Five
Fox Field Trials: Separating the Men from the Boys by

Six
Horned Heads and Twitching Tails: An Interpretation of

Seven

Eight
Small Game for Large Numbers: Stalking Squirrels and

List of Illustrations

At chapter openings:

Following Chapter 5:

List of Tables

Preface _____

WHEN I BEGAN this study in 1977, I had no single theoretical design or preconceived expectation about what I would find nor of how to bind my findings together. What I had was a Southern heritage, an early socialization in hunting under my father's tutelege, a "distance" cultivated by my youth and researches abroad, a curiosity about how hunting was linked with life and livelihoods in the community where I lived, and the need to connect what I spent most of my time doing—teaching at a small liberal arts college—with my larger interests and concerns.

The study began with hunters providing me with basic information about why animals and hunting were special to them. These initial explorations involved interviews and observations on deer hunters by several undergraduate students and me. Crucial at this stage, student participation in an out-of-classroom exercise contributed a critical mass of enthusiasm that got the project off the ground until fellowships granted me more time for research and reflection. Like the weather and relationships, hunting was a common topic in the daily conversations of men. Most of them had never given much thought to the topic of hunting, tacitly accepting it as part of their socialization as men and as an appropriate way to spend their leisure time. Hunters knew that I planned to write a book about them. Finding individuals who wished to tell hunting stories was easy compared to locating those willing to explicate the details of their hunting traditions within the context of their lives. But such interviews and observations comprise the core of this study.

The search for explanations led me beyond what I was witnessing afield. I read widely in Southern literature, history, politics, poetry, journals—I even searched archival materials—for clues and themes to synthesize my growing volume of words. The continuous interaction between observations, interviews, questions, and readings suggested new ways of asking and looking. As a masculine repository of individual and social constructions, hunting is an invaluable lode. Learning from and about it becomes an indeterminant process as long as one remains a participant. In 1984 I left the community that had meant home to my family for the previous fourteen years, and this departure brought closure to my interactive study.

The information I accumulated includes over nine hundred pages of field notes acquired through participation and observation with whites, blacks, and Lumbee Indians within Scotland County, North Carolina. I used these ethnographic details to form the basis for interpreting behavior and for relating the details to the broader tensions and frictions of community life. Individuals were contacted primarily through network interviewing. The process began with a sample of names drawn from hunting-license purchasers, and with acquaintances. These individuals suggested I contact their neighbors and friends, who in turn suggested others, until the networks melded into each other. I also joined hunting clubs (deer and raccoon), attended field events (fox, coon, dove), and participated in specific forays (for quail, rabbits, squirrels).

A second source of information consists of the materials I reviewed in local, state, and university archives. Although these collections were not specifically catalogued for hunting, there were occasional descriptions and references to the meaning, timing, and types of hunts in some of the papers. Such fragments, combined with a sense of Southern history, allowed me to ground the interpretations of the sporting texts in chapters 2 and 3. Certain pursuits of wildlife owe their social ranking and legitimacy to the myths of Southern gentility, traditions often accepted and perpetuated by Yankees and wealthy others. My search through the records of the past uncovered other ironies and paradoxes that are not likely to be tapped through oral sources. Local records in the county courthouse and printed in the local newspaper often provided the necessary substance for individual activities and suppositions.

A third source was a questionnaire I personally gave to a random sample of seventy-eight hunting-license purchasers during 1979. This sample, stratified by age, race, and location, provides a profile for further discussions on current attitudes and activities. This sampling connected me with hunters whom I probably would have missed otherwise, and their responses, summarized in chapter 4, suggest the continuity of some traditional sentiments.

My final source of information comes from some two thousand pages of transcribed conversations and interviews taken afield or with hunters reminiscing about their forays and what these excursions meant to them. These interviews and stories provide my point of departure in Part Two. I selected and edited these dialogues with care, wishing to preserve the flavor of individual voices and experiences. The words are those of hunters. I provide anonymity to the speakers by changing their names, but have described their status and role if they were important for context. I have occasionally rearranged phrases and omitted the normal conversational digressions, if these changes increased coherence. Many of these interviews and field notes are deposited in the Southern Historical Collection, the University of North Carolina at Chapel Hill.

These sources form the basis for the cultural analysis in subsequent chapters. I have sought out the behavior and words of hunters not in order to criticize them or disapprove, but to understand. The process has allowed me to confront my socialization as a Southerner, as a Tarheel, and as an academic; my training in the sciences and in the humanities; my comparative studies here and abroad; and it helped me reaffirm or resist some resolutions.

The study has affirmed my belief that individual abilities can transcend the tyranny of what is in vogue and resist the tribalization of knowledge now prevalent in academic life.

Wild animals have always played an important role in human existence, subsistence, survival, and well-being. They have been consumed as food, domesticated as beasts of burden, enjoyed as pets, and employed as symbols in human thought and ritual. In some preliterate societies, people have identified with the wild animals they hunt for food, and through their rituals they have celebrated the interrelatedness of life. Within the Western world, a major shift in such sensibilities occurred within the Judeo-Christian and Cartesian traditions, which insisted on the condemnation of animal idolatry and on the clean separation of human and animal domains. This shift led to the despiritualization of nature and its creatures, to the conception of people in a "supernatural" image, and to the relegation of animals as objects for materialistic exploitation. Stripped of any attributes they may previously have shared with humans, both wild and domesticated creatures became victims of exploitations unrestrained by the burdens of earlier traditions. Despite this sea change in Western sensibility, some of the old ideas survived, to be incorporated into the more humane attitudes of recent times. These attitudes are resurfacing at a time when human and animal spheres have been delineated and separated in space and by culture, and when the human domain has domesticated if not swamped that of the wild. The strongholds of these sensibilities are often found in the cities, where human contacts with animals, mainly those kept as pets or in zoos, serve as models and metaphors for what people presume would be their relationships in the wild.

This book is about utilitarian traditions and their transitions in the countryside, with a focus on hunters. The earlier embodiments of aristocratic pretenses, with their patterns and practices of prestige, largesse, and wealth by exclusion, have given way to more democratic, if not more ephemeral, modes. Furthermore, the complex interplay between individuals, local lifestyles, and land that contributed so much to the meaning of these pursuits in the past is being eclipsed by more corporate and cosmopolitan endeavors. This book, then, is about aspects of selfhood, about men, about metaphors of meaning, about power, and about display. It is also about winning and losing, and the form they can take on a small postage stamp of Southern landscape.

Acknowledgments _____

No BOOK is an individual endeavor. It is a social product and a testimony to others, who, in the midst of their busy schedules, take time to listen and to answer questions, to tolerate another's presence, to share experiences and stories. Consequently, I have accumulated many debts in the preparation of this volume, which represents over a decade of readings, musings, struggles, and conversations with friends, colleagues, strangers, and detractors.

As an interdisciplinary endeavor, my quest led to a few encounters with turf defenders. These "game keepers"—some adamant, others more constructively helpful—are due some recognition for lessons I learned. They taught me endurance, persistence, humility, trust in my intuition, new ways of looking at things—all qualities that contributed to the merit of the quest.

With even more gratitude I acknowledge those whose timely support made possible both the research and the writing. A year's grant for independent research from the National Endowment for the Humanities in 1977 (postponed until 1979) provided me with the initial opportunity for consolidating and furthering the studies I had begun with students. This support was followed later by a grant from the Harry Frank Guggenheim Foundation and from the Wenner-Gren Foundation for Anthropological Research, the latter enabling me to travel and review archival materials. Colleagues at St. Andrews Presbyterian College are due thanks for their influence and votes that granted me some financial assistance during the summers and leaves from teaching. A summer fellowship in 1986 at the Yale Center for British Art allowed me to spend a month using its Photographic Archive and Rare Book Collection on British Sporting Art. A fellowship year at the National Humanities Center in 1984–85 supported a shift from research to writing. My residence at the Center materially improved the quality of my writing and reflection through my daily contacts and discussions with other scholars in residence. The Harry Frank Guggenheim Foundation provided additional funds in 1987–88 so I could complete and revise the manuscript. I edited the final version while affiliated with the Institute for the Arts and the Humanities and with the Institute for Research in Social Science, the University of North Carolina at Chapel Hill.

To residents of Scotland County, North Carolina, I owe a special debt. Their friendships frequently extended beyond those given curious inquirers. In no particular order, I wish to thank specially the following: Joe Carpenter, Sr., Joe Carpenter, Jr., C. A. Purcell, James McRae, Ira Pate Lowry, Herbert Crabtree, David Evans, Tom McKinnon, R. F. McCoy, Bob Bullard, Nelson

Malloy, John Smith, Jim Bailey, Payton Gentry, Murdock Smith, Leo McRae, John Willie McNair, James Louis McLean, Maseo McCormack, Willie Fairley, Doug Clark, Tom Asheford, Glynn Paylor, Hubert Clemmons, Gerald Simmons, David Beaver, Jesse Lee, Roy Long, Junior Crouch, James Inman, Jr., Glenn Peacock, Charlie Stone, Phil Morgan, Chris Voss, James Leviner, Bill Newton, Mac Henderson, Lou Henderson, Glynn Grubbs, Edmond Langley, Robert Gordon, Norwood Wooten, Ron Mason, Nathan McCormack, Shaw Locklear, Hector McLean, Dunc Sinclair, Bill Purcell, Larry Benton, Allen Peele, Bobby Smith, Jerry Morgan, Randy Vest, Big John Carthens, David Pridgen, Roy Bostick, Gilbert Singletary, McNair Evans, Edwin Pate, and David Breeden.

Through their enthusiasm and energy, David McCall, Kim Johnson, Kathy Beach, Mark Powell, and Bruce Locklear, all former students at St. Andrews Presbyterian College, helped initiate the field studies. Former colleagues David McLean, Charles Joyner, Gerald Thurmond, Alvin Smith, Jack Roper, and George Melton assisted in many ways.

Finally, it is my delightful duty to thank those personal friends who have helped to make this book better than it otherwise would have been. They read various portions of the manuscript, offering valuable suggestions for corrections and words of encouragement. Kent Mathison, Jim Peacock, George Tindall, Bill Powell, Carlyle Franklin, Lawrence Earley, John Shelton Reed, Forrest McDonald, Jack Wilson, Tim Breen, Jack Roper, Bertram Wyatt-Brown, Peter Weil, John Sinton, Tom Beidelman, Karen Blu—all of them helped in this way. A special thanks goes to Helen Scogin, whose secretarial skills helped keep the momentum of the project alive with her transcriptions of tapes and lengthy conversations. Hers was a privileged earful of masculine gossip and activities within the county. Karen Carrol, Maggie Blades, and the typing pool at the National Humanities Center converted my earlier writing to legibility.

For me, researching this book, stalking its nuances, flushing its meanings, savoring its flavors has been a hunt, if only a symbolic one. The fieldwork, the long hours spent in transcribing and reading notes, the writing and editing have all taken its toll in other ventures missed, relationships not consummated, in peaks of inspiration and valleys of despair. During this time, my sons have graduated from elementary and high school and have become young men on their own. And Martha, dear Martha, was initiated early in our fieldwork among the Bisa in Zambia. She has stood by, watching, waiting, loving, reading, caring for the needs of the family; and as we have scrimped along, she has developed a career of her own in administration and counseling. She knows more about the gestation of this work and the labor involved than the reader ever will. And it is for her and for us that this book is dedicated.

SOUTHERN HUNTING IN BLACK AND WHITE

One

ON METAPHORS AND MODELS

Q. Mr. Faulkner, you seem to put so much meaning in the hunt. Could you tell us why you hunted when you were a little boy, or what meaning the hunt has for you?

A. The hunt was simply a symbol of pursuit. Most of anyone's life is a pursuit of something. That is, the only alternative to life is immobility, which is death. . . I simply told a story which was a natural, normal part of anyone's life in familiar and to me interesting terms without any deliberate intent to put symbolism in it. I was simply telling something which was in this case the child—the need, the compulsion of the child to adjust to the adult world. It's how he does it, how he survives it, whether he is destroyed by trying to adjust to the adult world or whether despite his small size he does adjust within his capacity. And always to learn something, to learn something of—not only to pursue but to overtake and then to have compassion not to destroy, to catch, to touch, and then let go because then tomorrow you can pursue again. If you destroy it, what you caught, then it's gone, it's finished. And that to me is sometimes the greater part of valor but always it's the greater part of pleasure, not to destroy what you have pursued. The pursuit is the thing, not the reward, not the gain.

(Interview with William Faulkner, in *Faulkner in the University*)

I AM INTERESTED in what animals mean to people and have chosen to study hunters, an important group within the context of a Southern community. The ways hunters, as individuals and as groups, relate to animals are keys that unlock some of the meanings in their social relations and in their lives. A man's position within a social group is an integral part of his self-image and identity. If he is a hunter, this image is buttressed with signs of land, firearms, special vehicles and equipment, dogs and trophies, together with club memberships and choices of partners. All these objects and choices are intimately interwoven and embroidered into the individual's identity and "selfhood."[1]

"Southern hunting in black and white" is a metaphor that helps my understanding of the dialectics and processes in this arena of community life whose traditions I have studied and shared. In their writings, anthropologists often use objects to capture a particular essence of a culture. In his *Forest of Symbols*, Victor Turner conveys the wide range of meanings that trees and plants have for the Ndembu of Zambia as they seek to contextualize health, strength, and productivity. For E. E. Evans-Pritchard, the spear is a metaphor to portray the idealized self among the Nuer of the Sudan. The spear exaggerates those personal traits—strength, speed, potency, permanence, the ability to command respect and to control the surroundings—to which its owner and other men aspire. In a similar manner, the many trappings, behaviors, and happenings of the chase frame and express the status and identity of those who pursue wildlife.[2]

The pursuit of prey is a major divide among these hunters. Scratch below the surface of any veteran raccoon, quail, fox, rabbit, or deer hunter and differences of caste, ethnicity, work, and life-style may be revealed. Individual choices of work, self, and community are anchored if not summarized in these recreational pursuits. These men may be Southerners, Tarheels (inhabitants of North Carolina), and members of the same community, but conceptions of what they are all about show in their methods and in their targets. Each species of game pursued is a marker, a visible bit of social differentiation.

Given the peculiarities of Southern history, racial/ethnic categories are part of the "figured knots in the lacework ribbon of social relations," to borrow a metaphor from Rhys Isaac. These boundaries often dictate who hunts with whom, what is hunted, the methods employed, and the relationships formed and sustained during and after a quest. Immediately adjacent to the community I studied is the homeland of the Lumbees, an Amerindian group that has carved out its own world of meanings, separate from that of blacks and whites. Their influences on hunting in the Carolina county of my study are not always direct or large, but they are still important. The majority of hunters within the county are white, and my materials for them are both extensive and rich. The unevenness of my information is an unavoidable consequence of living within a triracial community, wherein the races intermingle but mostly lead separate lives. Distances between them are perpetuated by various degrees of mutual suspicion and hostility. Given this background, my whiteness and frequent participation in white hunts, essential for gaining depth into my subjects, created some distance from other groups. My awareness of these barriers led me to search through surveys, interviews, and other means to overcome this social distance. Race is an important social discriminator, whether self- or other-ascribed, in this neck of the woods, and I use racial designations when they add substance to the attitudes and acts described.[3]

"Black and white" also serves as a model similar to that of a diagnostic X-ray portraying the bony structure of social relationships beneath the visible worlds of behavior and expressed thought. These bony structures are seldom apparent in everyday life, yet they are the stuff of scholarly discourse. They are experienced through the categories of culture, roles, and institutions, and through the boundaries that people place around their definitions of "we" and "they." The margins of these boundaries and categories are constantly moving, like the shifting sands, piled around the more enduring breakwaters of social structures and then eroded away and exposed by the changing currents of dramatic events. The problem with all analyses is that one must capture some of this constant negotiation—the essence of social processes—to grasp its eddies of change.[4]

My methods were ethnographic, that is, I recorded as completely as possible what I heard and observed, and used the language of those who permitted my participation in their lives and activities. Metaphors belong to and are understood by those who express their meaning within their daily lives. Like myths, metaphors are the graphics through which people control and expand their universe. Models are imposed from the outside; they belong to the monologue of knowledge, not to the indescribably intricate world they radically simplify by flattening it to the written page. Models are constructed from the truncated experiences and visions of observers and scholars. For me the tensions between these two modes of understanding remain. For expediency, I seek a blending of metaphors and models, letting the actors speak for themselves within the confines allowed for unity and clarity.

Hunting as an Ecology of Meanings

For many Southern men living in or close to rural landscapes, hunting is a passion. It is something that comes with the air and with the land and with the people who live there. Hunting is woven into the very fabric of personal and social history. Through participation, these men celebrate their relations with others, differentiate between themselves and animals, and observe their connections to the land. Through their learning, reciting, and contributions to hunting stories, men bend the beasts and circumstances to time-tested movements of body and verse. William Faulkner's eloquence to the contrary, the actual pursuit is but one of hunting's potent expressions.

For many men, hunting is the quintessential masculine activity, for it links their youth, when they were just learning about becoming men, with their presents (presence). It recalls that early learning, often under the tutelage of their fathers, the close associations of men engaged in a common pursuit, the triumphs over subjects capable of evasion, the mastery over technology and dogs, and the pleasures associated with the land. It recasts the stories of wild animals, of dogs, and of landscapes, and of people deeply etched into the conceptual imaginations of youth. To engage in hunting is to emulate, to defend, and to advocate what is a tried, proven, and proper way of becoming and being a man.

Hunting is also a way by which some men reaffirm their masculine identities. This is especially true today. Unlike their fathers, men today live in a world where the lines of demarcation between the sexes are blurred and where the presumptions of male "superiority" are being questioned. There are some women who also hunt and participate in the chase alongside men, but such incursions usually occur only within certain groups, in particular pursuits, or inside circumscribed conditions. Such anomalies are easily dismissed by men who seek more secure gender affirmations through their choice of group, target, and turf. In some forms of hunting the old order persists.

For these men, hunting is a timeless activity, for when the game is killed, butchered, and served, men still command the homeside turf as providers and benefactors. At a more inclusive level, skills of the chase allow these men to demonstrate their divergence and independence. The fact that they can still hunt, as their ancestors did, is "proof" that they will survive even if the rest of the world were to collapse.

Hunting is part of a man's commitment to locale and supports his other obligations to family, church, work, and friends. Like marriage, hunting is a way of integrating a newcomer into a rural community. It allows residents the opportunity to assess the stranger's behavior and to assign him to a known category of persons. In some circles, getting into the right group is important for sustaining one's reputation and source of livelihood. Therefore, if the stranger is not a hunter, it is unlikely that he will acquire the standing necessary to accomplish other things within the community. As a seasonal recreation and as a bastion of masculinity, hunting in many rural Southern communities persists as a product of history and of its associations within regional myths and values.

Through hunting, men enlist the past in the present, yet these pretenses are more than simply the survival of previous forms. Humans incorporate new ideas and novel types of technology into their pursuits and in the process may experience something new; therefore, the present is not necessarily a photocopy of the past. The past provides not a set of transcendent and immutable forms but rather a historically generated and malleable agenda of ideas, activities, and artifacts through which individuals cope with their moments. As with any ritual performance, to hunt is to demonstrate the potency of the past in an attempt to structure the future. Yet any attempt to structure that future in terms of that past puts its categories at risk. Traditions survive because they bend and blend with the times.[5]

Beyond affirming roles and perpetuating traditions, hunters serve an important predatory purpose. Like other predators, they cull back nature's production to numbers that can survive during the leaner months of a year.[6]

Perspectives help frame, momentarily if inadequately, human acts and sayings. As performed by some players on the neighborhood field and on more distant turf, hunting is about power. One need not be a Marxist to realize that the distribution of wealth, power, and prestige reinforces a multitude of social and cultural phenomena. Through its regulatory agencies, the state has emerged as the greatest holder and arbiter of power. Consequently, exercizing and putting to use one's organizational skills before legislative bodies has the potential for changing the name of the "game" and how it may be played. As an economic statement, sport hunting celebrates a transformation from humankind's earlier dependency upon nature, a condition that has prevailed for most of our existence. This evolutionary history is captured in Thorstein Veblen's observation that consumption, not production, has become the means by which people in industrialized nations define themselves.[7]

Like folklore, hunting appropriates parts of the "natural" universe and makes them a part of the "human" world. Except in men's minds, these worlds are never far apart, for the prey sought afield bears the stamp of human endeavors just as surely as those in pursuit. Stories and crafts draw people deeper into relationships with the places and life around them, and the use of local events and materials makes them significant. Folklife statements are often punctuated at the beginnings and endings of stories, and by the intensified language depicting wild animals, dogs, landscapes, and people, together with specialized vocabularies and productions. Through their ritualistic use of food, crafts, sounds, costumes, contests, and possessions, people everywhere enact conflicts, demonstrate shared experiences, and formalize their identities, be they of place, race, or grace. By contributing new names and nuances, people annotate their surroundings, building upon inherited glossaries while reclothing and reinvesting their landscapes with meanings. As Robert Ruark's Old Man was fond of saying, "the best part of hunting and fishing was the thinking about going and the talking about it after you got back. You just had to have the actual middle as a basis of conversation and to put some meat in the pot."[8]

In hunting, humans engage in activities of heavy significance. Their actions and thoughts are meaningful and connected to other things. Enculturation provides the ability to read these cultural emblems for the myriad meanings implied through the contents and conditions of their use. A person socialized in hunting reads its symbols for their formal, explicit signs as well as for their implicit meanings of rank and power, of wealth and status, of the boundaries between "us" and "them" that participants declare by the tone of their voice and by their actions, by the style of their clothes and by their dispositions, and through their use of space and time. Cultural empathy comes from deciphering words and artifacts, interpreting gestures appropriately for their implied significance, knowing a jibe from a joke, and reading social behavior for its multiplicity of meanings. One's cultural identity revolves around this recognition in role and ritual, in symbol and sign, in myth and metaphor. Ethnography is the craft of learning what to ask, the art of discovering the kinds of questions that generate meaning. Since there can be no singular interpretation, particularism and historical grounding are essential.[9]

Given this entangled background, what is one to make of this lode? For me, hunting provides the challenge of making sense of another, not so different, world; in the process, perhaps, to make a contribution toward the integration of knowledge. My quest is to apprehend, if only momentarily, the meanings of hunters; like the proverbial prey that hunters seek, it jumps conventional disciplinary boundaries, may elude some time-honored strategies, and it might even remain beyond capture.

Just as texts and contexts become shaped over time, hunting forms accumulate authority and mold social relations. History and contrasts often make meanings visible. The Old World aristocratic ideals of pursuit, which some Southern planters sought to emulate in the New World, offer a "subtext" of exclusion. The practical hunting activities of others stand out from these highly stylized performances. Likewise, the intent of the contemporary chase is often found in its conflicts and contrasts with that of other social groups. Through time and tone, I seek to elucidate the human issues in a subject that, like wildlife itself in an industrial society, has been relegated to an undeveloped frontier.

The Pretext of Place

The worlds of individuals and of social experiences may be understood as human constructions, as domains of historically developed categories and evaluations derived from a cultural reservoir of images and texts. We are not usually conscious of these symbols, myths, and rituals because we are immersed in them and because they have become part of our social and individual selves. Insofar as hunting is a social and learned activity, consisting of repetitive rituals, we can examine it like a collection of "texts" in which participants perform and make declarations about themselves and how they perceive their world.[10]

Dramatic and not so dramatic events mesh together in the consciousness and continuity of human social life. Dramatic moments in community life, their stresses and dislocations, are remembered long after they have occurred and may affect and guide behavior during less dramatic times. Coming to grips with the events and "texts" of individual and social life within one Carolina community is to contend also with the broader context of regional myths. As William Faulkner wrote, "The past is never dead. It's not even past."

Places and traditions associated with myths enable people to preserve their pasts.[11]

Place suggests boundaries and particularity, implies the shaping influences of lineage and landscape, affirms the crossroads of circumstances, and marks the experiences of groups and historical periods. Once a feature is named, it is distinguished from all others and marked in the mind. Attach a story to it and the place further serves human purposes. What keeps a place alive is not the preservation of its past per se, but the continual weaving of that past into the present.[12]

Scotland County, North Carolina, is such a place. Its name reveals an Old World legacy, a legacy begun with the influx of Scottish Highlanders into the Cape Fear River valley during the early eighteenth century. A local story has it that as these emigrants were pushing inland, some of them found a sign that proclaimed, "The best land lies 100 miles west of here." The legendary outcome was that those who could read found their way to what was to become the county of Scotland. This pride in education, at least among the upper crust, has been incorporated and institutionalized into subsequent generations. Before becoming a town, Laurinburg was the site of a high school where Professor William Graham Quakenbush taught some men who were destined for prominence. The Laurinburg Institute, founded in 1904 as a black preparatory school, is still run by the McDuffie family. The present generation has witnessed the merger of several other smaller institutions which now comprise St. Andrews Presbyterian College in Laurinburg.[13]

The hegemony of immigrants is visible in the preponderance of Scottish names in the county and in the large number of people, of all races, whose surnames begin with Mac. A strong sense of Presbyterianism remains awash in a subregional sea of Methodists and fundamental Baptists. Outsiders notice the locals' adherence to a doctrine of predestination, knowing and keeping their ascribed place in a hierarchy, and their clannishness. Other legacies and traditions abound within the county's triracial communities, but none is felt more than that for which the county was named.[14]

Although they provide the backdrop for various traditions, the physical features of the county cannot be claimed by any one group. Scotland County was one of the last counties created by the North Carolina General Assembly in 1899. At 319 square miles, it is also one of the smallest. The county's northern boundaries follow the irregularities of the Lumber River and Gum Swamp, while its southern border shows the imposed straight edge of a cartographic survey that separates two states.

Within the county are two distinct physiographic regions. The "Sandhills" constitute the northwestern third. Here the visible rise above the rest of the land and the sandy soils suggest a shoreline formed in the distant past. The "Flatwoods," as the residents call the southern two thirds, is generally level, punctuated with occasional depressions from old lake beds, meteorites, and stream courses. The smaller streams—Gum Swamp, Juniper, Shoe Heel, Leith's, Bridge, and Jordan Creek—drain in a southeasterly direction, eventually emptying into the Lumber and Pee Dee Rivers.[15] These streams show the imprints of previous attempts to harness their energy for human purposes. Today few dams survive, but the names of the entrepreneurs who built them are etched nearby on the county road signs. The county's best farmlands and its municipalities are in the southern section. The north remains sparsely populated, mostly covered by pine forests. Large sections of these forests are in the Sandhills Game Management Area, the site of seasonal hunts and field trials. Many of the roads in the north remain unpaved, evidence that it is the center for recreational, not economic, activities.

As the hub of economic growth and the county seat, Laurinburg is the axis for the major roads and railroads which transect the county. From Aberdeen and Fayetteville in the north, federal highways 15-501 and 401 merge within the city limits before passing beyond into South Carolina. The Seaboard Airline Railway and US 74 pass through Laurinburg, connecting Charlotte to the west with the seaport of Wilmington.

If Laurinburg and Scotland County do not have the coastal-plains sameness of their surroundings, it is because the county was the first to jump on the post-World War II bandwagon of economic and industrial development, and Laurinburg continues to attract the occasional slivers of industrialization. Beyond this good fortune, little distinguishes either the city or its countryside from many others throughout rural North and South Carolina. From the perspective of my study, the county's size and population were just right, enabling me to know and track individuals; it was sufficiently mixed with different peoples and places to provide revealing contrasts; and it was stocked with a diversity of wildlife and game to merit a scholarly stalk.

The Context of County

The town of Laurinburg predates the founding of Scotland County by a quarter century. When incorporated in 1877, the town was named after a prominent, wealthy, and influential Scottish family, and pronounced "boro" similar to the pronunciation of Edinburgh, Scotland. The building of a high school in 1852 and the construction of the Wilmington, Charlotte, and Rutherford Railroad shops in 1861 had already put Laurinburg on the map.

The earliest community developed around Old Laurel Hill Presbyterian Church in 1797. Old Laurel Hill was a thriving commercial center in post-Revolutionary War days. Here Duncan McFarland operated a tavern and stagecoach stop along the New York to New Orleans route. McFarland envisioned great developments for his property and staked it out in small plots, anticipating that his part of the world would rival New York and London as world centers. The Presbyterian churchyard served as the campsite for General William Tecumseh Sherman's troops when they passed through the county in 1865. They spared the church, for their target was nearby at Richmond Mill Dam, the site of Murdock Morrison's gun factory.

The railroad eclipsed the prominence of Old Laurel Hill. By 1861, most of the community had relocated south to Laurel Hill, then a depot along the newly built tracks. Here a turpentine distillery and a tub-manufacturing firm were established, and in the 1870s John McNair built his mercantile store.

West from Laurel Hill is the community of Old Hundred. The area received its name from a miscalculation, for its site was orginally scheduled as the 100-mile marker from the seaport of Wilmington along the projected railroad line. Although this error in location was corrected, Old Hundred retains some notoriety as a point along the longest straight stretch of railroad in the Western Hemisphere.

Astride another railroad track and the South Carolina border is the town of Gibson. Incorporated in 1899, Gibson is the county's smallest municipality. Its history is much older. The town was named for Noah Gibson, a merchant whose brother organized the local Methodist church. Nearby are the ruins of a Quaker town, Rockdale. The residents of this antebellum village left for Indiana when their slave-holding neighbors became intolerant of their divergent views.

Adjacent to fine farmlands, the Welsh communities of Hasty and Johns flourished as railroad stations along the Atlantic Coast Line Railroad. Both settlements had post offices and schools in 1886. Today the rails have been lifted from their rights-of-way, and the few remaining buildings retain little to suggest their more prosperous pasts. Near Johns is the Stewartsville cemetery, the county's oldest (1785) and best-known graveyard. Here the corpses of different races are interred in separate tracts.

Along the Seaboard tracks and US highway 74, immediately east of Laurinburg, is the town of East Laurinburg. At this site, Waverly Mills opened its textile plant near the turn of the twentieth century. Today the imprint of the town's mill-village origins remains. The residences of workers circle the mill, which had its own schools, churches, and stores.

In the northeastern section is the town of Wagram, originally known as Gilchrist. Its environs were settled by Scots during the American Revolution. The community of Spring Hill, along Shoe Heel Creek, preceded Gilchrist. It was renamed Wagram by a local admirer of Napoleon after the Little Corporal's victory in Austria. The Spring Hill Baptist Church, organized around 1813, converted many of the local Scots. Nearby stands the restored octagonal brick building of the Richmond Temperance and Literary Society, one of the first temperance societies when it was organized in 1855.

Near the Lumber River is the Laurinburg-Maxton Airport. Its runways and buildings were built by the federal government during the Second World War.

TABLE 1.1

Population of Scotland County, by Minor Civil Subdivisions, 1900 to 1980, Showing Percent Increase (Decrease) per Decade.

County and Minor Civil Division	1900 (%)	1910 (%)	1920 (%)	1930 (%)	1940 (%)	1950 (%)	1960 (%)	1970 (%)	1980 (%)
Scotland County	12,553	15,363	15,600	20,174	23,232	26,336	25,183	26,929	32,273
	(22.4)	(1.5)	(29.3)	(15.2)	(13.3)	(–4.4)	(6.9)	(19.8)	
Townships:									
Laurel Hill		2,571	3,182	3,398	3,332	3,401	2,923	2,539	3,222
		(23.8)	(6.8)	(–2.0)	(2.1)	(–14)	(–14.0)	(26.9)	
Spring Hill		2,300	2,617	2,907	2,985	2,827	2,488	2,949	3,651
		(13.8)	(11.1)	(2.7)	(–5.3)	(–11.7)	(18.5)	(23.8)	
Stewartsville		6,919	7,455	9,224	11,855	14,482	14,876	16,558	19,070
		(7.7)	(23.7)	(28.5)	(22.1)	(2.7)	(11.3)	(15.1)	
Williamson		3,573	2,346	4,645	5,060	5,626	4,896	4,883	6,330
		(–34.3)	(98.0)	(8.9)	(11.0)	(–10.7)	(–0.3)	(29.6)	
Municipalities:									
East Laurinburg		577	541	813	890	745	695	487	536
		(–6.2)	(50.3)	(9.5)	(–16.3)	(–6.7)	(–29.9)	(10.1)	
Gibson		—	264	417	435	609	501	502	533
			(58.0)	(4.3)	(40.0)	(–17.7)	(0.2)	(6.2)	
Wagram			120	309	388	397	562	718	617
			(77.6)	(25.6)	(2.3)	(41.6)	(27.7)	(–14.1)	
Laurinburg		2,322	2,643	3,312	5,685	7,134	8,242	8,859	11,480
		(13.8)	(26.4)	(71.3)	(25.5)	(15.5)	(7.5)	(29.6)	

Source: General Population Census Bureau and North Carolina Municipal Population.

Today the base is operated by a joint committee from the two towns, and its runways contain intercontinental jets parked between flights. In the northern tip of the county, Camp Mackall serves as the training grounds for soldiers from Fort Bragg, a military reservation in an adjacent county. These military bases, transportation networks, and the traffic within federal, state, and regional bureaucracies connect the county and its citizens to the outside world.

Locally, these linkages to elsewhere are experienced ambivalently. The local Chamber of Commerce uses Laurinburg's accessibility to lure new industries, while emphasizing the insularity of its labor markets from organized unions. Among county residents are world-class millionaires as well as those who have never crossed a county line in any direction. Most residents center on the more parochial and insular of these poles, coming and going and getting more knowledgeable as their means allow.[16]

Since the beginning, the county's population has shown a steady, if uneven, increase. The decade of the 1950s was one of heavy technological and social upheaval as many people were displaced from the land and their tasks

TABLE 1.2
Scotland County Employment, by Industry, 1970 and 1980.

	Numbers Employed	
Industries of Employed Persons	1970	1980
Agriculture, forestry, fisheries	534	341
Mining	8	35
Construction	392	431
Manufacturing	4,305	6,049
Transportation, communications, and other public utilities	540	522
Wholesale trade	246	376
Retail trade	1,277	1,779
Finance, insurance, and real estate	212	376
Business and repair services	86	205
Private households and other personal services	717	470
Entertainment and recreational services	40	33
Hospitals and health services	288	580
Elementary, secondary schools, and colleges	1,116	1,432
Social services, religious and membership organizations	107	144
Legal, engineering, and professional services	144	76
Public administration	221	458
Total employed	10,243	13,307

Sources: U.S. Department of Commerce, Bureau of the Census, 1970 and 1980 (Washington, D.C.: Government Printing Office), tables 123 (1970) and 178 (1980).

in agriculture. Laurinburg and Wagram absorbed some of this influx then, but most people went north for new jobs in the cities. Only Stewartsville Township, which includes Laurinburg, has shown continuous growth (see table 1.1). Agricultural work and ownership have been progressively consolidated into fewer hands (table 1.2).[17]

Today, most county residents find work in manufacturing, in education, and in retail sales. Both population and employment trends illustrate that the more regional dog wags the tail of community enterprise. Similar trends are found in adjacent counties. These shifts have enhanced the positions of those able to take advantage of them; most continue life as their blinkers allow.

In the following chapter I examine the literature for elements that shed light on the Southern hunting experience. The highlights are property and propriety, the distinctions and bounds by which wealthy planters sought to distinguish themselves. Consciously or not, all of us are creatures suspended in webs of thoughts and actions passed down from the distant past. How these cultural continuities, which have faced fundamental economic and political transformations, have endured is the basis for this inquiry into hunting. The ways in which structural changes have affected the rituals are no less important than the ways in which the persistence of the rituals themselves affected the course and pace of the structural changes. The reasons lie immersed beneath the actual practices themselves. It is fitting, therefore, to turn to the hunting narratives of William Elliott, an antebellum Carolina planter, as we probe into those deeper layers of meaning from which this enterprise leaps.

Part One

ON INCORPORATING THE PAST
IN THE PRESENT

Two

Propriety and Property: Hunting, Culture, and Agriculture in Antebellum Carolina

Southerners, like sportsmen everywhere, hunted for pleasure, for the joys of companionship, for the freedom of the field, and the excitement of pursuit. Yet, as with any cultural expression, their narratives of their exploits were constructed in a way that was consistent with their assumptions about human nature, society, and the world. When the Southerner became a hunter, he stepped into a role in which his own natural character was allowed a full expression and on a basis of which he could appreciate his own relationship to a much larger web of existence. He could deal imaginatively with his kinship to the other animals and get, as well, a sense of how one could be a strong-willed actor in a world of order and stability. In describing a hunt, then, the Southern writer made his society's theory of the universe personal and concrete.

(Dickson D. Bruce, Jr., in "Hunting: Dimensions of Antebellum Southern Culture")

AMONG THE EARLIEST and best-known books about sporting life in the antebellum South is William Elliott's *Carolina Sports by Land and Water*.[1] William Elliott (1788–1863) was born into a wealthy plantation-owning family in Beaufort, South Carolina, and, like many of his generation and status, was educated at Harvard College in the North. Upon returning to his native state, he served both in the South Carolina legislature and in the U.S. House of Representatives. He managed his family's plantations, building a reputation as a progressive agriculturalist and as an enthusiastic writer of gentlemanly sports.[2] Despite his position as a prominent cotton planter, Elliott opposed nullification, fought against secession and monoculture, and advocated industry. However, he supported slavery, which he viewed as "sanctioned by religion, conducive to good morals, and useful, nay indispensable"; he opposed Northern meddling, which he considered "wicked, unprovoked, and fanatical."[3]

Wealthy planters such as Elliott sought to emulate, to engage, and to surpass Old World aristocrats with their privileges and refinements in field sports. Planters' attempts to perpetuate aristocratic traditions in the New World against the strong democratic currents of frontier life are preserved in a few hunting narratives, in legislative papers, and in archival documents of the antebellum period. Recurrent themes in these hunting narratives and documents reveal the ideology of wealthy planters and attest to some ways in which they sought to distinguish themselves from other social groups.[4]

William Elliott's Hunting Narratives

To his sporting exploits, William Elliott brings keen animation and gusto. "The sportsman, who gives a true description of his sports," writes Elliott, "*must be an egotist*" (p. 181). For him, only personal experience provided sport its "liveliest expression." After describing the challenges of devil fishing and other aquatic sports along the Atlantic, Elliott begins the second half of his notable volume with a wildcat hunt in the environs of his plantation.

He begins his wildcat sketch apologetically, reminding us of the difficulties inherent in capturing the essence of past adventures. William Elliott chooses his field carefully from among his peers. On this February morning, his field consists of a judge, a doctor, himself, and two neophytes identified by the pseudonyms of Slash and Dash. Included are two drivers, presumably blacks, who manage the dogs and who beat the thickets. For this hunt, he brings a mixture of hounds—four couple (this is eight)—to track the cat, and in case it proves elusive, three pointers and a setter to flush birds, thereby adding variety to the outing. The sportsmen are prepared for either event, charging one barrel of their weapons with buck, the other with bird shot.

Arriving at a thicket, the hounds are let loose and soon find fresh evidence (a half-devoured rabbit) that a cat is about. The sportsmen surround the thicket. The sly cat presents itself to each of the hunters, except Elliott, who fire. After each report, the animated cries of the hounds reveal that the cat did not succumb. Finally Dash succeeds in killing the gaunt cat, whose leopard-like spots do not match the animal at whom the other "veteran" hunters claim they fired. The doctor and magistrate claim they fired on a black cat and that the dogs switched cats during the chase.

The skill of Elliott's hounds has been challenged, and his companions' charges are not taken lightly. Elliott allows his hounds to return to the exact sites where his peers claim their quarries appeared when they fired. When let loose, in both instances, the canine jury returns to the spot where the spotted cat now lies dead.

"Confusion!" says the judge; "must I doubt my own eyes?" The sequel shows, that it is safer to doubt our own senses, than the instinct of a hound; and that *his* inferences from the nose, are less fallible than those from human sight; for the cat, being duly subjected to a post-mortem examination, was found to have been struck by four out of the six shots fired at him—and the doctor's shot, of peculiar size, being lodged in his body, left no doubt of the fact, that the black cat of the doctor and judge was no other than the tawny cat of the rest of the field. (pp. 160–61)

With this challenge successfully rebuffed, the dead cat is stored in the fork of an oak. The hunt continues, interrupted by an occasional flush of partridge or rabbit, toward a thick, impenetrable gall. Here the hunters suspect another cat, for by their cries the hounds announce they are on the track of something special. The thicket is so dense that the hunters are unable to glimpse the quarry, and the fear of a quagmire keeps them on the thicket's edge. Suddenly the dogs halt and by their change in voice announce they have the chase at bay. It is Dash again, who, firing at something in motion near the leafy top of a bay tree, brings a heavy body splashing into the water. Standing on high ground, the field listens as the whole orchestra of hounds gathers full chorus, signaling a kill.

The suspense of what the creature might be ends when one of the drivers comes out "with a fat, over-grown raccoon; who thus paid forfeit with his life," writes Elliott, "for having imprudently crossed the hounds, when intent on higher game" (p. 163). Elliott leaves no doubt about the status of this quarry and of its intended consumers. "Strapping his prize across his shoulders, and smacking his lips in advance, at the thought of the high-flavored hams, into which he meant to convert his haunches," he writes, "our driver pushed again into the thicket with his dogs" (p. 163).

The field nears the end of the gall when Rowser, a favorite hound, suddenly bursts forth with a fierce cry. The other hounds rally and rush to the spot, as do the huntsmen. Elliott continues,

Gather, huntsmen! Now we shall see sport! The ground was favorable for the sportsmen, for a road ran parallel with the direction of the cry, and thus the whole field got placed, and took a fair start with the dogs. "There they go! Look! for the hedge! Rowser leads—he leaps the hedge—ha! he has overrun the track. Black has caught it up—it is all right! There they go—look at them!—listen to them! Huntsmen, is it not charming? Does it not make your pulse quicken? Is there not a thrill of pleasure shooting through your frame? Can you tell your name? Have you a wife? a child? *Have you a neck*?" If you can, at such a moment, answer questions such as these, you do not feel your position and are but half a sportsman! (p. 164)

Such flourishes of rhetoric, surely expressed more often in literature than in actual life, characterized and separated planters' hunting styles from those of other Southern groups. For planters, the process of the hunt, the chase, was the most important part of hunting. Participation in a chase meant being at the vortex of action, surrounded by the roaring swirls of peers and subordinates, of horses and hounds, all focused on a common objective. To planters, nothing was more detrimental to good hunting than to kill with practical intent. Such a motive might lead to market hunting or the sale of game, objectives which undercut the very privilege and largesse that aristocratic hunting assumed.[5] If most other whites and blacks hunted out of necessity, planters insisted they hunted for amusement. It was the ideal chase, the intensity of feelings and total involvement, that Elliott describes above.

After a splendid, exhilarating chase through an open field, the cat eludes its pursuers temporarily among the briers and palmettos of an adjacent tract. Rowser finally unmasks the stratagem of the quarry, which has doubled back to a thicket and temporarily lost the dogs by leaping from tree to tree above their heads and beyond their noses. A neighboring planter, attracted by the unusual din of Elliott's sporting troop, is the first to fire on the cat as it slips away from the dogs and mounts. The neighbor's two terriers chime in with the other hounds, and the pointers join the fray with their sharp, shrill notes. For Elliott, all this uproar is "delicious" (p. 167)!

The inexperienced, but previously favored Dash, tries his luck at downing the cat with a load of bird shot. He fails, whereupon the cat attempts his escape maneuver again. This time he is in full view and the field begins to close. Now Elliott takes the initiative. After apparently missing with one barrel, he lets fly with the other, catching the cat midflight between trees and laying it low. After a brief pause to admire the kill, the field undertakes the five-mile trek to town, and to dinner. Elliott's account ends, "And now, in high spirits, we dashed into town, our horns sounding a flourish as we approach—and our wildcats, flanked by the raccoon, showing forth, somewhat ostentatiously, from the front of the barouche" (pp. 168–69).

Elliott's description of this wildcat chase allows him to make certain points about plantation hunting—the identity of his hunting companions, the rela-

tionship between blacks and whites, the superior characteristics of hunting
dogs, the cunning of prey, the contentions between town and country folk, the
boastful displays of success, and the luck of novices. His choice of prey for
this first hunting episode is deliberate. The pursuit of this predator allows the
author to express in a clear and perfunctory way the essence of his culturally
based pursuit and the planters' modes of coping with the challenges to their
assumed prerogatives. Since no discriminating sportsman ate wildcat, its pursuit, like that of the fox in England, was enjoyed without thought of consum-
able compromise. Furthermore, wildcats were a menace to plantation livestock, poultry, and game and thereby a threat to the assumed tranquility of
plantation life, for which planters claimed responsibility as paterfamilias.
Elliott had no scruples about using guns against them because the cats sometimes climbed trees, defied the dogs, and fought when brought to bay. Epitomizing this species as destructive and evil, Elliott concludes with a classic
understatement that "the instincts of a man naturally differ from those of a
wildcat" (pp. 262–69).

Yet Elliott's favorite quest was for deer, and he left us four deer-hunting
sketches. These stories provide additional insight into a hunting style he
shared with other planters. Deer hunts followed a prescribed pattern, with
hunters taking "stands" surrounding a plot of land. Packs of dogs with drivers
were released onto the land to raise a deer and to drive it toward the periphery
and the standing hunters. Once a fleeing deer was wounded, the hunters
sprang onto horseback and chased it down.[6]

In his deer-hunting accounts, Elliott tells us about his differences with
Northern and city hunters, who marshal their forces on the barren turfs of
Jersey and Long Island and reap their rewards of "one brace of grouse, or
enjoy a *glorious snap* at some straggling deer that escapes, *of course*" (pp.
191–92). Then Elliott jests at city sportsmen who must import their game from
his native state for release. "What think ye of sport like this?" he writes. "Ours
was no *preserve* shooting! We were not popping over our own nurselings?
They were wild deer, of the wild woods, that we slew, this day at Chee-Ha!"
After gently chastising his readers, he solicits them to come for a visit and
participate in sport as it was intended—"mark the throb of a new delight
springing in your bosoms, as you sweep along with the rush of the hounds,
and fling the cares of life far, far behind you" (p. 192).

We read further about rituals—the daubing of a novice's face with the
blood of his first victim, the joshing with peers, the big bucks that got away,
the false pride, the nature of bears and deer, and the history of misdeeds that
haunt the Southern landscape, providing explanations for chases that fail to
end with the expected downed game.

Elliott reminds us that his position in society and his success afield are
based on achievement and skill, not on chance or luck (pp. 239–43). Aristocratic values sustain his position with reference to others in the South. Such

values include noblesse oblige, that is, a planter should not order his slaves to do anything if he himself is fearful of its consequences. He also affirms largesse. "How pleasant to eat!" he writes. "Shall I say it?—how much pleasanter to give away! Ah, how such things do win their way to *hearts*—men's, and *women's* too! My young sporting friends, a word in your ear: the worst use you can make of your game, is to eat it yourselves" (p. 191).

Deference and submission to those of superior social standing are other virtues. These values Elliott describes in an episode entitled "The Fire Hunter." He relates this story, he tells us, to expose to public attention "the dangers to property and to life" attendant upon the illicit practice of fire hunting (pp. 244–59). This practice, occurring at night, involved lighting a fire, placing it in a reflector, and carrying it to a site habituated by foraging deer. With the fire reflected in the eyes of the deer, the hunter is able to shoot the blinded animal at close range. Such methods typified the unsportsmanlike characteristics of those who hunted for their livelihood.

This particular sketch involves a plantation overseer who enlists, through fear of disclosure, the assistance of a slave, Pompey, to go fire hunting. Initially, Pompey refuses to assist for "Maussa count 'pun dem buck for heself," but is blackmailed into participating by the overseer's knowledge that Pompey had tried to secure the same deer by setting stakes to impale the deer as it leapt into the enclosed field (p. 245). The story begins with the white overseer receiving a note from his absentee employer, specifically requesting him to save the deer for his own ventures. The overseer expresses his indignity at being treated "as if I was a nigger" and in his indignation raises the question of propriety and ownership. Who owns the deer? What right does the planter have to reserve the deer for his own purposes merely because he owns the land? Why should an absentee landlord have the right to prevent those who live on the land from reaping its fruits (p. 246)?

The overseer wants the deer so he can sell it or exchange it for trade goods from a store, and his method is fire hunting at night. The slave wants the same deer for another purpose—as an addition to his meager rations—and he plans to get it by a different method: he will place sharpened stakes at sites where deer regularly leap across the wooden rail fences that enclose the crops. Both men are beyond the purview of planters; both are engaging in an illegal act. The illegality of such acts perpetuated an unholy alliance between slaves and subordinate whites—the type of alliance planters feared more than most other eventualities. Through his knowledge of Pompey's "poaching" activities and his offers of a foreshoulder and threat of bribes, the overseer obtains the compliance of the slave in this night venture.

Both the overseer and Pompey go fire hunting. The overseer shoots a buck, but also a colt by mistake. The death of the colt is disguised by the expedient roguery of impaling its carcass on a fence railing. Pompey is sent to the stage house to deliver the stag for sale. During his return, he comes across a dying slave, a brother out at night to purchase sugar for a sick wife. Another fire hunter mistook him for a deer and shot him. The unwholesome outcome of this tale, "illustrative of life," underlines, in Elliott's mind, the perverse consequences of not keeping one's place in the social hierarchy and thus becoming accountable for one's own imprudent actions.

Hunting and Social Relationships

Hunting texts, such as those of William Elliott, allow us to see the contours of social relationships in the Old South around the middle of the last century. Such accounts also permit us to recover and to interpret some cultural rules that made wildlife a special category of property, a source of recreation for a few while remaining a source of nourishment for many. Generally, planters left the most articulate records of their hunting exploits. These records disclose as much by accident as by intent.

Field sports in the Old South were largely the domain of men. While engaged in hunting forays, men left their women at home, with the exception of the infrequent fox chases close to the plantations.[7] Perhaps no arena of marital life was more problematic than the inclination of some men to leave their households for extended periods of time and to become absorbed in manly pursuits. A Virginia planter's wife lamented in the columns of the *American Turf Register* about the hunting habits of her husband. Although Providence had provided her with many of its bounties, "Juliana Rosebud" confessed she was not able to enjoy any of it because of her husband. "The unfeeling wretch," she wrote in 1831, "is devoted to his dogs, his gun, his horse, his grog, and everything but his wife. We never pass a day without some strife." She complained that her husband kept his favorite hounds in the house, objected to debts other than those for whiskey and hunting equipment, and kept friends who were boorish, crude, and contemptuous of all things she found of value. She pressed the editor to write her husband and advise him on his proper role.[8] Although this letter was undoubtedly a parody, beneath its humor was the cutting edge of marital conflict.

At other times, though, some hunting by men was not altogether incompatible with domesticity and marriage. "As to hunting I have been out once hunted all day and got home between 8 and 9 o'clock at night with one little fox," wrote L. J. D'Berry to his friend F. H. Whitaker in Halifax County, North Carolina. "Sufficiently amused since then I have stayed at home preferring the company of my wife to a fox hunt (My wife) how does it sound would to God that I could have said so 5 years ago."[9] Later, in October 1859, after mentioning a few kills of squirrels and birds, D'Berry wrote: "I am still enjoy-

ing the smiles of a contented and happy wife and would not be single again for
the world for a good wife is the best gift of God to man, save Jesus, and him
crucified."[10]

With the distaff connection with game confined mainly to infrequent fox
pursuits and to the kitchen, hunting was decisively the business of men, engaged in by all ages and races.[11] It was an important part of the male life cycle
as most Southerners experienced it and one that fathers shared with their sons.
More than most other teenage activities, participation in field sports signaled
a youth's crossing the threshold over into manhood. Participation in hunting
introduced young men into their fathers' fraternity, a circle of men endowed
with a special vocabulary, sustained by distilled spirits circulated from hand
to hand, and integrated by the ritual gossip about neighbors, guns, dogs, and
impediments overcome in the process of downing the game.[12] "The best of all
breathing and forever the best of all listening" is how William Faulkner was to
describe the experience later.[13]

The hunting expedition symbolized man's dominion over nature and nurture, just as the duel, scuffle, and verbal displays came to mean dominance
over men in other contexts. Its exhilarating moments became symptomatic of
other moments of courage and conquest.[14] In daily life, a woman's mission
might be to mitigate the behavior of men, but in the isolated hunting camp, the
distance from women was more than metaphorical. In camp, men could live
out their unremitting fantasies of self, of gender, and of group without confronting the realities of the homefront.[15]

The sentiments expressed through hunting, guns, and nature study between
a planter and his son is idyllically recorded in a scrapbook kept by George
Anderson Mercer of Savannah, Georgia. Mercer's father owned extensive
rice plantations, and young Mercer learned early to hunt, fish, and observe
nature. Accompanied by his cousins and by slaves, he hunted mostly small
birds, recording details of the numbers killed and whether or not they were
taken on the wing. Mercer went North, attended Princeton and Yale, and from
there recorded his reflections. From Princeton in 1855 he wrote:

Nature I have always loved, loved deeply increasingly: loved her woods—her
wilds—her fields—her floods. She has been to me a Mother from whose "bare
bosum" I could never take my fill. From earliest childhood, I delighted to wander
among her beauties, and long before my boyish arms had ever borne a fowling-
piece, I used to dream that, gun in hand I was a wild huntsman of the wilderness. My
childess steps loved to follow my Father and Uncle through the woods and fields, to
carry their game and to taste their growing pleasures, of which afterwards, I drank
the deepest draughts. I was never wearied, never satisfied; my poor feet would ache
and my legs smart with briers and the intruding yellow grass; still I trudged on,
hopefully looking to that glorious day, when with my gun, I could become a wild
wanderer of wilderness. Never, never, shall I forget the day when first a gun was

mine. It stands out brightly among the brightest scenes of my boyhood. I could not compute my happiness. My gun was a treasure without a price. We sallied forth, cousin Robert and I, to the loved scenes of Lebanon, as proud, as free as the wild eagle. Each report was a volume of sweet sounds—each little bird the object of a thousand hopes and fears; and so I became a hunter, a lover of Nature.[16]

For a planter's son, such as George Mercer, the fraternal ties across racial lines were often described in intensely personal and familial terms, especially his relationships with particular older slaves. While away in New York in 1850, he learned of the death of "an old negro named Prince," a slave belonging to his uncle. Mercer notes that much of his pleasure on excursions afield came from his association with Prince and that he would sorely miss him. He eulogized Prince in poem and prose and trusted "that his spirit has taken its flight for a higher and a happier world."[17]

Upon his return to Savannah later that year, Mercer wrote of a coon hunting expedition. This "very merry party consisted of five or six negroes, my two cousins and myself and many a merry laugh was heard ringing through the forests as we passed along." This foray produced no raccoons; the dogs had found it more propitious to chase hogs.[18]

Of course, familial affection was not extended to all blacks. Elsewhere, Mercer tells of an episode involving an outing with Master Nelson. In the woods, Master Nelson found a 'possum, dead for some time, and proceeded to extricate its corpse from a downfall. Mercer's account of the episode follows:

> The animal was perfectly dead and must have remained in the trap for sometime, but Master Nelson, without leave or licence, immediately placed it in a bag, which he carried with him, and slung it over his shoulder. Perhaps we were wrong in permitting him to do so—I fear that we were; but we did not think so then and the animal would have spoiled had it remained there longer, we did not forbid him to take it. . . . Having reached the fence which divides Lebanon from my cousin B's, we bade him goodbye and proceeded towards the house. Master Nelson immediately kindled a fire and putting on a pot, set about cleaning his possum, repeatedly warned by the other Negroes that if Mas. B's boys found him out he would have to settle the account with them.[19]

Although young whites and slaves collaborated in many plantation adventures, both had to cope with the eventual transformation of the affiliations demanded of participants in a slave society. As with young Mercer, whose educational and social development tore him from his erstwhile accomplices, a planter's son had a duty to demonstrate his manly skills, to affront dangers, and to show a sense of accomplishment befitting his ascribed place in the hierarchy of plantation society.

Field sports provided men an identity based on their demonstrated expertise

with horses, dogs, guns, and slaves. Self-identification included the personi-
fication and particularization of dogs, horses, and material objects such as
guns. Each was given a name and discussed as if it possessed anthropomorphic characteristics. If slaves were sometimes depicted as companions, animals took on human characteristics.[20] Skill in the pursuit, knowledge of terrain and game, tracking and marksmanship were all currencies useful in
ranking individuals within the local social structure. As with the exhibition
of skills, storytelling conferred status and inspired allegiance to the masculine ideals of friendly rivalry and fine fellowship. In commanding attention
from peers and others, these displays conferred a sense of power and a chance
for winning public admiration.[21] Such admiration for demonstrated feats of
hunting skills and storytelling was within the province of both blacks and
whites.

Good hunting in one's neighborhood was a potent image for any man aspiring to live the life of a "gentleman." After confessing the bliss of his recent
marriage and his meager returns from field sports, L. J. D'Berry wrote to a
friend on December 10, 1859, who had expressed an interest in buying some
of his land and two horses. Since he could "have neither of his children with
me," D'Berry confessed to thinking of selling "all and go to town and live a
Gentle Man the rest of my life." In this context he wrote of the sporting life
recently enjoyed: "I ran over a fox in less than half an hour and caught him the
other day and two days after I killed a fine Buck and two days after that I kill
a fine doe and two days after that my dogs caught one of the fawns and today
I left my dogs trailing in the care of another man and they failed to start the
deer so I got nothing. (Bad luck) but I expect to mend it up again."[22]

If all men in the Old South were not equal, these inequalities were expected
in the social ordering of everyday activities. As the main beneficiaries of the
"peculiar institution," planters through their reactions and rituals assumed responsibility for keeping the boundaries of propriety and property within their
self-ascribed limits. The function of the mounted foray within the political
economy of the plantation is shown in the hunting notes of Henry William
Harrington, Jr. The son of a prominent North Carolina family, Harrington
lived on a 13,000-acre plantation, Beausejour (Pleasant Abode) in Richmond
County. He kept a diary and at intervals took note of business and social
events, including hunting, in the Pee Dee region.

Harrington pursued primarily deer and fox with his hounds and shot an
occasional squirrel, goose, and rabbit. Whereas he reports few successful
conclusions to his fox and deer runs, he was more successful in bagging squirrels. He took particular pride in his pack of hounds and sought to improve
their stock with purchases of new bitches, trades with neighbors, and gift
hounds from guests. His mounted forays with hounds and guns served two
important purposes. First, hunting was a diversion from the boredom and
isolation of the plantation. On December 25, 1851, he wrote: "Another Christ-

mas come and I am still alive—rather dull times tho—Rode out with the Hounds this morning and walked out with my gun in the evening." There wasn't much else to do in the county but to fashion some excitement out of the materials at hand—the game, the hounds, the servants, with neighbors or guests. Second, his hounds and his gun accompanied him on many of his inspections around the plantation and on his other ventures. On October 5, 1857, he "rode to [the] plantation taking the hounds with me," and on November 6 he hunted in the morning before joining one of his companions to attend the burial of a neighbor. One can surmise how his appearance—mounted, armed, and with hounds while surveying his holdings—befitted his proprietary status. That other motives were present in his aristocratic displays are suggested in his notes for two consecutive days in 1852.

> July 6th   I cannot but regret the circumstances, coming to my knowledge yesterday, that elicited such a burst of indignation, rage, and contempt. Peridition seize the whole tribe of free negroes and mulattoes, abolitionists and all (MAN IS A STRANGE ANIMAL!)
>
> July 7   Performed a disagreeable opperation [sic] this evening and am fully determined to do more of the same whenever opportunity shall bring me up with the proper object.

Displays of armed might and a willingness to use force were prerogatives assumed by planters. Freed blacks and mulattoes near slave settlements were perceived as a threat to property by planters who ascribed to the doctrine of racial purity. Planters were not reluctant to use force in responding to challenges to their status or their "honor." While attending court in Rockingham on September 15, 1856, Harrington wrote, "That unprincipled scoundrel . . . offered me a gross insult which I brook indifferently, but am advised . . . that he is beneath my notice."[23]

Undoubtedly, the relationships between whites and blacks in hunting was particularistic and varied, as was the emotional and physical texture of all other relationships between whites, as privileged participants and owners, and their slaves, who coped in a variety of ways with their bondage. On some plantations, slaves may have received better material treatment and engaged in a broader scope of activities than their counterparts elsewhere. Despite the emotional and physical closeness often felt by men engaged in a common quest, the underlying social glue remained that of slave and master.[24]

Members of both races looked forward to the hunting season. For blacks, the experience of participating in formal hunts was different from that of whites; the experiences of both races were conditioned by the very nature of the hierarchical society to which they belonged. Slaves owned neither the land, the weapons, nor the game pursued. Furthermore, there was a difference in being free to join and being expected to—as beaters and carriers of the quarry.

All racial and social groups of antebellum Carolinians were fond of hunting, and game was an important part of most diets throughout the year. Some men hunted year round, but for most, hunting was an activity restricted to the fall and winter months, when they were not engaged in agricultural chores. Whereas planters had certain preferences and prerogatives in pursuing certain species, wild game of all sorts found its place on the tables of most social groups, and into the marketplace.[25]

It is difficult to show discrete disjunctions between social standing or race and the game pursued by each. However, there is a continuum along which one can place the clear tendencies expressed by most participants at each end of the social spectrum. Despite much blurring in the middle ranges, planters such as Elliott and Harrington exhibited a definite preference in game and methods of take. They took game in broad daylight on horseback, with guns, accompanied by trained dogs and retinues of servants. Whereas plantation masters in their youth might slip out at night against parental injunctions to run 'coon and 'possum with slaves, once they were grown these nocturnal excursions rarely occurred.[26]

Slaves, at the other end of the social scale, participated as drivers and subordinates for their masters during the daytime, and at night went after raccoons, opossums, and other game with dogs. Whites would complain in newspapers and journals about the packs of half-starved dogs found around slave quarters. Planters would grumble that slaves' dogs injured livestock, interrupted civilized traffic, and ruined "the constitution of the slaves, by hunting when they ought to (be) asleep."[27] But the objections led nowhere because hunting with dogs at night, and trapping, provided slaves a means of supplementing their sometimes all too meager rations. Some whites tacitly recognized the problem, turned away from disciplinary action, and preferred to be kept in the dark about specifics.

Blacks also took wild animals with deadfalls, snares, and other unobtrusive means.[28] In the slave narratives, one finds occasional reference to other types of hunting. Zeb Crowder was seven years old when the Yankees set him free. He recalls that "We had lots o' game ter eat. Marster 'lowed my daddy ter hunt wid a gun and he killed a lot o' rabbits, squirrels, an' game. We trapped birds and caught rabbits in boxes. Daddy caught possums an' coons wid dogs."[29] Yet the general tendency was, as Julius Nelson recounted when he was seventy-seven years old, that "De smart nigger et a heap o' possums an' coons, der bein' plenty o' dem an' rabbits an' squirrels in abundance."[30]

The Conflicts of Two Legacies

The English legacy that restricted the taking of wild animals to those of privileged social standing and the countervailing tradition of revolting against such prerogatives both made their ways across the Atlantic as part of the cultural baggage of the early settlers.[31] As the South developed into a society of greatly unequal men, men of property, who controlled the apparatus of governance, left little room for ambiguity about their vision. They saw the law as a means of creating a social world that embraced their collective image, and they enacted legislation to determine the contentious contours of property and status. The stark prose of legislative documents was another means by which planters sought to assure their ascendency and to press other groups into appropriate behavior. Whereas other groups have not left a literature or record of their activities to match those left by the gentry, the shadows of their acts are visible in the wording and boundaries of these legal declarations. Despite the gentry's attempts to exhort and control through legislative initiatives, the general trend in the judiciary was toward opening lands for public access and allowing the free taking of wildlife as an economic asset.[32]

The abundance of wildlife and the conditions of life on the frontier mitigated against most restrictions. These circumstances led John Lawson, on his journey through the Carolina hinterlands in 1700, to muse in his diary:

> Here property hath a large scope, there being no strict laws to bind our privileges. A qust [sic] after game being as freely and peremptorily enjoyed by the meanest planter, as he that is the highest in dignity, or wealthiest in the province. Deer and other game that are naturally wild, being not immured, or preserved within boundaries, to satisfy the appetite of the rich alone. A poor laborer that is master of his gun, & c., hath as good a claim to have continued coarses [sic] of delicacies crowded upon his table, as he that is master of a great purse.[33]

Opportunity and abundant wildlife were the providence of the frontier. Game there was more or less free for the taking. Residents of the frontier hunted for food and skins and protected, as best they could, their property from predators and pests. The early Southern trade in skins and furs was centered in Charleston, South Carolina. From here, agents dispersed into the back territories bartering Western wares for the products of Indian hunting skills. Deerskins were important items in domestic and foreign trade; exported skins reached a high of some 160,000 in 1784.[34] In addition to deer, meat, and skins, these hunters supplied other wildlife to the markets in the developing towns and settlements.

Acting in their own interest as landowners, colonial and state legislators sought to limit the conditions under which private rights to wild animals could be obtained, while at the same time encouraging citizens to destroy predators. Implicit in these acts was the state's proprietary interest in wild animals, an interest acquired by transfer from the English monarchy to the colonies and subsequently to the states.[35] Four types of statutes, repeatedly enacted, predominate in the colonial and antebellum periods. These laws include those that encourage the destruction of predators and vermin; regulate the harvest of valuable species, thus preserving breeding stocks; restrict the hunting privileges of certain groups; and regulate trespass.[36] Whereas enforcement of legislative edicts was possible in the more settled regions, recalcitrant individuals could move to areas where conviction was more problematic. The real watchdogs of these wildlife laws were the citizens who had land and property at stake and who, by acting as informers, received part of the perpetrator's assessed fines.[37]

To protect livestock on open range, the North Carolina legislators passed an act, before 1715, that offered a reward for the delivery of vermin scalps to magistrates. A similar act in 1748 established a bounty on the scalps of panther, wolf, and wildcat. The magistrate could give the bounty to a hunter only after administering an oath stating that the vermin were killed within the confines of the magistrate's county.[38] Despite these prescriptions, the cunning displayed by bounty hunters taxed the ingenuity of legislators, and their demands were a major drain on the tax revenues in county treasuries. Fraud was rampant; bounty items were often secured outside the boundaries of the county paying the award, and hunters killed and bountied the young animals while sparing the old, and recycled one corpse through repeated tenders.[39]

Indians and whites employing Indian tactics were among the first groups to experience the wrath of the General Assembly and have their hunting privileges, at least on paper, curtailed. At issue was the Indian technique of ring firing. This tactic of surrounding a promising deer locale, circling it with fire, and driving out the game ran the risk of incinerating not only the woods but also neighboring pastures and houses.[40] Ring firing was forbidden near white settlements, a prohibition resented by some Indians, who gave this edict as their reason when threatening to leave North Carolina in 1740.[41] As early as 1705, Robert Beverley in Virginia observed that Indians killed deer primarily for their skins, "leaving the carcasses to perish in the woods."[42] This remark was repeated by John Brickell of North Carolina, who linked the custom to fraud in the bounty system.[43]

Indians were not the only ones to receive discretionary treatment by the legislature. Most hunters and frontiersmen were suspected by lawmakers of lacking the attributes essential for participation in civilized society. According to this view, agriculture was the great civilizing force. Agriculture was held in abeyance by these wild men who pursued abundant game and were distracted from settling on the land to grow crops.[44] Legislators saw it as their duty to pass laws that prevented persons of inferior rank from squandering their time and protected them from idle behavior. Therefore, when the valuable stocks of deer declined in the eighteenth century, legislators promulgated laws restricting the time and methods of taking deer and exhorted would-be deer hunters to clear and settle the land.[45]

In 1745, the General Assembly sought to prevent the killing of deer at unseasonable times and to stop "many abuses committed by White Persons, under the pretense of hunting." The legislators left no doubt as to the identities of these people.

There are great Numbers of idle and disorderly Persons, who have no settled Habitation, nor visible Method of supporting themselves, by Industry or honest Calling, many of whom come in from neighbouring Colonies, without proper Passes, and kill Deer at all Seasons of the Year, and often leave the Carcasses in the Woods, and also steal and destroy Cattle, and carry away Horses, and commit other Enormities, to the great Prejudice of the Inhabitants of this Province; *Be it therefore Enacted, by the Authority aforesaid*, That every Person who shall hunt and kill Deer in the King's Waft within this province, and who is not possessed of a settled Habitation in the same, shall be obliged to produce a Certificate, when required, of his having planted and tended Five Thousand Corn-hills, at Five Feet Distance each Hill, the preceding Year, or Season, in the County where he shall hunt, under the Hands of at least Two Justices of the Peace of the said County, and the Hand of at least one of the Church-wardens of the Parish where such Person planted and tended such Corn.[46]

An act of 1784 that made it a misdemeanor to hunt deer at night was followed in 1810 by a more "stringent law."[47] Such laws had little effect on maintaining stocks of deer in settled areas, for by 1810 this species was already rare in the Carolina coastal plain.[48] Night and fire hunting were practiced by all groups, although planters were perhaps more circumspect in using these techniques. Henry William Harrington, Jr., of Richmond County participated in night hunting below Charleston while on a trip to Florida in 1833.[49] Nonetheless, planters such as William Elliott were opposed to such methods, which deprived them of their daytime sport.

Nothing provoked fear more readily in the minds of planters and other whites than the specter of armed slave rebellions. These fears were vindicated by sporadic and short-lived slave revolts and rumors of such throughout the first half of the nineteenth century. Weapons in the hands of slaves could be used violently against their masters as readily as against game. The peculiar institution was based upon force, and for whites it was essential that both the means and the potential remain within their own grasp.[50]

Fear of insurrection led whites to establish patrols to harass slaves. These patrols became part of the structures designed to perpetuate terror and to enforce the laws prohibiting weapon ownership and use by slaves.[51] Weapons kept by slaves were increasingly circumscribed by laws after 1831.[52] Free blacks lost their weapon-owning privileges in 1840.[53] In a slave society, free blacks were continually suspect by most whites, who felt their activities needed careful regulation and that the possession of any weapon by any blacks was indicative of their capacity to strike back. In effect, such laws were similar to the Black Acts in England, which sought to prevent widespread ownership of guns, to protect game from decimation, and to discourage uprisings.[54]

Despite the aristocratic pretensions of legislative acts and the planters' inclination to want exclusive rights in game, the wildlife laws allowed the free taking of game and the opening of unfenced lands to public access.[55] Restrictions were more easily sanctioned on paper than enforced on the frontier. Perhaps the proof in the pudding of wildlife policy was not found in the enactment of laws but in the ways the courts and public sentiments actually operated in the countryside.

Open land, which encompassed most of the land in the South, was considered as common property for hunting, fishing, and grazing.[56] As William Elliott complained, "The right to hunt wild animals is held by the great body of people, whether landholders or otherwise, as one of their franchises, which they will indulge in at discretion; and to all limitations on which, they submit with the worst possible grace! The 'ferae naturae' are, in their code, the property of him who can take them—irrespective of any conflicting right in the owner of the soil."[57]

As an avid sportsman, Elliott left little doubt that his sentiments and opinions were in the minority. To support his contention that the world should be construed otherwise, he disdainfully recounted a court scene as an instance of the popular attitudes toward hunting rights. An action growing out of trespass, this case described conflicting landowner and hunter rights. One of the hunters, a landowner possessing some property, is on the stand being questioned by an attorney,

> "Would you pursue a deer if he entered your neighbor's inclosure?"
> *Witness*—"Certainly."
> *Counsel*—"What if his fields were planted, and his cotton growing, or his grain ripe?"
> *Witness*—"It would make no difference; I should follow my dogs, go where they might!"
> *Judge*—"And pull down your neighbor's fence, and trample on his fields?"
> *Witness*—"I should do it—though I might regret to injure him!"
> *Judge*—"You would commit a trespass; you would be mulcted in damages. There is no law for such an act!"
> *Witness*—"It is hunter's law, however!"

"And hunter's law, is likely somewhat longer to be the governing law of the case in this section of country," continued a despondent Elliott, "for the prejudices of the people are strong against any exclusive property in game, as every one feels who attempts to keep it to himself."[58]

Elliott then describes the failed experiments of several acquaintances who sought to protect game stocked on islands and on the mainland. In all cases unrelenting poachers killed off their game. Poachers were impossible to convict without restitution against the landowner in the form of repeated offenses, fence burnings, the subsequent running of dogs on the plaintiff's private land, together with perpetual annoyance. For Elliott, the cause of such unwholesome public sentiments was "mostly an affair of inoculation."

It is derived from the laboring emigrants from England, who, mixing with the operative classes of our own white population, inspire them with their own deep disgust at the tyranny of the English game laws. When they descant upon the oppressions which have driven them from home, to better their fortunes in this land, this seems to be the sorest and best remembered of their griefs— transportation, for killing a hare or a partridge! The preservation of game is thus associated, in the popular mind, with ideas of aristocracy—peculiar privileges to the rich, and oppression toward the poor![59]

The Conflicts of Culture and Nature

To sustain hunting as an important mode of subsistence requires land and habitats bereft of much human interference. Human settlements influence landscapes and wildlife in many ways, generally resulting in a drastic reordering of the composition and abundance of plant and wildlife species. The most obvious effects occur when people kill wildlife or raise their own domesticates on land already supporting wild creatures. Other consequences stem from clearing the land, selectively changing the habitats, and burning of forests and fields. Some wildlife species adapt to human changes in the landscape, others do not.[60]

The accumulative impact of settlers' activities in North Carolina would change what they perceived as "wilderness," although previously domesticated and sustained by the Indians, into a landscape bearing the imprint of European interests. Settlement by whites and blacks set a paradoxical process in motion. On the one hand, an increase in the population, together with the expansion of agriculture, stock grazing, hunting, burning, and timber exploitation, progressively decreased the expanse of "wilderness" land and the types of wildlife that flourished there. On the other hand, as the landscape was reshaped, new forms of plants and animals were introduced and a few indigenous forms thrived. Consequently, changes wrought by settlers altered the ratios of wild species, were detrimental to most of the larger predators and herbivores such as the wolf, bison, and elk, and were favorable to many of the smaller animals such as the raccoon, opossum, squirrel, rabbit, and quail.[61]

Coming from a continent where game had become the preserve of the wealthy, European explorers were astounded by the variety and abundance of wildlife in the New World. As harbingers of a different cosmology and culture, the visitations of explorers along the coast of North Carolina were to affect drastically the scenes about which they wrote, particularly when they made it ashore.

William Hilton explored the Cape Fear River in 1664. Although he never landed, he found deer and turkeys "everywhere," a "great store" of partridges, and heard and saw where wolves "had torn a Deer to pieces." In the river, he "saw great store of Ducks, Teile, Widgeon, and in the woods great flocks of Parrakeeto's." Farther upstream Hilton was so impressed by "one Deer with very large horns and great in body" that, exercising the prerogative of explorers if not the later hyperbole of realtors, he named the place Stag-Park![62]

In 1700 John Lawson and a small party, guided by local Indians, left Charleston for explorations into the Carolina hinterlands. Although his journals are filled with descriptions of the wild animals he encountered, what impressed Lawson most was the prowess of Indians as hunters. His guides had no difficulty provisioning his expedition and he noted "a good hunter never misses of being a favorite amongst the women; the prettiest girl being always bestowed upon the chiefest sportsman."[63] As an Englishman, he thought the Indians were "the worst Dog-Masters in the World," yet he was impressed by how they treated their horses, which were well fed.[64]

Settlers followed in the footsteps of the explorers, and most of these were British by origin and descent. Before the turn of the seventeenth century, Lowland Scots arrived in small numbers. After 1732 the Highland Scots settled in family groups around the Cape Fear and its tributaries. Following the Battle of Culloden Moor in 1746, more Highlanders entered the colony and filled up most of the land bordering the lower Cape Fear and its tributaries. Meantime, the Piedmont and mountains became the habitat of the Scots-Irish, Germans, and English, who migrated along the Great Philadelphia Wagon Trail.[65] Finally the Lord Proprietors, whose motives were mainly commercial, recognized that a slave economy would enhance their interests. Accordingly, they gave "absolute authority" over black slaves to freemen who settled in the colony and allocated land to settlers on the basis of the number of people they brought with them.[66]

The Indians, whose hospitality made British settlement possible, suffered most in the initial struggles for dominance in the New World. Their numbers declined as numbers in the other groups swelled. Uneasy friendship, followed by increasing suspicion and hostility that eventually broke into warfare, characterized Indian-white relations. Warfare was followed by an uneasy accommodation and a repetition of the cycle. With each cycle, the balance tipped more in favor of the settlers, whose diseases killed many Indians and whose trade undermined their cultural independence. By 1763 only the Cherokees in the mountains remained as a viable buffer to settler advances. A few bands, such as the Lumbees of Robeson County, managed to survive the white onslaught and emerged again as active cultural communities in the twentieth century.[67]

Social distinctions were never rigid for most whites. Frequent fraternizing at court sessions, church services, taverns, and sporting events tended to blur the lines between them. Moreover, the uncertain economic conditions in a new and expanding frontier seemed to offer individuals the prospects for a quick and rapid rise in social status.[68] At the bottom of the social hierarchy, black slaves found that their welfare depended heavily on the disposition of their owners. Yet, despite the authoritarian structures within which they lived, slaves often created their own society and culture distinct from that of whites. For many slaves bondage became intolerable, and they sought to escape to other states or to hide in the backcountry. Escaping slaves posed a challenge to white society. In a society where they were often abused and accused of being escaped slaves, black freedmen and women often led precarious lives.[69]

Settlers' experiments with crops such as cotton, tobacco, rice, and indigo, and their cattle and hog drives to distant markets showed their commercial interests. During colonial times, commercial trends in agriculture were discernible among small farmers who grew wheat in exchange for sugar, molasses, and other necessities.[70] Among early imports, livestock became an important segment of commerce. Raised on the open range, cattle and hogs were driven to market, where their sale provided the means to purchase other products.[71] Highlanders along the Cape Fear raised livestock and horses and also cut the long leaf pine and floated its logs to sell downriver. Settlers in the pine forests also pursued the creatures living there. Some Scotsmen took to "living and hunting off the land where the cane brakes were a veritable hunter's paradise." Here some gained renown as "mighty hunters" through their exploits of deer.[72]

By the end of the eighteenth century, the forests of North Carolina had been altered by the axe and by fire, and their extent was somewhat diminished. However, the forested environments were not so changed or devastated that succeeding generations of settlers were unable to subsist within them.[73]

Although a few of the larger mammals such as elk and bison were extirpated from Carolina by 1750, wildlife remained generally plentiful during the initial centuries of European colonization.[74] Wildlife was a bounty that the settlers tapped for profit and for subsistence.[75] Its abundance on the frontier proved paradoxical. While many species provided settlers with an accessible supply of meat and by-products, others were pests around their settlements and gardens. Wolves preyed upon stock, and deer took to grazing enclosed crops. The practiced use of weapons for protection and for hunting became an essential survival skill for men living on the frontier. Weapons were the means by which men defended themselves and their families from hostile attacks, by which families were fed through hunting, and by which men protected their vulnerable livelihoods against vermin.

Of the game hunted, deer was the most important species in terms of pounds of food. Some localities of extensive agricultural lands were practically barren of deer by the early nineteenth century. Where swamps and thickets prevailed, deer flourished and hunters were able to provide venison regularly to the markets of Charleston and Wilmington.[76] Deer were taken and consumed by all groups, even slaves, albeit by somewhat different methods.

The ubiquitous rabbit was the favorite small game. The cottontail fared well within the mosaic of woodland interspersed with cultivated and abandoned fields. Rabbits could be taken by gun, with clubs, with dogs, and with a variety of traps, snares, and downfalls. Probably the most common method was the rabbit box, which, once set in good habitat, could keep a rural family in meat for most of the year. Their rapid regenerative abilities and ease of capture made rabbits a frequent meat on the tables of rural Carolinians, and rabbits were usually for sale in town markets.[77]

Squirrels were common wherever woodlot or forested stream provided suitable habitat. Gray squirrels abounded in the pine forests; the larger fox squirrels inhabited the forests of the piedmont. Both species were sought by country folk and occasionally shot by planters.[78]

The opossum and raccoon were taken chiefly by night hunters. Of these two species, the opossum was the more plentiful, easier to obtain and readily acquired without a gun. As scavengers, opossums often were caught alive, penned and fed for several days, before being butchered for the table. Both opossums and raccoons were taken with dogs. Once treed, they were shaken loose to the ground and captured. Both were common fare in rural areas.[79]

Numerous birds added culinary variety to the Southern repast. As the largest bird, the wild turkey was a popular target, typically secured by traps or with guns. Along the coasts and migratory routes, wherever they concentrated during the winters, ducks and geese were slaughtered in great numbers. Elsewhere, these birds were taken when conditions permitted. Quail and passenger pigeons were probably the most important small birds killed in the South. Of small size, quail could be obtained with traps, nets, or guns in sizable quantities. Although abundant in eastern Carolina, wild pigeons became infrequent visitors after the first decades of the nineteenth century.[80]

In the more settled regions of the state, numerous smaller birds frequented the fields and barnyards and these became targets for youthful "sportsmen." Writing of his youth in Franklin County, Kemp Plummer Battle described hunting with his brother around 1845 as "somewhat of a farce" with a "single-barrelled shotgun but no bird dog." Birds were few, with doves, robins, yellowhammers, and larks likely targets.[81]

Smaller birds were also captured with a variety of techniques available to slaves and poor whites. Probably the most ingenious way was by "bird blinding," a nighttime activity described by Zeb Crowder.

> I also piled brush in da winter time. Birds went in de brush ter roost. Den we went bird blindin'. We had torches made o' lightwood splinters, and brushes in our han's, we hit de piles o' brush after we got 'round 'em. When de birds come out we would kill 'em. Dere were lots o' birds den. We killed 'em at night in the sage fields where

broom grass was thick. Dem were de good times. No sich times now. We killed robins, doves, patridges, and other kinds o' birds. Dey aint no such gangs o' birds now. We briled 'em over coals o' fire and fried 'em in fryin' pans, and sometimes we had a bird stew, wid all de birds we wanted. De stew wus de bes' o' all. Dere ain't no sich stew now. We put flour in de stew. It was made into pastry first, and we called it slick.[82]

William Elliott's Closing Commentary

William Elliott ends his volume on Carolina sports with "Random Thoughts on Hunting" (pp. 277–92). In this conclusion, he defends sports hunting and expresses his concern over its prospects for survival. He realistically appraises the reasons for the gradual disappearance of game from the low country of South Carolina, which occurred with the destruction of forests and habitats and from the demands in the towns for wild game meat. This demand caused commercial hunters to slaughter the deer, and "it is too much to expect this class of men to refrain from 'firehunting,' though forbidden by law" (p. 285). In addition, the average citizen would not observe the sanctity of property lines; he considered it his right to hunt, whether or not he owned the land, and showed no respect for the rights of landed proprietors. Moreover, politicians flattered the prejudices of the electorate and refused to enact laws protecting private land. Neither would juries of citizens convict poachers (p. 292).

Yet Elliott closes on a more optimistic note:

I think there will be a reform in this matter—not that I shall witness it. It must be the work of time. When the game shall have been so killed off, that the mass of the people shall have no interest in hunting their neighbors' grounds—the law will be reformed; and when that time arrives, the juries will have no interest in construing away the law. So that we may yet hope to see the time when men may, under the sanction of the law, and without offence, or imputation of aristocracy, preserve the game from extermination—and perpetuate, in so doing, the healthful, generous, and noble diversion of hunting. (p. 292)

Although settlers and planters in the antebellum South favored agriculture over hunting as an economy, they competently harvested wild beasts through selectively absorbing Indian and African traditions, thereby creating amalgams of their own that allowed them to prosper in the New World. They opened lands to public access, allowing the privilege of hunting to slip from the exclusive grasp of the planters. These changes in Old World traditions were initially underwritten by New World plenitude and encoded as elements in the democratic new order. The Civil War and its industrial aftermath saw this abundance rendered into a hecatomb with the great commercial slaughters of game throughout the continent reflecting the newer democratic order. Yet, from these ashes was to emerge the phoenix of public power and sensibilities that was to save the game and to perpetuate the sport of hunting. It was for such sensibleness that Elliott yearned, but through means that he could scarcely imagine.

Three

Progress and Poverty: Sportsmen, Agriculture, and Development in Postbellum Carolina

PICKING.

The development came without fanfare of trumpets, and the men who brought it about had no genius for self advertisement. Instead of fulminating, they went to the root of the matter and set about Americanizing the misfit plan. In England the incentive for conservation came from the value of game to the land owner as personal property, and the land owner naturally saw to it that the laws made for his benefit were enforced. Here there was no corresponding incentive. But clear headed sportsmen showed that with game as the common property of all the people, it was the individual's obligation to preserve the asset. It was upon this basis of personal obligation that the problem was solved. Otherwise the predictions of game extermination would long ago have been realized.

(John B. Burnham, "Conservation's Debt to Sportsmen")

THE MILITARY DEFEAT of the Old South and the emancipation of slaves radically changed the relationships of planters like William Elliott to other groups and to the land. Planters did not readily confess such radical shifts, especially in their hunting narratives. Yet changes in methods by which they took game, in hunting companions, and in the switch from mammals to birds as prey suggest some of the larger forces at work on their play. We begin this chapter by recounting Alexander Hunter's youthful hunting experiences in the Old South, and then will interpret his pursuit of quail in the resurrected South of his adulthood. His account covers an important period of upheaval between prominent landowners and those who worked the land. Besides being a landowner, Hunter was also a sportsman, and, like all sportsmen, he sought to distinguish himself from those who worked the land, from factory workers, and especially from market hunters.

Through the expansion of the railroad system and the perfection of firearms, technology began to play an enigmatic role in the ensuing conflicts between sports and market hunters as wildlife populations declined. Having played an important democratic role in providing all hunters access to wild animals on the frontier, technology and the persistent development of frontier lands were now bringing about the restrictions and enforcement of hunting edicts sought by William Elliott of the Old South. The closing of the wildlife and range commons in the name of progressive agriculture became part of a calculus of change, trapping most blacks as laborers and slowly forcing the poorer whites into a market economy.

The structural legacies of slavery and of separateness in the South took a long time to reverse. The South's defeat and its separate labor pool fostered a distinct identity among Southerners that has lasted well into the twentieth century. The federal government's New Deal and the economic climate of World War II reversed the region's isolation and began to integrate the South into the national economy. Scotland County, North Carolina, was created by General Assembly fiat in 1900 amid the political and economic turmoil of those times. Regional and county histories are part of the cultural matrix molding the identities and behavior of the modern-day hunters, whose rituals will be described later.

Alexander Hunter and His Exploits with Quail and Dogs

Alexander Hunter's youthful exploits were on his father's plantation in Virginia, where his reminiscences begin, like those of George Anderson Mercer, by contemplating Nature's gifts.[1] Lacking Mercer's Princetonian gloss, Hunter begins with the thought that Nature's greatest gift to a child was "to endow him with a love of the forest, the field, and the stream, and to infect his blood with a longing for field sports" (p. 11). Alexander Hunter's youthful accomplices in mischief were the overseer's son, Sam, whom he describes in uncomplimentary terms (short, stumpy, carrotty-headed boy, with a snub nose, big mouth, large and knobby joints, tough as a pine knot), and two slave children, Robinson and John, given to him by his father. In addition to general shenanigans, Sam's favorite delights were the chicken and dog fights. Following Sam's imaginative leads, Alexander and his retinue got into numerous scrapes. "Sam had the imagination," he writes, "and I had the power" (p. 12). With Sam's collusion, Alexander brought his first gun and kept it hidden.

Their first hunt occurred one Saturday when Alexander's and Sam's fathers had gone to supervise an adjacent farm. The four gallants took to the fields after larks. When Alexander missed his shot, it became Sam's turn with the gun. Carlo, the house dog, joined them as they prepared to climb a fence. All made it across, except for Sam, who became concerned with his "galluses," or suspenders, holding up his pants. Carlo jumped a rabbit, and in the thick of pursuit Sam tripped on his breeches. Despite his impairment and the confusion, Sam fired at the rabbit. His shot missed the rabbit but scored on the slaves and on Carlo. Carlo got the worst peppering, but, as he could not talk, the subterfuge was safe. Robinson's and John's silence was bought with bribes and with threats of fieldwork (pp. 15–16).

Other scapes followed, including a close call one December when the gang attempted to board a skiff in the river. They were fired upon by a market gunner and had to flee home, naked and shivering. Alexander came down with pneumonia, felt death to be imminent, and let what was left of him join the Episcopal church. His throe is revealingly symptomatic of the landowner-black conflicts after the Civil War.

> I asked my father to summon the chief negroes on the place and let me bid them a final farewell. They thronged the room, and at my father's request a pile of gold was put on the bed, and when I feebly shook a bondsman's toil-hardened hand my father would hand him a gold-piece as my last gift. The emotional nature of the darkies found vent in muffled cries and sniffings, which discounted the mourners' bench at a camp-meeting. Having bade them good-by, and having settled my earthly account, I turned over and—went to sleep, a real cherub. I awoke safe and sound; but alas for a death-bed repentance! about a week after, when my pulse again made healthful music, I summoned my father to my bedside and asked him to make those niggers give back all the money. (p. 20)

The gang's revenge on the market hunter was also short-lived. Alexander was packed off to boarding school, Sam got the "derndest lickin' of his life" and left when his father moved west, while Robinson and John became field hands. But this youthful association would soon have been ended by the war. Alexander describes that transition:

> The winter of '60 and '61 ended my shooting days for a long time. The boys on the Southern plantations dropped their fowling-pieces and seized the musket, the saber, and the lanyard; the setters and pointers became house-dogs, the pack of hounds ate their heads off, and the game had a rest from their natural enemy, man; for the sportsmen, North and South, instead of killing game, were busy shooting one another. (p. 30)

The Civil War brought radical shifts in Southern society and its life-styles. Blacks were no longer commodities, a legal fact necessitating a new accommodation throughout the rural South, which changed planters from "labor-lords" to "landlords," causing a fundamental shift in their identities and behavior.[2] Thereafter, planters paid closer attention to their wealth in land than they had till now and shifted some of their paternalistic impulses to their dogs and their quail. Both land and animals responded to the planter's control without retribution. Like many others of his privileged position, Alexander Hunter survived the war and returned to the plantation in its reconstituted form.

Although Hunter wrote of other quarries, he was basically a hunter of quail, a bird he describes as "the most wonderful bird on the North American continent." His sentiments were not shared by those he considered of lesser stature: "The darky would whistle in answer and then declare that the colored man and brother 'didn't have no show nohow wid dem partridges' " (p. 113). A landowner's wealth in quail was pervasive and worthy of perpetuating. And it is about the financial consequences to the economy if the bobwhite became annihilated that Hunter begins his chapter on quail hunting:[3]

> Plain, unpretending Bob White furnishes at least one-half of the sport in both the North and South to-day. Exterminate him, and every gun manufacturer in the land would fail; every ammunition factory would go to the wall; half of the sportman's bazaars in the country would close their doors; hundreds of mechanics would be out of employment, and thousands of workmen would be turned out to the cold charity of the world. Not only this, but every kennel in the land, whose combined capital runs into the millions, would be broken up, and blue-blooded setters and long-pedigreed pointers would not bring the cost of their collars. The vast collection of guns would greatly depreciate in value, and the shrinkage in price of all sporting goods would be enormous. Yes! a wonderful bird is the little brown-coated, shy partridge, who is as much the friend of man as is his deadly enemy, the dog, who hunts him. (pp. 113–14)

Alexander Hunter's conception of nature and society was Darwinian, and the bobwhite quail provided for him the ultimate, visible expression for "the survival of the fittest." Despite their being "snared, gunned, baited, trapped, hunted, shot at and worried" (p. 114), quail, unlike most other game, were thriving. What, queried Hunter, could be the secret for this success? His rhetorical answer was that in being such a wonderfully adaptive species, quail had changed their habits completely. In quail, Hunter had found a metaphor for enduring on a capricious landscape, and he hoped that similar survival skills were present in his class of leisured gentlemen. In some ways he was right, for the plantation and its field sports, like John Brown's body, were lying amoldering in the grave, but their spirit continued to march in the veins and imaginations of Southern landowners and their Northern confederates.

Though it was the national game bird, Hunter notes that the habits of Northern and Southern quail differed. Southern birds were wilder, stronger of wing, and more wary. They had learned the trick of trusting more to their legs than to their wings. And such differences called for different skills in those who would pursue them and in their canine companions. Northerners, he tells us, selected for "fine carriage, free ranging, slashing style and staunchness," while Southerners chose those that exhibited "methodical hunting, careful trailing of the running birds, a capacity to push his way through briers and vines, good retrieving, and above all, toughness' (p. 116). A successful hunt in the South required careful planning and attention to detail.

Such planning began with the dogs. After nine months of leading a vagabond life, the long-haired setters were clipped, fed dry cornbread, and restored to their self-respect. Even so, it took several days to reinstate them to "thorough discipline." Dogs performed best when hungry and were kept under constant surveillance. By voice or by whistle, the shooter constantly let the dogs know of his presence. Otherwise, upon finding a dead bird the dogs would be tempted to consume rather than deliver it to their master. Hunter's prescription for a dog caught in the act of eating birds was a sound thrashing (p. 118).[4]

Attention to detail included overhauling the saddles and bridles, greasing the boots, and placing sufficient ammunition in the saddle pocket and in the hunting jacket. The choice of weapon was crucial. For Hunter, a No. 12 Greener with 28-inch cylinder barrels was the gun of choice, and No. 8 or 10 pellets the choice of shot. After giving these details, Hunter takes us on a quail shoot to a homestead "around which cluster only pleasant memories" (p. 120).

Hunter describes the "ecstatic feelings" with which a quail season begins: "The wild delight of the dogs, the whole household on the porch, the plantation-hands grouped around, everybody smiling broadly, and every heart light and interested!" Girls lay odds on the tally of birds each sportsman will bring back. This ritual "adds zest," for "nobody likes to disappoint the one who lays odds on him." The hunter pays off the bet with a pair of gloves (p. 121).

Besides Hunter, the party consists of two sportsmen, George and Whit "both of them were to the manner born" (undoubtedly a pun!), and Fred, a neighboring countryman whose fame comes from ownership of "the roughest, shaggiest, most un-cared-for setter." Whit and Hunter ride horses, George mounts a mule, and Fred is on foot. As they leave the yard, "a whole raft of little pickaninnies" in a show of deference rushes to open the gate, ushering the party and their six dogs into the sober business at hand.

The dogs run around at full speed and must be continually ordered behind the horses. Discipline of dogs must be rigidly enforced, for the sportsman, an efficiency manager, seeks "to husband his dogs' strength by every means in his power" (p. 122). The first covey rise procures only two birds as the pursuers lose the singles in a thicket. After a brief retreat, hunters and dogs regroup and work their way through several promising fields, enter another thicket, flush several large coveys, stop to rest and to smoke, and resume the hunt. The afternoon produces what Hunter describes as "the most powerful, artistic sporting picture I ever saw on the hunting field." It was a "beautiful stand" of "four dogs, side by side, touching each other, motionless, petrified, as it were; every muscle tense, every hair bristling" (pp. 126–27). The shooters are spellbound for five minutes, watching this freeze of natural instinct. Then lacking faith in their dogs and expecting to jump a rabbit, the shooters advance. The covey of a dozen birds bursts away without losing a feather as the men fire mechanically. Hunter muses that the quail deserved to escape for the potent point they stimulated in the dogs (pp. 126–27).

During the afternoon, Hunter notes the different skills and tactics of younger and older dogs. Each dog has its specialty and any exhibition of skill is praiseworthy. Yank's specialty is finding single birds. Even in open pine woods, where the birds match the pine needles, Yank "would often come to such a sudden stop that every muscle was thrown into bold relief, his eyes gleaming like coals" (p. 128). Where the birds remain unseen, the hunters accuse Yank of making a "false stand."

Unlike Yank, Range had to be disciplined persistently by Fred with a dusting of shot for exhibiting indifference. On this particular hunt, Range is disciplined twice by shooting before distinguishing himself with a magnificent stand over a "whaler" (a large covey of birds). Further along, the group secures a wild turkey and cripples a "Molly cotton-tail," which Range finds and begins to consume. When Fred confronts Range in the act, "He was the maddest man on top of the earth at that moment. He slung his gun around, and I am confident he would have put a load of shot, at short range, through the dog's head but for my intervention. I told him to cut a thick hickory switch and give the dog the worst hiding he ever had; that unless the vice of eating killed game was eradicated he might as well give him to some darky for a 'possum dog" (pp. 132–33).

Shooting ended at sundown. On the ride home, Hunter is struck by the conspicuous absence of hawks. Whit puts this observation in perspective by relating it to an increase in birds. "Darkies" were responsible for the absence of hawks, having shot them to protect their chickens (pp. 133–34).

Hunter closes his account with homely advice about bobwhites, hunting gear, feeding of dogs, and caretaking of guns. Through his writings, he seeks to distinguish sportsmen from all other seekers of game. Since all hunters killed their game, distinctions could not be based readily upon outcome. Instead, those privileged to mark their differences from others had to rely on attitude, motivation, and standing—characteristics not readily apparent except to aspirants of the new norms. Sportsmen of Hunter's stripes espoused a particular worldview, were wealthy, kept their subscriptions to sporting journals, and generally lived in urban areas. Alexander Hunter provides a glimpse of this new breed:

> I may say here, that when a sportsman goes for a month's shooting he goes for pleasure, and not for profit. He does not hunt industriously from morning until dusk, like a man who has only a few days to indulge in sport and wants to crowd a week's work into a day's shoot, and stuff his pockets with every possible bird that can be killed, crippled or run down. A sportsman who has the good fortune to be an inmate of a charming Virginia household, with his time at his own disposal, takes things easily; he hunts only on good days and loafs a good deal, and spends hours of the time lying at length on the heather under some tree, enjoying his pipe and reveling in the dreamy languor of a perfect Indian-summer day. Of course he rides; to tramp for hours on foot may suit a pot-hunter, market-gunner, or our African brother, but does not appeal to an amateur sportsman. (p. 135)

The threads of meaning in Alexander Hunter's writings are drawn from the larger cloth of changing political and economic landscapes. While his own vision focused narrowly upon his immediate turf, events and circumstances elsewhere impinged upon and eventually were to change the nature of Hunter's world. Wildlife was losing ground everywhere to new developments on the American continent and to overharvesting by hunters.

Wildlife and the Changing Cultural Landscape

The public's indifference to wildlife in the antebellum period, underscored by William Elliott, changed into a melee of crusades for the wildife that remained during the last third of the nineteenth century. The pendulum of public opinion swung away from game as an exclusively economic resource toward a more elitist tradition of sport for amusement and of species preservation. And this pendulum swing brought with it the force of policy changes and the establishment of new institutions.[5]

Beginning about 1870, an ideology of protectionism spread throughout the nation. It began in the North and spread West before flowing South. In each state, protectionist groups confronted local customs, existing statutes, and ingrained interests. Although there were many factions in the emergence of this new consciousness, the changes in the laws and customs may be followed through the activities and motivations of three main groups. These groups— sportsmen, market hunters, and landowners—had well-defined interests whose goals were sufficiently disparate to preclude accommodation. The sport hunter's favorite hunting site was likely decimated by the lucrative exploits of the market hunter, while both were equally vulnerable to changes wrought in the landscape by the landowner or his tenant.[6]

Before the Civil War, sportsmen were few. They kept in touch by reading and by contributing to *The American Turf Register* and *Spirit of the Times*. These periodicals reprinted the English sporting codes and provided images for American converts to the "proper world of field sports." After the Civil War, the spread of urbanization and industrialization, together with changes in transportation and weapons, made getting back onto the land and to nature attractive for many Americans.

Sportsmen shared a particular worldview defined by attitude, motivation, and affiliation.[7] Like Alexander Hunter, sportsmen tracked their quarries in a highly stylized manner, conversed with a technical vocabulary explicit about game and guns, demonstrated an abiding interest in natural history, adhered to a code of ethics, donned fashionable dress afield, often professed an interest in highly trained dogs, and belonged to cosmopolite associations. Only certain mammals and birds were worthy to test the skills of a sportsman and his dog. These prey were taken in a highly refined manner. Deer were given ground to exercise their natural instincts for escape, and birds were taken only on the wing. "The true definition is for one who seeks game, for his own pleasure, makes no profit from his success, giving to his friends, within that true instinct of noble heartedness that distinguishes every sportsman, one who finds it is that he has taken no unfair advantage of his friend," wrote George T. Nichols of the Georgia Game Association in his diary. He continued, a sportsman "never takes a mean one even of birds, giving that chance they should have! [*sic*] by allowing them to take wing before he fires—never shooting into a poor huddled flock of birds, on the ground, and then bragging of his success in the field. Out upon such sportsmen. They are not truly named—they should be called murderers—and not be recognized."[8] Sportsmen generally were urban, wealthy, Eastern, and professional.

Sportsmen took pride in their canine companions, often importing them from abroad. They kept detailed records on their dog's genealogies and breeding, and noted their desirable traits. Dogs were trained to locate and to retrieve specific game in a style befitting the refinements of their owners. A good retriever was to deliver shot birds "not mouthed torn and mutilated by curs, but laid in your hand by high breds, not a feather out of place, not even moistened by saliva," wrote Nichols.[9]

Representing other contenders in exploiting wildlife, market hunters took game and other wild animals primarily to sell. They worked for themselves, for the railroads, and for the lumber companies. They hunted either as part of small teams or as individuals.[10] Becoming a market hunter was comparatively easy, for most men already possessed the tools. Furthermore, hunters had access to unimproved land throughout the South until late in the nineteenth century. Along the coast, initial costs to enter the trade were somewhat higher, with the need for special weapons, large numbers of decoys, proper equipment, and with restricted access to waterfowl shooting areas.[11]

It may be difficult for city dwellers today, buying a limited variety of domesticated meats and fowl and maybe participating in an occasional hunt, to appreciate the omnipresence of wildlife in nineteenth-century diets and fashions. Virtually all birds and mammals were sold in cities, and their sale was a legitimate enterprise. Once killed, wildlife was readily sold to merchants, who were always receptive to new supplies.[12]

As a third group, landowners had a large stake in rights over wildlife. Their land produced most of the game which the other groups sought to pursue, trap, shoot, or ensnare. Although private property rights to their land were clear and defined, no such clear rights existed for the wildlife inhabiting it. As common property, wildlife was subject to local cultural norms and was generally available on a first-take basis. Whereas the lack of enforcement left the landowner to take wild animals at his discretion, local norms opened his land to the uninvited, who came to hunt and to fish.[13]

Landowners' actions influenced both the type of wildlife found and its abundance on their properties. They could modify their land as they saw fit, and they sought to retain this freedom. Furthermore, large landowners were organized and their influence was felt within local and state governments. Their strong disposition for private property rights in wildlife, like that in Great Britain, threatened the access that sportsmen and market hunters expected and exercised under rights of common ownership.

Small landowners rarely documented their hunting exploits, and if they did they rarely showed a sportsman's flair. In Gaston County, North Carolina, James L. Love recorded that he killed rabbits by tracking them in fresh snow and by shooting them in their beds. His purpose was to kill for meat, not to give "the rabbit a fair chance for his life." Others in his neighborhood hunted for squirrels in the day and for 'coon and 'possum at night, but Love did not care to participate in either of these events. Quail were caught by nets and in traps. Near Raleigh, Walton Stone is reported to have whistled for and killed quail during the spring. Killing quail or any other bird on the wing was seen as a waste of ammunition.[14]

Throughout the latter half of the nineteenth century, wildlife in the Carolinas and elsewhere was on the decline. Even the stocks of wild birds, which formerly frequented the fields and barnyards, were noticeably diminished. Reminiscing about his youth in Mecklenburg County, Dr. John Alexander wrote, "The civilization of the last fifty years will have much to answer for when we see the great coveys of birds driven from our country to make way for utilitarianism."[15]

The customary liberties of landowners and those of the sport and market hunters were brought to a showdown by the increasing scarcity of their common enterprises. The states assumed ownership of wildlife as common property, and the courts sustained that precedent. The ownership issue went against the grain of landowner sentiment. Eventually a licensing system provided the funds for a new institution, the state wildlife commission, whose agents became the vehicles for enforcing the game laws throughout the countryside. Landowners' acceptance of these encroachments on their proprietary rights suggests that they benefited from the situation. Perhaps such benefits were appreciated within the context of the trespass and stock laws, which worked in tandem with the capitalization and mechanization of Southern agriculture.[16]

The Changing Landscape of Technology

For the South, the decades following the Civil War were important ones for building railroads. In 1850 North Carolina had only 248 miles of track; by 1890 the state had stretched this mileage to 3,128. Postbellum railroads extended into the nonplantation regions, linking these interiors with Northern markets. With the consolidation of many smaller roads and the conversion of their tracks to standard gauge in the 1880s, rail lines enlarged the potential for commercial agriculture and industry, thereby making merchants into a powerful class in the countryside. The consolidation of Southern railroads also made them vulnerable to takeover bids by wealthy Northern entrepreneurs, who were in control by the 1890s.[17] This expanding network of rails and its new technology of cold storage facilities opened opportunities for railway managers, who sought to fill their boxcars with marketable produce and who actively promoted field sports through advertisements.[18] The second Northern invasion of the South came by way of refrigerated, Pullman, and private cars.

Through advertisements in journals and papers, railroad management sought to lure sportsmen "to visit the South and hunt game where it is more plentiful than in any other section of the United States."[19] In these pamphlets, North Carolina was depicted full of "hospitable people," who would assure Northerners of a "hearty welcome. All the world knows the latchstring of the South hangs out."[20] Southern Railway offered its customers a curious mixed bag of hunting and history:

> Long ago, when Cornwallis was in the lower Carolinas, Marion and his men were the game he tried often to bag. But his lordship, though he scoured the Palmetto State from its western fringe of mountains to its eastern skirt of sea, was never able to catch them. The partridge was not swifter than they, nor the hawk of keener eye. They dealt a quick blow and darted to the cover of friendly woods.
>
> To the hunter of this later time who traverses the lower Carolinas in quest of game birds instead of red-coats, there is given not a little pleasure in knowing that he is on Marion's stamping-ground. . . . Marion and his men lived on what game they killed, and sportsmen now, who hunt under the palmetto can easily do likewise.[21]

Railroad pamphlets offered a veritable saturnalia to Northern sportsmen, providing names of guides together with hotels and boardinghouses, summaries of game laws, and types of game found adjacent to the major stations along the railway lines. North Carolina was described as a place where "quail shooting is of the finest,"[22] and Laurinburg in 1921 was specifically noted for its quail and turkeys and as a place where dogs and guides were procurable.[23]

The response of some North Carolinians to these commercial ventures was positive, as demonstrated by the numerous listings of hotels and boarding-houses, by the rosters of guides and hunting-dog owners, and by the leased hunting preserves and well-appointed clubhouses in the mountains and along the coast.[24] Not all responses were so cordial, however. The whirlwind out-of-town excursions by sportsmen had the potential of devastating local wildlife, a prospect deeply resented by many residents and landowners. With quail the major attraction for outsiders, there were county laws by 1883 against the "export or transport from the State (of) any quail or partridge, whether dead or alive."[25] By 1905 most of the land had been "posted" against outside hunters.[26] Whether these laws were effective is doubtful, yet the increasing slaughter of game birds by Northern sportsmen and market hunters helped to crystallize public sentiments around the creation of a state wildlife management and law enforcement agency. One of the organizers of the Audubon Society in North Carolina, Dr. Thomas Gilbert Pearson, wrote:

> There were not, and never had been, any state officials known as "game wardens." It was extremely rare that any one was prosecuted for infractions of the game-laws, although such violations were numerous. Once in a while some pot-hunter aroused the ire of a sportsman who would get a peace officer to arrest him for hunting out of season. Now and then a Negro would get into trouble. Gentlemen hunted game for their dining-tables and to give to friends, or if too busy or too inert, would hand a Negro some shells and promise him a dollar if he brought back a good bag.
>
> There was considerable sentiment in the State for preserving the quail supply, this idea being fostered by sportsmen who did not want game to become scarce and by farmers who wanted to lease the shooting rights on their farms. However, birds were abundant and very good to eat; sheriffs were scarce, and, incidentally, enjoyed the flavor of game as much as any one.[27]

The rise of sportsmens' associations in the 1870s coincided with the heyday of their nemesis—the commercial or market hunters. During the last decades of the nineteenth century, the commercialization and exploitation of American wildlife was evident everywhere, with commercial hunters active wherever wildlife populations were abundant. Ironically, the same technical developments that made good wildlife habitats accessible to market hunters also brought them closer to sportsmen.

By the late 1880s, sportsmen could travel to their hunting haunts in comfort by rail and, upon their arrival, enjoy many activities of the hearth. Improvements in weapons—the breech-loading hammerless guns and center-fire cartridges—made shooting more pleasant and rewarding than had the previous arsenals of muzzle loaders and black powder. First perfected on the European continent in the 1850s, the breech-loading shotgun and its cartridge were refined in subsequent years and widely adopted by British and American sportsmen in the 1880s.[28] The various sizes of double-barreled, repeating, and automatic weapons became the means to ambiguous ends, depending on whether the hands that held the stock and pulled the trigger belonged to a sports or market hunter.

The postbellum revival of field sports in the South brought it in phase with the broader shifts in social movements and technology taking place on both sides of the Atlantic. The agricultural revolution in England and the extirpation of most English game mammals had led English squires to shift their fields to birds.[29] Beginning in the nineteenth century, this shift to birds became more than a mere shift in sensibilities.[30] We recall that William Elliott's ability to hunt deer in his backyard constituted an important part of his Southerness, an identity he projected to his readers in the North and in England. Both of these groups lacked the circumstance to hunt large native game animals within their neighborhoods.[31] In England, new incubating and rearing technologies made it possible to raise, manage, and shoot game birds in large numbers.[32] Furthermore, birds demanded less space than deer or foxes and could be taken sportingly on the wing and in battues after the breech loader and pointer dog were perfected. This efficient production and mass destruction of semidomesticated birds, from hatching to market, reflected emerging bourgeois values and the corresponding industrial metaphors of the developing social order. In England the production, distribution, and consumption of game birds became sporting commodities controlled by a relatively small circle of elites.[33]

Wealthy Northerners were attracted to the idea of the Southern plantation as a haven from winter weather and as a hunting preserve.[34] With game of all types, particularly deer, becoming scarce, Southern landowners grappled with their new identities. For many, such as Alexander Hunter, this new identity was buttressed by quail hunting and by their methods of take. This shift from fur to feathers in the South thus followed developments elsewhere and brought Southerners in line with the broader cultural and class norms of the times.

The *American Sportsman*, first published in October 1871, was the first national journal devoted exclusively to field sports, natural history, and conservation. Others soon emerged.[35] These national magazines provided sportsmen an important way to converse, to keep abreast of timely topics, and thereby to enhance their identity and function as a group. With sportsmen's clubs springing up in the cities, these monthly periodicals codified sporting ideals and helped to solidify sentiments behind conservation efforts in the political arena.[36] Northern sportsmen often took the lead in pressing for conservation legislation.[37] State game associations pressed legislators to pass laws protecting game and were often instrumental in bringing offenders to trial. That they were not always successful is illustrated by a case brought by the Georgia State Game Association in 1875 against a party having trapped birds (quail) in possession. The Game Association lost the suit because the law was not a general state statute. The association claimed a partial victory, alleging that before the legal decision was rendered, the party had petitioned to have the suit withdrawn on the promise never to trap birds again.[38]

Coalitions of organized sportsmen and naturalists in the cities influenced legislators to address the issues of wildlife declines in ways that benefited them. The conservation doctrines of preservation and wise use were initially piecemeal mixtures of nostalgic, scientific, and moralistic attitudes. The movement's various phases were fragmented until about 1890, when an awareness of ecological relationships, together with money, power, and political astuteness, provided the cohesiveness necessary to effect change on the federal, state, and, finally, county levels.[39]

The Changing Legal Landscape

The lack of uniformity in game laws, both among and within adjacent states, compounded the problems of law enforcement.[40] Within North Carolina, the General Assembly retained the authority over wild animals, but it delegated enforcement power to each county. When local government represented familiarity and trust to most citizens, this delegation of power to the local community was logical and expedient. Who would know better the status of game and be in the best position to assess the resource than those closest to it? A baffling array of county-specific laws that varied according to season, bag limits, game species, and trespass were the result. County citizens petitioned the state General Assembly for specific legislation, and some of these petitions were extremely local in context.[41] Fortunately, not all county petitions became statutes. Surviving petitions include requests to exclude fox hunters from trespass laws; to abolish all game laws pertaining to fishing, trapping, and hunting; and to make it unlawful to kill, shoot, trap, or net any partridge, quail, robin, mockingbird, bluebird, lark, wild turkey, squirrel or deer during an inclusive period.[42]

In 1900 the state court, in *State* vs. *Gallop*, affirmed that game was owned by the people and that the General Assembly had the right to grant, withhold, or restrict the right to take game. Furthermore, the court established that the legislature could prohibit landowners from hunting and fishing on their land at certain seasons, and that it could exclude nonresidents from hunting privileges altogether.[43]

New initiatives were contingent upon finding a source of revenue to support the new agencies charged with enforcing game laws in the countryside. This source of funds came from the sale of hunting and fishing licenses. In North Carolina, popular resistance to this new tax was avoided initially by requiring licenses only from nonresidents.[44] The General Assembly in 1903 established the Audubon Society of North Carolina to protect and to promote wildlife within the state.[45] The sale of nonresident hunting licenses supported the efforts of the society and its wardens. Yet the society proved increasingly unpopular and met mounting opposition from the counties. One by one, the counties prevailed on the General Assembly to have them exempted from the statewide provisions of the Audubon Society. This state program collapsed about 1909, with more than half the counties setting up their own license sales.[46]

Prior to 1903, the spectrum of bird species that could be legally taken in the Tarheel State included robins, flickers, bobolinks, meadowlarks, and blackbirds.[47] How did this once extensive range of forms come to be reduced to the smaller list of species hunted today? First, different groups expressed diverse interests in different birds, some showed concern for only a few species, others entertained competing concerns. The sportsman valued birds as objects of pursuit, the market hunter as commodities for profit, the farmer as controllers of insect pests and benefactors to agriculture, and the urbanite as a bestower of the esthetic and emotional pleasures inherent in watching birds. Second, because of the birds' migratory habits, their protection became a national issue, for uniformity in state laws was essential to ensure the survival of the birds throughout their ranges.

Ornithologists and sports hunters provided the defining characteristics for the new legal categories of game birds. In 1886 the Committee on Bird Protection of the American Ornithologists' Union drafted a "model bird bill," which defined birds as game or nongame species on the basis of the scientific classification of orders and families rather than by individual species. This model bill became the basis for designating game species in many states, including North Carolina, and was supported by the Audubon Society.[48]

After the counties abandoned the Audubon Society, a statewide game bill was introduced into the General Assembly every term for almost two decades before it finally became a law in 1926. Only after the state Supreme Court ruled that a county could not charge a resident from another county more than its own citizens for a hunting license, and at Governor Angus McLean's urging, did the bill finally became law. This law established the State Game Commission within the Department of Conservation and Development.[49] A state game warden was the commission's chief law enforcement officer, and he was entrusted with a major education program. The main appeal of this new bureaucracy to hunters was "the feeling that this system is based on the most democratic of principles in that it allows the persons that are most closely affected to initiate needed regulations by petition."[50] This new state law also established North Carolina's first resident hunting license.[51]

The new statute divided wild animal and bird species into three classes. Within the *game* class, including furbearers, were deer, bear, foxes, squirrels, rabbits, skunks, muskrat, raccoon, opossum, beaver, mink, otter, and wildcat, as well as quail, dove, wild turkey, grouse, and pheasant. The legislature, through its wildlife agency, set seasonal regulations for the taking and possession of game species. It became unlawful to buy or to sell any of these game, except for rabbits and squirrels, which remained for a time legal purchases during their respective open seasons. *Protected species*, generally all those not listed as game, were not to be taken or killed under any circumstances. *Unprotected species*, such as the wildcat, which was also designated as a game species, could be taken by any means except by poison. As a *furbearer* and as a *game animal*, the fox was intentionally left ambiguous and within the bounds of county regulation.[52] A special category was given initially to migratory waterfowl, with their management left to county and federal regulations. As a consequence, the northeastern coastal counties were exempt from the new agency's jurisdiction, and special licenses were required there for the shooting of these fowl.[53]

The State Game Commission set about its task of replenishing stocks of game through creating game refuges and game farms. By 1940, thirty-four refuges were in place throughout the state, including a Scotland County refuge of some four thousand acres. State game farms at Fayetteville and Hoffman dispensed pen-reared quail and turkeys to many prominent landowners around the state.[54] During the Second World War, the Game Division experienced financial setbacks, forcing closure of a number of its stocking programs and rationing of its personnel and supplies.[55]

In 1947, under heavy lobbying from sportsmen's clubs and the National Wildlife Federation, the General Assembly created the Wildlife Resources Commission, which took over all functions of game conservation in the state.[56] The democratic philosophy of the commission, "More sport for more people, with equal opportunity for all," contains more than just a twist of irony.[57]

Introduced as a democratic right on the frontier, hunting became more and more restricted and refined as life in Carolina society became more differentiated and institutionalized. Technological developments increasingly narrowed the scope and democratic access to environmental processes and products, among them wildlife. Each generation of hunters, reflecting the social and economic differences of the times, redefined the hunters' respective myths of "nature," "game," and "wilderness" and the boundaries of their pursuits in keeping with their identities of time and place. Representing hunters' interests, wildlife commissions operated politically and culturally despite their democratic pretenses and their management ideals of "sound biological principles." Inevitably, some interests and options were never heard.[58]

Hunting is not a timeless pursuit within a cultural void. Its means and practices have evolved in keeping with the political, economic, social, and cultural tempos of the time. Tying these human threads together within the cloak of hunting is the subsequent tapestry sought.

The Changing Political-Economic Landscape

The Southerner's passionate attachment to soil and to place was a post-Civil War phenomenon. Gavin Wright blames the South's postbellum economic miseries on the region's labor, which remained separate from the larger national labor market until after the Second World War.[59] This separate market for manpower had emerged when the South adopted slavery and sought to protect its "peculiar institution" from the preferences of the rest of the nation. Slave labor became the chief form of wealth in the Old South, and it was a highly movable asset. In Wright's terms, masters and planters were labor-lords, and because of the potential mobility of their wealth form, they were not tied to particular locales. All this changed after 1865. In the meantime, the dashing displays of mastery over mobile cultural and natural creatures found artistic and metonymical expression in William Elliott's wildcat and deer exploits.

Alone among American regions, the Old South made a desperate attempt to become a separate country. Its defeat on the battlefields and the emancipation of its bonded labor transformed planters and masters from laborlords into landlords, thereby shifting their slave-holding energies into local endeavors and investments in real estate. It now became necessary to enlist and maintain a cheap labor supply to work the now valuable land. It was a South in which the studied cultivation and sport harvesting of quail proposed by Alexander Hunter now made sense and became a meaningful metonymy for the localization of economic enterprises and control. Although Southern landlords encouraged the growth of towns, railroads, and factories, along with other enterprises, the South's labor force remained poorly educated, unorganized, and segregated. Industrial labor, like agricultural labor, remained typically low-paid and isolated from the relatively higher wages of the rest of the national market. It took the New Deal and World War II to shake the ship of the Southern economy free from its moorings in the regional past and to allow it to steam confidently into the American mainstream.

However, the economic and structural consequences of slavery took many years to overcome. Events of the past continue to influence individual consciousness and behavior. Memories remain selective and often benign, tending to forget the dismal side, especially if those plights occurred to others. Therefore, I begin by examining events and circumstances between the end of the Civil War and the close of the nineteenth century for eastern North Carolina generally before turning to events in Scotland County specifically. Shared historical experiences are the molds in which community identities are forged and which subsequently come to express themselves in distinctive attitudes, practices, and traditions.

North Carolina Generally

Reconstruction in rural North Carolina was a difficult period, characterized by uncertainty, violence, and confusion as whites and nonwhites attempted to cope with new conditions and formulate new roles. With slavery and its framework of social controls destroyed by the Civil War, both races now sought to define new economic and social relationships in a setting which neither completely controlled. Most Southern whites had not been slave owners, but they were also subject to momentous social change. Once tangential to the plantation system and largely self-sufficient, their independence now eroded and they were swept into unprecedented subordinate roles as tenants and mill workers.[60]

In the early days after emancipation, planters struggled to resurrect the old system as they knew it, while their former slaves tried to give some substance to their newly found freedoms. The planters still owned the land but had little money. The freedmen wanted land and economic independence. Through the passage of black codes, vagrancy laws, enticement statutes, and violence, landowners sought to restrict the freedmen's mobility, their alternative employment opportunities, and their access to other means of production and subsistence.[61] Sharecropping and tenancy evolved to meet the needs of a money-scarce society.

According to Harold Woodman, the period 1870 to 1900 throughout the South was a time marked by the emergence of a working class conprised of former slaves and once self-sufficient whites, and the formation of a bourgeois employer class of former slave owners.[62] There were many forms of tenant farming, but its goal was nearly always the same, with most blacks and many whites becoming wage laborers. The difference between tenant farmers and sharecroppers was important despite the fiction that both groups were actually wage workers. A tenant farmer rented the land he worked and was obliged to pay an agreed-upon portion of his yield to the landlord. The remainder was his to dispose of, subject to liens by others. The croppers, mostly blacks, were assigned a particular plot of land and were peons with no right to dispose of the crop. Here was another "peculiar institution." It resulted in the return of the plantation, not of the antebellum kind but of a large-scale capitalistic farm. It was distinctly Southern, influenced by the legacies of slavery, racism, poverty, and other peculiarities of its culture and politics.[63]

Changes in property rights provided new incentives that linked some seemingly disparate postbellum developments. The intensification of land use and the commercialization of agriculture led to the protracted political conflicts of the 1870s and 1880s and to the closure of the open range in many North Carolina counties. Previously, land rights were given lower priority than the rights of small scale farmers and herders who hunted, foraged, and fished on unenclosed land. Farmers were responsible for fencing their crops, while livestock were free to roam at large for their food and water. The stock laws, or "no fence" laws of the agriculturalists, reversed this tradition by requiring owners of livestock to fence in their animals and by protecting the inviolability of property lines. The closure of the open range deprived many poor, landless whites and blacks of valuable resources on which they had depended to sustain their life-styles. This loss was a serious blow to their independence and freedom, which in turn contributed to the political and economic turbulence characterizing the remaining decades of the nineteenth century. The stock laws not only changed the relationship between animals and crops, they also altered the mutual interdependence of people in the countryside.[64]

Landlords channeled their enterpreneurship into location-specific activities alongside other developments that enhanced the value of their holdings. With the shift to commercial crops, particularly cotton and tobacco, during the 1870s and 1880s, towns grew and prospered at strategic intervals along the transportation lines. Light industries and mills throughout eastern North Carolina were an outgrowth of this new entrepreneurial spirit and of changes in the countryside.[65]

The postbellum period brought expansion and prosperity to the manufacturing, transportation, and banking sectors of the state. In agriculture, however, chronic economic depressions followed declines in prices. Most farmers progressively lost their social position, wealth, political influence, and power to the urban business and professional classes. The deteriorating condition of small farmers led them to form coalitions that sought redress for grievances and for general improvements in rural life. They joined with black and white Republicans to displace the Democrats briefly from office during the 1890s, thereby creating a measure of democracy uncommon in the state.[66]

The Fusionists, as the alliance between the Populists and Republicans was called, restored some autonomy to local governments and increased the numbers of blacks voting and holding offices in the eastern counties. The visibility of blacks as office holders, together with a surge of racial tension, led the Democrats to focus their 1898 campaign on "White Supremacy." The populist movement was undermined and defeated by a variety of tactics, including discrimination, intimidation, fraud, and violence. Restitution followed repression, and black disfranchisement confirmed Democratic dominance in state politics until the 1970s.[67]

Scotland County Specifically

It is within the context of rising democratic coalitions and reforms of the Populist movement followed by political repression that Scotland County was created. The petition to create the county of Scotland from the eastern portion of Richmond County was introduced in the General Assembly by Hector McLean in 1899. It was not a new petition: similar petitions had been submitted three times before. A major grievance was that the county seat, Rockingham, was an inconvenient distance from its eastern section, placing a heavy tax on "the poorer classes." The petition stated: "It is a source of much anxiety to people living in the country, who frequently have to leave helpless families at home unprotected for several nights, while male members of the family are attending court."[68] White supremacy and the fear of black domination were the political codes. White fears of blacks ran deep.[69] This time the petition passed; the county was surveyed and began operation on December 10, 1900.

A number of family fortunes have been amassed within Scotland County, and probably more have been lost. One whose fortunes and influences are still felt was John F. McNair (1843–1927). Although McNair made a lot of money, his legend is that this fortune was at no one's expense. He enlisted in the Confederate Army and returned, like many others, impoverished. He stated out by running a small farm and using one room in his house for a store. His business and investments prospered. He was president of the State Bank, built the local Laurinburg and Southern Railroad, began the local oil and fertilizer companies, was a director of the local mills, and had other enterprises throughout the Carolinas. To many of his contemporaries, John McNair was just "a plain ole dirt farmer"—a self-effacing identity assumed by many leading citizens of the county today.[70]

Linked to the McNair family enterprises is the name of Z. V. Pate. He took over McNair's store in Laurel Hill, became his son-in-law, and expanded the company's land holdings into the surrounding counties. A name associated with industry is Mark Morgan, who came to the county in 1872 looking for "a place of healthfulness and renumerative work." He stayed on and became a partner with Colonel Mallory in the Richmond Cotton Mill and a leading manufacturer, banker, legislator, and agriculturalist.[71]

In 1924 the *Laurinburg Exchange* celebrated Scotland County's first quarter century by issuing a national publicity edition. The county was said to lead the state in various ways, including the production of more than two bales of cotton per person, an achievement that ranked it among the leading "counties of the world." In addition it produced more cantaloup and watermelons than any other county in the state, and the sandhills were being converted into peach orchards.[72]

Laurinburg had a large fertilizer factory, a large flour mill, the largest cotton oil mill in the state (independently and locally owned), four cotton mills, and various other industries.[73] Its first mill, Scotland Cotton Mill, was built in 1899 followed by additional mills in 1900, 1910, and 1920. According to the *Laurinburg Exchange*, all four plants were under the same "management and practically the same ownership and have been operated successfully since their establishment." In keeping with the paternalism of the times, the special edition noted that these plants were never known to "throw their help out of employment for any period of time." East Laurinburg was "a model manufacturing town" without labor problems. "The agitator and the propagandist finds little comfort there, where honest, hardworking, good American people believe in the golden rule and practice it." Finally, the editorial declared: "This is a God-fearing and religious people, who put first things first and make principle and right the rule of life. We are glad it is so."[74]

In the years after Appomattox, religion and God came to play an increasingly important role in pronouncements of local identities and in the interpretations of events. If before the Civil War, God's word had justified the peculiar institution of slavery, Southerners now sought to explain the failure of their cause. Southern apologists agonized over the question of why the South, as the inheritor of the best Western traditions and therefore God's chosen people, could have been destroyed by the Yankee barbarians. In this interpretation, the South had been conquered by might, not right, and the apologists were convinced that the South would surely triumph in the end. Religious idealism salvaged what the Northern defeat had denied the South on the battlefield and it became part of the persistent armor of Southern identity.[75] Within this context, hunting and its ennobling traits took on a quasi-religious redemption. The South may have lost on the battlefield, but civility, gentility, and grace were redeemable on the sporting field.[76]

Southernness was the substance of a Memorial Day speech in 1924 delivered by Dr. W. E. Hall, the pastor of the First Presbyterian Church in Fayetteville. On this occasion before a Methodist congregation in Laurinburg, Dr. Hall's topic was patriotism and the spirit of the South. He declared that the South was never conquered, rather its "resources were exhausted and its brave men were killed in battle, or wounded, and the staggering but unconquered remnant with Lee at Appomattox surrendered to the inevitable. But the undaunted spirit of the people marched on and is still marching to this day." Dr. Hall said he would not speak disparagingly of the North "for he admired Yankee grit, which after all was American grit and the common inheritance of all." Yet having laid on his audience that disclaimer, he admitted that he could name offhand six or more Southern military leaders who were unmatched by the North.[77] The cult of the Confederate War heroes, men of stature and statues of men, kept the issues of separate identities alive well into the twentieth century.

Unlike the boosterism of the local newspaper, the county's agricultural agent's report for the 1920s showed no rosy landscape. In 1920, 15,600 people inhabited the county. Only 17 percent lived in the city of Laurinburg and 61 percent of the population was listed as nonwhite. Many of the county's black farmers and tenants lived in the northern sandhills. They had their own separate agricultural fair each year. Even with low cotton prices, 50,000 to 54,000 of the county's 80,000 acres of cultivated land were in cotton in 1927, which were dusted against the boll weevil by aircraft. Despite the agent's best efforts, farmers refused to diversify their crops and livestock.[78] On the farm, the automobile displaced more horses than mules, and mules would remain the main work animals for several more decades.[79]

Many farmers eventually lost their battles against both weevils and bankruptcy. The census of 1930 showed a county population of 20,174, with 56 percent nonwhite, including 70 percent of the rural population. The depression of the 1930s was hard on small farmers, tenants, and sharecroppers. Many of the former lost their lands through foreclosures, forced sales, bankruptcies and outright purchases by larger landowners. During this decade, the percentage of nonwhites dropped and the percentage of people living in towns increased.[80] Blacks and Lumbees remained the main tenants on the land. Much of the marginal lands in the sandhills section was purchased by the Resettlement Administration as a reforestation and recreational area. Today these lands comprise the Sandhills Game Management Area, open to all hunters who purchase state licenses and permits.[81]

The Agricultural Adjustment Act of 1933 and the Soil Conservation and Domestic Allotment Act of 1936 paid landowning farmers to take their land out of production. These legislative acts by the federal government gave farmers strong incentives to displace most sharecroppers and tenants and to convert the remaining ones to the status of wage laborer. Farmers idled the land that was once cultivated by sharecroppers, who with no role in the rural economy migrated North in large numbers.[82] This "American Enclosure Movement," as Gunnar Myrdal called it, had "progressive" consequences even while it inflicted hardships on many. The demise of tenancy and the outmigration to the North of many sharecroppers opened the way for the mechanization of cotton farming, the Civil Rights revolution of the 1950s, and the rapid industrialization of the 1970s.[83]

The farm population of Scotland County declined further after the Second World War. Between 1950 and 1960, census figures showed a decrease of over 1,100 people, mostly blacks; the 1,686 farms of the former period had decreased to under 1,000 by 1960. Cotton continued to be the main crop and source of income for the 8,430 people living on farm tracts. During this decade, many farms were planted in pine trees and retired through the Soil Bank Program. Decaying and overgrown tenant shacks became the symbol of this passing era, for by the end of the decade most landlords were hiring only day laborers.[84]

Throughout the 1960s and 1970s the number of farms continued to drop as farmers continued to retire acreage through government farm assistance programs.[85] These conservation programs, together with a decrease in the number of people living in the country, extended wildlife habitat and allowed some species, particularly deer, to increase and to expand their range during the 1970s. In 1978 there were only 174 active farms in Scotland County, averaging 516 acres each. Farming was heavily mechanized, with cotton remaining the mainstay along with soybeans, corn, and small grains.[86] These drastic changes in the county's population and structure were part of the greater matrix of change that prompted county leaders to attract more industries during the late 1950s and 1960s.

County actions during the 1950s were built upon previous events.[87] The building of the Laurinburg-Maxton air base and the training of some thirty thousand troops within the county during the Second World War brought events of the outside world closer to many residents. Immediately after the war, county leaders were successful in obtaining state and federal assistance for a number of local projects. These projects included matching funds for the Scotland County Memorial Hospital, and housing for people with low income. The community was also successful in obtaining state and federal funds for roads, streets, and bypasses which enhanced its attractiveness to outside industry. The success of these community actions led to a sense of accomplishment among civic, commercial, and professional leaders. Their growing sense of community-oriented action and boosterism was dramatized by the selection of Laurinburg in 1956 as an "All-American City" and as the site for St. Andrews Presbyterian College.

Although there had been locally owned industries in the county since the 1870s, the first outside plant, Ingraham, began operations in 1959. In 1954 Scotland County lost a bid for an industry to a rival town; the explanation was that not all people within the community wanted the plant. With that loss in mind, the Laurinburg Chamber of Commerce reorganized to promote industrial development, which then became community policy.[88] The leaders and principal actors in bringing industry to the county were few. They modestly and quietly worked behind the scenes and channeled the energies of others. On the occasion of the hospital dedication, the Laurinburg Exchange editorialized: "The people know who they are and to whom credit is due. They are men who would be embarrassed by any mention of their names and who would prefer to remain in the background."[89] The noblesse oblige and somewhat counterfeit legacy of the "plain ole dirt farmer" prevailed.

In 1960 the Southern National Bank provided new sources of credit for business enterprises. Many of the activities mentioned in Laurinburg's presentation for its second successful "All-American City" award in 1967 (urban

renewal, hospital expansion, additional industries, improved recreational facilities, additional buildings at St. Andrews College) were activities begun
somewhat earlier. Among the new activities cited were the consolidation of
town and county school systems, a new library, and a mental health clinic.

It is ironic that the solution decided upon by community leaders in the
1950s to preserve the integrity of their ventures was that of industrialization
by national and eventually by international companies. Yet given the broad
trends in communications, transportation, technology, and economics that reduce geographic and cultural differences, for the county not to have boarded
the bandwagon of New South developments would have proved more problematic. By joining the trend, leaders now found themselves faced with new
questions of how to balance cheap, unorganized labor, low taxes, and minimal constraints on growth with expectations of rapid advances in the general
standard of living, increased social services, political stability, and other factors pertaining to the public's perception of "quality of life."[90] The gradual
passing from the scene of the inequitable economy based upon race and
county control ushered in new uncertainties. By the late 1970s, Scotland
County was showing that it was more than the small, caring community of
churchgoers and team players that its boosters had projected to outsiders. It
was a community in transition, whose citizens possessed a hodgepodge of
provincial and cosmopolitan attitudes. In many ways, the answer depended
on who and what was asked.

Gavin Wright reminds us that the new international economy resembles the
economy of the Old South in at least one way.[91] The disregard for place and
people implied in the ruthless use of mobile wealth by planters is like the
insensitive employment of mobile capital today. At one point, a community
and its decision-makers are favored to nurture another's capital; at another
time, they lose as the political and economic climates of capital growth
change. And this new mobile economic order must be accommodated by all
people, everywhere.

Four

Pursuits and Provincialism:
Contemporary County Hunters and Their Concerns

My daddy was a hunter. He even hunted before he had a bird dog and he'd walk up this quail and he'd wait until a coupla quail crossed each other, and he'd get two at one pop. He'd come home maybe with nine birds and he hadn't used but six shells. So when I got large enough, he took me along. He gave me a light gun and some shells and we'd get up a covey of birds and they'd fly off and he'd pow, pow, and the birds would fall. He'd turn around and say, Did you shoot? And I'd say, Well, I didn't this time. He said, Well, you got to shoot you know. You can't kill them unless you shoot. And from then he trained me out there in the woods. He trained me to fish and how to hunt, and finally got him some bird dogs.

(A Lumbee professor)

PEOPLE LEARN from their histories. The political and economic upheavels throughout eastern North Carolina that began in the nineteenth century and lasted through the 1960s produced generations of ordinary citizens who shied away from anything political. Lacking an effective two-party system and subject to Jim Crow laws that disfranchised many of them, rural citizens in Scotland County learned that dissent was not welcome and that politics was something left to those in power. Rather than become involved in politics, they turned to activities such as family, religion, or some form of recreation through which they might achieve control and distinction. Whatever one's choice, the individual controlled it and felt sheltered from society's power. Politics and government were synonymous with potential danger and with reductions in personal freedom. These sentiments remain today, especially among the older generation.

As a form of recreation, hunting arose directly from the fabric of common interests and sentiments of rural life. Most men of earlier generations developed their basic sense of social identity in the small, tightly knit, rural communities where they were reared. This world of face-to-face contacts derived its unifying force from common experiences, from seasonal routines, and from a shared culture. People's social relationships stemmed mainly from the ties of family, neighborhood, and church, and by those formed in the course of earning a living. Hunting and fishing were a release from the constraints integral to an agricultural way of life. In hunting, a person's character and accomplishments provided the stuff that forms enduring bonds. Men were criticized or praised, respected or reproached, as a consequence of their success or failure in well-established roles. Thus, the small peer group was the canon for assessing masculine abilities and tastes. Participation challenged individuals to try new and powerful roles, each initiated under the aegis of a rough-and-ready social equality before generating a hierarchy of its own.

In this chapter, we examine the characteristics of hunters in Scotland County during the late 1970s, using information gathered from the Wildlife Commission, from hunting licenses, and from a questionnaire administered to a sample of license holders. From these sources, we can refine our understanding of the hunters' world, including who hunts, how hunting is learned, what some of its boundaries are, the types of equipment employed and the prey sought, and, finally, hunters' attitudes toward their game, hunting, and locality.

The North Carolina Wildlife Resources Commission

No understanding of local hunting is possible without some reference to the state's institutions and their power over the lives of ordinary citizens. Despite the hunters' strong inclination to keep politics off their personal turf, wildlife belongs to all the people in the state. As common property, rights in wildlife are vested in the General Assembly, which stipulates the conditions under which these resources may be pursued and possessed by individuals. Once the General Assembly enacts the laws, the details of wildlife assessment and management become the province of the Wildlife Resources Commission, which has broad regulatory authority to resolve management problems and to make some regulatory decisions.

Candidates for the position of Wildlife Commissioner are chosen at public assemblies of sportsmen held in each of the nine districts throughout the state. The slates of candidates and the number of sportsmen voting for them are forwarded to the governor, who decides which commissioner to appoint in each district. Two additional commissioners are appointed at large by the governor and one each by the Speakers of the House and of the Senate. Commissioners, who serve six-year terms, assemble monthly, review information, and make decisions regarding wildlife management. The daily functioning of the Commission is vested in an Executive Director and his staff.

In general, the Commission follows a standard procedure in establishing hunting regulations. The process begins with the gathering by biologists of statistical information on the major game species, using a variety of direct and indirect counts, and comparing them with counts from previous years. On the basis of these trends, the Commission proposes regulations on bag limits, seasons, and other matters, which are then aired each spring before public assemblies of sportsmen in each district. Summaries of these hearings are presented to the wildlife commissioners for their consideration. Once set, the regulations are publicly announced, and are enforced throughout the state by "wildlife protectors."

For the public, the most visible arm of the Wildlife Commission is its enforcement branch, which employs the majority of its personnel. The wildlife protector is the keystone of current wildlife management, for two reasons. First, hunters do not obey laws and regulations without effective enforcement. Fear of being apprehended and fined remains a deterrent to illegal behavior for many hunters. Second, many of the Commission's programs are financed from sales of hunting and fishing licenses; consequently, enforcement is essential to maintain this flow of revenue.

Wildlife protectors are stationed in most counties of the state. They wear distinctive uniforms and are furnished with radio-equipped patrol cars; occasionally they employ other equipment such as boats and aircraft. In addition to enforcing the wildlife regulations, protectors give talks to schoolchildren on nature topics and perform other "public service" functions. All fines for violation of game laws are paid into the school fund in the county where the trangressions occurred. The wildlife protector's work has been described by a mix of biblical and wildlife metaphors: "Perhaps of all occupations, it is the one most requiring the wisdom of Solomon, the tact of the diplomat, the cunning of the fox, the patience of the hunting owl, the courage of David, and most likely, no matter what he does, to result in the lamentations of Job!"[1]

As hunting has become more of a sport and less a necessity, the rules governing its manners and its seasons have shifted from local norms to formal laws enforced by uniformed strangers. Although both norms and laws continue today, state laws circumscribe the boundaries within which game is taken. Some types of sportsmen are more influential than others in establishing the laws to which all conform. These influential sportsmen have the foresight, time, money, and organizational acumen to affect directly the decisions made by the legislators and commissioners in Raleigh. Other sportsmen may attend district hearings and have their viewpoints summarized for the Commission. Yet for many others, such regulatory protocols remain mysteries. For members in this latter group, hunting remains largely a traditional activity, local in content and context. Their prospects for transmitting their passions and traditions to succeeding generations seem as problematic as their access to the surviving game.

Hunters and Their Game

At intervals, the Wildlife Commission solicits information from hunters concerning their targets and successes. The Commission summarizes and publishes these data in its magazine, *Wildlife in North Carolina*.[2] Annual license duplicates, kept in Raleigh, provide demographic and residential information on county hunters. Together these sources provide a first glimpse of Scotland County hunters and their pursuits.

The Commission mails its questionnaire to a sample of hunters. The information that is received, summarized for the state by district, provides estimates of what was hunted during the past season and of the number of game killed (table 4.1). During the 1970s popular species sought within Scotland

TABLE 4.1

Ranking of North Carolina Wildlife Species, by Numbers of Participating Hunters, Hunting Trips, and Harvest Success Rates, 1972–73.

Game Species	Participating Hunters	Hunting Trips	Harvest	Trips per Hunter	Success Rate
Squirrel	197,155	1,309,280	2,072,110	6.6	1.6 squirrels / trip
Rabbit	178,925	1,227,920	1,461,780	6.9	1.2 rabbits / trip
Deer	145,296	1,163,400	47,469	8.0	24.5 trips / deer
Dove	141,107	716,516	3,064,510	5.1	4.3 doves / trip
Quail	119,639	963,225	1,981,910	8.1	2.1 quail / trip
Ducks	32,454	183,152	195,593	5.6	1.1 ducks / trip
Raccoon	30,172	304,430	168,437	10.1	1.8 trips / raccoon
Fox	10,332	85,033	NA	NA	NA

Source: *Wildlife in North Carolina* 38, no. 1 (1974):25–26.
NA = Not given.

TABLE 4.2

Harvests of Major Game Species in North Carolina's Wildlife District Four
(Includes Scotland County).

	Wildlife Species					
	Deer	Squirrel	Rabbit	Quail	Dove	Ducks
Number of hunters	18,267	26,409	24,330	21,437	21,229	8,749
Number of hunting trips	130,001	227,533	167,076	161,640	126,681	54,337
Kills	5,802	270,538	145,594	329,409	592,026	44,877
Trips per hunter	7.1	8.6	6.9	7.5	6.0	6.2
Kills per trip	0.04	1.2	0.9	2.0	4.7	0.8

Source: Mail surveys of hunters, 1970–71, reported in *Wildlife in North Carolina* 37 (January 1973):22.

County's district, as measured by the number of trips hunters made to take them, were deer, squirrel, quail, and rabbit (table 4.2). By the early 1980s, this order had shifted slightly to deer, squirrel, rabbit, dove, and quail. If a game's popularity is measured by the number of its hunters, deer hunters were followed by those after squirrel, dove, rabbit, and quail, in descending order. Yet in numbers of game killed, dove was the most popular, followed by squirrel, quail, rabbit, and deer.

Dove shoots begin the season for most sportsmen. Dove shooters kill more than four doves per hunting trip. With a daily bag limit of twelve birds, a marksman usually does not find it difficult to kill a legal limit. At the other extreme in terms of kills are deer hunters, who make many trips for each deer bagged. As "big game," deer are sought by many, but obtained by only a few. Quail hunters averaged two birds per trip. Squirrel hunters averaged slightly more than one squirrel per trip, while those after rabbits and raccoons averaged less than one animal per foray.

The popularity of hunters' prey has shifted gradually since the 1940s (table 4.3). Squirrel hunters, the largest segment of license purchasers when the commission began its mail surveys, were outnumbered by deer hunters during the 1980s. This shift reflects the expansion of deer throughout the state and the growing popularity of "big game" hunting. Quail and rabbits have declined in population and popularity, reflecting changes in land-cultivation practices, availability, and "taste."[3]

Scotland County License Purchasers

As the main revenue for the Wildlife Commission, hunting and fishing licenses have substantially increased in cost in recent years, along with inflation. In 1977–78, the Commission issued twelve hunting licenses. The Resi-

TABLE 4.3
Changing Popularity of Species Hunted.

Start   **Finish**

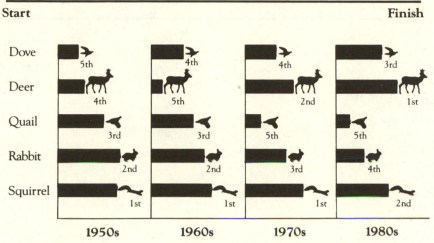

Source: *Wildlife in North Carolina* 50 (February 1986): 27. Reprinted with permission.

dent Sportsman License, the most expensive at twenty-five dollars a year, allowed its holders to hunt and fish, with few restrictions, throughout the state. Other licenses, scaled in costs, restricted its purchaser geographically, to a particular time, to the use of certain weapons, or to taking certain species. The licenses sold in Scotland County during 1977–78 reflect the demographic and residential characteristics of their holders (see tables 4.4 and 4.5).

The majority of license purchasers were white (74.7%). Whites purchased combination hunting and fishing licenses and were the main supporters of the Resident Sportsman license. They bought the full range of licenses and they, together with a few Lumbees, were the county's trappers. About 20 percent of the whites purchased county hunting licenses, as did 16 percent of the Lumbees and 36 percent of the blacks. Blacks accounted for 16.5 percent of license holders, with half purchasing combination hunting and fishing licenses. As indicated by their purchase of county licenses, blacks mainly pursued small game, mostly rabbits and squirrels. Almost 9 percent of license purchasers were Lumbees, who sought both hunting and fishing privileges.[4]

In 1978 the proportion of male hunters by race in the county's population was 63 percent white, 33 percent black, and 4 percent Lumbee. By 1981, 60 percent of the male hunters over ten years of age in the county were white. Why are there proportionately more whites and Lumbees than blacks among license purchasers? In light of the region's past history of racial repression, it is not surprising that comparatively few blacks hunt. Moreover, blacks are not likely to congregate in large armed groups and engage in quasi-military activities, as many whites do. Such overt militant displays by blacks are likely to

TABLE 4.4

Distribution of Hunting and Fishing Licenses Sold within Scotland County, by Race and Residence, 1977–78.

| | Race | | | | Residence | | | | |
Type of License	White	Lumbee	Black	Total Number	Laurin-burg	Rural or Town	Maxton	Other County	Total Number
Combination of hunting and fishing	468	73	87	628	201	330	38	59	628
Resident sportsman hunting and fishing	121	5	6	132	31	92	1	8	132
Resident state hunting	67	5	30	102	44	51	2	5	102
Resident county hunting	173	17	70	260	50	192	4	14	260
Game-land permit	—	—	—	118	33	63	—	22	118
Resident big game	—	—	—	367	82	223	16	46	367
Resident state trapping	22	1	1	24	4	17	3	—	24
Country resident trapping	5	2	—	7	1	4	1	1	7
Primitive weapons	8	2	—	10	1	7	2	—	10
Nonresident 6-day hunting	16	—	2	18	—	—	—	—	
Nonresident hunting	8	—	—	8	—	—	—	—	
Controlled shooting preserve	5	—	1	6	—	—	—	—	
Totals	893	105	197	1,680	447	979	67	155	1,648
Percentage	74.7	8.8	16.5		27.1	59.4	4.1	9.4	

Source: North Carolina Wildlife Resources Commission, Raleigh. Information used when legible on licenses.

provoke countermeasures by whites seeking to sustain black subservience and dependency. Reconstruction and its aftermath brought new levels of racism and violence against blacks, and this has affected hunting as well as other walks of life. Hunting and hunting rights were particularly important in establishing new social lines between blacks and whites. Ironically, in the Old South, blacks and whites had been able to hunt together and mingle in ways that were no longer acceptable when blacks were freed. As a consequence, one rarely sees blacks hunting, and rarer still are the occasions when they are found hunting with whites.[5]

TABLE 4.5

Distribution of Major Hunting and Fishing Licenses Sold within Scotland County, by Race and Decade of Birth, 1977–78.

Type of License	Race	Decade of Birth						
		1900–19	1920–29	1930–39	1940–49	1950–59	1960–69	Total
Combination hunting	White	28	70	76	137	124	33	468
and fishing	Lumbee	4	6	13	26	22	2	73
	Black	11	24	10	32	10	—	87
Sportsman hunting	White	9	11	21	45	29	6	121
and fishing	Lumbee	—	—	—	3	2	—	5
	Black	1	1	1	2	1	—	6
Resident state	White	3	3	5	19	27	10	67
hunting	Lumbee	—	—	1	—	4	—	5
	Black	3	3	3	10	9	2	30
Resident county	White	6	9	21	30	64	43	173
hunting	Lumbee	1	3	3	1	5	4	17
	Black	9	4	12	10	27	8	70
Totals		75	134	166	315	324	108	1,122
Percentage		6.7	11.9	14.8	28.1	28.9	9.6	

Source: North Carolina Wildlife Resources Commission, Raleigh. Information used when legible on licenses.

Most (60%) license purchasers lived in the country or in small towns. Many were there because of economic circumstances that allow few choices. Men who have few years of formal education and are experienced only in mill and farm work have few marketable skills and choices of residence. Yet rural lives, embedded in dense networks of kin and friends, have the advantage of easy access to hunting land and to jobs requiring menial labor.

Hunting is mainly a young man's sport, with two-thirds of the license purchasers being under forty years of age. For most, the zeal for pursuing game diminishes with age, as demands of work, family, and other obligations encroach upon their time. Yet the fact that 20 percent of license purchasers continue to hunt after their fiftieth birthday lends credibility to the saying that "a man's a hunter if it's in his blood."

Finally, hunting is largely a masculine domain. Of the approximately twelve hundred license purchasers in the county, only fifteen (one percent) were women. Thirteen of these women were white, one was black, and one a Lumbee. The majority (thirteen) were under forty years of age, lived in the county, and purchased licences permitting them to both fish and hunt.

Data from county licenses show that hunters are predominantly white, male, of rural residence, under forty years of age, and pursue local game and fish.[6] I tried to flesh out these categories by asking additional questions from a sample of license holders.

A Sampling of Scotland County Hunters

The general attributes of hunters one gets from licenses convey nothing of the reasons and value systems that motivate hunters. To gain deeper insight, I sorted licenses by race because race continues to be an important indicator of life chances in rural North Carolina. Then I divided licenses into age groups (over and under forty years of age) and further sorted these by residence (Laurinburg, town, or rural address). Using these categories, I interviewed a sample of seventeen blacks, fifteen Lumbees, and forty-six whites and asked each of them to respond to a series of statements and questions while I also encouraged informal comments and discussion.

Information obtained from my sample supported several regional stereotypes (table 4.6). Whites had the highest level of education, with almost half having had some college, and they belonged to the more favored economic and professional ranks. Lumbees were intermediate in position between whites and blacks in both education and household income. Blacks had less formal education and were employed as menial workers in local industry and agriculture. Until the county system was consolidated in the late 1960s, schools were segregated. More than half of my total sample had no formal education beyond high school.[7] Those completing their formal education at this level found their choice of work and occupational opportunites limited. A third attended courses at local technical colleges to enhance skills in their current jobs. Whites with college and professional degrees had attended institutions within the state. These educational attributes indicate a decided provinciality, at least within my sample.

Children's attitudes toward animals are strongly influenced by their environment.[8] About one-third of my sample grew up within Scotland County and over half in adjacent counties. Four whites, reared in cities, came to North Carolina while in military service at Fort Bragg, married local women, and worked in local industries.

Most respondents belonged to the three major Protestant denominations and attended church regularly. Although Baptists predominate throughout the South, Scotland County is one of the few counties in which Presbyterians are in the majority. Their Scottish heritage and faith predominate in many county activities.[9] A quarter of my sample claimed fundamental and evangelical faiths.

An individual's dwelling is an indicator of his economic status.[10] Within the county, Lumbees resided more frequently in mobile homes than did blacks or whites, suggesting with historic irony that they were among the more recent arrivals. All racial groups resided in largely segregated neighborhoods, with the majority of blacks and Lumbees owning no land. About half the whites owned land, most of which they leased to agribusinessmen seeking to consol-

TABLE 4.6

Socioeconomic Information Provided by Questionnaire Respondents, by Race.

	Race		
	Black (N=17)	Lumbee (N=15)	White (N=46)
Highest educational level obtained			
Primary	6	5	6
Secondary	8	6	14
College (number with degree)	3 (0)	3 (0)	21 (12)
Graduate school	0	1	5
Household income			
0–$9,999	7	5	8
$10,000–$19,999	6	2	17
$20,000–$29,999	4	7	51
Over $30,000	—	1	10
Childhood environment			
Urban	—	—	4
Scotland County	6	3	18
Rural other county	10	12	23
Urban and rural	1	—	1
Age			
39 years or younger	5	10	20
40 years or older	12	5	26
Religious affiliation			
Baptist	4	4	12
Presbyterian	2	1	17
Methodist	8	1	5
Pentecostal Holiness	3	2	7
Church of God, other	—	5	3
None	—	2	2
Current residence			
Trailer	4	9	3
Wooden frame house	3	3	13
Cinder-block house	4	3	3
Brick house	6	—	27
Landowner? (Owns 3 acres or more)			
Yes	5	6	26
No	12	9	20
Voted in recent presidential election (1976)			
Yes	9	7	43
No	8	8	3

idate their holdings in mechanized operations. A few white professionals re-
siding in Laurinburg retained farms or cabins in the county.

That only half the blacks and Lumbees voted in the 1976 presidential election is no surprise, given the disenfranchising history of the region. Participation in local elections is generally lower.[11]

Sixty percent of my sample were taught to hunt by their fathers (table 4.7).
For many youngsters, learning begins as soon as they are able to accompany
adults afield. Induction by fathers was the main avenue into the hunting world
for whites and Lumbees. Initiation by friends or peers was more common
among blacks, and to a lesser degree among whites. Five individuals claimed
to have no mentors. They were largely self-taught and absorbed hunting skills
as part of their youth.

With more ready access to guns, land, and dogs, whites and Lumbees
began to hunt at an earlier age than did blacks. The earliest age of a first kill
was by a white, who was six years old when he shot a dove. Most whites had
made kills by their eleventh birthdays. Generally, blacks started later, and
their group included the person who was the oldest (thirty) when he made his
first kill. He killed a rabbit while out with a group from work.

The initial kill is a significant event in the life of a young boy. Beginners
usually go after squirrels as well as rabbits. If run by dogs, rabbits can be
difficult targets, but they can also be spotted and shot in their beds or taken in
rabbit boxes. Rabbits were the most frequent initial targets for blacks and
remain the species most hunted by them. Doves were the most frequent initial
kills of young whites. Many of these youngsters took song birds with the BB
guns that were given to them as birthday and Christmas presents.

What is it that motivates men to hunt, especially since it no longer constitutes an essential economic activity? When posing my question about why
individuals hunted, I suggested three answers: for meat, for sport, for contact
with nature.[12] Most described themselves as sport hunters, frequently combined with the other two categories. Certainly, sport hunting was the most
socially accepted answer. It lacked the stigma attendant to those who hunted
exclusively for the table, known perjoratively as "pot hunters." However,
most game taken *is* eaten, within the household. Within white households,
game frequently has important gender significance in marking the dependency
of family members upon masculine abilities. Hunting for meat was the reason
given by over half the Lumbees. Perhaps their answer underscores the
staunchness of their traditions and the insularity of their cultural norms. Only
four respondents, whites and urban professionals, claimed to hunt for the contact with nature it brought them.

Because hunting begins as a family- or peer-oriented activity, its styles,
skills, and techniques have the potential of remaining a local expression or of
encompassing more cosmopolitan values. For some hunters, traditions remain
provincial; others are drawn into larger networks, becoming part of larger

TABLE 4.7
Hunting Socialization and Initial Kills, by Race.

	Race		
	Black	Lumbee	White
Person who most influenced informant to hunt			
Father	6	12	29
Close relative	4	—	3
Friend or peer	6	3	10
No one	1	—	4
Informant's age when first kill made			
Under 10 years	—	4	17
10–11 years	2	1	10
12–13	2	7	8
14–16	7	3	9
17 years or older	6	—	2
First animals killed by informant			
Squirrel	6	11	19
Rabbit	10	2	9
Raccoon/possum	—	1	—
Dove	1	—	8
Songbird	—	1	5
Quail	—	—	3
Other	—	—	2
Rationale for hunting			
Meat	3	7	3
Sport	9	3	24
Contact with nature	—	—	4
Meat and sport	5	2	1
Combination of all rationales	—	3	14
Belongs to sporting organizations or subscribes to hunting magazines			
Yes	9	5	37
No	8	10	9

organizations and special interests. The organizations they join may be local, such as county clubs, or regional and national, such as Deer Unlimited, Quail Unlimited, or the North Carolina Wildlife Federation. Within these organizations, a person may become actively involved or may simply read its literature. My sample shows that whites were more avid joiners of sporting organizations and readers of sporting magazines than Lumbees and blacks. About half the blacks joined organizations and only a third of the Lumbees.

Once learned, hunting may become part of an individual's identity, used to reference him socially and economically and to place him within a specific group. Within the group, roles are vetted, affirmed, or denied in competition with close associates. If affirmed, the activity may be undertaken as an appropriate role and seasonally expressed, or more actively and consciously interwoven into one's life-style and biography. This absorption of hunting into an individual's personality and his purposive engagement in perpetuating its traditions are clear in the following interview with a lawyer, a wildlife commissioner appointed by the governor:

Well, I started with my dad when I was seven or eight years old. He always kept bird dogs and was an avid quail and deer hunter. We had bird dogs in the yard all the time, family pets as well as hunting dogs, and he started taking me with him when I was just a little fellow. I couldn't keep up with him at all. There was just something about the outdoors that drew my fondness. I sometimes think that maybe it's all in how one is brought up as to what he likes in life as far as hobbies. I hunted and it just grew on me and I grew to love the outdoors, especially quail hunting, and I love to watch the dogs work and I love to watch the quail. I think quail is a beautiful bird, and there's just nothing like being out on a cold, crisp November day when fall's in the air and there are beautiful colors everywhere behind a good bird dog in search of a rare bobwhite.

My dad also took me to his deer-hunting club when I was about eight. I usually went with him about every time he went that school didn't interfere. Some of the older hunters didn't particularly like it that I was tagging along. And I loved the fire, the fellowship, the big tales they told, sleeping out in a shed filled with pine straw. There was just something about the atmosphere that I became enamored with and learned to love more and more as I grew older.

SAM: *The things you look back on that were important were your father, identifying with the dogs, a rural background, getting away from home.*

Right, small town. I had plenty of woods around me. There was a lake down the road. It was not very populated then, and I had a dirt road and woods to roam in and dreams to dream of being alone in the woods, sort of like Robinson Crusoe. At my very earliest, starting with a BB gun and slingshots and graduating up to the .22 and .410 and .20 gauge.

SAM: *Do you remember the first animal you killed?*

I remember several animals. I remember very vividly the first quail I killed. I would say that probably the first thing I killed was a squirrel. I was probably seven or eight. I slipped up on one I saw in the woods not far from my house. It was sitting there beside a branch. I had a .16-gauge double-barrel shotgun. I saw him stop on a limb not too far from me and I killed him. And I remember having some remorse about shooting him with a shotgun because he really didn't have a sporting chance, so to speak. I remember another time killing one with a .22 rifle, almost at dark. He was way high in a pine tree. He was crouched on a limb that you could just barely see the outline of his body. I was down to my last shot. I had missed all of them but that one. I had a single shot and I put it in and downed him with the last shot. And I remember very vividly the first quail I killed. I was about ten or eleven then. How the covey got up and how I picked one on the right and he fell and the old setter that wouldn't retrieve found him and I had to run to get the bird because he wouldn't bring him back.

SAM: *You hunted deer and quail with your father.*

Yeah. Now, I do remember. You asked me about my first animal. I remember that I killed some with a BB gun. What we called not the best sort of birds—a sparrow, blue jay, or mockingbird occasionally. One time I slipped up on a female cardinal. I could see the bird through the shrub and I shot. Damn it if it wasn't a cardinal and I felt terrible about that. But I used to waste my BB's primarily on the little sparrows that you see so frequently. I remember one time, I told my mother that I hoped that all the birds that I was killing with my BB gun were bad in the eyes of the Lord so that I wouldn't be killing the good ones. And I remember overhearing her tell that to my father when I wasn't in the room!

SAM: *What other values are associated with hunting? You mentioned your meaningful relationship with your father.*

I think tradition to me has a great deal to do with it. I came along to hunt with my dad about the time that the great quail hunting was on the wane. I heard the tales of the great hunts in days gone by and the great experiences out-of-doors and the great bird dogs that pointed with one in his mouth and retrieved two dead birds at one time. All that wasn't purposely ingrained in me, but I just fell heir to it by virtue of being around to hear the tales. My father and I had a very close relationship and when he went out to see his friends, he'd carry me along no matter how bad they cussed or anything. He figured I had to learn it sooner or later. I subconsciously dreamed of the days when a man had a frontier to conquer, much as we did in the West. I often wonder how much that plays in getting out-of-doors and feeling that frontier spirit even though it's limited.

SAM: *You came along when wildlife began to wane. How has that made you feel in terms of coping with circumstances when you know that you'll never replicate those days which your father and his friends talked about?*

Well, that's one reason I feel like my years on the Wildlife Commission are worthwhile in trying to leave some heritage for the younger generation. It's going. Habitat's shrinking, the pesticides they're using are killing a lot of small game. I wonder if when my son gets to be my age, or younger, if he'll have the opportunities I had. He won't have the ones I had when I was his age now, when you could go out and find covey after covey of quail in the open woods that had been burned, and the big longleaf pines that you could see a quarter mile through. Those days are gone. It bothers me. I worry about it sometimes, the fact that I may be seeing the last of it.

SAM: *Does it worry you that your son will be hooked as you were on his father's tales of yesteryear?*

Yeah, possibly so. He's probably heading along the same path that I headed. He's gone bird hunting with me. I've carried him to the deer-hunt club. He's fished with me and he loves it all. The next question is always, when can we go again? But I have encouraged him to get interested in other things—baseball, football, something which I have an interest in because that may be all he has to enjoy. At least, I think he'll always be able to fish, and I've encouraged that. We probably fish more together than anything else.

SAM: *In your mind, is hunting related to your identity with the land or the perpetuation of landownership?*

That's a good question. I never thought about that. I don't relate the hunter's activities to the perpetuation of the land, but I relate hunting to the beauty and the quaintness of a place. I had favorite coveys that I've shot year after year, but there's a certain attachment to a tract of land. The tract of land that we control in the Sandhills we plant feed patches every year. But I've never hunted those quail up there. I do it just for the pure enjoyment of getting out there, planting the stuff, seeing what it will do, and seeing what wildlife it feeds. Watching for deer tracks, looking to see how many coveys of quail we can run out of one feed patch. We also feed ducks up there on the big pond. We don't shoot ducks there either. We've got wood-duck boxes up there and usually every year they're full.

SAM: *Would you tell me about those "bad" birds you shot as a teenager?*

Yeah, like the worst of the lot. I didn't hate them, but I find a lot of times, like the birds I killed as a small boy, that I sometimes regret killing a buck deer. To take that thing away, to snuff out its life, although I'm aware that if we don't harvest a few that it will lead to some destruction by nature. I don't kill anything that I don't eat, and I enjoy quail and I enjoy dove. I enjoy venison and I've had some of the best venison tenderloin this weekend that I've ever had. I don't care for rabbit, I don't kill rabbits. Now, I'll shoot one occasionally when I'm out bird hunting because I know either my companion wants the rabbit because he likes it or a friend wants the rabbit. But I don't kill rabbits for me. I don't hunt squirrel any more. I just try and hunt those things that I enjoy.

I've asked myself this question, how to get down to the nitty gritty of taking something that you also turn around and try to protect. And I think, maybe subconsciously that you protect so that you can take or you take so that you can protect. And for the beauty, for the fact, that you want your son to see a dog point and maybe his son see a bird dog point.

Reflections on Wild Animals, Hunting, and Community

On my survey, I read to hunters statements from a variety of sources that seemed relevant in sorting out respondents' attitudes about wild animals, about hunting, and about community life.[13] They were asked to tell me whether they strongly agreed, agreed, had no opinion, disagreed, or strongly disagreed with each statement. I used the responses to these statements, together with comments contributed during the course of the interviews, as sources for putting these hunters and their community into context. (See the Appendix.)

Hunters expressed an ambivalence in their relations to wild animals. In some ways, wild animals and men inhabit separate worlds, with each domain having its own attributes. In other ways and at other times, the actors in each domain are joined and interact. For most of the year, however, wild animals are left to cope on their own with a few inroads of assistance by farmers, who may plant some wildlife foods in patches, and by others who may decide to leave some vegetative cover for the game. In the wild, animals predict and cope with severe weather, an attribute my respondents thought was superior to that possessed by humans. Other attributes of wild creatures—their freedom, smartness, wildness, beauty, and adaptability—are admired within the context of their survival beyond the limits of human protection. The opening of the hunting season removes this insularity. Hunters now seek game and through their contests and conquests acquire some of its attributes. By their returns, they come to distinguish among themselves.

About half of my sample denied the overall superiority of men over game. To attest to hunter superiority goes against an image of game as "worthy opponent." A few sportsmen affirmed that "some animals are smarter than man, all of them to a certain degree, and one on one most animals are smarter." The smart animals in mind were the deer, the fox, and the raccoon, not birds. Most small game coped through "instincts" and were less adaptable than the larger forms when faced with changes in habitat and challenges from humans. The ability to reason was restricted to humans and to the larger and more elusive mammals. These mammals "have more sense than people generally give them credit for."

The domains of people and wildlife were separated more for blacks than for Lumbees and whites. Fewer blacks agreed that affection was an appropriate emotion toward wild animals, and 40 percent thought animals didn't feel pain to the same extent as humans. In his nationwide survey, Stephen Kellert found blacks had a "negativistic attitude" toward wild animals, expressed through less general interest and affection.[14] Perhaps those at the bottom of social hierarchies need to distance themselves more from "inferior" creatures, while those near the top can afford to feel a closer affinity for them.

As the hunters' analogues in the natural world, predators were dangerous and efficient killers. As a consequence, most respondents thought that a decrease in nonhuman predators would benefit their sport. In particular, rabbit and quail hunters blamed foxes for the low numbers of their favorite species, a conviction they and trappers often voiced in public hearings during the 1970s. They wanted to get the fox reclassified as a furbearer (from that of a game animal) so the fox could be trapped legally.

More than half of my respondents were supportive of trappers and their ways of securing wild animals. As expressed by one sympathizer, "Some people makes a living off that (trapping) as a way of getting money for dog food. Animals remaining loose are doing damage to farmers' crops." Another expressed a typical reservation, "The only thing that bothers me is when they catch the wrong thing, like my hunting dog." Pain in animals became brutally apparent when their own dogs suffered.

When pursued, all agreed, wild animals should always be given a fair chance to escape. Therefore, any chemical or mechanical items that took advantage of animal "instincts" should be outlawed. Yet, a few individuals carefully exempted some devices, since decoys, callers, and even bait were frequently used to attract or to concentrate game. My respondents linked sportsmanlike pursuits in nature to appropriate gentlemanly behavior in society: "It's important to give animals a fair shake. I don't know if you could trust another person to give you a fair deal if he wouldn't give it to the game."

With its weapons, tests of skill, dominance over dogs, and conquests over wild creatures, hunting is in symbolic opposition to the traditionally ascribed roles of women in the homeplace. Respondents overwhelmingly agreed that through hunting, male youngsters learned important attributes of sportsmanship—including a sharp sense of observation and the development of self-reliance, fair play, patience, and unselfishness.

Some respondents felt that most women they knew distrusted guns, abhorred violence, and depended upon their men, as fathers or spouses, for protection. A machinist, married to a local woman, expressed this informing ideal his way:

I think women have much more love for life than a man does. A woman ain't never had to be a protector. It's never been bred into the woman that she's got to be the food supplier, in the case of hunting, or in the case of war, the protector. It's just never been bred into her.

My wife won't go hunting. She's scared to shoot a gun. I tried to get her to shoot a gun, but she's scared to. I don't know why. We live out here by ourselves, and because we hunt and stuff so much that I bought her a little .22

hand pistol. She was scared to pick it up. She wouldn't shoot somebody if they came in the house. I said, "Woman, you've got to be crazy. You and Chris are by yourself and you mean to tell me if somebody came in through that door you wouldn't cut loose with them on a gun?" I told her that I could show her how to shoot somebody and not kill them. If you cut their legs out from underneath them, you're not gonna kill them but they're not gonna get you either. She's just scared of the gun because she knows what the potential of that gun is.

Many men believed that sex roles reflected the biological and evolutionary pasts in which women stayed around camp gathering while men hunted and killed the important parts of the shared meals. As a consequence of this belief, people engaging in these subsistence activities today found a source of "innate" satisfaction. Guns and hunting were less important to the identities of Lumbees and blacks than they were for most whites.[15]

Marriage was a major, often disruptive, transition for a man's previous hunting commitments and associations. One informant said he knew friends "who hunted up to when they got married. Once they married, hunting drops off. It has something to do with family, the wife herself and what she says about it. Lots give up hunting so women won't hassle them about it." Another claimed the marriage might "have slowed him down a bit, but if you live to hunt, if it's in your blood, then marriage won't make no difference."

Membership and participation in hunting clubs provide some men a haven from their wives, children, and job-related responsibilities. Surrounded by peers, men find diversion in playing cards, in drinking, in forays for game, in gossip about other people, and in animated accounts of notable successes. Less than half my respondents claimed hunting was an appropriate means to get away from women; other activities served that purpose. Most men feared competition from women if not their appearance in what is traditionally a masculine arena. A member of a deer-hunt club explains his reluctance to accept women as members:

I just don't think that's the place for a woman. I don't believe in women elders or deacons in the church. I'm just that conservative. There's been some up here when I've been here, but it seems to cut down on the looseness of the men. They tend to be watchful of what they say and what they do and that restricts me. I just like the relaxed atmosphere of getting away. You can say what you want to. If you want to cuss, you can cuss. If you want to step behind a bush and take a leak, you can do that without having to worry about someone peering around looking at you, or some woman being there. To me, it just puts restrictions on things and I like to be more fancy free.

Half of my sample agreed with the statement that women would find hunting difficult to understand. Men blamed women themselves for their lack of participation in the field.

Given the cultural barriers surrounding the masculine turf of hunting, how does one explain the few women who did purchase licenses? In 1977–78, eight women purchased combination hunting and fishing licenses, five got county hunting licenses, and two, state hunting licenses. Seven were reared as protégés of their fathers, who had taught them to hunt as they would have their sons. Five younger women hunted during courtship with their boyfriends or with their spouses. Fishing was a more acceptable activity for couples to engage in together. Therefore, if women hunted, they did so in company with a particular man, rather than as an activity sanctioned for women.

Hunting Dogs

If respondents felt ambivalence about their interactions with wild animals, they held no such feelings for their dogs. To them, hunting dogs are conceptually different from pets.[16] They are specially trained to make game visible and to track it down when wounded. Such dogs are believed happiest when performing hunting tasks and when exhibiting these skills.

An owner invests both money and ego in his dog. The dog is kept and fed all year; this devotion by his master is expected to be matched by the dog's performance in the field. When performing well, dogs are petted and verbally praised. On the other hand, a poorly performing dog may be abused, cussed, kicked, traded, or even shot.

In addition to performance, obedience and respect for the master's authority are synonymous with good breeding in dogs. Respondents generally agreed that "the more obedient the dog, the more kills he will make"; yet for a few, it was more important for dogs to be able to locate game than to obey or show respect.

Today there are specialized breeds of dogs for pursuing each type of game. Like the prey they are bred to seek, each breed is ranked. Generally, the more specialized the breed and the more restricted the pursuit, the more prestigious and costly the dog. At the top of the canine hierarchy are those with aristocratic pedigrees, including the pointers, setters, and foxhounds. Below these apical creatures, the ranking gets rough and in general expresses the wealth and standing of the owner. Near the bottom are the all-purpose mutts, including those used for chasing raccoon and deer out into the open.

Satisfactions from Hunting

Two-thirds of my respondents thought hunting was different from other sports. Yet they found these differences difficult to define except in general terms (different skills and results). Two thirds disagreed with the statement that blood sports "all represent the destructive and cruel energies of man directed toward the pursuit of more helpless creatures."[17] According to them, wild animals were able to best man on their own turfs and to escape his best-laid plans. Fair competition and meaningful challenges were vital aspects of the hunt.

Participation within a group allowed individuals to rank themselves according to skills associated with downing the game. The numbers of small game, particularly birds and rabbits, killed by an individual on a given day or during the season were tangible evidence of the hunter's competence and skill. "If someone kills more'n me, I'm proud of 'em" is how one sportsman put it. The image of killing an eight- or ten-point buck and mounting its head for placement within the house was a dream shared by many sportsmen. I interpret this image of a deer head mounted within the house as a tangible assertion of masculine dominion within the woman's sphere of influence; it is also a class statement about the existence and location of gender conflicts. Downed game as a symbol of conquest seemed less important among Lumbees. Hunting as a component of land ownership was most important for Lumbees, and least so for blacks.

Seventy percent supported the proposition that hunting organizations were important as a means of getting access to dogs and to land. Half the blacks thought so but cited lack of money as the major detriment to their wider participation in the sport. For three blacks, patronage and "friends of long standing" provided access to land. In general, the larger the hunting group, the less skill was required of each individual. Yet this assessment was conditioned by the types of prey the hunters sought. Dove shoots required many people scattered throughout a field to keep the birds flying, and the main skill was to hit the birds. Solitary deer hunters considered their observations and tactics to be superior to those participating in large drives with dogs. Yet small game pursuers of a utilitarian bent knew that "more hunters are more likely to get the meat."

Who hunts what appeared contingent upon many factors, including socialization into a tradition and into a network, social and economic status, and access to land and equipment, including dogs. Almost two-thirds of my respondents were in agreement with the statement that the rank of the game pursued reflected the social standing of those in pursuit. Yet the overall rankings of game depended upon whose opinion one sought. The most prestigious prey within the county was quail, but most hunters had to settle for other targets. The following conversation records the musings of three mill workers, all of them deer hunters:

People are big on quail down here. A lot of people will tell ya, they'll give you permission to hunt on their land and the first thing they'll tell you is don't shoot my quail. You can hunt my rabbits, the squirrels will eat here, but don't mess with my quails now 'cause that's something I'm aholding for myself.

Quail hunting is a nice sport, just a leisurely walk. The dog never gets out of sight of you, you can just set your own pace. You can talk to your friends, and just keep right on talking and your dog won't quit searching until he finds the birds. And they're good eating too.

SAM: *How would you rank the types of game in the county in terms of prestige? What would be number one?*

Deer hunting would have to rank number one, I think. I tell you, 'coon hunting would push it close. I mean there's a lot of 'coon hunters.

SAM: *When you're talking prestige, are you talking about coon hunting?*

No. If you are talking about prestige, it's your quail hunter. A lot of people who go with the upper class, your lawyers, some of your politicians and commissioners, quail and dove hunt. A lot of these dove hunt. They get together with the big farmers, the big landowners on the first day of the season. I've never been to one, but you hear other people and a lot of names mentioned at the dinners they have. The dove hunters are the politicians, your lawyers, your doctors. When I'm talking prestige, I'm thinking money.

Race and class are also recognized as important factors in determining who hunted what. An immigrant from the North who came to stay linked both caste and class:

You know, you've heard, there's a sort of racial barrier in there. The white people don't go for coon hunting and rabbit hunting as much as the blacks. The black people don't go for deer and bird hunting as much as the whites. You could say that coon hunting and rabbit hunting is a poor man's sport, really, because almost all the blacks I know that's all they do, rabbit and coon, and very few of them deer hunt. You've got to buy a real expensive rifle. You've got to buy clothing for it, you know boots and all this, where if you're out there rabbit hunting or coon hunting, you just throwed a pair of old duds on and go out there and stomp around and shoot your rabbit with a little old .22 or something like that. So it's a big difference.

Hunting and Its Management

Over half of those asked strongly agreed with the statement that without game laws and their enforcement, wildlife would have disappeared by now. Although formal laws provide the legal boundaries for the taking and possessing game and most men verbally accepted those limits, it was left to officials to catch violators. Yet the informal sanctions of peers were feared more than apprehension by outsiders. Informal sanctions on an individual usually meant his alienation from the local group. They reflected notions of "good sportsmanship," a collection of relative ideals that expressly excluded selfish individuals who "hogged the game" or the most favored locales. Among close associates, the notion also included everyday behavior and conversations. Contempt and disdain were expressed for those "who shoot, kill, but do not retrieve."

Still, many respondents were reluctant to turn over to authorities a companion who had violated a game law. Blacks seemed more vocal in their opposition to outside game authorities than whites and Lumbees. One black explained: "We have never done that—turned a buddy in—never had anything like that happen. We discuss it before we goes in the woods. If a guy has killed ten rabbits, we wouldn't give up the rabbits to the game warden, but would distribute them among the rest of the hunters." Another individual expressed his concern: "Anyone is liable to make a mistake—like in deer hunting. One should allow him a coupla breaks."

Sixty-five percent felt strongly that it was improper for poor families living in rural areas to trap and to take game out of season. Poor economic status generated no sympathy from sportsmen, who thought the poor were adequately cared for through food stamps and other welfare programs. Like the colonial aristocrats encountered in Chapter Two, sportsmen believed that the resources of the poor were improperly invested in hunting when a better investment came with finding and keeping a job. In addition, by trapping out of season, the poor were "depriving me of future hunting for you are killing adults and dependents. That would be comparable to digging corn before it come up."

Most sportsmen considered the egalitarian ideology of their recreation important. Blacks and Lumbees, who often face discrimination in finding good places to hunt on private lands, were strong in their support of "equal opportunity and access to hunting privileges." Whites were less inclined to agree. Those owning land felt "equal access" ran counter to incentives for providing habitat and food for wildlife; the game their land produced was not available for public taking.

Attitudes toward Self and Society

Rural Southerners generally tend to think of themselves as different, particularly from Northerners, whom they often use for comparison. Undoubtedly, many of their cultural traits, including conservativism, religiosity, a tendency toward violence, suspicion of government and of outsiders, preference for the concrete over the abstract, and the strong sense of tradition and place are typical of rural societies. Yet when these traits are combined with poverty, a particular history of sectionalism and racial relations, and the legacies of defeat and dependency, their expression remains uniquely Southern in context and place. There are many studies of Southern communities and about the South. My intent is not to review these, but rather to discuss the attitudes that my sample of Southern hunters tended to affirm or deny.[18]

Localism has been defined as "a tendency to see communities as different from each other and to prefer one's own."[19] This attitude, closely associated with a "sense of place," is sensitive to the circumstances that make one's community unique. Often this uniqueness comes from a mesh of friendships and kinships that are impossible for individuals to duplicate elsewhere. The fact that 35 percent of those questioned by me were reared in Scotland County and that an additional 57 percent were reared in adjacent counties suggests a large measure of endemism. Although endemism may act to constrain behavior and to moderate it toward conformity (if an individual's actions reflect upon the reputation of his relatives and friends), there are other facets to localism. As John Shelton Reed observes, "Localism may reflect limited experience and narrow horizons, but it may also be a manifestation of geographical particularism—an appreciation of the qualities of one place as opposed to others."[20] Although I did not attempt to untangle "affective localism" (based upon narrow horizons and life experiences) from "instrumental localism" (based upon knowledge of alternatives, with individuals making their choices in the light of other alternatives), I suspect the former is more operative among rural residents and industry workers and the latter among professionals and businessmen.

Sixty percent of my sample responded favorably to the statement that their present location was the best county in which to live and work. Lumbees expressed the highest agreement with the statement (80%), blacks the lowest (59%). A 1971 survey by Reed and Glen Elder asked North Carolinians to name the best thing they liked about the South. "More than two-thirds of our respondents," Reed claims, "mentioned natural conditions: the benign climate, the clean air, the forests and wildlife, the easy pleasures of a life lived largely outdoors. There's nothing uniquely Southern about this taste: the frequent mob scenes in our nation's parks tell us that. But, Reed continues, "Southerners can indulge themselves more easily and more often than their less favored brethren—and our data show that's important to them."[21] According to Reed's research, the accessibility of nature, the low incidence of crimes against a person by strangers, and the more agreeable texture of life result in powerful personal and territorial bonds among a population that is fairly homogeneous. Reed found that strong majorities of both white (59%) and black (65%) Southerners agreed with the "best state" and "best community" labels. This high level of positive black response was surprising but consistent with the composition of his black sample and with the changes in race relations during the 1960s. A higher percentage of blacks than whites had not finished high school, many had never traveled outside the South, and most were still living in the same state in which they had been raised—all of which suggested bonds forged by familiarity, affection, and attachment to life in their native state.[22]

"Very few of our respondents mentioned politics or economics when we asked them for what they liked about the South, and nearly a third mentioned them when we asked what they liked least about their region. All in all," Reed continues, "I read these data to say that state and local politics don't make much of an impression on most folks just living day-to-day, except as an entertaining sideshow (perhaps especially entertaining in the South)."[23]

The image of "community" is particularly strong among the privileged groups within the county. Their image is that of a hierarchical society, part of the ordered nature of things, with those at the top expected and authorized to take a special and dominant role in decision making and governance.[24] Most respondents agreed that differences in income and social standing sowed the seeds of hostility and distrust and tended to concentrate political decisions in the hands of a few individuals. Yet they valued the ideal of community over the goals of a few ambitious individuals and distrusted radical politics, particularly when construed as liberal challenges to the conservative order.

When asked whom they most respect and admire, Southerners are more likely than individuals in other regions to choose among their kin and neighbors.[25] People most admired by my sample were close kin, preachers, then national politicians. Their choices of movies and TV shows were sporting events, Western movies, and the "Dukes of Hazzard." Whereas strong kin and religious networks remain important community symbols, these were becoming submerged in more diffuse networks. New jobs brought into the community by light industries and the ease of travel now allowed affiliations beyond kin and neighbors.

Although recent studies suggest that the South is becoming less different culturally in comparison with the other regions, some persisting traits illustrate its legacies of economic and social marginality within American society.[26] These traits are indirectiveness and individual independence.[27] Generally, Southerners seek to avoid confrontations. Ninety-six percent of my respondents agreed that "a person should generally seek to avoid direct confrontation. Conflicts should be resolved without fighting through the church, among kin, in the workplace or neighborhood." In contrast, half my sample agreed that it was usually better policy "to turn the other cheek" than to fight. The possibility of striking back was left open, contingent upon who constituted the "other party."

Although as a region, the South leads the nation in rates of homicides and assaults, Reed argues that these regional differences "owe more to regional cultural differences than to differences in the effectiveness of socialization or other mechanisms of social control."[28] Though Southern homicide and assault rates are higher than elsewhere, the crimes are often committed by someone the person knows and for reasons both the killer and the victim understand. Three quarters of my sample agreed that "war and aggression are inherent in human nature," the rest affirmed their opinions with "isn't that what the Bible says?"

A strong sense of independence that emphasizes the individual's role in securing a good standard of living may also reflect the South's legacy of marginality and isolation. Most respondents agreed that the pioneering values of self-reliance and political and economic independence were important goals for men. Until recently, most Southerners have sought independence through their religious and kinship networks rather than through dependence on government agencies.[29]

Two thirds strongly agreed that obedience and respect for authority were essential for children to learn within the family. Obedience and respect are traits required for most menial jobs. Although respondents wished for interesting work and for some choice in the workplace, many realized these wishes were unrealistic. A man might think of himself as the major decision maker within his household, but he couldn't entertain such expectations on the job. Sons were important for carrying on family names, a statement strongly subscribed to by men with daughters. The ownership of land, as security and as a heritage from previous generations, was a strong goal for most rural men. For Lumbees especially, land ownership was an important objective, symbolizing their links to the past, their ancestors, and their rural orientation.[30] A few urban whites, who owned extensive tracts of land, considered other forms of wealth more desirable than land.

Religious institutions remain an important part of the social and cultural fabric of Southern life.[31] Church attendance and membership continue as an essential part of community life, with most Southerners likely to be found in church on Sundays. Over two-thirds of interviewees strongly agreed that it was "important for our modern society to restore its faith and belief in religion and in God" and there was almost unanimity with the statement "our society needs more activities which combine traditions and feelings of togetherness."

Samuel Hill attributes a large measure of individualism with its emphasis on "getting right with God" to the large number of Southerners who have joined evangelical churches. In these churches, individualism has both theological and organizational consequences. One organizational consequence is that, through its implicit and egalitarian accent, the church becomes a gathering place for individuals who share common problems. Within this community, the basic distinction is between those who are saved and those ripe for proselytizing.[32]

Maintaining appropriate relations within one's congregation and religiously attending church on Sundays are in conflict with the aspirations of some sportsmen. Such was the case for an inveterate raccoon hunter who partici-

pated in late Saturday night competitions to improve the competitiveness of
his dog breed:

You know the biggest thing that bothers me a lot is like when we go out to
these championships or field days down here. God says in the Bible, seek He
first and all other things will come. It bothers me because when we're out on
these late Saturday night hunts, and we go off somewhere, the times that we
come in, often being out all day and night, and when you come in at day light
or after, it works on your attendance in church. And it's awful hard for me to
curb that down, to cut back. A lot of times, I'll just simply refuse [to hunt] and
say I'm not going. I try to cut that down because it does interfere with things
a person should do around the home and social activities and one thing and
another. And a person that's dedicated to an organization or breed of dogs, it's
really hard for him to curb those things, especially if he really loves it like I
do. It's hard to say no, I'm not going to meet Joe tonight. I'm going somewheres else. I really have to watch myself to keep my church attendance
active.

Other than affirming dominion of man over nature and its creatures, the
Bible provides few guidelines in this community of churchgoers. If new behaviors and attitudes toward other creatures are to emerge in the future, they
will undoubtedly come from the outside and bear the philosophical underpin-
nings of outside developments and the sanctions of reinterpreted older texts.

The attitudes of county hunters toward themselves and the animals they
pursue are part of a more regional culture. As with other cultural traits, these
attitudes and behaviors did not come about through individual contempla-
tion.[33] One is not born a hunter, nor does the knowledge of what goals a
person should pursue and how to do it come with the genes (or jeans!). Such
ideas are garnered from others while growing up and from peers later in life.
Hunters who share cultural and biological landscapes have learned more or
less the same lessons.

Part Two

ON INTERPETING THE PRESENT

Introduction to Part Two

THE SEARCH for understanding others is at the heart of the humanistic impulse. Through making observations and through asking questions, the ethnographer seeks to lay the ground work for interpretation. Translation is ethnography's fundamental task; those perplexities its greatest challenges. Culture is more than words and deeds. It encompasses techniques and technologies, dress and demeanor, and a host of other codes by which members convey meanings and significance. In coping with another cultural world, the ethnographer pays particular attention to disciphering these codes as well as to what people say and do. Translation and interpretation are parts of an inescapable circular process in which understanding at one moment is refined and restructured through further discriminating appreciation of subtle nuances in cultural forms.

The ethnographer's field notebooks and tapes are filled with accounts of the doings and sayings of particular people in particular circumstances. The task is to identify the encompassing metaphors that locate diverse opinions and actions on a more or less coherent map of experience. Metaphors inform and shape sayings and actions and are in turn reciprocally shaped. At any given time, there is an economy of metaphors within a cultural scene reflecting its time and place. Yet it would be arrogant to suggest that the text of even a simple cultural scene could be captured on the flatness of the written page.

For each of the subsequent cultural scenes, I select a primary theme and sort my materials accordingly. The choice is often an engaging opposition such as winning/losing, male/female, and inside/outside expressed within each recreational activity. It is also fair to say that the same themes are expressed to some degree in each of the other hunting scenes.

Some categories and evaluations are prevalent, particularly those of land and dogs. Land is a basic commodity within a rural society and in the minds of those who continue as actors within such landscapes. Land has both legal and substantive boundaries. It can be bought, sold, or lost depending on one's circumstances. In the memories of some county hunters are the painful recollections of their families' separation from the land and from agriculture during economic transitions. For these men, their seasonal forays back to the land brings pleasurable associations of social roots and a play world of action. This sentimentality was voiced by one who told me, "I'd sure like to find a job I enjoy as much as hunting!"

Land on which to hunt is of four categories: *private land*, owned by individuals or corporations who may restrict access; *leased land*, rented by a group or hunt club for exclusive use by members; *game management land*, owned by the state, managed for wildlife and publicly accesible for a fee; and *open land*, generally not restricted or posted against trespass. Private and leased land are the most valuable because their controlled access normally means that they harbor more wildlife. Hunters owning or leasing land generally enjoy higher status and success than those on state or on open lands.

Dogs are human allies on many hunts. Although most young dogs can be taught to chase wildlife, each chase has its own breeds formally sanctioned by the kennel societies. Hunting dogs may be lavishly cared for, but their existence in a kennel is usually contingent upon performance in the field. Hunting dogs are strongly identified with men and masculine ideals and reflect the status and style of their owner. "A dog's as good as his master," is how a fox hunting acquaintance expressed the correlation.

We begin the next chapter in a patch of seeming anomalies. There are no practicing foxhunters currently resident within Scotland County and those described in Chapter 5 are outsiders, from Kentucky and elsewhere. Attracting national and regional fox field trials and keeping their patronage for a decade or more involves more than an abundant fox population. The prospective hunting area should be devoid of deer and other creatures likely to detract fox hounds from their competitive missions. Furthermore, participants require access to large open spaces where they may follow their charges, who are no respecters of property or boundaries. Last, the area must contain a solicitous organization which enters competitive bids for hospitality, publicity, and other enticements to the sponsoring group and acts as liaison between locals and strangers. The southeastern portion of Scotland County meets all of these basic prerequisites and the local Chamber of Commerce possesses the skills which make the sojourns of fox hunters so profitable for a few local businesses.

By most accountings within the county, hunting is masculine turf. Yet within competitive fox trials, women often accompany their spouses, assist with the daily chores, participate in the games, and may even hold some of the higher symbolic ground. Their participation is a different class statement about economics and gender from what pertains for most county residents, whose relations are described in the subsequent chapter.

Within North Carolina, the fox is a creature with an anomalous, if not checkered, past. The fox has been listed as a game animal, a furbearer, and as vermin depending upon the local county option. Currently, the fox is listed under "small game and other species" with no closed season on taking them with dogs, but with no open season except as permitted by local laws in certain counties. Scotland County allows fox trapping under special provisions, a determined local response to outsider interests and to a strong pro-fox legislative lobby.

Five

Fox Field Trials: Separating the Men from the Boys by Going to the Dogs

Now there's just hundreds of fox hunters that wouldn't go to a field trial, and it's not because they know something, it's because they have heard something. They've heard the talk that the judges are crooked, and so and so's gonna win, and the poor fellow don't have a big Cadillac automobile and a big, brand new, four-wheel drive truck. If you don't have that, there's no use to go because you're not gonna win anyway.

SAM: *Would you allow that some of what they have heard is true?*

Right, but the poor man can't win, simply because he hadn't paid some judge. What is true is that the man with a whole lot of money can enter a whole lot more dogs. His damn percentage of winning the thing is a whole lot better if he's got fifteen dogs entered. The poor man enters but one or two dogs. He stays out at the kennel. He don't mingle with nobody except his little group and they're poor boys like he is. Maybe every twenty-five times some poor fellow wins the damn thing, then after a while everybody forgets it. There's so many people that does not go to field trials and they could care less about it and wouldn't go if you'd pay their expenses. But if you could get that same man to come to three national hunts, you wouldn't have to ask him back. If he could make friends at all, he'd be back. You know, there is people that just can't make friends under no circumstances.

(Conversations with a fox hunter, 1979)

THE ENGLISH tradition of equestrian fox hunting was an early import into the New World, and it provided fashionable recreation for the well-to-do on the East Coast.[1] Yet within its shadow, among the less socially refined yeoman farmers and slaves, a more democratic and informal tradition evolved.[2] Centered more on dogs than on horses, these neighborly traditions developed into regional and national competitions when the railroads and motorized transport made possible the coordination of events over greater distances.

Initially, the breeding and keeping of hounds were local, family enterprises. Hounds were bred for their working qualities, centering on performance in the chase. In time, conformity and standards became important when some fox hunters developed canine lineages embodying desirable qualities and competitive traits.[3]

This chapter is about foxhounds in competitions and about reflections on the ideals of their owners. Interpreted through their practitioners, these contests are about life-styles, about the self and change, about power and social structure. The bench-show competition is an exercise in show and tell, about the men some of whose ambitions are fulfilled by the hound. To paraphrase Oscar Wilde, field trialing is more than the pursuit of the inedible by the unmentionable.[4] In these competitions, hounds bear important cultural messages and are the embodiments of human rivalries.

The Walker Hounds

Among the first families to improve their hounds, by careful recordkeeping of their crosses, were the Walkers and Maupins of Kentucky. In the early nineteenth century, the Walker family migrated to Kentucky from Virginia and brought with them black and tan Virginia hounds, descendants of the original stock of English foxhounds in America.[5] The Walkers settled next to the Maupins, where they followed their hounds in the pursuit of the native gray fox.

Through a fortunate conjunction of chance and expediency, the Walkers injected new traits into their hounds. About 1850, Mr. Walker was fortuitously given a "stole dog" as a gift. While it was in pursuit of deer somewhere in the Tennessee mountains, this dog was captured by a neighbor of Walker's, a livestock trader, while returning from a cattle drive. The gift hound, named Tennessee Lead, had "all the qualification necessary for a high class dead game foxhound" and served as a "breeding outcross."[6]

Around 1856, the red fox began to spread into Kentucky. The local strains of hounds, ideal for tracking the gray through swamps and thickets, were unable to capture this new quarry. This dilemma called for a resolution. The resolution came with new blood and tactics brought about through the importation of two dogs with English bloodlines, renowned for their speed and discipline. Rifler and Marth, the names of the imported pair, were bred with local hounds to obtain the desired qualities. These crosses produced the Walker lineage, a line known for its "self-reliance, cold noses, refusal to pack, and a fondness for skirting."[7]

The development of this bloodline was particularized by a descendant of the originating Mr. Walker, now himself a venerated member of the fox-hunting fraternity:

It was my grandfather, John W. Walker, and Uncle Wash Maupin who started the Walker breed of hounds. Grandpa was born in 1802 and Uncle Wash in 1807, and they hunted together in Madison County (Kentucky) all their lives as boys. The hounds are 150 years old now. Grandfather married my grandmother, who was a real fox hunter, and he had four sons. And they started running these hounds. Uncle Ed took them east, Uncle Steve went west to Texas and West Virginia, and my father went south with the hounds. The greatest publicity people ever had for the Walker hounds was Sam Woods, who had lots of money and took the hounds everywhere. The publicity man that named the Walker hounds was Colonel Jack Chinn. He was a racing steward. He got to hunting with Papa and them about the turn of the century. And he told everybody, "If you want to have a good fox race, go down to Kentucky and run with the Walkers." Well, the Maupins kind of got peeved with us a little as they had always felt like that maybe the Walkers stole the publicity. And I said, "Now Julian, Colonel Chinn, your father and you boys, and your grandfather out of Madison County, they didn't have much company to run the hounds with, and therefore, they lacked the form of public relations it took to spread the fame of the dog."

SAM: *How does it feel to be the third generation in a tradition established by your grandfather and father?*

I've been born with the hounds and I don't usually volunteer information because the people worry me to death everywhere I go. I'm not great or nothin' like that. I've had to make my own living. My father spent a fortune. My grandfather was an extremely wealthy man in Kentucky.

SAM: *From hounds or from farming?*

Oh, no! They had land and horses, good horses, good cattle, and good everything. When my grandfather died he left all four of his boys pretty richly endowed with stuff. But my father was the finest, best-looking man I ever saw, but he cared nothing for money. The rest of them kind of took care of what they had and they died in good shape. But my father, he was just a horse and dog man and loved his friends, and he had to have people from all over come visit us. Consequently, he didn't have much money when he died, so I had to start and make my own way. I'm in the banking business now and I quit the dogs after he died. I hunted with him as long as he lived and when he died, I quit the dogs for twenty years until I could get a start myself. As soon as I saw I was gonna have money enough to last, I bought me a pack of hounds and started breeding and running hounds myself.

SAM: *Is there someone like your father, or grandfather, who has a passion for hounds and is devoted to improving them and keeping the Walker name alive?*

Well, I run them but I don't breed them. I just buy a good hound when I see him so he can run good for me when I go. I've bred a few good dogs, but I just quit. I'm the last member of the family that's hunting. The tradition was passed on to thousands of fox hunters. From the standpoint of sporting fox hunting, I'd say that these men that's running the Walker dogs are the mainstream of fox hunting in the United States.

I think fox hunting is one of the outstanding national diversions, and fox hunters are kind of a different breed of people. They are all friends and friendly. They visit each other whenever they want to and they're very liberal people from the standpoint of entertainment and furnishing pleasure for each other. You see, there's one thing about fox hunters that I want to straighten you out as much as I can. The fox hunters years ago were pictured as people that sit around a wood fire with a half gallon of whiskey, drinking whiskey and burning up rail fences, and they were not known to be very high-type people. But now some of the finest vocations in the world, some of the finest lawyers, judges, doctors, and everything else you'll find right up here in this motel. The finest class of people in the world have turned into fox hunting. A lot of people make their living looking after the hounds. And the horse industry that follows the fox hunting is a big industry. These people that ride these nice horses and follow the hunts. They spend a lot of money wherever they go and they're a big help to the local economy.

SAM: *Has fox hunting enabled you to do anything that you wouldn't have been able to do otherwise?*

I don't think I would have been able to meet the quality of people extended over the whole United States that I've met, and the quality of people that visits me in my home and every other way. As I have told you, the old-fashioned picture of fox hunters are of people that sit on a high hill with a jug of whiskey and a bunch of scraggly dogs with very little background running a little fox. But the whole thing has changed, changed to upper class, lawyers and doctors, and judges, financiers, and everything.

SAM: *Why has it changed? Any ideas?*

I think they realized it's a whole-hearted, genuine sport, close to nature. They realized it has good fellowship and they realized they have a chance to meet aggressive people, see.

SAM: *Meet aggressive people?*

I mean aggressive people in the business world, in the medical world, in the financial world, in the world of engineering, the world of all kinds of industry. The personalities that I have met in the world of fox hunting has been one of the broader experiences of my life. I meet new people everywhere with new ideas and new philosophies. And you meet people like Aaron Briar, brilliant of mind and everything but still a fox hunter, see. He comes from a fine family. He's just let himself go since he's been fox hunting. He's given up everything. He used to court every girl in the country and now he's quit courting and his life is just around those damn dogs. He's let his best habits and his mentality and everything drift until he's just in a world of dogs. He's letting his house run down, he's letting his farm run down, and he's letting everything run down just because he's a typical bachelor. He's not interested in anything but these damn dogs. Of course, when I leave here tomorrow, I'm going back to the business world. It gives me a change in the mental picture for me and I enjoy my dogs. The first thing I'll do is I'll go down and see about them dogs. But I'm not gonna let them take charge of my life.

This account tells us about more than the nature of hounds. Initially a local product, Walker hounds were dispersed by men socially and spatially positioned to champion their qualities. A local tradition of rivalry between neighbors turned into regional and national competitions, a transformation made possible by changes in transportation and the media. These changes in time and space differentially affected individuals and groups. Some, like the Maupins, lost; some, like the Walkers, gained; and still others, like the teller of the tale, regained what he had once lost.

The foxhounds no longer belong exclusively to the Walkers. The economic spinoffs from a sporting interest in dogs and horses, like for Alexander Hunter's quail, are pervasive. As education transformed some farm boys into moneyed professionals, the older fox hunting images no longer fit the new circumstances. The isolated figure of a fox hunter on a hilltop, burning rail fences and drinking home brew, became inappropriate for those destined as movers and shakers in society. From his own history, the teller reminds us that inherited status and wealth may be transient, an insufficient means of securing a permanent role in prestigious circles. A person's presumptions must be underwritten by resources and a vision, which unlike Aaron Briar's, remain broader and deeper than mere identification with hounds.

On Hounds, Men, and Field Trials

For participants, fox hunting involves deep psychological identification between themselves and their hounds. The domain of the latter provides a pool of potent metaphors that can be transferred to the domain of the former. As with all interpretations of symbolic transfers between domains, the individuals making the transfers reveal through their choices as much about themselves and their placement within a competitive hierarchy as their remarks about the "other." Calling a competitor a "son of a bitch" may be interpreted variously, contingent upon its tone, circumstance, and the gestures that accompany the utterance.[8]

As a class, foxhounds are assumed to be noble and to possess high status, a legacy of their origin within the aristocratic Old World. In describing favored hounds, owners use the same terms of reference as they do for esteemed peers. Hounds are loyal ("more loyal than most men"), possess consciousness ("never cuss in front of them for they know what people say"), are goal oriented ("broke dogs only chase foxes"), and can discriminate ("she discredited some for lying and many more she saved from threshings by confirming the presence of a fox"). Fox hunters disdain other types of dogs, and their terms for them—"potlickers," "cur," "mongrel," and "grade dogs"—embody their invidious distinctions. Their insistence to casual outsiders that fox hunting canines are hounds rather than dogs reinforces this distinction.[9] Formalized competitions end by separating hounds into winners and losers. Attributes of winners, and sometimes of losers, are transferred from the participating hounds to their owners. These metaphorical inferences between human and hound domains are circular and begin with the assertion that foxhounds are special and separate from the rest of the canine class.[10]

Whether on the bench or in the field, hounds and owners share a common purpose—to win over the others in the competition. Bench-show owners rarely admit to their persuasive abilities before a judge; however, the handler is as much on "show" as the hound. The handler controls and positions the hound so its best qualities are displayed. In the field trials, hounds serve as proxies for their owners, who vicariously follow the races as best they can. The hound's objective is to find fox scent, trial it, and when the game jumps, to pursue it doggedly until it is captured or escapes. Owners follow the proceedings by sound, preferably by sight, and claim their hounds enjoy the runs as much as they do. Bench-show enthusiasts praise characteristics that epitomize physique and showmanship; breeders extol profundity and the hound's potential for competition; field trialers applaud courage, endurance, stamina, and the skills of fox finding. Good breeding and bloodlines are essential, but the most valued characteristics in any hound are developed through practice.[11]

Beyond winning and performance, a hound endears itself by characteristics that distinguish it from all others. In the field, a hound is located in space and is identified within a pack by its mouth. A distinctive voice is desirable and commands a good price. Hounds "tongue," "yell," "squall," or "chop" (rather than "bark"); any tone or frequency that rises above the others is valued. Whereas a distinctive voice is an important asset, it is linked with the wisdom of knowing when and where to use it. The most unconscionable trait is for a hound to babble. Defined as "giving false tongue," babbling is a trait without redeeming value. To be caught babbling is to cast doubt on the hound's other qualities, and on its owner.

Besides babbling, hounds may show their incompetence by chasing other game ("not-broke dogs"). Overcompetent hounds offend by "swinging" out of a pack, catching "wind" of the fox, anticipating its direction of movement, and shortcircuiting the chase. These "smart dogs" do not signal their intentions to either their owners or peers, and if their tactics prove wrong, they "dry up" the track, confuse the pack, and cut short the runs. Incompetent and overcompetent hounds are equally disdained.[12] If either flaw is found in an individual, the hound is usually destroyed. Otherwise, owners risk having aspersions cast on their own reputations.

Exemplary hounds are sources of conversation and envy. Their competitive abilities reside, as among humans, in the hound's individual character, which is transmitted through "blood lines." Upon the death of an esteemed hound, its body is interred in a special place such as the Foxhunters' Hall of Fame Cemetery in Texas. Those not having the means or the inclination to honor their hounds in Texas inter them at home, decorating the grave appropiately.

The Quarries

Unlike the anthropomorphic similarities that men share with their hounds, decided ambivalence describes the fox hunters' attitude toward the fox. While fox hunters recognize that their sport depends on the courage and wiliness of the hunter, they also realize that their prey is stigmatized as "vermin," sharing the negative attributes of a villain and thief.[13] Yet as wild mammals go, the fox has been pampered and protected as few others. The 1979 North Carolina Legislature, under heavy lobbying from fox-hunting associations, classified the fox as a "game animal" (rather than as a "furbearer"), stipulating that it could be taken only by hounds.[14] Fox hunters speak proudly of their nonconsumptive goals: "Fox hunters is the only group of people that would rather not take their game." Yet this assertion is tempered by the realization that some foxes eventually succumb to the hounds: "We regret the death of a fox more than any Sierra Club member."[15]

Today there are two species of fox in North Carolina. The red fox is probably not native but an import from the Old World. It flourished in the newly cleared landscapes of the settlers and gradually expanded its range westward from its original release along the East Coast. This Old World heritage assures its ascendancy over the native grays. The red fox likes high ground, where it depends on its speed and "going to ground" to escape the hounds.[16]

The gray fox is a native with no pretenses of aristocratic blood or bearing. This common species inhabits the coastal plain and piedmont areas of the Carolinas and has a relatively small home range, which often includes thickets and swamps. Furthermore, it readily climbs trees to escape the dogs and rarely gives long chases. Consequently, it is a "poor man's fox."[17] Foxes are cunning tricksters, aware of their pursuers' abilities, and are said to enjoy the chase. The fox is considered a noble adversary whose pursuit and eventual capture and death confirm the equally sterling qualities of its conqueror:

I think the fox is a real good opponent. He's not said to be sly for nothing. The stiffer the competition, the better you become. You become more. You have to put up the best in you to overcome the fox, the best in your dogs, and the combination of dog and brain to overcome the fox because he's really a good opponent. In the process you learn something. Sometimes you learn more from defeat than you learn from victory, which is not what they say much in this day and time. If you compete with somebody better than you are in a particular sport, eventually you become better yourself. And it'll help you become stronger in your particular line, to improve yourself.

The fox is the best sport of any of us. He runs because he loves to run. He's the gamest of all the game animals and he's a real sport.

The successful staging of a field trial depends upon live foxes, some of which may be caught and killed by the hundreds of hounds let loose during successive days of an event. During the fall of 1980, Scotland County was chosen for three major field trials within the space of six weeks. Such pressure takes its toll on local foxes. This inevitable fact is not overlooked by organizers, who must insure an adequate supply of foxes. Their means include the feeding and care of the local fox population, the release, immediately prior to the trials, of live foxes brought in from elsewhere, and informal exclusion of those now seeking to purchase land in field-trial territory.[18]

The National Foxhunters' Association

The National Foxhunters' Association (NFHA) began informally around 1893 and was incorporated in Kentucky in 1929.[19] An early accomplishment was its publication of the *Foxhound Stud Book*, a registry establishing confirmations and standards. The Association's purpose is the promotion of "wholesome and heartful outdoor sports and pastimes in season," including field trials for foxhounds, bench shows, horse shows, and other sports. These sporting events "promote the health of and encourage sociability among the members," and "provide for their amusement, entertainment, recreation and diversion."[20] Today the NFHA is an affiliation of individuals and groups who agree to conduct sporting events according to its rules. Its members are those whose passions are horses and hounds, yet its annual events are attended overwhelmingly by those of the latter persuasion.[21]

The National sponsors bench shows and field trials for hounds and various contests for horses. Each competition has become the domain for a distinctive set of enthusiasts, each with similar life-styles and having somewhat different expectations. Each set is composed of many groups and individuals who compete for prestige, esteem, and prizes, including elective and appointed offices. Each group recruits new members, seeks conformity to its norms, and discusses politics and boundary maintenance within the organization. The successful politics of some come at the expense of others. In some cases, a group's successful and successive political ploys enable it to have a degree of institutionalization within the parent organization. Boundaries between groups become visible, entrenched, and reaffirmed with each bone of contention and conflict. Yet some individuals transcend these boundaries, seek new alliances, and eventually change the nature of these internal political games. Beyond their continuous tasks of caring for hounds or horses, fox hunters spend most of their time in the company of a few associates. These bands, linked with others through the social glue of politics, provide the alliances through which presidents are elected. And the election of presidents, with their powers of appointments and visibility, is not a randomly distributed skill.

Those serving the National as elected officials are aware of its internal dynamics and boundaries. They are mindful of the ways key issues are interpreted by the different groups and how they are likely to act. Group dispositions become evident at election time and when rule and organizational changes are discussed in an open forum. Then boundaries become tangible and personalized as individuals interpret one another's words and behavior and become suspicious of motives. The persistence of boundaries is clear in the following conversation with a former president, a judge by profession. I asked about the issues before the Association:

Well, I think internally, there's some unrest. That's true in fox hunting the same as it is in life. The young must be heard and the old are not ready to hear them. You may have sensed that last night. I'm a man of gradualism. I think they can accomplish their purpose by doing it by degrees instead of having a revolution and blow everything up. The young could phase theirselves in and I think they're doing that. Last night one of the North Carolinians came to me and said, "We've waited long enough now to get the young into this," and he's a man in his fifties. I said, "By God, you beat the whole executive committee, ain't that good enough?" "Well, what about the directors? What about those people that don't have a dog?" I said, "There's nothing wrong with them being directors." "Yes, there is, every man there ought to be running hounds if he's a director." So that's the internal part of change. I think the change that we have no control over is the encroachment of civilization on wildlife areas. And it's not only our sport, it's every sport going.

SAM: *Returning to the events that happened last evening, there was only one candidate put in nomination for each office. Will you interpret that situation for me?*

Yes, I can not only interpret it, I can tell you why. It's like every organization, including the church. There's two factions and they spend the first two or three days jockeying for power to see who to elect. A lot of people want to make it a rider, or society hunter, against the man who has the dogs in the back of his truck. I don't interpret it like that because I own horses and rode horses, and 90 percent of them riding out there are my personal friends. But there's one expression, "Forks of the Creek Foxhunter" or "One Gallus Hunter."[22]

SAM: *Those are the old-timers, the traditional county fox hunters?*

Right, that can't afford to dress up and they hunt just for the love of the hunt and no social activities, no nothing. But see, the theory behind the National, it's not supposed to be something where we come down here just to have a good time. It's supposed to improve the hounds. And we come down here to see and watch everybody else's hounds, and if the judges do their jobs right, then we're supposed to have the dogs to breed to. We find out who's got the better blood. There's one worry and it worries all hunters. If you're gonna go for theory, maybe all of us are breeding a little too much for speed, for front-end hounds and not enough for nose and the ability to carry a track in a dry field.[23] But I think it has improved the hounds. I'm in it for about thirty years and I know that I have better hounds than I did.

SAM: *So you're saying that a lot of things go into improving a breed of hounds that are not appreciated by the One Gallus Hunter?*

Right, the opportunity he has to improve his hounds is limited because he only knows his hounds and whoever hunts within a ten-mile radius. This way we know hounds in all the states. By no stretch of the imagination is there fox hunters in every state, but there's some method of use of the hound in every state.

SAM: *To return to the elections of last evening. There was just one candidate. Was there some kind of reconciliation between the two factions?*

Really there's no reconciliation except this. Both of the leading contenders are fine gentlemen. The losing candidate was put on the Executive Committee. The one just elected president was in the Kentucky State two weeks ago.

You don't ask for the job, you don't lectioneer for it, but a bunch of the hunters asked him if he would take it. And he said yes, that he'd be honored to take it. And the Kentuckians committed themselves at that time that they were going to be for him. Well, the other contender belongs to another faction, which has been running this organization for a long time and includes the immediate past president. They went to the president and said, "Hell, they're gonna beat us if we don't get some hunter to run. Let's try and split the hunters. Try and split these kind of people that carry the box."[24] All of them are hunters. But what they was trying to do was to get someone, a dog man, to run against the one from Missouri. Well, we're in North Carolina and if they could have got a good candidate from here, it would have been a whale of a race and he might have beaten the other man. I could live with either of them.

SAM: *So how did they exclude the nominee from North Carolina?*

I think this is what happened. He came to me with another fellow. He said, "Are you fellows got anyone you want for president?" I said, "At the Kentucky State, we all agreed to back the boy from Missouri." He said, "I figured that and this suits me exactly. They're trying to get me to run and I said I don't want it. I'm gonna retire in six more years and then if the National wants to honor me with that, and if my health is good, I'll be delighted to do it." And he went back to the current president and said, "Hell, my friends are all for the boy from Missouri and I like him. He's my buddy, I'm not gonna get in any contest with him." And that's when they folded their tents and crept silently into the night.

SAM: *So those kinds of struggles are resolved before they come up on the floor for public vote?*

Right. Because it's good for the organization. The more open votes you have, the more fights you have, the more divisions you have in the organization. I don't think anyone wants that.

SAM: *Are there other groups of fox hunters?*

Well, maybe there's more. There's the Forks of the Creek, and then there's the Field Trial Hunter. And I would say that they intertwine. I would like to think I'm a Forks of the Creek Hunter. For instance, I go out twice a week, if I can get away and run my hounds with three or four people, or I run by myself. So I do some of the Forks of the Creek stuff, but I love Field Trials. I love to see my friends and I love this part of it. You really can't be a good hunter and be just a Field Trial Hunter. There's not that many field trials. You can't stay away from home that much. You have to be a home hunter too.

A LISTENER: *Could I say something? Because you are a Field Trial Man, while you're out there listening to your dogs, you say, ''Well, I hope this young dog,*

Old Joe, he'll make something fit to carry to the field trials.'' But on the other hand, the gentleman that don't take part in field trials, that thought don't ever cross his mind. He just hopes to have a good dog.

He goes out there just to hear them run. When you look at them in the box from the time they're whelped until the time they're weaned, you ought to think this is going to be the litter. This is the one that's gonna do the job. I think if you breed them you have that kind of faith in them.

LISTENER: *But the Forks of the Creek Man, now, he's not that particular about the breeding.*

That's right. They don't really care that I've got pedigrees. The third type of fox hunter is the Organized Pack. Others can tell you more about this than I can because I never belonged to one. It's a type of club hunt. The doctors and lawyers and the millionaires down there that have made a lot of money and maybe don't know one end of a hound or horse from the other, but is what I call "nigger rich." They feel good and want to do something. They've got a big club house, got ground, and they've got a pack of hounds there that don't belong to anyone. They belong to the club. They start working hounds in what they call couples. They have a master, they have a joint master, and they're good on horseback, and they have what they call whips. They teach their hounds to travel in packs, tight close-knit packs. They put a young hound in coupling with an old hound. They move from field to field as a unit. They do it on horseback, and they go for the formal thing you've seen on television, the red coats and black hats and the riding boots. They hunt every Saturday afternoon in hunting season. During the summer, if they can't hunt and they want to drink and party, they go out there and have what they call 'exercise the hounds.' They take them up and down them country lanes while they're educating them for the fall. The riders are riding and watching and when they come in, they've got a bar and they've got a restaurant, not open to the public, and they all party.

I hope you will understand that the Field Trial and the Forks of the Creek overlap. Probably the best foxhounds in America are the Forks of the Creek hound for their purpose of being prolific. For our purpose, the field trials, they would not be the best hound. The secret is to get one that can do both. Here, they've got to run the full five hours each day. At night, the Forks of the Creek hounds have got to run until the race is over. If it's fourteen hours, they've got to run fourteen hours.[25]

As within other formal organizations, groups of the NFHA vie and conspire to enhance their positions relative to other groups. The boundaries separating them vary with time and with circumstances. Some men move freely and comfortably between and among groups in ways that are impossible, inconceivable, and an anathema for others. Learning the politics of the association becomes a few, comes slowly to others, and has no appeal at all for the rest. For a perceptive few, learning of decisions made "behind the stage" comes with time, with holding office, or with close association with those of political bents:

When I started coming to the field trials, I thought that what I visibly saw and heard was all there was to it. But shit, that's just the beginning, especially the last part of it. Anything you see has already been shuffled around and argued inside and out before that meeting. Years ago when I first started, I thought that everything that took place was there at the meeting.

SAM: *How did you learn differently? Who got you on the inside?*

Well, it came through showing dogs after so many years. Dr. Kelly and myself become good friends, and I began to understand more and more. He just didn't sit me down and tell me. He would include me in a lot of conversations he would have with other people, where maybe three years before that he walked away to talk to somebody. Later, it got so that I was included.

Another fox hunter relates that when a friend became president, he was asked to accompany the president on his rounds to parties:

Everywhere he wanted to go, I'd take him, and you talk about somebody having a good time! This was kind of the start of me getting in on the ground floor of a bunch of crap that goes on. All those top guys, all of them knew me anyway and they figured well, I'll just go ahead and say what I want to in front of me, he ain't gonna say nothing about it noway. Hell, a lot of the fellows said, damn so and so. I said, "Hell, don't talk to me, boy, I'm a bigger nigger this week." And them boys, they'd laugh.

SAM: *Did you ever wish to become president yourself?*

No sir. Not under any circumstances. I think it might be the reason I don't is because I know too much about it. When you get to be president, there's a certain group of people that's gonna tell you what you gonna do and what you can't do. And what they tell you might not be what you want to do at all, but you're gonna do it, or else.

SAM: *Otherwise they remove you?*

Well, it's not in the rule book that you get to be president for two years because they actually elect you every year. They go through all that shenanigans the second year of voting to keep you in as president. I've only seen it happen once and that president said he stepped down for personal reasons. He got to where he stayed drunk and made a damn ass out of the year.

The office of the president is the most visible position, and its assumption by an individual is formally the apex of his power within the organization.

And with all formal roles, election exerts its price in conformity and distance. Yet the office of president is a viable option for comparatively few fox hunters. Other roles are more probable, and that of judge is a highly visible, if not more contentious, one.

The Judges

One prerogative of the president is to appoint, subject to the approval of the board of directors, judges for the bench show and the field trial. The bench show is generally the initial event at the National and takes place the afternoon before the field trials begin. The bench-show judge chooses an assistant, the ringmaster, to implement his decisions and to place hounds in order on the benches.

The bench-show judge evaluates hounds in each of four classes—derby dogs, derby bitches, all-age dogs, and all-age bitches—for their conformity to the published standards of an ideal foxhound. The winners of the four classes are shown together to enable the judge to select the "Best Hound in the Show" and the "Best Hound of Opposite Sex." This selection is the main bench show event, with the top dogs receiving silver trophies and trays upon which their names are engraved. This judge also selects the "Best Couple" and the "Best Two Couples."[26]

Although the points allocated each trait on the ideal hound are given in the bylaws, a judge's evaluation is somewhat subjective and contemporaneous. As I watched from the sidelines, another judge, an acquaintance from an earlier state contest, responded to my questions about judgment calls:

The feet, legs, back, just like you'd be looking at a woman. You look for a dog with shape. He's got his quarters. He's got his deep chest. Feet goes a long way with me. I like a good-footed dog.

SAM: *These characteristics are all allocated according to a point system, so much for the feet, so much for the head?*

That's exactly right. If you've read your rule book, it's five points for the head, fifteen points for some of them. But he ain't adding points. He ain't got that much sense. But he, just like I, what he sees is what he's looking at now and that's the way he's placing it. He's got his rule book in his mind, he ain't adding no points.

SAM: *He's working from what an idealized hound should look like?*

Right. If somebody would make him tell how many points his front dog had, he couldn't tell to save his life. He'd just say he's better'n to me than the rest of them is.

No separate entry fees are charged for the bench show. Hounds entered for the bench, however, must be registered and pay their fees for the field trial. And it is expected that each hound placed on the bench will compete in the field trial until eliminated there by a field judge. To do otherwise is to lose one's standing on the bench. As a consequence, only the hounds on the front benches usually are entered for the field trial.[27] Field trials are a risky business, and the winners on the bench watch anxiously until their hounds are eliminated. Bench hounds are judged on appearance and know very little about the practicalities of chasing foxes. Yet, with these rules, the NFHA keeps alive its fiction of combining show and performance qualities within the same body.

If he wishes, the Master of Fox Hounds may appoint two assistants to facilitate his control over the field trials which, if separated into derby and all-age events, last for six days. These assistants coordinate the work of an additional twenty to thirty field judges appointed by the president and directors from the names submitted by the affiliated associations. During the five hours of the daily field trials, these judges scatter to follow the hounds. Afield, they score the hounds, identified by numbers painted on their sides, for fox finding and chasing behaviors and eliminate others for misbehavior.[28] The association compensates judges by paying for their room, board, and transportation costs. For most men, it's an honor to be selected as a judge, a status maintained by appropriate distance from those who enter hounds. To remain a judge, one must remain circumspect and above partisan disputes:

Take for example Robin, knowing him like I knowed him. Of course, you've done heard him talk. He talked right out in front of you about how he had figured out what was gonna win this race. And he didn't know you from Adam's house cat. But Robin has already gone as far as he'll ever go. He's on the downhill now simply because he talks. He says a lot of things out loud that he don't know what he's talking about. He's just digging his hole that much deeper every time he says anything. Said he was gonna wring that fellow's ears that turned him down as a judge. There ain't no way he's ever gonna know because he's just not the type of fellow to be able to find out.

Being a judge has its own rewards and headaches. In the following conversation, a Master of Fox Hounds talks about his role and its chores:

I started judging in 1952. Hell, man, that's twenty-seven years. Where I was raised at, every farmer around us had hounds. We'd run rabbits with them in the daytime and foxes at night. When I went to work as a game warden, I really got interested in fox hunting and I'll tell you why. I couldn't never hunt nothing else. If you had a day off a month and you went hunting, somebody would say that's all you ever did was hunt. And wildlife protectors had a hard time deer hunting and stuff like that. If you go with a crowd, somebody would shoot over yonder and worry you to death and wouldn't leave you alone until you get it straightened out.

SAM: *What are some of your biggest headaches as Master of Fox Hounds?*

Well, you've got twenty-five judges and invariably you gonna have some that don't know what the hell they're doing, and if you don't watch yourself you're gonna get in one of the wildest scenes. Some of them trying to impress somebody by making up a bunch of stories or something. And these fellows that come regular, time will test them. And then too, you make a damn mistake. There are five hundred hounds out here and I don't have any feelings about any of them, but some old boy borrowed some money to come down here and been training these dogs and thinks he's got a good one. Everything should be set so he gets a damn fair shot at it. It's important as hell to somebody.

I don't know no other thing like it that the effort is put to make the thing come out right. Horse shows, I've fooled with a lot of horses, but I don't know anything about showing them. It seems to me that them things are crooked as hell. I mean, you can take a girl and put her on a mule and she'll beat the hell out of some old ugly boy on the damn best horse in the country. But this thing, hell, I don't know whose dogs they are out yonder. These judges don't know. So some old back country woods boy in the overalls [a reference to the One Gallus or Forks of the Creek Foxhunter] that borrowed money to come here has got just as good a chance as the damn doctor down the street. I have actually had to break up fist fights in the judge's room over a score given a dog because somebody thought somebody was giving him too much and he wasn't being fair to the rest of them.

Everything we do in that judge's room has to be a majority decision. I can't make no decision about whether they scratch this dog or not. Anyone in the room has the right to contest a score that's given. All's he got to say is, "I'd like to talk about that." They'll get a judge in there maybe from inexperience who begin to score dogs too much and gives every dog a maximum score. And you're gonna have one of them stop us and say, "Look, I'm not questioning you, but we try to do this thing uniform and we have a right to vote and call for a discussion and a vote on that score." And if there's twenty-five judges and I call the vote and thirteen of them says "no" and twelve of them says "yes," it's "no." And when we come out of there, it's pretty well united.

The hunters think of these dogs like they do their kids. Man, they get all upset about one being eliminated for a fault. They take it personally. And they don't believe the dogs do what they do, and sometimes dogs will do things here with all these other dogs that he wouldn't do at home.

SAM: *Do you have problems with the owners of dogs putting squeezes on judges?*

There's some problems, and over the years if any of that occurred, it would get to be a real problem. But now in all my years of judging, I've never had but one man to offer me any compensation for helping his dog. And the way he did it, when he brought it up, I couldn't prove that's what he said. But there's no question in my mind what he meant. He showed me this number which I didn't want to see and said this is a fine dog and would really mean a lot to me if he was to win and he would appreciate anybody helping him with that. And I said, "What?" And he said, "You know what I am talking about." And I said, "I know exactly, damn it, what you're talking about," and I said, "I'll tell you something else, you can box up those hounds you've got here." He said, "Well, I didn't mean to be bribing you or nothing." I said, "The hell you didn't. Let me tell you something. Don't you ever approach me like that again and I'm not gonna fail to tell the committee what you said. They can determine what you meant." He was pretty big in the foxhound business and if he ever run another one in a field trial, I don't know about it. He got the word.

There's people here that would pay $25,000 to win this trial. I'm not saying there's a lot of people here would pay $25,000 to win honest. I doubt that there's many here who would pay that to win it crooked. But it would be worth that much to them to win it. But we don't take no shit off these damn people. If one come up to one of us right now, I'd just tell them right out and no questions. I'd tell everybody tomorrow morning what he did.

SAM: *The judges have to be circumspect in what they do and say?*

Right. After a while the hunters get to know the judges and the judges get to know each other. If one old boy talks out of that group, they'll do what they call "blackball," and they won't fool with him. He'll get a hunt all messed up and see, when you come out of there and say, "Look Bob, so and so scratched your dog," you're telling him that you don't agree with what the rest of the judges did. This is a democratic process and we don't care which side you're on. The majority wins and you have to realize that you're no smarter than the majority, and whatever the majority votes is right. And if you can't agree with that, then we don't want you in there to begin with. Sometimes the tempers fly a bit. But if he isn't right, he doesn't make it but three or four times before they learn him and don't fool with him no more.

The competition's so fierce and they get so close to the hearts of these hunters that if they make a few mistakes they don't need them no more. And there's no question they make mistakes. They misread a number. Most of the fellows get a little age on them. They've got to be to have enough experience to judge one of these big-time hunts. Take me, I can't see as good as I used to and if I see 530 go across there, that's what I'm gonna write down here. I know that's what it is, but it could be 580 that I misread. If twenty-five judges in three days and everybody's honest, I wouldn't say the best dog here will win, but a good hound should win. If everybody does what he's supposed to do.

In theory, everybody has an equal chance. Of course, people through experience are sharp enough to take advantage of the little breaks. I'm not talking about crooked things, but paint their numbers on the sides of their hounds better. Know what type of hound to bring. You hope to get your hound just as soon as the hunt's off. If you don't get him until the night sometimes, he ain't got much time to rest. Another break of the game is the hounds being where the judges are. If you have an average hound and he gets out there with eight or ten poor hounds and jumps a fox, he'll show up real good. Where's an average hound get over there with five or six good dogs, he won't show up so good.

One of the things that a man can do if his dog runs up a lot of score, he can take him out of the country and hide him so he couldn't get eliminated. But don't forget, I've got two hundred hound owners here that's helping me watch for that. And they will report to me anything he saw like that. You hardly would be able to see your dog all day if you looked for him among these six hundred hounds. And if you did, you wouldn't never find him in a place where you could catch and load him without somebody seeing you do it.

SAM: *What would be the point of loading your dog?*

To keep him from being eliminated. See, we haven't gotten to that point, but we'll eliminate them for anything that they do wrong. If the judges see a hound do something wrong, he scratches him, and he don't run no more. So if he had run up a lot of score and was getting tired and quit, that guy'd put him in the truck and carry him home or something. His score would stay and he would very well win with it. Of course, lots of them are going to get eliminated.

A hound is eliminated for anything that's a fault to an ideal champion. Loafing, that's probably the most prevalent. Loafing, not going hunting, quitting, laying around, standing around the road, trotting up and down the road after trucks, showing no inclination to hunt a fox.

Now, babbling is probably considered the worst fault. That's a dog tonguing when there isn't any track, giving lie, and giving false tongue. They get excited and tongue when there's no track. Running the back track, running the track the wrong way, is a fault. Running any kind of track except a fox, wolf, or deer. And a deer, you won't score them or scratch them. It's normal for them to do that. He can get scratched for being handled. He can get scratched for interfering with the race, doing something to distract the other hounds. I don't care what it is, coming in season or heat or standing in the road barking, anything that interferes with the chase.

Judges are the "gatekeepers" for the established standards among competing houndsmen and horsemen. They evaluate behaviors and stances, discriminate between class and taste, differentiate winners from losers, and solemnize their choices by ceremoniously passing out trophies. These trophies are the visible symbols in the currency of competitive esteem much cherished by their owners.

Society Hunters

Wealth, gender, horses, and expensive life-styles distinguish society hunters from the other groups. Most are women from Kentucky, horse riders who enjoy the freedom of following the hounds unencumbered by the heavy hierarchical rituals of their hometown clubs. In Kentucky, they belong to exclusive clubs where participation for both humans and hounds is highly regimented and structured. Their nickname of "Tally Ho" is an epitome whose envy is expressed in a hound owner's remark that "we would all be Tally Hos if we could afford it."

Society hunters belong to tight social circles and often attend events as a group. They truck their horses and accessories from Kentucky, often bringing servants to attend their animals. While following the hounds, their riding attire and bearing set their small parties apart from other mounted individuals, who are often the judges. In the evening, they gather for room parties where their conversations turn to what others are wearing, their chores at home, speculations and jokes played on colleagues, good runs, the advantages of being "so close to nature," past affairs, and current events. At parties and in the field, they socialize mainly among themselves and with a few celebrities of the NFHA.

Horse shows are not mandatory events and their occurrence is at the discretion of the president. With few participants in recent NFHA horse competitions, there was talk of discontinuing them as separate events. All riders participate in the Best Hunting Horse contest, the winner chosen by field judges, whose names are known only to the president.[29]

My conversation with a rider begins as she is recuperating from an exhilarating morning run with the hounds. I ask what riding means to her:

Pure pleasure. We just love to be able to take out through the country and follow our own line. We do organized fox hunting at home with a pack of hounds and there you have to wear your uniform and you have to stay behind the huntsman and the field master. We jump, which is fun, but down here you can come dressed as you are and go wherever you want with whoever you want and the only ones you have to look out for is the fox, the hounds, and the judges.

SAM: *Are there differences between these hounds and those you run with in Kentucky?*

The others are bred to run as a pack, and these are not. They're bred just to run and to hunt a fox. They'll hunt individually most times, and if they strike something they'll begin to speak on the line and then other hounds will hark unto them. Then you wind up with a big pack on a hot run like this one was. As a rule, our hounds hunt and run as a pack and they are what is called Whippers—in that answer to the huntsman, and they sort of keep the pack together. They ride on the fringes and keep track of where the hounds are.

On our particular hunt back home, we do not have good sport, so we hunt to ride. Down here we ride to hunt. We plan this from year to year and it gets in your blood. It's a big effort getting up at three o'clock every morning for six or seven days and we drive 550 miles to get here. This year we brought ten horses.

It used to be when we first started coming you had 100 to 150 of us riders. The hunters call us the Tally Ho Riders because when we see the fox we say "Tally Ho," which is an English term.

SAM: *Any reason for the decrease in numbers of your group?*

I think the diminishing started when the hunt first came here. Probably 80 or 90 percent of the people who come to these hunts ride a little while and then they socialize a lot. We ride and we take care of our horses and we socialize a little.

SAM: *So there are different factions within the Tally Ho?*

Right. And also the accommodations here don't suit the social crowd. The motels are not fancy enough and there's no place to eat dinner. We bring our own breakfast and we have sandwich makings in our cooler for lunch or we go to the church luncheon.

SAM: *Do you have a way of making a living besides horses?*

Well, I am fortunate that I have an independent income. I work for my sister, who owns a farm, and we work alike and think alike. We breed horses on a very small scale. We're not equipped to handle a lot of horses and you feed a brood mare and foal for several years before the foal becomes useful. It's much more profitable to have boarders or to lease horses. We own five or six horses that are good for beginning riders and they're pretty much in demand. We have a lot of young mothers who lease from us and can't afford and don't have the time to own and take care of their own horse. So we provide them with that service. There's a lady down here with me that used to have horses and then she got divorced and she can't afford and doesn't have the facilities to keep a horse. She just leases one from us. It's very convenient for her and less expensive and less trouble because we get the horse ready for the hunt and take it to the hunt and all she has to do is get on and ride and then get off and hand us the horse. She doesn't have to clean the tackle or the horse or the stall.

SAM: *Here there seem to be more women into horses and more men into dogs. Can you explain?*

Right, well, I think the men that are into dogs are for the most part farmers and small-time businessmen. Their wives are perhaps more old-fashioned homebodies that stay home pregnant and barefoot and mind the house and the kids. I may be all wet, but that's my opinion. And the women that are into hunting, into horses, are sportswomen. Sportsmen, by and large, are more interested in basketball, football, golf and those things rather than into hunting [term used in the English sense of game pursued by hounds]. You see very few boys because there are so many other things for boys to do and they can do them all with their dad. But little girls and horses seem to click and it's something that women can do without big competition with men. Handling horses is something that anybody can do with a certain amount of knowledge.

SAM: *So it's something that women can do and not face much competition with men?*

Well, I don't know that that's a reason, it's just a fact. I should think that women have the time and the interest. They don't have a business to take care of and it's something they can do with their daughters while the men coach football and soccer and things with the boys.

SAM: *There is also a competitive side to horse riding.*

Oh yeah. There's a tremendous competitive side, but it's still dominated by women. Now there are some mighty good men equestrians in all phases, but they are a small percentage. I think it's because the women, the girls, grow up with the horses and they grow up doing it and not too many men do unless their parents are into it professionally. So that's all they're exposed to because the parents aren't interested in taking them to football and things like that. So they're sort of victims. It's just a known thing that there are more women into horses than there are men.

It was an unfortunate thing, fifteen years ago when I started hunting. There were, like I said, 100 to 150 Tally Ho Riders, and they had the wrong outlook on this field trialing. All they wanted to do was to get to the fox when it was killed and get the trophies. In organized hunting, the head and the tail and the feet are prized possessions. Some of the riders would get a little out of hand. They'd run over the top of the hounds and over the top of the judges and interfere with the chase. We got to be very unpopular with the hunters because of that and they thought we were blood-thirsty. Jumping and grabbing the fox and cutting it up and putting some blood on your face is a sort of initiation rite in our kind of hunting. Oh, it really was a bad scene. And my sister and I made a concerted effort over the last several years to be friendly with the hunters. We even get out of their way. Instead of galloping down the middle of the road and making the trucks stay behind, we get off the road and we're friendly.

And instead of trying to get there when the fox is killed, we sit out here and enjoy the cry. We love to see the fox and see him cross the road and everything. If we're there at the kill, then fine. We love it. Our purpose is to follow the hounds, hear them run, which makes me tingle and goose bumps. It's like you're in an auditorium with quadraphonic sound. It's just something you have to experience. You can't describe it, but that's what we love.

This conversation reveals composure, a comfortable life-style, self-assurance, and privilege. It also assumes deference, although that attitude has changed with the realization among the remaining riders that the pursuit of the fox at field trials was more than just their show. Within the association, society hunters are a minority group, yet, their symbols—the black hunting helmet, the hunter's horn, and riding stick (crop)—adorn the NFHA's seal, above its motto, "Good Fellowship." A legacy from the past, this seal portrays a time when hounds and horses were more readily kept together by most sportsmen. Today few houndsmen can afford the upkeep of both animals, although the hidden costs of the horsepower under the hoods of their four-wheel drives must rival such expenditures.

It is the aristocratic image of the huntsman (now a huntswoman) and his (her) mount that legitimizes these sporting activities and gives them standing. Thus the presence of the society hunter sanctions the field of competitive houndsmen. Such a mixture of animals and gender, women mounted on horseback and men afoot with dogs, a few rich women in a sea of masculine rivalry and competition, are the stuff making for a structuralist's field day. Academics of the structuralist persuasion would be tempted to find meaning in the oppositions between men and women, hounds and horses, mounted and prone, sign and symbol. The meanings are there, played out between these symbolic poles, and support for their significance can be mined from the statements and behavior of the constituent groups.

Rituals are fertile fields for the flowering of ironies. For many county residents, the message of the society hunter above is probably missed, for in this type of hunting, class is more relevant than gender. The obvious symbolism is that of a few rich women, mounted on horseback, epitomizing what hunting, in its strict, formal sense, is all about: the pursuit on horseback of a wild animal with the aid of hounds.[30] Undoubtedly, the original intention of the NFHA was to confirm hounds that had both show and performance qualities. Yet these goals run counter to stronger cultural currents of social differentiation through the acquisition of differing products. This process, what Marshall Sahlins calls *la pensée bourgeoise*, proceeds according to a meaningful logic of the concrete, in which the significance of observed objective differences is considered an appropriate sign for emerging social distinctions.[31] In time, the means by which hounds of the bench and hounds of the field became distinguished developed into two separate and unequal tracks, with the boundaries between the two reinforced by human conceptions of class and style.

Bench-Show Fox Hunters

Among houndsmen, those investing in the bench show are generally wealthy and belong to the professions. Their group includes lawyers, bankers, doctors of medicine and veterinary science, wholesalers and managers of large corporations, and a few of lesser economic means admitted by performance if not conformity. The breeding, raising, and training of "high-class" foxhounds is an expensive hobby. It is a hobby that enthusiasts can afford to, and do, trust to someone else.

Although bench showers are comparatively few, this deficiency in numbers is overcome by their facility with social and organizational skills. Their contest, the bench show, lasts two hours on the opening afternoon of the annual meet. Subsequently, these houndsmen have the rest of the week to follow casts in the mornings and to attend parties in the afternoons and evenings. There are consequences to these activities, for, in conjunction with society hunters, some men discuss tactics to control and manage the association. They seek ascendancy through alliances, through splitting the more numerous votes of the field trialers, and through parliamentary maneuvers in association forums. Measured by the succession of their candidates elected as president and as directors, their tactics may be judged overwhelmingly successful.

Winning on the bench is a cherished accomplishment and readily absorbed into the identity presented to one's peers. Winning also has its promotional side, with the champion's owner often advancing within the hierarchy of the association. I asked one such winner, a subsequent president, what it meant to win:

It means you've got the best-looking hound in America. I won the first dual championship on record at the National. That's the field and the bench. That is the greatest honor a fox hunter can have, to win a dual championship. I had a bitch that done that and I was more proud of her than any dog I ever had.

SAM: *Is it more important to have a dog rather than a bitch?*

Oh, yeah. You can breed a dog to a lot of bitches, but you can breed a bitch not over about onced a year.

If the above gentleman was somewhat reserved in his conversation with me, his partner, who raised and trained the winning hounds, was more eager to talk. He talked about the nature of their partnership and the meaning of winning:

He furnished the dogs and I furnished the know-how, because he didn't know his ass from a hole in the ground about dogs. And what little he knows now is what I taught him, if he still remembers anything. He just heard that I knew how to raise puppies. We done our part of the winning, oh, good God yes. I raised the dog that won the National bench show in 1965 in Texas. In 1960, I raised the dog that won the bench show in South Carolina and we still owned him at the time. But the one that won in Texas, we sold that thing when he wasn't but 5-½ months old for six hundred dollars, and hell, at that time that was the most outrageous price that had ever been paid for a dog. So I've had my glory and I'm awful proud of it.

SAM: *You sold the winning hound?*

That's right. After you win the National bench show, there's nowhere for you to go then, except to keep him for breeding purposes.

SAM: *You decided not to go the stud route?*

A man would have to have a hole in his head to go that stud route. Course, I've got a big enough hole in my head, but you have to run to the airport and pick up dogs and breed them and take them back to the airport and ship them. Tom, Dick, and Harry drives four hundred miles and knocks on your door at three o'clock in the morning and all that crap.

They make money, but hell, that ain't that important. It's important to some of them, but it ain't that important to me.

SAM: *Your satisfaction comes then from having won and from watching others begin to climb the ladder toward success?*

Yeah, it's all glory. Stars will shine in your eyes every time you think about it.

SAM: *What does it take to produce a National bench champion?*

Course, you have to have the breeding stock to begin with. You got to feed them. Back when I started, you had to invent your own formula for growing puppies, before all this fancy puppy food came into existence. Yeah, it does me good to see these fellows wanting to climb the ladder. Course, I know what he's gonna have to do to get there, but there's a lot of them starts out. They're burning up the wind. They're gonna do it, and they get half way up the ladder and it gets too complicated and they quit. They finally realize that it's costing them a whole lot of money. You know the old saying is that you're not gonna get anything for nothing. You got to pay for what you get. I'll tell you one damn thing. You pay dear to have a National bench show champion.

SAM: *And I guess there is a social price as well in getting to know the right people?*

Yeah, you can have a National field trial winner at 10 percent of what a National bench show winner cost. See that guy with the raincoat on? He's the only man that have ever raised, owned, and showed three National bench champions. I raised two. It took him forty years to do what he done, and it took me ten years to do what I done.

My third dog would have won if the fellow had taken him down off the bench and walked him around a little bit. I raised and trained that one too, but it didn't win. Come damn near winning though. Course them near misses don't count. That second place bench, it ain't worth a shit.

SAM: *So winning is the important thing. You tend to grow conservative at that point.*

Yeah, it happens that way. If we'd been out there among the benches Sunday afternoon, every time the show judge would say that's it, hold your place, if you and I had been standing out there mingling with those children while he was still out there on the floor, you could have heard some of them way back there, even the man in tenth place, say, "Damn, I did all right, didn't I? I put one on tenth place!" And he did do all right. But if he ever gets on top he don't think he's done so well back then. But you've got to start somewhere.

Even the owner of the hound in tenth place stands to win a ribbon, a small symbolic return for competing in the high stakes of the bench show. The competition that owners face to place a hound on the last few benches of each class is not generally stiff. These places are usually sought by field-trial owners hoping to place in the field and win a Dual Champion, an award won infrequently.

The skills and time for working a hound to the top of the bench show are similar to those used in the social circles of their owners. Sociality, hospitality, conspicuous consumption, largesse, and networking are all skills used to enhance the standing of man and hound. Most of the hounds entered get on the bench and receive ribbons, an affirmation of participation. Bench hounds may be beautiful and refined animals, but they hardly know what a fox is. Breeders have played a large role in differentiating the bench show and the field-trial hounds.

Breeders

Breeders play for high stakes. Unlike the other groups associated with fox hunting, breeders are unashamedly commercial and retain some distance from prospective purchasers of their products. Their reputations are based upon their abilities to produce winning hounds consistently and conspicuously. Breeders bring more hounds to the meets than they enter. They are prepared to sell their stock at prices reflecting their reputations and momentary standings in the stakes.

Most breeders are reluctant to talk about money, and they are particularly zealous about the amounts which others suspect they make. When pressed, they willingly discuss the presumed fortunes of others:

If you have a champion like Louis has, it's possible to make some money. Of course, I haven't gone at it to make money. It's just more or less for sport and prestige, which is all I ever got out of it.

SAM: *Money helps, doesn't it? In terms of making that prestige and status worthwhile?*

It gives you something to work to. It gets you recognized and you get a lot of friends, meet people you wouldn't no other way. And then it seems like when you win with a champion and then he goes to producing winners, the price goes up. Just being a champion means a little, but then he's got to prove himself that he is a stud dog. And he also has to be a bloodline that people will hunt with. Before you can do any good with them as far as making money's concerned, he's got to prove hisself and get other people's eyes on him, get them to look at him.

Reg had an old black female that went and bred to Lewis's copper dog. That thing produced Hornet, rather that thing produced some puppies that just won everything. Everywhere they went, they'd win, and damn Jackie, he seen far enough ahead that he bought up all that breed of dog, although he paid two and eight thousand for a dog. But he got them all bought up and now he can sell puppies. I'm talking about puppies now, six or seven weeks old, for four hundred and five hundred dollars a piece just as fast as he can produce them.

SAM: *Who buys those dogs?*

These damn guys that's got all this money, that drives all these four-wheel drives, and a lot of these other folks around here that don't look like they got a nickle.

SAM: *So winning is the important first thing?*

That's right. Yes sir!

The Chase magazine, the official organ of the NFHA, caters to the breeders' aspirations by sponsoring the Chase Futurity. This event runs for three days, beginning on the morning following the bench show. A hound may be entered only once and must be under two years old. In addition, entrees must be registered in the International Foxhunters' Stud Book and nominated several months in advance of the event.[32]

Some kennels are consistent producers of futurity winners. This enviable reputation is obtained by only a few:

Charles and his boys, they have a lot of winners. And Wooly wins a lot. I'm talking about a whole lot, that's what keeps him selling puppies.

SAM: *Is part of their strategy to get their names associated as winners so that people will bid high on their dogs?*

If Wooly's got a good futurity puppy, a man has to go plum crazy with his pocketbook to be able to buy it from him, because he's wanting to keep it himself so people say, Wooly's done won the futurity. He can sell fifty more dogs just because that one won the futurity, although he's gonna be selling the same breed that he's been selling. Where is he'd sell you that dog and you win the futurity, then eventually part of that credit would go back to him, but you would actually get credit for the dog winning. This costs him a whole hell of a lot of money to start, but he stuck with it and kept pounding at it until everybody knows that if you get a dog from his kennel, more than likely you're gonna win a trophy. Not necessarily win a field trial, but you gonna win a trophy.

Consistent winning in the futurity has its price. Kennels specializing in derby dogs fare poorly in the other competitions:

I think everybody's got a different opinion why Edgar and them can't win the all-age when they can win the damn futurity every time they want to. I mean that's the way it appears. But hell, they do good to even place a dog in the all-age.

SAM: *What are some of the opinions?*

Well, they figure that the dogs, by the time they keeps them until he's over two years old and got him in shape to run in the all-age, he's done wore out. The dog's either wore out or they're bred so they can't take it after they get a certain age. Most anybody can breed a dog that, until he's two years of age, will run through a briar thicket, run through a barbed wire fence, run through everything. Running's his game. But you'd better breed that thing right. Just watch for him anytime after he's two years old, he's gonna blow up and wouldn't run a damn thing. Maybe just completely quit. And they don't take no part of the bench show. They specialize in futurity and I'll be durned if they don't win their part of it.

Both bitch and dog contributions are recognized for improving the breed and performance, yet these qualities are mostly discussed in masculine terms. Stud performance is particularly exonerated. For men, dogs are the performers and the main carriers of bloodlines and skills. Pressed, some men will allow that desirable traits benefit from nurturing by bitches. Bitches produce few litters during a year, consequently their production is limited in comparison with that of dogs. Dogs can provide almost unlimited stud service, for which prospective clients pay fifty to two hundred dollars.

Foxhounds exist in a highly artificial and selective state. They are selectively bred for configuration to an ideal type and for their ability to pursue a fox. Maintaining standards and perpetuating them incurs risks and great expenditures of time, training, and resources.[33]

The growth of fox hunting and field trials depended on recognizable improvements in speed and stamina. While a preoccupation with animal pedigrees has its practical aspects, other considerations suggest more mundane and expressive goals. Through the purchase of stud rights, an individual lays claim to connections with other prominent fox hunters and kennels; thereby he gains entrance into an esteemed group and enhances his own standing. And given sufficient time and resources, he may build a genealogical entity of his own design with identifiable characteristics of color, size, shape, or voice.

For hounds, matches can be arranged without taking into account motives external to breeding and without the complications inherent in human marriages or sexual alliances. Unlike their human counterparts, bitches produce litters, both sexes are polygamous, undesirable offspring may be eliminated, generational time is short, and crossings with hounds of note can be easily arranged or purchased.[34] Given these considerations and sufficient resources, a fox hunter can put together a bloodline bearing his name within a comparatively short time. He can provide this lineage with a history and a special set of physical and behavioral characteristics. With meticulous skill and luck, an enthusiast can take a transient entity (hounds), provide it with an identity (his own name), and create a salable commodity that outlasts his lifetime. Through the focused energies of men of means, a transient resource becomes a durable one.[35] Such achievements are the legacies of the founding fathers of American fox-hunting bloodlines whose names we recall today as the Walkers, Triggs, Julys, Henrys, and Birdsongs.

Field-Trial Fox Hunters

Field trialers are the most numerous of the participants in regional events. There are two recognizable types, which are often discussed as distinct. But, as a former president told us, each is coalesced with the personality and experiences of individuals. The "One Gallus," born and reared in small towns and the rural countryside, continues to reside and work there. They are mostly blue collar, nonunionized mill workers, service station attendants, truck drivers, small farmers, and lower-level civil servants. With their main stronghold in the mountains, these individuals keep small packs of dogs for private rituals called "hill-topping."[36] Some provinciality and patriarchal presumptions show in the following conversation:

Well, a fox hunter is a person that loves the outdoors. He loves the cry of the hound. It puts a tingle up his spine. He hears things that the ordinary person will never hear. There's something about the cry of the foxhound that pleases his ear, and God gave him the fox for the hound to run. They say a dog's as good as his master. Because if he's a sorry master, he'll keep a sorry hound. But if he's a good master, a good strong one, he'll have a good strong hound.

SAM: *How would you describe a good master?*

Well, a good master's a man that puts everything in its place. Everything has got a place and a place for everything. Now you study over what I said. Let me give you an average fox hunter. An average fox hunter is a man that he's got a wife and three kids and a pickup truck. He works five days a week somewhere and he buys a little dog. Maybe he's got five or six good hounds, and he just can't wait till the weekend so he can hear them run. And he tries to run on Friday night and he'll come in Saturday and gather up his hounds and Sunday morning gets up and goes to church, take his family to church. Nine times out of ten, they're that kind of people and they don't harm no other soul. Now the old story about a fox hunter drinking, now that's something out of the storybook. I can show you men on this ground that's never touched a drop of whiskey, including myself, and I've been hunting all my life. In the mountains where I hunt, if we even smell whiskey on your breath, you'll never go hunting with us again.

SAM: *Have you ever had any champions, winners?*

Not any, no champions, and don't care whether I ever own one or not. I'll tell you why. In the country where I live, we cannot produce a field-trial hound. The mountains up there, we run red fox at night. We call it hill-topping. When you go hill-topping, you don't produce a field-trial hound.

The austere tastes and provinciality of the One Gallus provide substance for jokes and barbs as other fox hunters josh and jostle. Nonetheless, some other characteristics are admired, especially the Gallus's independence and the ability of his generalized hounds (referred to as "honest") sometimes to outperform all others. The intermingling of One Gallus traits in the field trialer becomes apparent in the following conversation:

Now, all the fox hunting that's done is not done by three or four people or a big group of people. A lot of fox hunting is did by one man going out here and taking his pack of dogs and going out maybe fifteen miles from home, back on a dead-end road, and he'll sit there all day by hisself or all night, and it don't make any difference whether it's hot or cold weather, be by his lone self and not a damn soul to speak to and don't want nobody to speak to. He wants to hear them dogs. And he's just as soon go with his buddies, but if they don't want to go that night, he's gonna go anyhow. When he leaves the house to go hunting, if you want to come along and bring yours, you're welcome. Why he's a fox hunter is because he likes to hear them dogs run. It's not because he likes to get out there and shoot the bull. Of course, the bull's included in it, but that's not really the reason. The real reason for becoming a fox hunter, or calling hisself a fox hunter, is because he likes to hear the dogs run. And of course he likes the fellowship, but hell, he can do without that. When the dogs are running, he wants everybody to be quiet until the dogs goes out of hearing and then he'll talk to you a little.

Although many share interests with the One Gallus, field trialers are usually financially better situated and in more control of their time. As a consequence, they can afford the time and money it takes to keep and to enter hounds in regional and national events throughout a season of competition. Occupationally, field trialers are agribusinessmen, farm implement dealers, rural schoolteachers, insurance salesmen, with an occasional lawyer and veterinarian in the mix.

Keeping hounds healthy throughout the year is a time-consuming business, involving other family members. On a daily basis, hounds require feeding and watering, cleaning of pens, and checking for signs of disease. On a less frequent basis, hounds need training and running to keep in shape, trips to the veterinarian for shots and consultation, and searches for prospective mates. Many of these daily chores fall to wives, who frequently accompany their husbands to field events. Reared on farms, many of these women spend a lifetime associated with the manly sports of their husbands:

My father was a hunter of all kinds—a fisher and a hunter. I was almost born fishing and hunting, and I've went and stayed all night many a time. I just enjoy listening to the dogs. I'm into it head over heels the same way my husband is. I learned a long time ago, if you can't beat one of them and you don't work, you just as well join them and go on. And when I did, I learned to enjoy it.

SAM: *Would you say that it's rather unusual for a woman to be as involved in fox hunting as her husband?*

It is. It's more unusual than maybe another sport, but there's an awful lot of ladies that attend field trials, and they help with the dogs. Well, maybe at home they do more for the dogs than their husbands do. I talk to all of our'n at home. I give them all the shots, and I breed them and give them the hookworm shots. We raise puppies. I do all that. We had to give a hundred shots last week of parvo vaccine. It didn't work so good, so we lost some dogs and we got the blood sent off and they identified it as being that. It's that feline [*sic*] distemper and they said it would be alive for seven years and the only thing that would get it would be Clorox. So we got barrels of Clorox and mixed it with water and my son has a six-hundred-pound pressure spray gun there and we sprayed it all over. We didn't have another one take sick. But that one was enough, just losing that one.

SAM: *Do you participate with your husband in other kinds of hunting?*

We don't do nothing but fox hunt now. It takes up most of the time. Time
to see about the puppies and feed the dogs and when you go fox hunting you
don't never know when you're coming back. It may be all night long. I've
stayed out all night many a night. We farmed all our lives and we've retired
now. Our son's running the farm.

SAM: *If you couldn't fox hunt, what would you miss the most?*

Well, I would miss the sound of them dogs clapping that tongue. I got some
good tapes. I sit up in the house and play them tapes when it gets so we really
couldn't fox hunt. Since we're living in such a densely populated farming
area, we don't get to run our dogs year round. We have to run them after the
neighbors get their tobacco up high enough that the dogs can get through the
fields without damaging it. So we're handicapped in that respect, but then
sometimes we fox hunt half the day and then hunt the dogs. They'll eventually
come back, most of them, where you cast at.

I find as good a friendly, more down to earth bunch of people that do this
thing. The whole bunch, that'll take an animal like that and care for him and
feed him and treat it like these animals are treated. They're treated as good as
some humans, and when you lose one of them, you lose a part of you. You
learn to love it just like you love anything else. You know, with a different
kind of love. Now don't misunderstand me.

For most field trialers, their sport needs no elaboration nor justification.
Most discuss their participation as an inheritance, a legacy from a father or
from a neighbor. Field trialing for them is part of a total social phenomenon,
to use Marcel Mauss's terms, an activity in which they invest considerable
time, talents, and their egos.[37] For them, life becomes a paradoxical mix of
close neighborhood ties and incessant strivings for an advantage and the competitive edge, thereby enabling them to get a leg up (my doggy metaphor) on
rivals. Their field events are scheduled during the late fall and early winter
when men, and families, leave their scattered farms and engage in competitive
ventures in which winners are sharply divided from losers:

It's the thrill to me. If I got one to turn loose Saturday morning and I don't
think he got scratched, I'll listen for that number till the last thing. To me, it's
a thrill. And be competitive. I just love to. I want mine to be competitive.
They ain't gonna worry about their groceries. They'll get their groceries even
if they don't do nothing, but they can do it.

SAM: *Does that competitive spirit spill over into the other activities you are
concerned with, such as farming?*

Yeah, exactly right. I love to come see these people. I didn't come to play
with them. I come to whip them if I can, honest. I don't want it no other way.
But now they'se a few that has accused some of us of being dishonest. But
they didn't know what they was talking about. But I love it straight.

SAM: *You play by the rules.*

I want it straight. I sure do.

SAM: *With the expectations so high on winning, but with the chances of winning so low, do fox hunters ever play tricks on leading dogs so they can't win?*

We had a dog who could outrun and outdone any dog that was out there in Mississippi. The Master of Fox Hounds thought we'd won, for he had scored so good at the end of the third day. They come to us and said, "I wouldn't leave him in these pens tonight. Somebody'll do something to him." But they didn't. There they was accused of taking your dog and hauling him out of the country. Say I was scoring good. Catch him the second day of the hunt and haul him miles away, put him out knowing that he can't be back here tomorrow to meet competition. They've been accused of that, but now I hadn't never put that on nobody. That's wrong.

I've heard tell of one maybe like he's out there in the woods doing something and had his dog under his overcoat. Now that's wrong. He's been called on that, or according to readings he was. And he's supposed to be a Christian man right now. If mine come up here now, see me, hear me talking, switching them tails, I'd get in my truck and I'm gone.

Now my dogs won't stay with you, not even if you take them. But they hear me, they'll come to me. They love me to death, I guarantee you that. They'll switch them tails. Them things are almost like a person. Probably more loyal than most people.

In the field trials, fox hunters may enter unlimited numbers of hounds provided they pay their entry fees. Entered hounds are randomly assigned numbers, which are painted on their sides. These numbers serve as identification markers when the hounds are encountered afield by the judges. After a roll call at daybreak on the casting grounds (as the place of release is called), the hounds are turned loose and are expected to exhibit fox-finding behavior for five hours on three consecutive days. To do otherwise, hounds run the risk of being eliminated by the judges. Points are assigned to hounds for hunting (persistently searching for a fox where expected), for trialing (when a trial is struck, hounds work the line and give tongue), and for speed and drive (when the fox is started and the pack is in hot pursuit). Each of these behaviors is part of a graded series, with maximum scores going to the hound closest to the fox during speed and drive and to the other categories of fox finding when observed late in each five-hour sequence. Judges sum up the scores for each hound on a daily basis and post the score by hound number in the motel lobby. Theoretically, only the owner and the secretary know which numbers belong to which owner. Hounds successfully finishing the three-day race and accumulating scores in two or more categories are given endurance points worth a quarter of their overall score.

Fate and chance play a large role in winning with field-trial hounds. A championship field trial is chaos in that all kinds of things can and do happen. Elimination by judges from the competition is a great risk; between one-half and two-thirds of hounds entered do not make it through the three days. Many fall victims to accidents, to predators, to abandoned traps, or are caught in fences. There is also the risk of foxhounds becoming lost or, worst of all, of being killed while crossing a highway or railway track. Field trialing is a marathon. For those hounds concluding the races, ten prizes are awarded for each category of hunting, trialing, speed and drive, endurance, and highest general average. Unlike the opening day when each hound begins the competition on an equal footing, field trials end with few winners and these receive multiple trophies.

Reflections on Winning and Losing

Fox hunting is a game currently played by strangers on the landscapes of Scotland and adjacent counties. Its undertaking brings in new money for a few established businesses. It is tolerated by the majority of residents out of curiosity or amusement, and may be damaging to some whose property gets run over in the heat of the chases. Foxhounds are part of the passing scene of the fall season.

Among fox hunters, hounds are the mediums by which the scores of their owners are settled. Points scored by field-trial hounds become the measure of the men whose investments underscore a chancy game, in life as in sport. The more staid games of the bench show depend on another currency, one where social standing depends less on risk and more on refined discrimination. The winners in either competition, both hound and man, are assured a place in the annals of regional and national fox hunting lore.

There are other ways of winning, if one interprets success in a broader context. This connection includes the prospect of gaining esteem from peers, of maintaining a position of status within the association, and of maintaining social ties with particular peers and friends. In addition, one may be appointed a judge and thereby serve as a "gatekeeper" to another's pretensions. And if one has social, organizational, or political skills, he may be elected a director or a president. There are also many ways to lose. The epitaph "going to the dogs" is reserved for those whose pretensions, once advanced, were not sustained through the hurly-burly of time.

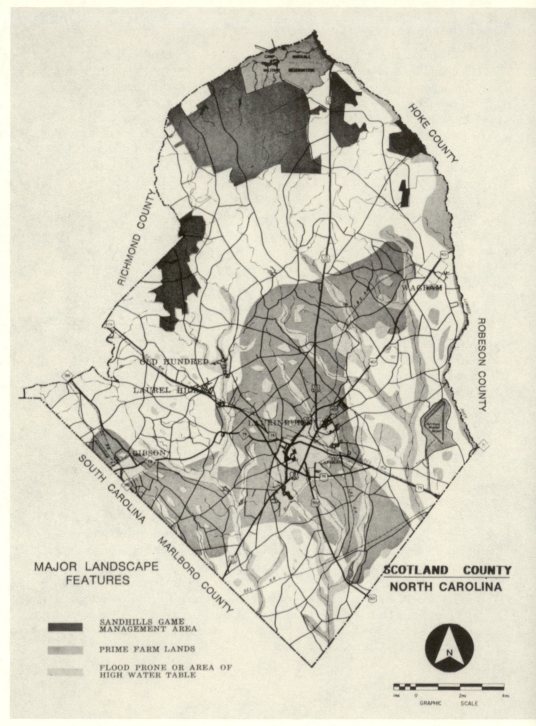

MAJOR LANDSCAPE
FEATURES

SCOTLAND COUNTY
NORTH CAROLINA

SANDHILLS GAME
MANAGEMENT AREA

PRIME FARM LANDS

FLOOD PRONE OR AREA OF
HIGH WATER TABLE

1 mi.   0   2 mi.   4 mi.
GRAPHIC   SCALE

1. Map of Scotland County.

2. Bench-show competition, National Foxhunters' Association, 1979, in Laurinburg, N.C. The event was held inside the National Guard Armory because of inclement weather. The bench-show judge and ringmaster (left) are discussing the placement of hounds.

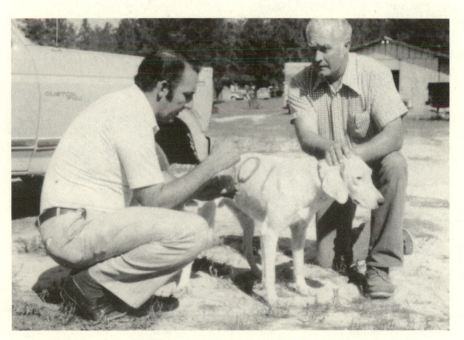

3. Painting numbers on the sides of field trial hounds, National Foxhunters' Association meeting, fall 1979, hound kennels, rural Scotland County.

4. Drivers releasing their dogs at the start of a deer hunt, Carpenter's Deer Hunt Club, fall 1980.

5. Standers inspecting and discussing deer killed as the carcass is delivered to the clubhouse, Carpenter's Deer Hunt Club, fall 1982.

6. Ritual of cutting a shirttail after missing a buck, Carpenter's Deer Hunt Club, fall 1979.

7. A "still" hunter showing off a large rack to admirers at Carpenter's Deer Hunt Club, fall 1980.

8. Putting down a brace at a Pinehurst, N.C., field trial. (Courtesy of North Carolina Collection, University of N.C. Library at Chapel Hill)

9. Hunters and politicians in line for a barbecue on opening day of dove season, Labor Day 1981, Henderson Club.

10. Close network of friends toasting the memory of a deceased landlord and mentor after a successful hunt, Henderson Farm.

11. "The Discussion Settled," *Leslie's Weekly*, December 19, 1891. (Courtesy of Photographic Section, North Carolina Department of Cultural Resources)

12. Rabbit hunters working the edge of a field with their beagles, winter 1980.

13. Skinning a raccoon carcass after a successful "buddy hunt" sponsored by the Rockfish Coon Club, winter 1981.

14. Trapper confronting Wildlife Protector about his arrest on three counts of illegally trapping foxes, State Line Coon Club, winter 1980.

15. Socializing outside the Coon Clubhouse before competitions, summer 1979.

16. Owner positioning a coon hound for a bench show, winter 1980.

Six

Horned Heads and Twitching Tails:
An Interpretation of Buck-Hunting Rituals

All of a sudden I thought about how maybe planting and working and then harvesting oats and cotton and beans and hay wasn't jest something me and Mister Ernest done three hundred and fifty-one days, to fill in the time until we could come back hunting again, but it was something we had to do, and do honest and good during the three hundred and fifty-one days, to have the right to come back into the big woods and hunt for the other fourteen; and the fourteen days that old buck run in front of dogs wasn't jest something to fill his time until the three hundred and fifty-one when he didn't have to, but the running and the risking in front of the guns and dogs was something he had to do for fourteen days to have the right not to be bothered for the other three hundred and fifty-one. And so hunting and farming wasn't two different things at all—they were jest the other side of each other.

(William Faulkner, *Big Woods*)

ARCHIBALD RUTLEDGE begins his story of the Whitehorn Buck by describing the elusive creature that swells in the minds of its persistent pursuers. This creature's head is adorned with large and handsome antlers whose color, white, provides a transcendental quality. For buck hunters, the size and shape of an antler epitomize the greatness, smartness, beauty, and majesty of its bearer. Shed antlers, once found, are tangible evidence of a monarch's survival, and they are proof of the memorable yarns spun over his dimensions and dexterity; they become the substance for subsequent strategies. The death of a monarch is only a temporary triumph, when the head and antlers are mounted in the place of honor within the hunter's den. It becomes a tragedy when remorse is felt in losing an old protagonist who has deeply stirred one's emotional base. Like the "big bucks" of a financier's dreams, the quest begins anew after each conquest.[1]

Most large bucks remain at large, unrestrained by property lines, and free to roam the minds of men who are themselves restrained. For most buck hunters, these large creatures remain beyond their grasp and, through time, come to symbolize the ones that always get away. As Archibald Rutledge remembers, these magnificent animals are most vulnerable to the poachers and tenants who share the bucks' space and who spend time trying to figure them out.

The practice of restricting deer hunting to the killing of bucks first emerged as part of the sportsmen's codes in deference to the customs of wealthy gentlemen and outsiders.[2] Slightly later, regulations regarding bucks became codified to enhance the expansion in deer numbers. Today, with deer plentiful again, the state of North Carolina encourages the taking of does in addition to bucks. Yet somewhat paradoxically, state intervention designed to increase the deer harvests and to improve the chances of individuals has met with resistance by many buck seekers.

My perspective begins with the dawning realization verbalized by William Faulkner's twelve-year-old boy whose thoughts introduce this chapter. The sentiments and behaviors in buck hunting are not divorced from the rest of one's life and livelihood; work and play are sides of the same currency. With this insight I seek to clarify some of the cultural contradictions displayed "on the horns" of such changes in policies and customary practices.

Some Boundary Lines in Land and Animals

Distinctions among deer hunters follow the contours of land ownership and are determined by the sex of the deer pursued and the caliber of the dogs in pursuit. Let us try to understand some of the cultural rules involved.

The ownership or access to land and its location with reference to the deer herds are important criteria for determining the rank of clubs and the success of participants. The deer herds are found mainly in the forested northern part of Scotland County, and their absence from the cleared lands south of US 74 makes that terrain ideal for fox field trialing. The Sandhills Game Management Area, state controlled land accessible for a fee, is also on a large chunk of this land. Deer hunters pursuing their quarry on private or leased land surrounding this management area have higher status and prospects for success than those on state and open lands. The deer season opens earlier on the former, giving hunters there the "edge" in securing wide-ranging deer.

There are usually two animals involved in deer hunting—dog and deer. In their relation to humans, each is differentially located in social space yet both are strongly identified with men. Neither animal respects land boundaries; their movements across boundaries cause conflicts.

The dogs of deer hunters belong to no particular breed; practically any dog can learn to chase deer. Moreover, many dogs assume this role after failing to perform on other game. Besides food and housing, these dogs receive little care from their owners, although a few individuals may be championed for their tracking abilities. Owners seek a pack with diverse traits, including some dogs known as "cold trailers," "long and short winds," and those rarest of the breed that "open" only on the tracks of bucks. The taxonomy of dog mixtures (cur, feist, drop) and their given names indicate their diverse origins. The given names in one pack were those of the person giving the dog (Watson dog), a diverse background (Heinz, or 57 varieties), an annoying habit (Colonel Sanders, for chasing chickens), or an ability as a "trailing machine" (Axelrod).

Hunters are unable to control their dogs' wanderings once they are turned loose to find deer, although deer clubs use individuals, known as drivers, to follow the dogs and to encourage their looking in the right places. Sometimes dogs take off in pursuit of other animals or cross boundary lines on to another's property, leaving them unaccounted for at the close of a hunt. Inevitably some dogs get lost and become feral, and such occurrences cause enmity between county residents and hunters. To reduce this problem, some hunters capture all the dogs they find while hunting and exchange them for their own that someone else caught. Others simply shoot the dogs, particularly if they are without visible identification.

Some hunters do not use dogs in their quest for deer. These deer hunters cannot afford to maintain a pack of dogs throughout the year or prefer to test their own skill (or luck) against the animal. Although it may be illegal elsewhere in North Carolina and in other states to drive deer with dogs, within Scotland County hunting with dogs is the norm.

Deer, though they are hunted for food or trophy, fall into that special category of creatures that is wild only in a relative sense. They live on the margins of human habitation, where they frequently do damage by feeding on crops

and raiding house gardens and, worse, cause automobile accidents on highways. Deer are vexing problems for some landowners, who not only suffer
losses from their crops but also endure the disturbances of trespass on their
land by hunters during the day and by poachers at night. Clubs plant special
crops to attract and sustain deer on their land or may bait them so they will
hang around certain areas. Clubs view deer as "property," which they protect
through quasi-vigilante efforts by posting their land and patrolling their
boundaries.

As "big game," deer are bounded by other conventions. They are products
of the land, yet rights to deer, which can cross boundaries, do not come with
land ownership. Like other game, the state determines when and how deer
may be caught by individuals. Venison cannot be bought or sold legally, a
sign of the boundary marked out by sport hunters in their conflict with those
with more mercenary interests. Unlike other comestibles, venison belongs in
the masculine domain within the consuming household. The cleaning, cooking, and serving of venison is within the province of men, where it features as
seasonal fare at reunions and other ceremonial occasions. Therefore the distribution of venison within a community reflects many cultural aspects of relationships between givers and receivers, between men and women.

Among deer, only males bear antlers (see table 6.1). This visible biological
difference is an important one, and the state uses it to distinguish between
buck and doe hunting. Although in the past all deer were legal targets, at the
turn of the century the focus narrowed to bucks-only, a practice enforced in
the interests of conservation. Today, "deer hunter" in its generic sense may
pejoratively designate someone who kills does and fawns as well as bucks.
The injunction limiting the killing to bucks-only is based upon the biological
observation that among most ungulates, there is a "natural surplus" of males
over the number needed to reproduce the next generation. This fact is coupled
with the perspective that smart, and particularly large, bucks are the ones that
survive and do most of the breeding. A large rack is symbolic of virility and
survivorship, emblematic of a buck who stays around to get "the job done."
Theoretically, buck hunting improves the quality of the deer herd and provides a harvestable surplus without depleting the population. However, actual
practice provides many exceptions.[3]

TABLE 6.1
Deer Antler Terminology for Scotland County.

Spike or Botton	Short, first-year antlers
Cow horn	Longer spike with no branches
Rack	Any antlers longer than a spike, such as a 3-point, 4-point, etc.
Rocking-chair rack	Any larger set of antlers, visible above the sideboards of a pickup truck, "so large one can get up in them and rock"
Rubin	A large buck that always escapes

Deer Hunting and Buck Hunters

Generally deer hunters belong to one of four groups: club hunters, hunters on game management lands (usually outsiders from other counties), "still hunters" (individuals hunting from tree stands), and "poachers." These categories are established according to how hunters pursue their quarry (with or without dogs, choice of weapons), with whom (individually or in groups of peers, relatives, or strangers), and where (on private or state land).

The Hunt Clubs

By 1980, there were a dozen hunt clubs within Scotland County, each with its own berth in a locally recognized hierarchy of prestige. Those at the top began in the early 1950s, at a time when deer became a plentiful commodity after decades of scarcity. Prestigious clubs are well organized, with written rules and structured roles. They control the best territory on private land surrounding the Sandhills Game Management Area. Initially, local doctors, lawyers, and businessmen—and outsiders of comparable social status—comprised their memberships. Most of the outsiders left when the deer herds declined during the 1960s. They were replaced mostly by outsiders of lower social stature, yet still all white. Clubs with less prestige are of more recent origin, composed mostly of county residents, including some Lumbees and fewer blacks; they are more transient and are a local response to the perceived monopolistic plot of outsiders. These local members share similar outlooks, work in similar mill jobs, live in the same neighborhoods, and attend the same church. Their hunts are informal and entrepreneurial. Furthermore, they do not always follow the state's injunctions (i.e., they are said to "deer" hunt)[4] for their lands are not in areas that assure them access to a steady supply of legal bucks.

Club members pay annual dues ($75–$125) permitting the hunt master to lease hunting rights on land and to pay for the upkeep of a pack of dogs. The land broker is a local resident, who leases land and provides members with a refurbished tenant shack as the clubhouse. Leased land is posted and its boundaries are patrolled against intruders. Policing borders is time and energy consuming and a constant topic of conversation. If caught, a trespasser is generally reprimanded, verbally assaulted, sometimes manhandled—depending on who he is—before being released. Rarely is one prosecuted for trespass.

Normally, clubs have well-defined roles. The main decisions are made by the *hunt master* or president. He is the acknowledged leader who organizes and oversees the hunt, makes the decisions as to which parcels of land to hunt, supervises the various functions of the club, and directs the distribution of venison. The other members are divided unevenly into relatively few *drivers* and many *standers*. Drivers are experienced with dogs and know the lay of the land. They release and follow the dogs within the areas designated by the hunt master. Drivers occasionally get a shot at a "sneak" or "slip" deer which evades the standers stationed along the periphery of the hunt. Someone familiar with the marked points (called "stands") places the other participants at intervals of 100–125 yards (outside of shotgun range), surrounding the territory within which the dogs are let loose. These standers are the key producers in this team play. Their duties are to remain alert and to kill bucks as they are flushed to them by the dogs and the drivers. Although gossip among standers is that some locations are better than others, the hunt master and drivers maintain that each stand is of comparable value. According to them, the stander's attentiveness makes the difference between securing a buck and its "slipping away." From experience, some older bucks seem to know the locations of stands and are said to "slip around" the boundaries defended by standers.

Members keep tabs on each other's activities, with some acquiring reputations as winners, others as losers, during a season. Gradations of success are recognized, such as killing the buck with the largest antlers or most points, killing the most bucks, or consistently drawing the best stand. A good winner attributes his success to luck; thus others can assess their lack of success to a bad draw. A few may attribute their success to skill, thereby needling those who do not score.

Clubs have distinctive rituals. These rituals include seasonal feasts or barbecues in addition to smearing blood on the faces of initiates. The most discriminating ritual is reserved for individuals failing to produce a buck flushed by his stand. This person faces a kangaroo court of peers. He is marked by having his shirttail chopped with a large hunting knife. The amount of shirttail removed and hung in the clubhouse is contingent upon the offender's reputation. If the culprit has an otherwise enviable reputation or is a prankster, the jury may demand everything except the collar. A few clubs levy an additional fine of several "bucks" (dollars) to feed the dogs.

"MANY A DEER DONE GIVE HIS HEAD,
MANY A HUNTER DONE GIVE HIS SHIRT"

My field notes for the opening day of buck season, October 15, 1979, provide the following details on the structure and context of club hunts.

———————

When I arrive at the clubhouse about 7:15 A.M., members and their guests are standing around in small groups. Many had not seen each other since last season, and a few had driven over a hundred miles to be present this opening day. Talk centers around happenings since last season, on events of mutual interest, on new jokes and stories. The hunt master, who lives adjacent to the clubhouse, moves among the groups, welcomes individuals and their guests, and exchanges pleasantries. After his rounds, he stands on a table and counts fifty-three people present.

The hunt master calls for order. He welcomes the members and says this group is the largest one ever assembled by the club. He expects some success but hopes that not everyone will get a shot or kill a deer. The large assembly forces the issue of where to hunt. The hunt master decides to hunt simultaneously the two tracts of land in front of the clubhouse (1,200 acres) and behind it (800 acres).

A red shaker containing numbered black balls passes among those present. Each person selects one of the balls from the shaker, reads its number, and places the ball in a slotted tray. The number on the selected ball becomes the individual's stand number. The hunt master clumps standers by their consecutive numbers and assigns each group a vehicle and driver to take them to their stands. Stands are numbered at intervals along a road that circles the area designated for hunting. Humorous jibes and recollections about acquaintances are shared as the new groups assemble for their trips to the periphery.

7:45–8:00 A.M. By truckloads, the fifty-three standers leave the clubhouse. For the rest of the morning, they are to remain at their posts until they are fetched for lunch. Four groups of drivers (nine men) assemble the dogs. Each driver favors some dogs over others, knows their temperaments and tracking abilities. After loading the dogs into four vehicles, the drivers converse before departing for separate release points. Humor shared is at the expense of the standers. Drivers banter about their ineptness, about standers facing the wrong way when the buck slips past, about falling asleep on the stand, about their personal and smoking habits, and about their inexperience with deer.

8:15. I leave the clubhouse with Ronnie and James and a truckload of dogs. We proceed down a dirt road to the main highway, from there we turn onto a small track, eventually stopping in the middle of an expansive tract. Ronnie relates an episode from last year. He had turned onto this track when he saw a pair of legs beneath a dense stand of blackjack oaks. It was a buck and he "let 'im have it with a full load o' buckshot."

8:25. We park and release the dogs. The drivers load their shotguns. James proceeds toward a sawdust pile, the remains of a cutting site thirty years earlier. Ronnie and I move in a circle around him. The ground is covered with fresh deer tracks. Around the margins of the sawdust pile are saplings which bucks have scraped with their antlers, called "scrapes" or "rubs."

From the sawdust pile we walk along the margin of a swamp and blackjack oaks. The dogs run ahead, with the drivers occasionally rushing into the brush encouraging the dogs to enter the swamp. Ronnie has several puppies and is anxious for them to get sight and scent of deer.

"These dawgs just hunt close. I've got two or three dawgs wif me that don't even know what a deer is. Course they will find out before the day is ovah. . . . The dawgs don't ever make your major jumps. If a deer was in hyar and ya comin' through the woods, it's gonna be up yonder a couple haundred yards and he goes to move. The standers will see dat deer dat the dawgs h'ain't thought about seein'!"

SAM: *Are the chances pretty good of getting a shot at a deer while driving?*

Yeah. It's not as good as if you were on a stand, but there's always a possibility. It usually takes two to three frosts before the dawgs took to arunnin' good. It will take these puppies several hunts before they turn into real deer dawgs.

8:45. A shot is heard behind us. For the drivers, one shot is a good sign, suggesting a stander has downed what he shot at.

8:47. Along the swamp's edge, we hear a rustle. Within a few seconds a large doe springs out of the swamp some fifteen paces from us. She runs into the blackjacks. Ronnie levels his shotgun instantly, but sees no horns. The dogs are elsewhere and did not pick up her scent. We continue along the swamp's edge.

9:00. A spike (first-year buck) emerges from the swamp out of range. Ronnie hurries forward with his puppies. They pick up the scent and begin trailing.

9:10. We hear another shot in the direction of the standers.

9:12. Drivers from across the swamp yell and alert us to expect a deer. James separates from Ronnie and moves further along the swamp margin.

9:19. A doe jumps from the swamp between Ronnie and James. Ronnie yells, "I couldn't put nuthin' on her head." The dogs that were running the buck return and begin trailing the doe while we work our way along a drainage ditch.

9:35. Three shots follow in quick succession. They are fired by a stander over a rise from us. As we ascend the rise, the drivers point to deer tracks, where deer have scratched for acorns on the ground, and where bucks have rubbed their antlers against small shrubs.

"Bucks are slippin' 'round fer sure. Standers haf to be on der toes for bucks will slip by even wifout da dawgs chasen 'em. Bucks try to stay close in. Slippin' from one place to the next and trying not to get the dawgs too close or to have to go to the edge and cross dat road where da standers at."

"I've seen right smart o' fresh tracks. In da thick o' blackjacks only see da flick o' white tail—dat's mostly what ya see and get. Dat dawg is atrailin' little ole rascal. Doz puppies o' mine are a settlin' in now, not playin' as much as da first. Dat also goes for me, as I'm asettlin' in now too. Bucks come up in des thick blackjack ridges and gets down 'n' hides. Hafta walk up on 'em and flush 'em out."

James and I pass by a stander on the ridge. We ask if he has seen any deer. He says no, that the shots heard earlier were behind him and not on our hunt. We walk parallel to the line of standers. "Does will run all ova da standers. Buck will smell 'em and know where dey's at. Dawgs must be pushin' bucks pretty hard for dem to run past a stander. You're huntin' in his backyard and there's no way you're gonna know as much as he does."

10:17. While moving through a stand of blackjacks, we "flush" (force into the open) a small deer. It runs at an angle toward us. Instantly, Ronnie levels his gun on it, but can't see well because of the thick cover. "It come out low aflyin' like a bird. Dis one come out on his knees," Ronnie says as he hurries forward to encourage his puppies to get on its trail.

10:25. We come upon fresh deer sign: "This is where some deer done did his job. He must be in here somewheres." A beagle finds a recent pile of deer feces and rubs his head in it. James confesses that he doesn't know why dogs mess themselves like that.

10:30. We return to the truck and wait for the dogs. In a few minutes one dog appears, followed by another and an old beagle. Ronnie is concerned about having to leave before his puppies return. "You pick up puppies at da truck first time out otherwise dey will be expected to be picked up elsewhere. Maybe dey got da scent of dat deer and went afool."

Ronnie places several slices of bread where the truck is parked, expecting his dogs to remain there until he returns.

10:50. We depart in the truck and proceed toward Mr. Goober, a stander. Before stopping to talk, the drivers allow that "he ain't shot nuthin' " from their previous experiences with him. Mr. Goober says the buck slipped past at the top of the hill. He couldn't see horns until the buck cleared the rise. Yet he proclaims that elsewhere a stander killed a seven-point buck and that a driver bloodied another. We proceed to the clubhouse.

11:00. At the clubhouse, I circulate among the groups and listen to the gossip from the morning hunt. A buck was killed in the abandoned field below the clubhouse, and its story retold as each truckload of standers arrives. The stander took his stand and walked into an open field to relieve himself prior to the hunt. That's when the buck flushed. "He had his pants down ataking a shit when the buck got up" is the version passed around. It makes the point that bucks appear when least expected.

Another story circulates about the buck that was bloodied. The hunt master followed the buck for a hundred yards into the swamp until he could find no further blood. Some standers say that when a wounded buck stops bleeding externally, it begins to bleed internally, disabling it from further travel. The hunt master persists in his version that the buck was wounded only superficially. Upon hearing this story, five men, including a driver and dogs, leave to look for the buck. The buck is not found, but as the men are late in returning to the clubhouse they delay our departure for the afternoon hunt.

Standers returning from the morning hunt join the company of their original groups. They now converse about happenings on their stands, share jokes, and eat lunch. A few of the older members gather to talk while discretely lacing their "chasers" with liquor. The hunt master circulates, spending a few minutes with each group, and winking at me, he says, "Ya gotta be a politician for this job."

Inside the clubhouse, a group crowds around a small table, pulls the change from their pockets, and plays seven card stud with "wild cards." A judge, who, along with his two sons, is an invited guest, coughs and moves outside saying, "It's against my morals to be in a room when someone is breaking the law."

Outside, Chester McLaurin, a retired mill worker, tells of the whippin' his father gave him as a youth. He had accomplished his assigned task of plowing a field behind the family mule and was returning to the house when he heard some dogs running a fox in a nearby swamp. McLaurin followed the hounds all that night and reappeared at eleven the next morning. His father took his belt and really "whupped" him for "not adoin' what ma pappy learned me to do."

Another story was told about Jesse Len. He took a preacher raccoon hunting one night. He let the dogs loose, they took up the trail and began hollerin'. The hollerin' stopped suddenly. The preacher asked Jesse what they was adoin' now. Jesse allowed "they're arunnin' on posted land!" A raccoon hunter among the listeners commentes that when the dogs start to run deer, that's when we "get shed of 'em."

Tom, a stander, shows pictures of the buck he killed earlier with a bow and arrow. He carries the arrowhead, which killed the deer, in his truck among his shotgun shells.

An elder tells about a recent trip to the Outer Banks. In the next room, the story goes, a young girl and two boys giggled a lot. The girl repeatedly said that she wanted the boys to get over their bashfulness and take a "hard stand." One boy got on top of her and he "must have had what she wanted because she sure lost her giggles." The old stander admitted that listening almost gave him a "hard-on." The story was repeated, with its teller encouraged to tell about "his almost hard."

At one o'clock, the hunt master lines up the standers for the afternoon hunt. A young club member drives into the yard and presents the hunt master with a big cigar. His wife has just had a baby boy (his first was a girl) and he is proud. He says the baby weighed nine pounds and takes after his father, for it was sure ugly. "It didn't have no neck to speak of."

The hunt master passes the red shaker around and the standers draw their numbers and reassemble in small groups for transportation. The site for the afternoon hunt is some two miles away on a tract of eight hundred acres.

1:15. I leave the clubhouse with the assistant hunt master, Ronnie, and some standers, whom we plan to place on stands. A red truck approaches. The assistant walks over to talk to those in the other vehicle. Upon his return, he tells us they were "still hunters," hoping to place themselves along the periphery of our hunt so our dogs would run deer to them. The assistant indicates the club's boundaries and subsequently places our standers in positions to intercept any deer should it run toward the outsiders. We then proceed on a dirt road toward the center of a tract now surrounded by standers.

1:45. We turn the dogs loose along the edge of a swamp. Ronnie has saved his best dogs for this hunt and says, "We've really got some trailing machines."

I ask about the recent marriage of the assistant. He replies that he planned his marriage and honeymoon to give him a week off at the beginning of the deer season. Proceeding along the edge of a swamp, we pass the place where he killed his first buck when he was nine years of age. He recalls its details vividly.

2:01. We hear a shot behind us while flushing an unseen deer across the swamp.

2:10. A spike buck springs out of a small bay directly in front of us. Immediately both drivers level their guns on it. The buck runs up the hill, parallel to a stander, who fires three times as it passes broadside.

2:14. The dogs pick up the scent and begin trailing.

2:15. The buck passes another stander, who fires a single shot. The drivers proceed up the hill to the stander who missed.

"He was acomin' right up beside me, then he cut back the other way. That's when I seen his horns, when he cut back that away."

"You didn't seen his horns when he was coming towards you?"

"It was a spike or three point. It was anodder point is what it look like."

Ronnie: "I could've shot 'em when he got up, but I couldn't see nothing. He was acomin' like dis to me and I couldn't seen any horns. When I was started to shootin', then I didn't know exactly where he was. That's the reason I ain't done shot. Damn, that's three shirttails—shirttail, shirttail, shirttail!"

"Nope, not my shirttail. He was too damn far off. I thought he was just a mile off or I wouldn't have shot 'em. You ain't getting my damn shirt. I believe I done hit dat damn deer, otherwise problems."

"Get your damn knife out, Tommy."

"Damn if you don't get that knife outta me."

"Get that damn shirt."

"That thar was a big sonofabitch, did you see it? It was a big deer to just have a spike, did you see it?"

"Yeah."

"Well, why didn't ya shoot it?"

"I wish that sonofabitch would have come right straight up that bank."

"Damn, don't be greedy now. Somebody done dusted his ass further up yonder, where them dogs done gone."

Ronnie kicks a doe skeleton and says that it probably was hit by a car on the road and ran here to die. The assistant suggests it was probably poached and left wounded.

2:20. On our return to the swamp, we scare a fawn, which runs, stops some 125 yards, and attempts to hide. We move to keep the dogs from chasing it. The assistant hunt master proceeds along the edge of the tract to intercept any deer before they reach the outsiders whose stands are nearby.

2:30. Ronnie and I walk to the crest of a ridge and circle back. Close to a road, we stop the hunt master, who, along with his grandson, is driving along the periphery of the hunt. He tells Ronnie that his puppies which left this morning were collected and that the last shot killed the spike.

2:45. We separate and walk in a line so we "can kick around dat head" (a small depression).

2:55. We hear two shots in the distance. The assistant hunt master tells me that his ability to hunt helped him during his military duty in Vietnam. Since he was accustomed to wandering in the woods and looking for signs, he was better prepared for combat than most soldiers. He attributes these skills with saving his life on several occasions.

2:59. We hear three additional shots as we return to the truck. The stander who killed the spike is there.

"I knowed I seen his horns. Ya might call it a five point, or a four point, or a three point, but I would call it a three point."

"You're just acting up there something, ain't cha."

"That one was ahawling ass, man. I ain't like ma daddy-in-law. I don't shoot 'im but one time."

"You better stop talking shit."

"I'm gonna tell him all the way home, just you wait."

"They done shot at 'im right thar three times. Now I told ya that ya got the best stand on the hunt."

"He come right outta dat corner. Well, he'd acome straight off dat road, but I was asitting down right where I left ya in there behind dat big pine. One come across disaway and she stopped down there in the middle of the field and I finally scared her off and then he come dusting outta the corner there."

"Did he come out wif a doe?"

"Naw, there was one done come across disaway and she stopped out dar in the middle of the field. When I shot 'im, you know, he just rolled and when his head bobbed up that last time, I couldn't see no horns. I reckon his ears were up ova his horns and I couldn't see no horns. I said, aw hell. And I knowed I seen horns the first time I shot at 'im."

3:03. The drivers and I leave to walk through another section. Out of hearing from the stander, we comment on how excited the stander is. Last season, he missed a deer when his gun jammed. He took the gun to a blacksmith and told him that he would give him a box of shells if he could make the gun not jam again.

3:20. We pass through a terraced field once worked by mules. It is now planted in quail food. We jump two does. Ronnie can't see the first deer but he keeps his gun aimed just in case he spots antlers. In the field, thick sumac and tall patches of broomsedge seem likely cover for deer. "If a buck's in dar, you would have to step on 'im to get 'im to move."

3:30. We return to the truck. We leave and pick up a load of standers on our way to the clubhouse.

3:50. We are the first group to return. In a few minutes other trucks arrive and unload their standers, who reassemble in small groups. They discuss the numbers of shots heard, the stand numbers where each occurred, the killing of bucks, and the number of points on each rack.

I talk to a stander, an acquaintance from previous hunts, and ask him what part of hunting he values the most:

Well, I just love to see deer. It encourages me, even the does, and I also like to hear the dogs run. And another thing, you meet a lot of interesting people. Now, the hunt master's had people down here from lawyers, doctors, judges, and other people as poor as I am. I mean it's a variety of people and most people that hunts around the organized hunts, you'll find that they're fairly straight people. Now there's a lot of deer hunters. I know you've heard probably some people say they aren't nothing but just as shitty as they come. Kill anything or anywhere, but I mean the people that hunts in an organized hunt here, you'll find that most of them are pretty nice people. Kind of like the doctor told my wife. The subject come up, you know, about me liking to hunt and he said, well, don't discourage him. Said I never heard tell of many people getting in much trouble while they was ahunting.

SAM: *And your wife believed him?*

Well, I don't know about that now. I couldn't honestly say whether she fell for it a hundred percent or not. My wife, she's understanding about me deer hunting. Now a lot of women's not and totally against it, you know, being gone maybe on Saturday when you're both off and stuff like that.

SAM: *You may have let her know that there wasn't much she could do about your deer hunting?*

Well, I guess that's probably so too, but you hear women talking about the 'other woman,' girl friends, etc., maybe he even goes hunting with her. But after they get married, they just raise hell about it.

SAM: *Why do you think this is? Do you think it's mainly women that raise hell about it or is it men that raise hell?*

Well, I don't know. The tales I've heard it's been women. I've never run into that problem. She's always been very understanding about it, and I guess we both have to compromise a little bit, one way or the other.

4:05. The trucks bearing the slain bucks arrive. As each truck pulls around the clubhouse, a group of standers gathers to discuss where it was shot (stand number) and the name of the stander. For the afternoon hunt, a father and son exchanged stands and both killed bucks. The hunt master tells me this coincidence is worthy of note. Usually only one swapper is successful and the other is left to bemoan his luck.

One of the drivers in the morning shot and missed a buck. He assembles the other drivers to demand that they are immune from shirt cutting.

When the third carcass arrives, the hunt master congratulates himself on an excellent prediction. He looks over to Tom for affirmation. Tom laughingly says that a kill of four bucks was his prediction.

While the carcasses are flayed into six sections each, the hunt master assembles the standers for the last time. He calls for his shirt-cutting knife, an eighteen-inch machete, and demands order in his court. He asks those who missed to assemble in a line. One culprit remains out of the lineup. When his name is called, he yells "he's just left!" and is then dragged by his buddies into the line.

Six shirttails are to be cut this afternoon. For each offender, the hunt master asks how he pleads. "Guilty" is the usual reply. The first shirttail is cut by Ronnie, who is anxious to perform since the offender cut his shirt last season. Ronnie folds and cuts a broad strip from the offender's undershirt. The next offender pleads "not sure." The hunt master allows him to consult a "lawyer." When his friend steps forward to take his picture, the offender says, "I want a real lawyer, not a half-assed one." His shirttail is cut high. Mister Goober, who in the morning let a buck slip, is summoned. While threatening to cut his shirttail, the hunt master sentences him to two years suspended verdict.

When all the shirttails are cut, everyone returns to the butcher shed. Sections of venison (classified as ribs, shoulders, or hams) are given to some standers whose names are checked on a large board listing the membership. By keeping records openly, the club assures itself that the venison is evenly distributed. One stander remarks that this is the first time that he has missed his game and is returning home with venison.

The distribution of venison concludes the day's hunt. Standers return to their vehicles and begin the journeys back to their homes. Drivers pen and feed the dogs for the next hunt, scheduled for Wednesday, for those who live close by, and for Saturday.

Hunters on Sandhills Game Management Lands

Those pursuing deer on public lands may be locals, residents of adjacent counties, or from more distant places. They hunt on game lands for many of the same reasons as those who belong to clubs. Yet they do not control the land and their quests are always at risk to disturbances from others. The way to avoid frequent interruptions is to find inaccessible locations and to get to a site first with the largest number of men. In addition to controlling a site, large groups maximize their chances of securing deer. Luck plays a large role in the success of these hunters as their territory is a "commons." Their tactics include still hunting from stands and drives by dogs or by men.

The insensitivity of these hunters to local boundaries, their seemingly large numbers during the open season, and their lack of accountability contribute to the resentment that clubs feel toward them. Their behavior is unaccountable within the local frameworks of power and prestige, with individuals appearing and disappearing with no recognizable pattern. Whereas most outsiders may be well intentioned, when encountered by clubs they are usually out of place. Club members take the attributes of a few (they say many) desultory (they say purposeful) encounters and apply these characteristics to the whole category of outsiders. Furthermore, locals and clubs are left to contend with stray and feral dogs. Although gameland hunters consider their activities "sporting," clubs say they are "predatory" rather than "stewardly." Locals suspect outsiders of being unprincipled types who would just as soon kill does.

I interviewed these hunters as they came on to the road between their forays. The following interviews with successful groups illustrate some of their life-styles and demeanor.

"LIFE HAS TWO TYPES OF PEOPLE—LOSERS AND LIARS"

The following is a conversation recorded on opening day of deer season, November 19, 1979, on Sandhills Game Management Area with four hunters.[5] One hunter has just killed a buck. All four work in the Greensboro mills; three are related (father and his two sons), and one is a lifelong friend of the others. The men are between the ages of thirty-four and fifty-nine. They have taken off work for opening day. The recording begins with the successful hunter describing his kill:

I saw the deer. I thought it was the buck acrossin' the road. So I lit out and I just followed it on down. So when I got next to the pond I stopped and sat down. And I said, well, it's time they started shootin' over there. He's got to go down to the pond because there's a bunch of men up the pond, and I knowed he was agoing down that way. I heard my brother starts shootin' at another one over there. I seen two deer just all of a sudden comin' down the hill just like that, you know, so I grabbed my gun up and the first one was the biggest but I seen there wasn't no horns on it. And just like that I looked behind and he was behind the other one. So I just shot him and downed him and he jumped back up and started to get away and I shot him again. That's when I hit that horn, and I throwed the gun on the other one. I would say it was about seventy yards away and I had my gun right on that deer, just like that on the back of his head. I couldn't see no horns. Aubrey said he was a buck. He could have been a camel. And I heard him shootin'.

SAM: *They say this is your eighty-fourth deer. Do you still get excited with the prospects of deer hunting?*

Deer huntin' is like the fever. It builds up all year long and then has to be released. It's like buildin' up for 'a piece.' Once ya laid one, you move onto the next one that may be harder. Huntin' runs in the family. Both my fathers and grandfathers were hunters. It gets into the blood stream. It's important to keep young folks away from pool rooms, beer joints, and from gettin' started wrong in life. I recommends huntin' for younger people. It gives them somethin' to look forward to and to enjoy. They will work harder and plan harder and it gives them a chance to prove theirselves. It is the biggest challenge I've ever run across in my life. Life has two types of people—losers and liars.

FRIEND: Yeah, that's what you go for to feel good to have success. Anything, you know, that you go at you're gonna have success, and if it don't, it defeats you.

SAM: *Would it be fair to say that you feel the same about success on your job?*

Yes I do. Yeah, when you do a good job on anything you feel, you know, secure. I killed a big one last year, weighed about two hundred pounds dressed out. I had his head mounted.

SAM: *How would you describe a buck? His qualities?*

OTHERS: Umm, smartness.
   Yeah. He's slick, when they want to be, can't they?
   Yeah. But we always outsmart them for some reason.
   There ain't but one thing that takes a buck's mind off of a human being, or a gun, and that's a doe when he's in rut.
   Yeah, but she talks to him. When he's runnin' like that through the woods she's atellin' him this and that and when she sees anybody out there, she'll ah, ah [gestures with his hands] and he'll either turn around and go back or he'll cut one.
   When she puts that tail up she let him know that there're runnin' into a person up there. Somethin' dangerous.
   And she won't give a darn, she'll come right on by. Or she'll throw that tail up. When they run up to you like that and they smell you, they'll throw up their heads, they go wild.

SAM: *Which is smarter, a buck or a doe?*

OTHERS: Oh, a buck, two to one. A buck's a hundred times smarter. He never takes the lead, and just like if you seen two does acomin' together, the buck can be either forty yards behind them or he can be one hundred yards to the side agoin' with them.
   Well, see, it's like this. What makes them so smart is that the buck will send them does out first to check things out.
   He's the boss of all of them. See, when he starts roundin' up all his does and he fights for the herd, and if he wins that herd, then them does has to go with him. And he controls them from then on, the matin' and all that stuff. Fights off the other bucks. He definitely establishes a territory and then they have to stay with him.

SAM: *Would you say that this relationship is true of the human situation, between men and women, as between bucks and does?*

OTHERS: Well, I would say this. It used to be that way, but not now. Because there're more women out here in society, the big wheels, that are equal with men. In another five years there'll be more women than there is men, because men's gettin' lazy in politics.

No, no, you're gonna have to go back to the olden day, a thousand years. What the Bible says.

Yeah, but a woman can't lift and go like a man. The Government made these laws, we can't change them.

Well, that's like it was when they hired the first lady out there where I work. I said is this woman gonna do the same thin' I'm adoin'? She said if she gets the same pay she'll do it.

Well, she might come in there and say, hey, where does this part go, where does it belong? I don't mind tellin' the woman because she's doin' the best she can. I agree with you that a woman can drive a truck.

SAM: *Any reason why women aren't along with you?*

Women always ask us why we hunt when they's so prutty. The longer a man stays married the less women are likely to ask them to give it up. We tell our wives not to believe anything that anyone says about us.

The following is a conversation with three hunters, roughly of the same age, from Winston-Salem. One of the hunters has just killed a spike and they are busy loading it into their truck. All three are employed at the same firm, two are related (uncle and nephew).

SAM: *This happens to be your lucky day!*

Yep, yep, but we happened here several times before and we didn't have any luck. We hunt onced or twiced a year. Maybe get down here onced more. Pretty good ways to go, ya know.

SAM: *How do you feel? Like a winner?*

Oh well, I'll have to think a minute. There's a whole lot of luck in it. And I put a whole lot of damn work into it. I'd like to get annoder 'un. We saw four. Only one buck. They're rare. Ya come to a strange place and you are sure lucky to get one. That's all.

SAM: *What would have happened if you had missed that buck?*

I would have laughed like hell at 'im. We've missed ourselves. There ain't no tradition of cutting shirttails. Now that's more for kids, that is, buddy. There're a lot of hunting clubs that go for that stuff. Now when they starts acuttin' on us, we start acuttin' back. That's the only tradition we'z got.

SAM: *Anything else you wish to tell us about hunting?*

You haf to go one time and about freeze your ass off, starve to death and you'll know what I mean. There's nothing ya can tell about it. Just gotta experience it one time.

SAM: *What keeps you coming back? Is it that you've made a kill?*

OTHERS: That one's got two horns. We're looking for one with four horns. I reckon we'll come back next Saturday. See, that's a young one there. We'll gonna look for an older one now. His daddy, then his granddaddy.

We don't hunt with no dogs down here for if we lose them it's too far to come back to look for them. And we all took off the day to come hunting.

AN ACCOMPANYING STUDENT: *Y'all didn't bring your wives with you?*

OTHERS: Sure would have liked to had mine last night, or somebody's. Hell, no, a big fat damn nigger. It wouldn't had mattered. Something fat for sure and warm.

We're just old country assed boys. We ain't helped cha much, but getcha a gun and get out here about six one morning and be able to write that up.

Still Hunters

Still hunters pursue their quarry on private and public lands as individuals and as members of small groups. They depict themselves as outdoorsmen testing their skill and knowledge on the buck's home territory.

Still hunters are craftsmen, often blue-collar workers and farmers, who both in their vocations and avocations take pride in expressing themselves through their accomplishments. In hunting they frequently limit their means in order to maximize their enjoyment of success when their skills pay off. Before and during the season, these hunters spend much of their time in the woods, charting deer movements and behavior. After scouting and selecting promising deer trails in an area, they spend hours in "tree stands" or on the ground awaiting the appearance of their prey. It may require years for them to outsmart a particular animal, usually a big buck. When it comes, success validates their acquired knowledge and skill.

The state sanctions their enterprise by opening the season early to those who use primitive weapons, such as muzzle-loaders and bows and arrows. The early season enhances their chances of success, while their options are increased during these days when either bucks or does are fair game.

"I'D RATHER HUNT THAN BE MARRIED"

The following is an interview with a machinist in a local laboratory. Although he was reared in Pennsylvania, he married a local woman after he was released from his tour in the military at Fort Bragg. The interview takes place in his living room, surrounded by buck and turkey mounts on the walls:

Most of the hunting up there [Pennsylvania] is all hill hunting. It's all still hunting or you drive with men. Down here it's flat land, swamp hunting, and you drive with dogs. Which I don't see no sport in driving with dogs myself. To me, I'd rather get out there and walk my own game up rather than let a bunch of dogs do it for me.

Down here, I more or less get the feeling that a lot of these hunters just do it to have something to do, to get out. Up home they take it more like a sport. There's a lot of illegal stuff goes on down here. Just like hunting with shotguns. I don't like hunting with shotguns on deer. Up home they use high powered rifles. If you hit him, he's dead, he's done. Here they wound so many game that it's beyond belief. You can go up to the Sandhills any time and find dead deer all over the place right after hunting season, during hunting season, and a lot of that's does. That goes back to the story of the dogs. You take them out and put them in the woods and you turn a pack of dogs loose. Everybody's all hyped up because they hear the dogs howling, and the next thing you know you see a brown flash in front of you. You throw the shotgun up and empty the shotgun at the deer and you walk over and it's a doe. Because the deer's running. You don't have time to see what it is, you're all excited, you want to shoot it. Where with your still hunting, the deer comes walking by you and you can see it and shoot it and you know what you're shooting at.

SAM: *Is hunting related to the land in any way?*

Yeah. A hundred years ago that was the only means of getting food, and especially if you wouldn't have all the cattle ranches and stuff, everybody would have to hunt for a living right now. If you wanted to eat you had to hunt and, to me, it's born into everybody if you want to stop and think about it. [He tells about the one hundred acres owned by his wife's aunt. Most of the land is cleared for agriculture.]

There's always been deer there. I haven't really hunted it myself because it was so far away and because of the trouble with the poachers on it, but I have gone up there and put stuff out for the deer. I've been up there several times and seen them guys. You could see where they were driving through the field at nighttime, hunting stuff. You know, they can really ruin it for you. You can post it all you want but that won't stop them. That's another thing down here. Nobody has any respect for the other man's land. Like this private land up in the Sandhills belongs to a buddy of mine's father-in-law and he give us the right to hunt on it, me and him, and a hunt club has all the land around it leased. Well, they're always running their dogs across his land. They come over there and shoot game on his land, but if we go over there on their land they want to take us to court and all this and that, because they have posted signs and stuff up. A hunt club has 90 percent of the land around here leased and there's really not that much land available to hunt on.

SAM: *How has hunting changed during the years since you came to live in the county?*

I think that hunting's gone down for the worse, really. I mean, I can tell a big difference between it now and what it was like. Every year it gets harder and harder. The deer are being pushed out of the wooded area into the city. I can go anywhere within one mile of my home and show you all the deer you want to see. The game managers and commissioners of this state, I don't know what they do with the money. They increased the license this year, but you don't see no better game management control. They don't feed them during the winter, they don't do nothing for them during the summer.

SAM: *Is hunting related to your work?*

No. I would rather hunt than work, to tell the truth. That's how much I love it, and I just like to be outdoors. At work you've always got somebody looking over your shoulder, dictating over you and stuff and I just like to be free and when I'm out in the woods I feel free.

I'd rather hunt than be married. My wife, she doesn't understand what I get out of just going out into the woods. I put a lot of hours into deer hunting, and then come home with nothing. I can go up there and sit eight hours a day and never see a deer and I'm still happy. But she doesn't understand how you can be happy going up there sitting in the woods, looking at the birds fly around.

SAM: *Do you think there is resentment on her part that you spend so much time out there rather than at home with your family?*

Yes, very strongly. She thinks I should spend more time here at the house with her and the little boy, but I just can't break it. I love it too much. Actually, I've been trying to beg my wife to go hunting and fishing with me. She goes fishing with me but I get fed up with it because I've got to bait the hook and take the fish off. But I can't get her out in the woods with me to go deer hunting because she says, how can you shoot something like that, look at them big innocent eyes. But when I do bring it home and cut it up and put meat on the table, it's a different story then. If I go out deer hunting every day and don't get no deer and then come home, I get all this and that, but when I come home with a deer, I get a pat on the back and it's let's eat. They just don't understand it.

SAM: *Would you say that hunting for you represents an accomplishment? For instance, that deer rack mounted on your wall?*

Yeah, I wouldn't part with it. It's like being in a fight. I've been fighting with two of them for four years now and they beat me every year. But if I get him I'll put him on the wall. I don't kill nothing I can't or won't eat.

SAM: *What about deer? What qualities does a deer have that compel you to hunt them?*

Deer's real smart. I've had many a deer walk right by me and I ain't ever knowed it. They're aware of their surroundings. A deer and a turkey is about the same but a turkey's got a little bit more edge on the deer. Turkeys are such a dumb-looking animal but he's got that edge. I'll say the difference between them is the mating season. When a deer goes into rut, he's foolish. He's just like a man or a male dog chasing after a female in heat. He'll walk on you and he'll look at you. He just acts stupid. He's a completely different animal when he's in rut. But turkeys keep their smartness in rut and at other times. They don't ever turn dumb. A buck just goes plum stupid. When a deer's in rut he's not aware of anything around him. The only thing he cares about is that doe in heat and making scrapes.

SAM: *Are people that way?*

And people are the same way. People do funny things, you know. If you're out there with a good-looking woman and some dude comes up and tries to take her away from you, you're gonna fight. You're gonna protect her. And you act a little bit more foolish then than if you were just out with Jo Snow down the street and you didn't care if you lost her or not.

SAM: *Is it true that the doe protects the buck, or is it that the buck is smart enough to know where the doe and hunter are?*

The buck is smart enough to put the doe in a situation where it looks like she's protecting him.

SAM: *So she's being used by the buck?*

She's being used by the buck. They all get together and running down a trail. He'll be behind, he knows the dogs are there, and he'll make one great big leap and jump off the trail and let that doe continue running. Same way when they're hunted. If they're running down a trail and all of a sudden he sees a man with a gun up there, he'll jump and put himself on the opposite side of her. He's using her. I've used my wife several times. Every man does that.

SAM: *What is being a buck all about?*

He's the king. He's the law, order, king, provider. He's on top of the throne. He's the main man.

SAM: *Is any of the hunting you do related to the work you do, or how you do it?*

You asked me this before and I'm gonna answer it my way. Anything that I do at work I always take my time on it. I strive for the time to make it look good. I do a lot of machine operations and I can slap that thing together and it'll be burnt and holes in it, but it'll still work. Now I'm not like that. And it's the same with hunting. If I find a deer—like that twelve point I've been hunting for four years and I'm still after it. I'm the only one that hunts that land besides a particular hunt club. I keep tabs with him in the hunt club's land. I know he's there. I've seen him this summer already. [He tells of his present living arrangements, renting from his wife's aunt.]

I would have to sell all my hunting equipment, the money I put into it, the time I put into it, and invest it into living over there in Camellia Acres or Lakewood Hills. Me and my wife make enough money, but I can't do it and do this too. Me and my wife like to live practical. I don't care what people think, what kind of house I live in or nothing like that. But we're living comfortably and I've got money in my pocket and if I want to go to the beach tomorrow, I can get up and go to the beach. I ain't got to work. I've tried living up there in high class. I couldn't enjoy none of that. I couldn't fish. I couldn't do what I really loved in life.

SAM: *Why was that? Was it such a drain on your pocketbook?*

We had so much money when I first came here, we didn't know what to do with it. We had people over here all the time. Had big hams and big turkeys, free beer, and parties. I told my wife, shit, let's move up to Camellia Acres and have us a decent house. It's a different story and we're right back here again. I'm happier now than I was up there. See we were doing all right, but I couldn't do what I loved most in life—hunting and fishing. If I can't do that you might as well lock me up in jail.

Poachers

Poachers are on every sport hunter's derogatory list, for they unashamedly broach the boundaries of what the quest should be about. The norms and behavior ascribed to them are often inversions of expected behavior and norms. Poachers, they say, take advantage of the game and they are relentless pursuers with any means. They hunt at night, with lights, and on other people's property. They kill game to sell and to turn a profit. Their tactics indiscriminately take deer without reference to its size or sex. If in the process they happen to kill a large buck, they mount and sell its head to other interlopers who know the prestige of a big rack without having earned it. In these ways, poachers, men without context or social concerns, undercut the virtues and currency of what buck hunting should be all about.

The world of the poacher is a shadowy one; consequently, their boundaries are rather impermeable to intrusions and inquiries by others. No one openly claims the status of "poacher." Nor have I ever knowingly interviewed one.

On the other hand, I have witnessed their alleged automobile tracks in plowed fields, listened to persons describe their actions and accuse others of being "them," read in the press about their infrequent capture by wildlife protectors, and spent long nights staked out with concerned citizens expecting a poacher's imminent disclosure.[6]

———————

The following transcript was recorded from a conversation with long-term community resident. The resident is an "outlaw" to the main deer club proprietors while remaining an independent-minded individualist to others, who read about his prowess with deer in the local paper. He is in his mid-thirties. He relates his version of an earlier encounter with a hunt master:

Him and Bill pulled a shotgun on me one day. The hunt club's land runs into government land and I had parked at the end of the road and walked down the road. Bill's land is on the left and Albert's is on the right. Right as you get to the end of Albert's land there's a streak cut through, and it separates his land from the government land. The government went in there and cut a fire lane. I was walking the fire lane, ahunting because, you know, the dirt was soft and I wasn't making no noise when I was moving. Well, I killed a six-point buck on government land and he ran across and fell over on Albert's land. From where I was at, there was like a hundred yards straight out to the dirt road, and if I didn't I would have had to drug that deer across two hundred yards the other way to get back to another road where I could have took him out. So I drug him across Albert's land, about a hundred yards, and out to the highway and laid the deer down on the highway, on the side of the road, and gutted it out and threw the guts over on Albert's land. Well, I don't think nothing of this because the raccoon and 'possum and stuff will eat the guts, see. I'd rather do that than bury them. Well, the next day I went back. There was two bucks running together and I killed the small one, but I was after the bigger one. He was about a ten-pointer. I'd seen both of them just time and time again. I never could get a shot. I'd jump them, and they were traveling with a herd of six does. I had them pretty well figured out where they'd be at a certain time eating and I could always jump them, but I couldn't never jump the bucks.

Well, I had parked at the end of the road and was walking down the dirt road which belonged to the government, but their land's on both sides. They passed me in the jeep and pulled right in front of me and got out. I thought they were gonna ask me about one of their dogs they lost. Well, old man Albert gets out and he walks right past me. He don't speak or nothing. When he gets past me, I'm walking up the road, he turns around real quick and throws a shotgun in my back. He said, stand still you son of a bitch, and I said, what's wrong? Then Bill comes up and he crams a shotgun in my face, and then Tim's standing over there to one side with a shotgun in his hand. He said, you're the son of a bitch that killed a deer on my land yesterday, wasn't you? I said I was up here hunting yesterday, Albert. I killed a deer over on government land. I did bring him out across the edge of your land, but I didn't kill the deer on your land. I drug him out across here because it was easier than dragging him four hundred yards the other way to get him out.

He said you've been coming up here for a long time hunting my land, hadn't you? I said no. I ain't never come up here and hunted your land. I always hunted government land. He said, well I'm a goddamned tired of it. I just believe I'll kill your ass. That's what he told me. I said, well, if that's what you're gonna do there ain't nothing I can do about it. And Tim said, naw, let him go. Said I believe he's telling the truth. Albert said, no, said I'm taking his ass to town and take out a warrant for him.

So he said, Bill, take his gun from him. And I shove the safety off my rifle and I dropped it down, holding it with one hand, and I said, Bill, if you grab the barrel of my gun, I'm gonna kill you. Albert said, go ahead and get the gun, Bill, he ain't gonna shoot you. I said, Bill, if you pull my gun out of my hand, you'll kill yourself. I said, I'm not giving y'all my gun. He said, well, you get in the car, we're taking you to jail. I said, let me tell you something, you ain't taking me to jail either. They'd done made me mad then. When they seen that I was mad and wasn't going to let 'em have my gun, they said if we catch your ass back up here one more time, said we gonna shoot you and say it was an accident.

So I got to thinking about it, and I go back into town. He told me when he was talking that he had the right to arrest me, he was a deputy sheriff, so I go up to the Sheriff's Department and ask him is Albert a deputy sheriff? He said, well, I kind of deputized him so he'd kind of look after that night hunting in that section for me. Said we been having a lot of trouble up there with that. I said, well, they pulled guns on me and they tried to kidnap me and put me in the car and bring me to town against my will. And I thought I'd come up here and tell you that if it happens again I'm gonna kill one of them.

I still wasn't satisfied, so that night about four o'clock I called Albert up on the telephone and said, you know who this is don't you? I said, I've been thinking about killing your goddamn ass and I might come up there tonight and do it. He changed his phone number.

I called him up two or three times and later on somebody put some dynamite in one of his mailboxes and blew it up, I think. Then after we had the run-in, I went back up there the next day. I told them I'd be up there hunting again and be sure for him and Bill to come on around there that I'd be waiting for them. I went up there and parked and waited for them to come and they wouldn't show. It tickled the shit out of me after it was all over with. I had him sweating though. He thought I was gonna come and get him and he didn't know when. He's pulled guns on two or three people out there. Get out and just slam the gun right in their face and tell them he's gonna blow their head off if he catches them back on his land again.

On Being Male in the Human and Animal Worlds

Hunters express and define their identities variously. Yet certain cultural themes recur in their recreational pursuits, their home life, their work, and what they're about. These themes in diverse expressive forms confirm the centrality of some preoccupations.

Like most men, hunters are concerned with two basic problems of identity. They are absorbed with their place in a social hierarchy of other men and in their relationships with women, most often their wives. Some men emphasize the differences between the sexes and seem to believe that these are fundamental biological, rather than cultural, differences.

Some folklore about animals assist people to know who they are as sexual and social beings. It reflects shared assumptions about gender and gives these assumptions a concrete reality. When a man listens to a joke or participates in a hunt, he is confronted with an image of himself. Even if only for a moment, the uncertain becomes sure, the ambiguous becomes obvious.[7] The vivid images of men's stories, the obscenities and violence, the ethnic and racial jokes, and the lewd sexual fantasies exemplify a masculine world and a deep-seated dependence on women. Some hunters equate abstract entities like masculinity with concrete realities as in their images of buck and doe behavior and in their ideas of the buck hunter. What are some of these projections?

Bucks are beautiful creatures; big bucks are majestic and smart. They are the emblem bearers for their species. On their heads they bear the physical badges of their prowess and their rank attesting to their authority. A large rack symbolizes a longlife of doing what it takes to survive and to "make it" in the real world. Smart bucks know where the boundary lines are, and when those boundaries must be crossed they know how to "slip" around their adversaries. Bucks, therefore, are the great discriminators, evaluating each other's moves and putting subordinates in proper coordinates. Little bucks need controlling, particularly if they become overly assertive and exhibit "uppity" behavior.

Such discriminating abilities and knowledge set big bucks apart, and for this reason they are usually encountered alone. Their weakness is predictable. During the rutting season their one virtue becomes their vice. They become "horny" and do "plum foolish things" in their pursuit of immortality. Catching a big buck off guard or out of context, "doing it in," becomes another's claim to fame.

In many ways, the domain of does is the opposite of bucks. Does are non-discriminating, "all does look and act alike," and they don't possess those magical antlers. They are "inferior," often do stupid things, are passive producers of bucks, and are "done unto" often as the result of male violence. Yet, each doe is potentially a peril, for she has the capacity to undermine bucks, thereby showing how frivolous and ephemeral their "standing" really is. In particular, does are a real threat to big bucks and their ascribed attributes of freedom, male autonomy, and status.

The buck hunter is the epitome of a masculine mystique. He is cool and collected in the trying and risky moments of performance. He uses his mind instead of his emotions in situations where discretion is essential before action. He is active and assertive in the appropriate context and shows control in any situation likely to compromise him. He knows how to win appropriately, and does not cause others to become jealous or envious of his triumphs. These characterizations are hardly new revelations about Southern men or buck hunters. In a telling way, William Faulkner illustrates them in *Delta Autumn* through his characterizations of Uncle Isaac McCaslin and the renegade Roth Edmonds.[8]

These ideals of masculinity were learned by the current generation of buck hunters from their fathers, whose formative years were passed when deer were scarce and bucks were the appropriate, if the only legal, deer to take. Because its tenets were absorbed at an impressionable age, this masculine mystique has a semisacred quality they now try to emulate in their present life and choices. For these individuals, failing to live up to the norms embodied in this ideal is to slide down the slippery slopes toward feminization. For men to consider altering its dimensions to fit changing gender and societal roles is a difficult cognitive exercise.

Folklore also suggests culturally acceptable outlets for frustrations and tensions, as cultural barriers may prevent the perception of class or gender ambiguities. As a consequence, some buck hunters feel the need to protect themselves continually against what they perceive as a threat of being physically and morally undermined by women and against the boundaries that allow their games to be undermined by others. As one venatic sportsman expressed the context, "It's the politics of cunt and hunt!"

Hunting and the Household

Although the relationship between spouses shifts in response to changes that partners can and cannot control, the domestic unit is normally composed of a man, who works outside the home for wages, and a woman, who initially stays home to raise the children. To financially support a family, the husband finds work; his job is often repetitive and boring, and, just as often, brings meager returns. These men express a sharp dichotomy in their attitude between the work they must perform to sustain their families and the leisure they control and value for themselves. For some men, survival in a family unit depends upon remaining employed. Yet their economic and emotional well-being may be subject to sudden changes.

The economic dependence of women on men is a consequence of structural constraints on women's economic choices. If women work, their earnings are much lower than men's and their choice of occupations is more limited. After their children reach school age, many women find jobs outside the home. Yet the claim of women on the earning power of their husbands is an extremely important aspect of the household economy, as is the home's gender distinctiveness.

Two buck hunters summarized their sentiments this way:

The main point is if they [women] cared anything about you, that they wanted to be with you. Nowadays, the way things are a man and his wife has to work. He don't see his wife during the day. The only time he sees her is at night after she cooks supper and got the youngins off to bed. Then, more or less, they have time to sit down and talk their problems over and spend time with each other. Saturday's the only time they would have together, and here's the man getting up at 5 A.M. crawling out of the bed beside of a warm wife to go out in 10-degree weather. She says he's got to be crazy. If a man's got any kind of heart at all, he can understand it like that, yet he still expects her to be understanding.

I believe that if my wife had a hobby that she enjoyed as much as I enjoy deer hunting, I'd probably be single. We expect, or demand, the wife to put up with a whole lot more than he and to be submissive to their husband. When I go to the woods, she goes to town. That's every woman's hobby. A woman don't have but five dollars and will look all day. She might come home with four dollars and ninety-nine cents, but she's looked all day. She enjoys it, and deer hunting is what I enjoy doing. It costs me money and gas and shells and license and stuff like that, but to me it's worth it.

Ideally, the disposition of money within a household is decided by agreement between the spouses. In practice, household money constitutes a "domain of contestation" between husband and wife and results in frequent disputes, which may erupt into physical beatings and fights. Wives have acknowledged and legitimate claims to household money for the support and well-being of the family unit. They press these claims forcefully and are critical of their husbands for wasting money on beer, tobacco, and other nonessentials which, in the wives' view, includes hunting supplies, dogs, and other women. Wives are also critical and suspicious of the amounts of time and money their husbands spend in the company of their peers.[9] As explained by buck-hunting husbands:

They get aggravated at us being off on Saturday, every Sunday, and holiday. I tell my wife, it's just like this. I love to hunt and I love to fish. I said I don't go to no bars, I don't come home drunk, I don't whore around with the boys. I said if I can't go to do something decent, hunting and fishing with two of my best friends that you know don't do that, then tell me and I'll quit. I'll then go to them bars instead. I said you can take me like I am or you can change and it's all right. It don't make no difference to me. I love her and I want to stay with her, but ain't nothing gonna take me from hunting and fishing, I don't believe.

I'll tell you how my wife is. If I work on Saturday, I go in an hour earlier, she'll get up and cook my breakfast. If I'm going hunting, I have to get up and cook my own breakfast. As long as you're going to get that money, it's all right, you know.

Some men obstreperously structure their time outside the family in such a way that it becomes a year-round activity. It begins with dove hunting and target practice in early September. This is followed by scouting for sites during the bow and arrow season, then deer season until January, and concludes in March with the quail and rabbit seasons. The rest of the year is filled with peer get-togethers, which include fishing expeditions. From the men's perspective, women waste money and spend it indiscriminately. They are frustrated that as soon as their earnings enter the "domain of household money" it is quickly spent.

There may be other funds within the household. Wives may have their own sources of funds from inheritance, crafts, odd jobs, and work. Husbands may also have funds about which their wives have no knowledge. Money may be kept outside the purview of the other by it never arriving in the household in the first place. In this case, the spouse spends or allocates the money before it becomes a part of household finances. The latter may be a private bank account or prior claims on the husband's check for vehicles, hunting gear, or club dues.[10]

Household money, over which the husband has general authority and the wife a strong legitimate claim, can be described as a "domain of contestation," a private fund for women, and sometimes a secret fund for men. A spouse's time may be distributed and contested similarly. The time that the husband has not committed to his work or to his peer group also falls into a "domain of contestation." His wife may seek claim to his unallocated time to do tasks around the home, visit relatives, or shopping. Given the strict gender boundaries within the household and between work and play, the husband's control over his time and money becomes an important part of his identity as a man.[11]

A man labors under two economic necessities: to support his wife and family and to secure economically and socially his capacity for work. Within this view, investments of time and money in the company of his peers help a man to accomplish both objectives. He seeks his place in a community of peers through his network of social relations, his patron-clientships, and his status.

In his view, no other means of coping seem as effective, and other options may be closed to him because of the cultural blinders of a "masculine mystique."

Time and money left for the household fall within the "domain of contestability" described in note 10, where a man's control is compromised by the claims of his dependents. Every time he yields to the demands of his family for his time and resources, his self-worth and identity are contested in the midst of an intrahousehold struggle. He experiences these demands as an assault on his masculinity and on his identity as "head of household." He is concerned about becoming "feminized," and his peer group supports this view. A challenge to his hunting-cash-time allocation threatens to toss the whole domain of the husband's exclusive rights into contention.

If some males have an interest in preserving the inviolability of their domain, some women (maybe not necessarily their wives) have an interest in destroying or eroding this privileged construct. Whereas some men seek to protect their prescribed privileges as men and to allocate their resources to support this perpetuation, some women lay siege to them, pressing their claims for immediate needs. When a man comes home with venison, his wife may be glad to see him since, in her view, it is tangible substance that he was hunting and his money and time were not squandered on beer and carousing with other women. Such wifely rationality can lead to many types of conniving and deception by husbands.[12]

The sometimes petty-sounding quarrels within a household are in reality, genuine arenas of gender contestation in politics, economics, and rhetoric. They are battlefields in which "traditional" rules and roles are invoked, but at the same time also challenged, renegotiated, and re-created in the course of married life. Since marriage is a process of becoming, the marital bonds are either strengthened and given legitimacy with the passage of time and events, or they disintegrate into divorce.

Many forces operate to stress and change marital bounds as they do in any other type of social relationship. When change comes, it alters the rules and structures and maybe even the contents and contexts of the arguments. Some women are blatant in their tactics to gain control. The woman in the following account successfully prevents her husband from joining his friends, whose activities would have taken him out of her control.

A still hunter tells of a friend who wanted to join him and his small band. The would-be joiner practiced shooting with the band and even went with them to Tennessee to purchase his bow and arrows. The hunter telling the story brought his friend a Sportsman license as a gift.

"He was going with me. I went over to pick him up. His wife hollered at him and told him, said, if you leave, I leave. I cooked your supper for you, but if you leave out of here I'm gonna rake your supper to the dogs. And he hollered back and told his wife to put his supper on the stove and that he would eat it cold when he got back. That should have satisfied her. And we turned and walked out the door and started to get into the truck and looked back. She held up her word. She was raking his supper to the dogs when he got in the truck. And that was the first and last time he went ahunting with me."

Hunting and the Community

Hunting is embedded in social relationships involving other people and sometimes large plots of land. The joining together of men into clubs to control access to deer habitat and to sort themselves into roles is just one form these relationships take. Through their participation in club activities, men take advantage of the distance from home and work, establish patron-client bonds, and "play games," sorting the winners from the losers. In some ways, the space and time devoted to buck pursuits is a play world that provides men a temporary sense of domination and control, which they may lack in other important spheres of their lives.

Buck hunting teaches men the importance of control and sanctions a culturally appropriate means of its expression. As a recreational activity, deer hunts may be *expressive*, with participation in the activity bringing its own rewards, or *instrumental*, with the activity providing the occasion to take or make new clients or friends, for learning new things, or for finding new jobs. Having a place to go and feeling a part of a larger group are important. They are also costly. Yet hunting is an important investment because it provides a man with the opportunity to establish social bonds within a larger community of his own choosing. In some ways, membership within a club has no price. For example, it is impossible to buy one's way into the most prestigious clubs, while less status-conscious groupings still exhibit various degrees of selectivity. Once membership is obtained, however, a man is tied into relations with a patron who becomes his sponsor or hunt master.

In rural areas, a man who owns land and huntable habitat is more respected than another who owns a comparable amount of money or other commodities. Wealth in land "belongs" in a wider sense to other community members and, for that reason, a landowner is generally circumspect in his prosecution of trespassers over the boundaries around his land. A large landowner is not respected exclusively for the amount of land he owns but for his "sociability." If he appears overbearing in his exertion of property rights, ingrates may retaliate by setting fires, damaging property, or flouting his domain, as we saw earlier in the interview with the "poacher."

Prerequisites for a club include land holdings, dogs, memberships, and sufficient habitat of the right kinds to sustain deer. The maintenance of those assets and other chores are taxing and continuous tasks if the club is to endure. To ensure the survival of his club, a hunt master must maneuver successfully within the circles of power and prestige locally and elsewhere. The "durability" of a club demands that the group stick together to accomplish tasks that few could accomplish alone. In this game of persistence, some clubs are more successful than others. Formal clubs stick together and take a stand at regional wildlife hearings. They vote in blocks to elect wildlife commissioners (four commissioners within a five-year period were members of Scotland County deer clubs), and they get local ordinances passed which benefit them. Local hunt masters use their influence to pass county laws that prohibit shooting from road right-of-ways and ban the use of lights at night to spot deer. In 1977 clubs were instrumental in shifting the opening date for deer season on the Sandhills Game Management Area to a month later than the opening on the surrounding private lands. Their political savvy for increasing their deer kills at the expense of hunters hunting state lands is immediately apparent from kill figures kept by the state (table 6.2).

And yet boundaries and social structures are never permanent. They wax and wane with the times and circumstances, and they may even collapse. To understand the movements through time, we contend with the forces at play within them—their contradictions, their ambiguities, their oscillations. This task demands a slightly different perspective than the forces one engages immediately on the ground level.

Some forces within a community help to maintain the status quo. Within the clubs, egalitarian and democratic values predominate. Such values are shown when stands are randomized and venison is equally distributed. Despite these pretenses, men, as individuals and as groups, will argue and place themselves in cliques and debate issues of the moment. Individuals may drop out of clubs for financial or family-related reasons, and cliques may find interests or pursuits closer to home. These ruptures in the membranes of prestigious clubs are soon healed by others who are eager to join. Not so among the less durable

TABLE 6.2
Deer Kills in Scotland County, by Sex and Location, 1976–81.

Season	Total Killed	M	F	?	State Gamelands	Private	Unknown
1980–81	280	275	5	—	85	194	1
1979–80	223	221	2	—	85	138	—
1978–79	212	211	1	—	60	151	1
1977–78	174	171	3	—	56	117	1
1976–77	208	199	8	1	105	101	2

Source: North Carolina Wildlife Resources Commission files.

clubs or groups, whose memberships are composed of neighbors who work and worship in the same closely knit communities. With them the joshing and antagonisms penetrate the many dimensions of their social lives and may develop into long-term feuds.

A prominent landowner may die. Since some arrangements for hunting access are not legally formalized, the heirs of a distinguished citizen might dispose of his land in their own interests, thereby disrupting a hunt master's control over contiguous land. Clubs monopolize the prime deer range on private lands, and yet their harvests of bucks are supported by the herds on public lands. Through its mandate to manage the deer herds and to sustain its revenue from license sales, the state wildlife agency has different priorities from that of the clubs. The state's interest, supported by the work of its field biologists, seeks to expand the deer harvest to more people, and that objective includes the taking of does. Such propositions are anathema to the clubs. For them, the situation becomes a replay of the cult of efficiency versus the premodern codes of chivalry and tradition.[13]

Clubs attribute the decline of the deer herds in the early 1960s to the doe days held by the state wildlife agency in the Sandhills. The decline in buck harvests then led to the disbanding of several clubs and their loss of prominent people. In the late 1970s, biologists championed again the idea of thinning the herds with doe days. They pointed to an outbreak of a gnat-borne hemorrhagic disease as symptomatic of an impending imbalance between herd size and habitat.[14] Support for "doe days" came from other deer hunters. Most clubs fought this proposal, for they knew their enterprise was based upon the expansion of the deer herds on game lands. As the chief architects to the boundaries of unequal access to the deer in the county, clubs were also the main beneficiaries of these structures.

Nonetheless, clubs and biologists watched and pondered over the meaning of this latest outbreak of deer afflictions. The sentiments of one hunt master were summarized in his comment, "Damn cruel disease, all that meat to ruin." Such men are mindful of the ephemeral boundaries on which they place such high stakes (or steaks!) and which consume so much of their time. When the club kills of deer did not suffer significantly the year following the outbreak of disease, hunt masters remained adamant in their rejection of the biologists' theory of causation. Yet the wildlife agency had succeeded with a limited doe hunt on its game lands.

Summarizing a Point

I have described buck-hunting rituals in terms of boundaries and existing structures. I have also sought to explain some of the forces that account for their persistence as well as change. These boundaries are continually being challenged, argued, and renegotiated as the masculine mystique is defended and attacked, and in economic practice, as couples and groups come into conflict about decisions over power, land, and resources within the household and within the community. Such conflicts may not be the sign of disintegration or crisis. They are processes of making and re-creating "traditions." Traditions are never simply residues from the past. If they are to persist, traditions, such as those governing buck hunting, are *made* to persist. Continuity as much as change must be created and fought for. Rules among people and boundaries between groups and on the land are always at issue, their resolutions at stake.

Seven

A Bird in Hand: Coveted Covey and Flying Furies

De dove he bill an' coo a sight,
　And make all kines er love,
An' he win er gentle bride wid ease—
　De sof'-voiced cooin' dove:

But w'en he wins dat gentle bride,
　He puts her on er limb,
Wid er few coa'se sticks fer a settin' room
　Fer de young on's, her an' him.

De pa'tridge is a business man—
　'Pon dat you bet yo' life;
He do his talkin' to de p'int,
　An' git a hustlin' wife:

An' he takes 'er to er cozey nest,
　Way deep down in de grass,

What's cool by day an' wa'm by night
An' hid fum dem dat pass.

Den gimme de pa'tridge eb'ry time,
An' 'way wid de cooin' dove;
For a business man an' er wa'm snug nest
Beats de col' rain mixed wid love.

(John Charles McNeill, *Possums and Persimmons*)

TWO GAME BIRDS, the bobwhite quail and the mourning dove, are indigenous to North Carolina and to the South, where their current status reflects a change in the agricultural landscape. The quail, a small gregarious bird whose restricted range responds to the patrimony of human husbandry, is a quarry associated with status and wealth. As in the poem by Scotland County native John Charles McNeill, the quail is a metaphor for the protected preserve of the businessman, the gracious and generous life-style of one successful in the pursuit of specie.[1] Out on the other limb is the dove, somewhat clumsy with the tasks of perpetuating itself, yet today more plentiful than the quail. It breeds on the same turf as the quail, yet is a momentary and migratory species. Dove shoots open the fall hunting season and are open to a wider cross-section of hunters. Compared with the apollonian reserve of quail pursuits, dove shoots often have a festive atmosphere punctuated by excessive shooting, by danger from packing so many men and guns into the same field, and by games of one-upmanship. The pursuit of these two birds illustrates two powerful forces at work in community life, that of divisiveness through exclusion and that of incorporation through participation in mutually shared events.

Quail Hunting as a Literary Tradition

Quail are the stuff of Southern traditions. The pursuit of quail is linked in the myth of the Southern gentleman whose land ownership is his source of wealth, prestige, and independence. The fidelity of quail to place (small home range), their response to habitat improvements and to stewardship (favorite coveys shot year after year), their pursuit with special breeds of dogs (pointers and setters) that "honor" each other's points and with paternal heirlooms (father's double-barrel shotgun), their sudden bursts into flight (separates cool sportsmen from their pretenders), and their cockiness and pronouncements of presence (they whistle their own names!) are some of the characteristics seized upon to construct durable structures of emotion and ritual. The irony is that the prestige of quail hunting is of recent vintage and one in which Yankee wealth played a large, creative role.

The basic structures of quail hunting began in the 1880s. Slightly earlier, the modern shotgun was perfected and the railroads linked the urban sportsman with his hunting sites in the countryside throughout the South. As the new gun was deployed by sportsmen, so were new breeds of dogs. The first field trial was run in October 1874 near Memphis, Tennessee, and *The American Field*, a magazine that chronicles such events, was established in the same year.[2] Most of these developments were contemporaneous with the growth of Thomasville, Georgia, as a winter resort and as a quail-hunting center. The purchase of Southern plantations by Northerners and their use as retreats and winter residences perpetuated the image of quail hunting as a recreation for the leisured and privileged classes.[3] The first secretary of the Audubon Society in North Carolina, T. Gilbert Pearson, noted the many large quail preserves in Guilford County owned by wealthy Northerners and was aware of the vast revenue brought into the state by outsiders.[4]

As quail became a sporting mainstay within the Southern landscape, writers elaborated upon its styles and developed a literary tradition centered on its pursuit. Alexander Hunter was an early contributor to this tradition, depicting quail hunting as the epitome of a leisured life-style. Work was important only insofar as it allowed more time for what really counted: being out with the dogs, going after quail.[5] Many Southern gentlemen vindicated their superiority over visiting Yankees on the sporting fields of quail, thereby contributing to the rebuilding of their cultural confidence after its shattering defeat in the Civil War.[6]

The aristocratic assumptions of quail hunting are revealingly told in Robert Ruark's book of childhood reminiscences, *The Old Man and the Boy*. In this literary masterpiece, Southport native Ruark is guided tenderly and wisely by his grandfather, the Old Man, in the arts of hunting, fishing, and training dogs. It was the bobwhite that brought out the best behavior in men and dogs.

> This little bobwhite, the Old Man told me, was a gentleman, and you had to approach him as a gentleman to gentleman. You had to cherish him and look after him and make him very important in his own right, because there weren't many of him around and he was worthy of respectful shooting. The way you handled quail sort of kicked back on you.[7]

According to the Old Man, quail hunters had to keep remembering things about their dogs. For one thing, a quail hunter should never shoot rabbits in front of his dogs, for that would distract the dogs from their appointed task of finding the quail. Another thing was that any dog that wouldn't "honor" another's point was worthless, but a hunter should never underestimate his dog. If a dog came from a family with a nose and a sense of decency, any mistake he made was probably the fault of his owner.

As for quail, the Old Man allowed that any *man* with sense would never force quail to leave an acre on which they wanted to live. As a member of the farming family, quail expected to be fed and cared for as creatures who are rather set in their ways. Yet quail, like people, had to have the sound laws of economics laid on them, otherwise they would destroy themselves by starting fights in the family that would eventually eliminate the lineage. So you shot quail down to half their numbers when the season started, and if you cherished them enough and didn't get greedy, a landowner could keep quail in his backyard forever. In a symbolic sense, quail hunting allowed for the postbellum continuation of paternalistic traditions and may have served as an oblique compensation to landowners for losing control over laborers.[8]

Keeping tabs on one's hunting opportunities in the 1920s was problematic, but the Old Man had mastered even those contingencies. He had the whole county as his private shooting preserve. In those days, tenants and sharecroppers generally weren't interested in quail. They looked after the Old Man's quail, suppressed brush fires and predators, and planted food patches while the Old Man reciprocated with gifts, game, the return of stray hogs and cattle, and favorable credit references. This system produced quail for a few privileged individuals and led Ruark to write admiringly that the Old Man didn't believe in sharing his wealth in quail with everyone. He shared them with his friends because he could control them. Those quail were "*his* birds, and not for nonappreciative short-time murderers to shoot into extinction."[9]

The heyday for quail shooting occurred around the turn of the century. Wild quail were plentiful then and pursued by both sport and commercial hunters. Several people I interviewed around Laurinburg in 1979 served as quail guides in their youth for twenty dollars a day to Yankee sportsmen from Southern Pines. In subsequent years, the quail populations within the state experienced a series of roller-coaster fluctuations on a descending slope. At least since Alexander Hunter's times, quail have been changing their habits at frequent intervals.

Changes have also occurred among the dogs, their owners, and the landscape. According to some raconteurs, such as Havilah Babcock, Yankees are responsible for corrupting all these entities.[10] In his parable of the "stink sparrow," described as a Northern tourist in Southern bobwhite country and as a "lowly groundling and hedgehopper," Babcock shows how Southern dogs and men may be misled by impostors of various stripes. Outshooting Northerners and "Yankee fleecing" were honorable ways of striking back at these crafty invaders and their ways. What worried Babcock the most, however, was that Mr. Bob was "degenerating into a skulker, an ignoble groundling, and a denizen of horrendous brakes and thickets" through changes in the landscape.[11] Therefore to remain a quail hunter necessitated becoming a politician. With Bob (localism for bobwhite) no longer plentiful, what was left had a strong inclination toward self preservation. One had to figure with Bob rather than against him.[12]

In 1938 *The State* magazine devoted several pages to a discussion of the quail situation in North Carolina. According to the game commissioner, the decrease in quail resulted from overhunting by "game hogs." Therefore, he favored more enforcement and a farm game program designed to encourage landowners to provide food and cover for quail. Other theories pointed to the selfishness of sportsmen ("You can't expect the farmer to feed and provide cover for quail when it is a deplorable and well-known fact that many other-wise law-abiding citizens become outlaws when hunting"), adverse weather conditions and inappropriate plantings, stray dogs and cats, and the greedi-ness of hunters together with the increased efficiency of their weapons ("Un-less this type of machine-gunning is eradicated, it will soon be easier to find a polar bear in North Carolina than a covey of birds").[13] Similar complexities surfaced again over the scarcity of quail in the 1980s as the Wildlife Commis-sion grappled with changes in seasons and regulations.[14] As the Old Man would have said it, the problem was that people were no longer treating the quail and its habitat in a genteel fashion.

In the past, quail thrived when and where the land was hand and mule worked, the countryside was crisscrossed with overgrown ditches, and fence rows provided cover between the fields. Modern intensive farming with its pulpwood, pasture, intensive crop plantings, cleaned fields, and chemicals have reduced much of the habitat containing the birds' needs. Many hunters believe the state contributed to their woes by introducing new strains of quail, strains which do not "stand" for the old genteel behavior of dogs and men. These other breeds, known as Mexican quail, are "runners" and seek out in-accessible places. Given such genetic and environmental predispositions, it is not surprising that quail have changed their habits so frequently while trying to keep abreast of their habitats.

On Boundaries between Quail Hunters and Others

The scarcity of quail, along with its other perceived attributes, undoubtedly contributes to its social value for Carolina sportsmen. For a few privileged individuals and landowners, the pursuit of the bobwhite is a reflection of the best traditions of the Old South. Today when these individuals assert their identities as quail hunters, they lay claim to a genealogy of status and control over the good stuff of life. Such associations are clearly stated in some of the interviews below. We begin with the views of a venerable county patriarch, influential in banking, merchandising, and politics, and in bringing industry into Scotland County:

I hunted quail largely with local friends of mine. I started as a boy, I guess, hunting rabbits and got interested in quail hunting and then in the duck and goose hunting on Core Sound and Lake Mattamuskeet. I've an interest in all kinds of hunting except deer hunting.

SAM: *Any reflections on why you're not interested in deer?*

Well, I didn't want to shoot a deer. I've been deer hunting and had an opportunity to shoot a deer, but I've never shot a deer. I went along for the companionship of the other hunters.

SAM: *Does a deer mean something different to you than a quail? Is it that you feel more distance from birds than you do from deer?*

Well, yes, it would be against my desire to shoot a deer or a dog or any animal of that type. Birds are different to me. I do not believe I can explain that. It's just a personal feeling.

SAM: *Let me ask you about quail then. Most of the people who own a lot of land and are prominent in the community seem to hunt quail. Is there something about quail in that context that has particular value?*

Well, it's rather relaxing. It was exercise. Watching an intelligent dog work quail was very interesting and the thrill of a covey rise is just something you can't explain.

SAM: *You mention the dogs and the relationships between friends. Is there something to do with the land, also symbolized in quail hunting? Let me suggest one form this connection may take and maybe others will come to mind. Quail hunting takes place on a piece of land and, if you are careful, you don't shoot out all the birds. You can harvest them year after year and establish a relationship with them on your land. Do you sense this connectedness in quail hunting—a long-term relationship that involves personal friendships, dogs, quail, and the land?*

Yes, I think that's true. Of course when you hunt quail, you usually hunt on your land or some friend's land. You learn the land, you get interested in the timber, the trees, and get interested in the streams on the land. And in my case, since we hunted largely on our own land, I learned a lot about land lines and the developing of the types of farming we were doing. So there was that connection as well as the pleasure of hunting the quail.

SAM: *Has hunting quail enabled you to do anything that you would not have been able to do otherwise?*

I reckon the main advantage to me has been the exercise and the ability to get out in things other than the routine business that was in the office, and to learn about the location of our various real estate tracts and learn something about farming.

SAM: *Some people have said hunting is a great way to get to know another person. Do you agree?*

Yes, an excellent way. You learn about your neighbor's sportsmanship also.

SAM: *What does it mean to learn about your neighbor through sportsmanship?*

Well, I think a good sportsman is one that doesn't try to eliminate all the game. For instance, in quail hunting, if he finds a covey late in the season that's down to about five birds, he shouldn't shoot. He should leave some to produce the next year's crop of quail and, of course, you shouldn't leave a wounded duck or goose on the water that he thinks might die. He ought to make a special effort to get that goose. A good sportsman would not shoot his dog, as some people will if their dog makes a mistake or flushes something besides quail, because it's a lack of that person properly training his dog and the dog's having respect for his commands.

SAM: *Would you make a distinction between a sportsman and a hunter as not being the same thing?*

I think they're entirely different. A hunter's a man after maybe meat for his table and will kill anything that he sees. If he's quail hunting, he'll shoot anything that appears before him, such as rabbits or anything else, and I think a hunter is just a killer, where a sportsman is not. He does not want to eliminate the game. A sportsman's character would be entirely different from that of a hunter. For instance, a hunter can work in a job in which he's employed and he can produce a lot more game than he can do out hunting in the woods, but they hunt just for meat, and sometimes sell the quail, you know, and sell deer. That shouldn't be done.

SAM: *What did you like best about hunting?*

Well, my best recollections, my best pleasures from hunting, is companionship of the hunters and also learning about the habits of quail, ducks, geese, and wildlife of all kinds.

SAM: *So the kill is irrelevant?*

Yeah, that's right.

SAM: *With whom did you quail hunt for the most part?*

I hunted with a prominent Presbyterian minister [named], now deceased, a number of years. I hunted with a prominent landowner [named] and of course, other friends came in from the outside. They're too numerous to mention. Unfortunately, I'm here and they're not.

SAM: *Was bird hunting an activity that you could offer out-of-town associates as a turn of favor? It was good for business and they wouldn't be able to quail hunt where they were?*

No, I did not bring in any outsiders for business reasons. I brought in my friends that I enjoyed being with and I thought they would enjoy being with me. I didn't use it for business purposes.

We permit some hunting on our land. It's up to the discretion of the land manager. They take quail, deer, rabbits, that's about all there is here. A substantial amount of land is leased for deer hunting.

SAM: *Are there any problems with leasing your lands out to hunters?*

We've had no problems. There have been deer hunters and I think as a whole there's been no problems.

SAM: *I would imagine one problem a landowner might have is if someone gets mad at him that he would do something either to his stock, his crops, or burn his forests. Would not the leasing of land to a group be a way of protecting it and therefore one of the incentives for letting other people lease your land?*

Yes, if you did not lease land there would be the possibility you'd have a lot of poachers on there and if you prosecute them in violation of posted land, why occasionally there might be a person that would resent it to the extent that he might burn the property.

SAM: *So leasing land to other people is a way of designating to them the responsibility of keeping it productive for wildlife?*

Yes. That's part of it and also you have the feeling that you don't want to cheat the fellow that's on a forty-hour a week job to keep him from having any place to go to enjoy hunting. In other words, you have to have some feelings for your fellow man.

SAM: *Has hunting provided any particular revelation to you? Is hunting related to your other values or life-style in any way?*

That's a real hard question. I think that hunting, as a sportsman, does tend to create a relationship maybe. Your relationship between the wildlife has a tendency maybe to mellow your relationships with people. I think to that extent it does, yes.

SAM: *How does hunting wildlife mellow one's relationship with people?*

That is not easy to explain. But you have a feeling, when I said mellow the relationship, you know, leaving part of the covey of birds, not killing all of the game so there'll be some next year. You think about survival, you know, and if you have a wounded bird or animal that creates sympathy for you and I think anything that will create sympathy for wildlife will create some sympathy toward your fellow man. It's a hard question to explain, not being a philosopher but just a common dirt farmer that I am.

The "common dirt farmer" is the façade behind which lives a man who presumes his social standing and behavior are beyond explanation and public disclosure. It was a reluctant interview, revealing little beyond what was al-

ready assumed. Yet the interview touches upon the obvious images of sportsmen and quail. The sportsman is not excessive in his kill, is concerned with
retrieving downed birds, and is aware that the dog's behavior reflects upon his
master. The pursuit of quail is tied to the ownership and management of the
land; it also provides the social context for recreation among one's peers and
perhaps for an awareness of those less fortunate. Birds differ from mammals,
such as deer, with birds considered the only worthy targets. These themes and
more are elaborated upon by another prominent citizen, who is related by
marriage to the largest landowning family:

I saw so much hunting going on all the time, being around it when I was a boy.
My father used to take us out when we were very young and show us what
hunting was, show us what a gun was, what it would do and how to handle it.
So I got indoctrinated at a very early age. I had four brothers and they all went
into hunting. It was a family-oriented and community-oriented activity because so many people in the community did hunt.

SAM: *Do you still remember the first animal you killed and the circumstances?*

I remember the first bird I ever killed, which was killed out there on a
neighbor's farm. It was a .12-gauge shotgun and I was sixteen or seventeen
years old, and was hunting with my oldest brother. It was a quail. Now any
time I say bird it refers to quail. I never started shooting any others.

SAM: *So you're exclusively a quail hunter?*

A quail hunter. I went dove hunting one time and I've never been since.
[WHY?] When I grew up we didn't shoot doves. Well, we were told that dove
wasn't a good eating bird and there wasn't any reason to kill them.
One reason I didn't like to shoot dove is I felt like if I'd go out there and
wait, somebody would give me a dozen dove. I'd be doing the same thing I
would if I were shooting. No challenge at all. A dove flies over in a straight
line. You see which way he's going and you hit him. It's not really skill.
I've had one shot at deer and I went out on a stand and sat down on a stump,
put my gun across my legs, and opened the morning newspaper to read it until
the hunt started. And I heard the dogs bark way off in the distance and I looked
and there was a big buck reading the newspaper with me. And I sat there
looking at him and he was looking at me, and I was trying to figure out how
to get that gun up and the newspaper down in time to shoot him. And I finally
dropped the newspaper and picked up the gun and he was gone. I have never
seen a hunt start that fast in my life!

SAM: *Is there any particular significance or value that quail has for you?*

I think the reason people love to shoot quail is because it presents a real
challenge. A quail gets up, it sort of scares you when it gets off the ground,
and he flies so fast. It's very difficult to shoot him.

Now, when you say "value" I think I might give a different slant on it, but I think that hunting is just something that has been handed down for many generations and it was just a way of acquiring food. We were taught to not take any game that we didn't either eat or give to somebody else to eat. I've never killed for the sake of killing.

In this part of the country, I've never known the social class of hunters to make any difference whatsoever when it comes to hunting animals. In fact, throughout my life, some of my most enjoyable hunting times have been with people who were extremely poor, and when I would hunt with them, they'd carry the meat home because I knew they needed the meat.

SAM: *Does hunting relate to the land in any way?*

Oh, yeah. It gives you a chance to walk over the land, take a good look at it and see the timber, see what's wrong with it, what's right with it, and it just gives you a wonderful opportunity to get in the outdoors with some degree of frequency, which most people enjoy. I certainly do. I don't hunt my own land as much as I do other people's land. The only land I own is up in the Sandhills and they are Mexican quail and they do not hold very well for the dogs. So I like to hunt them down here where you have larger quail and they hold a little better for the dogs.

SAM: *Any changes in hunting during your lifetime?*

Yeah, vastly. I've noticed the last fifteen or twenty years I don't care as much about killing as I did, and I very frequently go hunting now without a gun. I just go with somebody and carry a camera. I haven't killed a bird in five or six years. Now wait a minute, I take that back—except on a preserve.

SAM: *So you hunt on a preserve?*

Well, I hunted once a year in the last three years on the preserve. But the only reason I do that is I invite somebody down to hunt, and you field hunt in the morning and go up there in the afternoon. The chancellor of N.C. State University, he's a great hunter. And the only reason I shoot up there on the preserve is to help him carry some birds back with him. We'll kill anywhere from two to fifteen in the field and then we'll get some twenty to thirty more in the preserve. Of course, one thing that contributes to my hunting on the preserve is that there are so many people hunting nowadays and quail are not as plentiful as they used to be, and I just want to be sure that the quail are delivered while our friend is visiting.

We have some land that's reserved strictly for people who we want to hunt with. We very seldom turn down anybody hunting on any of our other land unless they are just notorious. A person that would go in there and start fires and kill the game indiscriminately. That's not too big a problem, but some people just don't care.

SAM: *So some of your land is reserved for your business associates and guests.*

The reason we do that is so nobody will disturb the birds. We know they're not disturbed when we go in there. When the chancellor gets down here once a year, we'd certainly like to see that he got into a good covey. But if we didn't have it that way, some of them might stir them up and the coveys wouldn't be together.

SAM: *Your family is said to own the most land in the county. How was it that they obtained so much land? Was it through purchase, foreclosure, or?*

Through purchase. I guess we'll always be credited for being the ugly land-lord, but actually, if you go down and look at the Register of Deeds office, you'll see very few Class A farms changed hands in 1932 and 1933. And what few did change, the family just left the door open. I've been here forty-three years, and I have foreclosed one mortgage. And that was twenty or thirty years ago. I did that at the expense of a runaway owner, who had gotten mixed up with liquor, and he was talking when he should have been listening, and somebody slipped around and burned his house down, which is a common way of treating somebody. And he heard about it and ran and caught the bus and went to Washington and nobody knew where he was, not even his family. He got so scared that they were going to kill him. He called me from Washington and pledged me to secrecy and asked me to get his wife and children put on the bus and buy them tickets and all so that they would not even know where they was going. He had to wait it out, and then he asked me to foreclose on his farm so that nobody could look at the deed and see where he was.

SAM: *Is it true that your firm is the largest landowner?*

This just happens to be the largest farm. It's no more than 5 percent of the county. That's a fact!

This interview is more forthcoming, perhaps a testimonial of an individual who marries wealth rather than inherits it. For him, quail hunting remains the challenge, creating and reinforcing boundaries against other types. Deer and dove hunting remain outside the cultural borders he has self-consciously con-structed, although he acknowledges participating in them at least once. And through his ties to the leading landowning family, he recognizes the intangible rewards of hosting dove shoots for employees, who would present him a limit of doves out of deference should he show at a shoot.

While his personal interests in wild quail has shifted to photography, he provides quail as part of the currency of reciprocity with outside benefactors. Public institutions are often a means by which some acquire private gains. Among his benefactors is the chancellor of the state's land grant institution, whose faculty supply much of the expertise upon which his business of agri-culture depends.

On Preserving Quail

Quail may be hunted as wild birds or as semidomesticates on preserves. Given the unpredictable nature and number of wild quail and the limited time busy men have to pursue them, the preserve shoot becomes expedient. The nature and values of preserve shooting are elaborated upon in a conversation with a prominent banker. Although he was born in the community, he now resides elsewhere, returning seasonally to hunt with friends on a preserve:

I've been hunting on a game preserve about twenty to thirty times this year. We kill lots of birds. The reason there's a lot of quail hunting is the activity. In the first place, you get a lot of good exercise when you're hunting. Then you have the dogs to watch and there's something going on all the time, even when you haven't got a covey of birds on the point. Then the excitement of the birds getting up and staying with it. Oh, it's just such a fine diversion—the best I know to take my mind off of everything else. That's what I use it for. Now I've gotten down just to quail hunting because I'd rather do that than something else. You can't do everything. You have to restrict yourself to what you like most and that, for me, happens to be quail hunting. Of course, the preserve has been a great boon to the quail hunter. There's nothing quite like them, those that are run correctly, and the shooting is fine, and, of course, you can have much better dogs. When you're on a preserve, you do get shooting, and the dogs have a lot of birds killed over them and that's one way to train a dog. You can't train a dog with artificial means. You have to hunt birds to train a dog.

SAM: *One of the things people have told me about preserve shooting is that it offers them the chance to compete with each other and see who can down the most birds. Is that a part of quail hunting for you?*

Well, the skill of killing the bird, that has to be some of the euphoria of the hunt, and it helps keep you young and helps you feel that you are in the swing of things if you can hit the bird. They're not easy to hit. Of course, the more you practice the better off you are and that's bound to be some of the euphoria of that. Insofar as the competition between hunters, we use a different system on that. This is our own system, and we score the percentage of birds taken on the hunt by the number of birds that we bring back. In other words, the number of birds that are shot and that fall without trying to tie it down particularly to one individual. We have a sort of hunting creed. You have a backup man, you have two up front. And we found that way you kill more birds and you really have more fun if you don't hold back and say, all right, Joe, this is your bird, and John this is your time to shoot. All hunters, if they can shoot with safety, shoot at every bird, and we kill more birds that way and have more fun. Now, you can tell who got the bird, but you are always very chivalrous and gentlemanly about it and say well, that's your bird when you know in your own mind that you killed the bird, but that doesn't bother you. You don't hold them to competition and count, now you killed so many or I killed so many. We like the system and it works well. Bring back a lot more birds that way and nobody gets mad with anybody else if they drop the bird right when they're getting ready to shoot.

SAM: *So it's a corporate effort?*

But you get the fun individually. You get it collectively and individually and it's a real pleasure. The finest recreation I know of is quail hunting. I don't have much time to go and do all sorts of hunting. You establish your priorities and when you have a limited amount of time you do what you like to do best. You can't do it all unless you don't do anything but hunt during the hunting season.

We use mostly a holiday hunt. We go out in the morning, not too early. We get to the place we're going to hunt about ten o'clock in the morning and we'll hunt two or three hours and have a festive lunch, good lunch, sit around and tell a few stories and have fine fellowship, and then go back in the field, say about two o'clock until dusk and kill a lot of birds and have a fine time, and get the exercise and all the activity with it.

SAM: *Do you hunt with your business associates?*

It's entirely different. You cut yourself off completely. Now, you may hunt with business associates, but you don't do any business on the hunt. Business is not even discussed. What's discussed on the hunt is usually the hunt and stories about hunting and all that's happened in the past or things that come to mind that you experienced before on a hunt, or is usually associated with wildlife in some way.

I can't help but feel that a quail has an awfully good chance of outwitting you. He does it by instinct and you can't tell where he's gonna fly, and he's got a good chance of getting away and there's that intrigue. You're really in competition with that bird. He's gonna make it and you've not hit it and, of course, the dog furnishes part of the competition with the bird. Is he going to find him or is the bird going to get up before you have a chance to shoot him? You've got all that intrigue and there's so much going on. I think an experienced quail hunter has a better chance of not being hurt than any other I know of. But it does take experience. I tell you, you take a big chance hunting with people who have not had experience. It can be very, very dangerous.

In deer hunting, you're too much like a spectator. In a good quail hunt you are absolutely a participant. You're matching skill and wits and everything else against not only the game but the terrain, the weather, and everything else rolled into one. Just the outing itself, what you do and the activities, it doesn't get boring. You're sitting there waiting for a deer to come along and you can get bored. You don't get bored on a quail hunt because you're moving and you're gonna find some birds. Of course, if you're doing preserve hunting, you're definitely going to find the bird. Even if you're doing just plain wild hunting, you may not get to shoot at them, but you're going to see some and your dogs are going to be working all the time and you get excitement and all that. If you do much of it, you've always got some unusual incident that takes place. Something that's happened that's amazing where your bird will react, flight path, or particular shots. And there's euphoria in that, when you make a shot that you didn't think you were going to make.

SAM: *So it's not just the reactions of quail, it's also the relationship between you and the dogs.*

You use the same dog. You know the dog's name and behavior. You know what the dog will do. I had one dog that would go off and point and if you didn't show up pretty soon, the dog would start barking and give you the signal to come find him. Wonderful dog! Things like that are not all that unusual for people who hunt quail very much. The dogs enter into it a great deal. There's nothing more intriguing and exciting and pleasing than to see a good bird dog work and the way they handle it. Then you have to praise your dogs and depend on your dogs and all that sort of thing.

SAM: *Does land play any role in that tradition of hunting?*

I think so. I think the love of the land carries over into hunting. You just like to be out walking through the woods and fields and that feeling that a person has when he likes the land, and he likes outings and closeness to the land. I think that's all a part of it.

We seem to have that idea that one hundred years ago in this part of the country that it wasn't any problem much to go out and kill your game and have it for supper that night. But I've come to the conclusion that's not true. In many game animals, there's more now than there was back then and even back then they weren't running everywhere. Now as far as quail hunting, I think the preserve type thing, a managed preserve, is definitely the answer. The wild bird population has just gotten so low and there's no way to keep it up because they've cleared up the habitat, and intensification of farming and pesticides and everything else. It's just ruined the wild quail hunts. But a preserve is the answer and the more of it done, the less expensive. And you use the means that you have to resurrect it and it really works out and can provide more pleasure. You can't go as often or as cheaply, but when you do go, you certainly get your money's worth.

Preserve hunting is costly exercise; to become cost effective it must be engaged in frequently and on a grand scale. As the banker allows, preserve hunting extirpates his contingencies and dangers. Few such benefits may accrue to the preserve owner. To turn a profit, a preserve owner looks upon his quail as a business commodity and charges for each bird killed in the field to compensate for his losses of released birds, for the training and upkeep of dogs, for land, and for equipment costs. Killed birds are but the tip of the iceberg of those produced by efficient means. Diseases, predators, and circumstances may take as many, if not more, birds than hunters. Luck, location, and assured patronage allow few full-time preserve operators to prosper beyond the short term.

Preserve shooting is a legacy of the Progressive Era. During the first decades of this century, many quail estates in the state were operated by Yankees. In the 1930s and 1940s, state game farms delivered most of the birds produced to large landowners. When it became inexpedient for the state to produce birds for mass markets, the enterprises reverted again to private hands. There are a few ways to temper the costs and benefits for individual landowners. A few farmers now raise quail part time, with their town clients covering basic costs. This type of preserve shooting is not for profit, yet the farmer gains in his access to professional services, which his town contacts bring in the form of reduced legal, medical, dental, and other fees.

Our banker mixes his metaphors in combining the chivalrous and gentlemanly behavior of yesteryear's quail quests with the efficient and bourgeois values of his profession. Are these contradictory values, representing Old South/New South sentiments, articulated with quail as the mediator? I suspect so, but the possibility became a question only after I had left the field.

On Social Relations and Bird Hunting

Social relationships are at the core of bird hunting. The paternalistic forms emphasized by Robert Ruark between the Old Man and county residents belong mostly in the past. These long-term human relationships are not replicated in the more tenuous arrangements between businessman and farmer. The constants of time, place, and relationships of the older forms are revealingly told in an interview with an eminent resident, of third-generation wealth, and his family's protégé, Tyrone McQueen:

My father was a hunter and he thought hunting was more important than hanging around the house. And my older brother hunted, but mostly it was the relationship with my father. We just hunted quail.

SAM: *Do you remember the first quail you killed?*

I remember who was with me and where it was. I was about thirteen years old and I was quail hunting. My older brothers had been with my father, and the first time they shot they killed birds. And so my turn came, and I made the mistake of going without my father. I shot two or three boxes of shells and I couldn't hit them. My father, of course, had killed the birds for my brothers by shooting at the same time they did. But they came home and they had killed their first one, you know. I killed my first bird up in Wagram with my father and Mr. Banks. Everytime I see him, which is three or four times a year, we talk about killing my first bird.

SAM: *What are the values or meanings associated with hunting? One of them is your relationship with your father.*

Yes, it's very true, and now the relationship is with friends. Of course, I only hunt quail. I don't shoot doves and I don't think of that as a sport. Take your bird hunting where you have a dog and the dog is trained and sometime you can hunt all day and never find the birds. It's a good experience anyway.

SAM: *Do you keep your own dogs or does someone keep them for you?*

I keep them in the backyard, particularly during the fall and winter months, and then during the summer months I keep them out in the country with Tyrone McQueen.

SAM: *Tell me about your association with Tyrone McQueen. He was very close to your father, wasn't he?*

Tyrone McQueen taught me how to hunt. Tyrone kept my dogs and trained them. He and my father hunted together and then when we would come home from school we would spend every day with Tyrone. He'd take us hunting and supervise the dogs. Very close friends.

SAM: *Any other meanings or values associated with hunting?*

I don't know how to articulate it. I'm not a meat hunter.

SAM: *You like to eat quail, do you not?*

Oh yeah, I do, and enjoy being successful at it, but if I kill one or four or eight, it doesn't make any difference to me. I like to see my dogs, but they need to be my dogs. I don't enjoy your dogs nearly as much as I enjoy my own. It sounds kind of selfish or something, but when I come back from hunting—like the golfer tells you what he did on the ninth hole—I would tell my father about the dogs working and where we were. I can remember hunts specifically, and I pretty much hunt the same area, and I can go out there and see a familiar tree—the woods look the same to me—and I can remember where I was last year, ten years ago, twenty years off, from the experience I had right out there in those woods. I shoot the same covey of quail that I've shot for thirty years, and there's a companionship even with the quail itself, and we're very careful not to shoot down a covey of quail too much, because we know that they've been there for decades and we want them to stay there.

One of the sad things I see is that land is being cleared. We are concentrating on farming that's chemical. Farming practices are not compatible now with live or actual habitats like we really need, so that's a real conflict. And I can see that I'm gonna lose some of my best territory in the next three years to the bulldozer. So I've staked out another area that I've got control of that I know nobody can do anything to it but me.

It's almost as if the purer tradition is gone forever. I'm really the only one in this very large family that is serious about hunting. For me it's identification. It's a tradition. I know my father loved it and I think that's the reason I love it. I know his father before him was dead before he was even born but he was also a hunter. My mother's kin I don't think were hunters. My father was twelve years old when his grandfather gave him a double-barrel shotgun, and my father hunted all his life and that's the only shotgun he ever owned in his life. And when he was sick, I told him, I said Daddy, there's one thing you've got I want. He started getting nervous and he thought maybe I wanted the farm or something, but he said, what is it? And I said, I want your shotgun, and he said well, go get it before anybody else gets it. But I'll take that gun—I won't shoot it—but I'll clean it up and put it away and someday I'll probably mount it and put it in a den somewhere, and maybe that's part of the nostalgia or something. I just enjoy the memories.

Quail hunting for me is a very personal thing. To be honest, I'm not trying to create anything. It probably is selfish, but it's a very pleasant and personal thing. What I'm saying is I'm happy to be a hunter, but I don't think many people feel about it like I feel about it. My satisfaction comes not from killing. It comes because of the hard work and the nature and the trees and familiar places. I can just head out and walk for ten miles, spending the day, going to the country store, and maybe even playing a game of checkers if Mr. Banks is down there playing. And I've enjoyed bringing friends from the North down here. I've kept up with my classmates and they just check in now and then. Making them eat sardines and crackers!

Tyrone McQueen is in his 80s. He is a tenant, a dog trainer, a hunting companion, and the protégé of a prominent land-owning family. Moreover, he has played all of these roles, all of his life:

Why I started huntin'? I was about twelve years old, I guess. I'd be late to school. I had seen white folk huntin' but not colored folk in those days. Had to be careful and without a dog I'd walk 'em up. That's when I bought ma first dog for five dollars. Most I ever killed? Christmas Day I killed sixteen rabbits, sixty-three birds, shot all but two shells I had from my .20-gauge gun. Strung birds around and danglin' from ma waist, rabbits tied together and strung along behind.

SAM: *What does hunting mean to you?*

I remember huntin' with Mr. Herbert, right by ourselves. He told me that when he died he wanted me to be a pallbearer at his funeral. That if I was sick or somethin' and couldn't carry the coffin, that I should touch it and stay close. That's what happened too, for I was sick and his sons were the ones who carried it and I walked behind. He said I'd done helped raise his chillun. I'd spend half time wif 'em and he'd spend half time. Whenever I was huntin', we would always pause towards the end of the season to count the birds in the coveys before shootin'. We would leave five or six. We would take four or five out of a covey. We wouldn't kill the last birds from the coveys, usually fifteen or twenty a day. Didn't matter who had done most of the killin' for they were shared at the end of the day so everyone would get a mess.

SAM: *What has changed noticeably during your long life?*

Land's openin' up and whole lots better now. A poor man gots to be 'umble. Got to honor other people in the goin' and comin' and to get together in peace. Some of ma folks get too impatient. When the Laud make one he make 'em all from the same stuff, even Adam. A poor person must be 'umble, honor 'im and 'is girl and everythin'. Only way he can get anywhere. I'se married for forty years. Never get anodder one. Neither in mischevious acts. I'd be gone for long time and dat woman o'mine she reared de chillun and no problems.

White folk always been good to me. Give birds, always have rights to fish in deah ponds and hunt in deah fields. In return I'd give dem a mess o'fish or quail. I have no land. It wouldn't be right to kill all you have and not offer any to you. People today don't kill all dey birds on deah place, but dey come to your place and kill all o'dem. Maybe you wasn't a hunter, but one day I'd kill nothin' and then two or three anodder day. Then you would welcome some birds. If you'd good enough to feed and raise birds then should be given some in return. I had good fortune could hunt anywhere I wanted to. Mr. Herbert used to issue invitations to come for a feed. I'd catch all da fish and kill da game and cook it for all the guests. Would happen four or five times a year. Also would have dignataries, important people, come down here for huntin'. Would spend haf day with Mr. Herbert and haf day with me. Governor killed his first bird unda me. Blew 'em up.

Paternalism and personalism have always been the privileges of power and wealth. In the agrarian South, land ownership often procured both privileges. Quail hunting supplied the landowner with both a means of recreation and reconnaissance. It also provided the stories to personalize their landscapes. Whatever the motives behind the quest, cultivated relationships were desirable. Landowner and tenants need not belong to different racial groups, but given the probable composition of rich and poor in Scotland County, such differences were likely. Obedient blacks were described by paternalistic landowners almost as members of the family, in warm and affectionate terms. Some blacks, like Tyrone McQueen, spent their entire lives under the aegis of patronage, reciprocated in kindness, and trained several generations of landowners and dogs. Both partners shared the same values when it came to quail.

The relationship between father and son is likewise an enduring one. The boundaries of a privileged landowner's identity are particularized in the familiar landscapes, in his dogs, and in his friends, including such as Tyrone McQueen. Yet the attempt to conserve the landscape tamed by one's father and to uphold his traditions has increasingly become a precarious exercise, presumptuous if not consumptive of wealth. It is an exercise fraught with emotional and practical problems, as illustrated by a middle-aged farmer trying to carry on in his father's footsteps:

I used to hunt every day. I did that for one main reason, because Daddy hunted every day. And I said, well if he hunted every day, his son will hunt every day. But things have changed, two things. Daddy was financially able to hunt every day and he found plenty of birds every day. For two reasons I can't. Now I started doing it this year. I'd go out and beat the bushes. It might not be but a couple of hours, but I would try and do it every day. And that's one reason my hunting partners are really tickled. They wouldn't want to tell me that I was hunting too much and pushing the birds further into the swamps.

I do enjoy going by myself on occasion even though you can make that perfect shot and nobody's there to see it and you can't describe it to them how perfect it was, how pretty the dogs worked. But finances too. This past year farming, I realized that I've got to make more time and let one "boy" go and do his work myself. In other words, not pay him. Which is fine, for I love to work on the tractor also.

SAM: *If I have listened well, what you've told me is that the farming and hunting you're living is your father's tradition. He gave you not only a farm, land, but also something to do with it. When you hunt you celebrate his presence if nothing more than in your memory.*

That's exactly right.

SAM: *And some of the problems you're currently facing relate to your trying to provide continuity for that, to push those traditions into the future. I was reading last evening some of Robert Ruark's book on growing up in North Carolina. In that book, the boy, now a number of years older and wiser, comes to realize that he is not able to carry forward all the traditions of his grandfather. Times have changed and so has he. Have you come to a similar sense in the hunting you do now?*

Yeah, I have a great deal. Let me go back a little further. He was my closest friend plus a father, and he and I did things together so much, and he had a heart attack, and, five years before he died, I said if you die, my world is gonna fall completely apart and I'm gonna die with you to a certain extent. Well, he kept up right on me for a long time. He had another heart attack, a couple of more strokes that kept him where he couldn't get out at all. So he started weaning me off.

SAM: *Do you think it was conscious on his part, or on your part?*

It was something he couldn't help. It wasn't that he tried to wean me off, but the Good Lord looked after me and weaned me off of him where instead of me depending on him for a good time or financially, he depended on me for a good time. I neglected my children. I neglected my wife, I neglected my friends. I took care of Daddy, and I'm glad it was like that. He wasn't bedridden, but he was in a wheelchair where he couldn't get around everyday. And I'm not bragging or anything. I was glad to do it. I regret that I neglected my family, but they understood too, bless their hearts. But every day I'd ride him around. I would cater to him. Anything he wanted to do. I spoiled him, you might say. I did it to make his life, his last couple of years more pleasant.

He was a wonderful father and that's all you can expect. If he'd adied when I was a kid, I'd missed all this, every bit of it. Or if he'd abeen an old sorry son-of-a-bitch that I ought'n to cared about, it wouldn't have made any difference. I wouldn't have had any memories at all, but the good memories I never shall forget. Just like I say, he was like a brother to me, a best friend.

Whereas the landowner above was able to make the transition from his father's leisurely agrarian tradition to a multiple-crop quasi business, others are not so fortunate. A second-generation landowner, who inherited a farm from his father, was in his forties when he experienced financial difficulties making ends meet. Some of his difficulties stemmed from his attempt to shift abruptly from tenant farming to commercial livestock production. In the end he was to lose the farm and his family. His ruminations upon his pending loss are revealing, especially after telling of his inhibitions against taking more than his limit of quail:

We've had some pretty difficult times in the last four years, in particular in our livestock operation. We don't even have the livestock we've been raising. We've sold out and are intending to repopulate. I think that during the last four years I would have used any harmful chemical products or anything available to help me survive in what I was doing at the expense of every quail that's ever been. And knowingly would have done that. It's a very selfish thing, but when you get down to it, I think people do some rather foolish things when it's survival time. If I could farm successfully and had leisure time and could hunt and be more in personal touch with wildlife, I might forgo some of my profits for the sake of wildlife. I would have to be able to afford some of it. I wouldn't give it away at the expense of my family or my survival. You know, there's a matter of wealth and well-being involved. I think when you get poor your values shift, needfully so. If you get hungry enough, you'd trap every quail in Scotland County to put on the table or sell.

On Dove Shoots as Volatile Events

The mourning dove is a widely distributed game bird and thrives in most states. Its migratory wanderings place dove in a different management category from quail, which by comparison are provincial homebodies. The boundaries for hunting doves are defined by the U.S. Fish and Wildlife Service, and infractions of their regulations are federal offenses.[15] Although these federal edicts are subscribed to by some shooting parties, for the most part, like federal taxes, they are to be evaded unless apprehension appears likely.

Because of their cosmopolitan background, doves are not approached with the same sense of husbandry and stewardship as quail. Doves lack visible signs of good breeding and refined tastes. In consequence, their pursuers have not been inspired to leave many signs of a literary imagination. Rather, one acquires the word on dove from the mass media journalists of radio, television, and newspapers.

For Robert Ruark's Old Man, the opening of dove season was like "a community party, like a house raising or a cane grinding or quilting bee."[16] Today, its significance is attested to by its opening on Labor Day weekend. The event is heralded by advertisements and articles in the local paper and on radio. Local merchants purchase space and time for "specials" on camouflage shirts, shells, guns, and other necessities. Typescripts supplied by the Wildlife Commission advise shooters on the conditions of the local dove population and fields, on regulations and methods, on dangers from strangers shooting in overly packed fields, and on legal liabilities if shooting takes place over "baited fields."[17]

The opening of dove season remains as much a community event as it was in the Old Man's time. Yet with so many men and doves packing into the fields, it is difficult to keep all the behavior within bounds or even to know where the boundaries are. Unlike the aristocratic pretenses of chivalry and refinements among quail hunters, the behavior of dove shooters packs all the potential of the battue, unleashing bourgeois bursts of competition for the most game bagged rather than for the challenges presented.

Even a shoot takes some preparation. Previous to the event, landowners harvest some fields, leaving weed seeds and spilled grain to attract large flocks of doves. For some landowners, cultivation and harvest practices are deliberately inefficient and contrived to corner the local dove population.[18] Then on opening day, the landowner or sponsor prepares a feast or barbecue and invites neighbors, acquaintances, friends, and friends of friends. Labor Day festivities, socializing, barbecues, and dove shooting are likewise linked in the seasonal rituals by which employers or agribusinessmen host their workers and celebrate the turn from the summer's heat toward the coolness of fall.

A noon feast is followed by a mad scramble to the open fields for the likeliest "stands" (or "sits") for those who have done their scouting of dove flight paths. Positioning oneself within a dove flight lane becomes part of the early bird route to outshooting one's rival, and besting him to a potentially profitable stand is part of the grandstanding openers. Yet the assumption of a well-situated stand must be validated by behavior appropriate to it, for an open field allows no cover for discretionary shooting. Bets are shouted from stand to stand, and wagers (sometimes in more than words) are taken on the first shot of the season, the first bird taken, the most misses, the first limit, and the last out of the field. Under some field rules, those rounding out their legal limits are free to take up a neighbor's.[19]

Successful shooting takes a large pool of gunners spread through a field habituated by doves. The spread of gunners keeps the doves (mostly immature birds reared in the surrounding shrubbery) circling and looking for an undisturbed place where they can land and feed. When they appear, doves are likely to occur in droves and in numbers unlikely encountered with other game. Encounters with doves remind one of yesteryear's clouds of passenger pigeons or hordes of bison. And with those images in mind, bourgeois impulses are blatant. Conservation must be tempered and cultivated.

The play of norms, personality, and ideals of sportsmanship is interwoven in a conversation with an agricultural salesman. He came to the county as a teenager and was in the thick of peer activities in his twenties and thirties. As he approaches his fortieth birthday, he finds his travels take him increasingly away from the county. He begins by telling of changes in his hunting targets and describes a dove shoot in which he participates:

I don't know how old that particular dove hunt goes back, and I'm not real sure why I was ever invited. Maybe it was through a mutual friend. Somehow or another I ended up over there, and back then if you had thirty or forty folks for opening day that was a gracious plenty. And they introduced me to dove shooting. From there I was invited to go on a quail hunt. So in terms of my hunting evolution, I guess it started with rabbits and moved right into dove shooting, which took me quite a while to master, and on to quail.

SAM: *Do you see your hunting as a kind of evolution or maturing, or do you see quail hunting as running with a better mix of people than those you went rabbit hunting with?*

I've never thought about it in that context, but now that you bring it up, in rabbit hunting we did join up occasionally with some, if you will, blue-collar friends. The fellowship was good. It never really occurred to me in terms of thinking of it as a power trip thing or in terms of social strata.

SAM: *You mentioned that you don't hunt as much as you used to. What has happened?*

It seems harder and harder to not so much find the land, and maybe not even the time, but as my life-style changes, as much as I love to hunt with my old hunting companions, we just seem to be going, although we're headed down one path in terms of age, we're off on different directions. Benny and I used to hunt religiously ten or twelve years ago, two or three times a week.

SAM: *In dove hunting, do you find yourself competing with or against your companions?*

I did initially, because it seemed to be an ego feeder to walk back over to that truck and have the limit in the shortest amount of time, so you could sort of look down your nose in a condescending way at the rest of the fellows when they walk up to the truck or cabin. You literally see fellows out there not only wasting ammunition, but just destroying everything that flies in range. And it looks to me like there's a certain degree of madness. I'm sure I'm a little overzealous here, but I think they've lost sight of what they're doing out there. It's not R and R the way they're going about it.

SAM: *What should they be doing out there?*

Well, I enjoy smelling the breeze and looking at the caterpillars, and if I'm in a soybean field, trying to figure out what kind of herbicide or pesticide I've got in my nostrils. Gosh, I wonder if this crop's gonna make, does it need rain? All sorts of things come through my mind. And then, totally unrelated things to hunting happen to me when I'm out in the field.

SAM: *When you're out in a dove field and someone shoots more than his limit, would you call in the Wildlife Protector or would you confront the individual with his offense and exclude him from further shoots?*

It turns out that one of my hunting companions is also a wildlife commissioner. Of course I hunted with him prior to his wildlife commitments, but I'll have to admit that he's had an influence not only on me but a lot of guys in the group. I can remember as a younger man not adhering to the limit at all. It got to the point that it didn't matter back then, but it mattered as I got older and began to become a little bit more involved and as conservation became more in the media and as a general topic of conversation. I became a little more self-conscious of what I was doing and adhering to the rules was easier.

SAM: *The commissioner has his reputation at stake and, in a sense, so do you insofar as you wish to remain his friend and stay in the same circle.*

He does, that's right. You don't want to embarrass him. I feel like I could speak for the entire group that hunts on the shoot on the opening day dove situation. I would feel very badly about anybody jeopardizing not only his, but anyone else down there that could be possibly subject to a fine or to embarrassment.

SAM: *And that would put him on the spot.*

That would put him on the spot and he certainly doesn't deserve that because he's not only a good friend, but he's a good, if you will, a "good hunter." And his dad obviously instilled a lot of sportsmanship traits to him and I enjoy it being passed on down to his boy and his peers.

SAM: *What is being a good sportsman in reference to dove shooting?*

Let's say the dove field's been scouted and everybody's been placed and then twenty minutes later someone makes a late arrival and he'll look and see where people are to an area where he can't see anybody, figures it's safe, and will holler, Hey, is there anybody here? And somebody will pop their head up behind a corn patch and say, Yeah, I'm here and this fellow will move on. He will address himself to the distance that's required for safety in a dove shoot. I consider that a "good hunter" and a "good sportsman." Picking up another man's bird on the other side of the ditch. I've seen fellows unload their guns, get off their stands, and move over and pick up a bird and throw it across the ditch to the other man.

SAM: *Is retrieving crippled birds part of sportsmanship?*

Yeah, in my eyes it is. That was something that I was taught by that group.

Through the discussion of his hunting "evolution" and through the easy mixing of the terms "sportsman" and "hunter," this individual reveals his station. His discriminations in language and behavior are not those of someone expressing and defending the faith of the fathers.

Dove shoots are exercises in marksmanship, testing one's abilities to place a bead and connect with a fast-moving and whimsical target. As Ruark's Old Man explained, doves "are the easiest hard shootin' in the world. Or maybe it's the other way around. Maybe they're the toughest easy shootin' in the world."[20] Figuring the angle and distance to lead doves comes readily for some shooters. For most others, the calculations are more difficult and learned with "an awful lot of gunpowder" during each shoot.

As the opener to the fall hunting season, dove shoots are characterized by numerous excesses and nominally poor shooting as men seek to get back into the swing of things after a sweltering summer with fishing rods. The opening day is usually still hot. Most shooters come with folding stools rigged with compartments for extra shells and for cool beverages, including beer. Many shooters do mix alcohol and gunpowder, despite the maxims against such mixtures heard while in the company of other sportsmen. Perhaps as a consequence of this mix and the greater proximity to each other, dove shooters are at greater risk than most other sportsmen. Accidents on dove shoots, as with other forms of hunting, remind participants of the tragedy of unconstrained reactions; but rarely does the possibility dissuade them from continuing to shoot.[21] One shooter described the accidental shooting of his grandfather:

Granddaddy was almost seventy and had gone out dove hunting. They'd finished the hunt and he and this young gentleman were talking together on this little embankment there by the field. A flight of dove came over and they both got up to shoot and this fellow slipped on that embankment while trying to keep his balance. And Granddaddy died instantly from the shot. He died in the field. I really felt sorry for the young man.

Some shooters justify their excessive takes of birds by explaining that a few days of shooting is all their time allows. One sportsman, whom we both knew had killed an excessive number of doves on an opening day, rationalized his action this way:

Well let's face it. You've got more respect for the laws of big game than you have for small game. And then you have good and bad years. I've got my own laws and the ways I judge a person as to whether or not he's really unsportsmanlike. Dove shooting is the only case where I might be flexible. I'm sure shooting over the limit on doves is probably the most common violation of any game law and I have done that. I haven't done it in several years, but I used to do it, especially as a teenager. It's not something that I go around bragging about and I have been conscious of the fact that I did it when I did it. I guess it's what I would compare with what some people would call a little white lie, if there is such a thing. It's still illegal as if you killed a doe.

In my opinion, if everybody killed a hundred it wouldn't hurt the population. So I don't consider it really damaging wildlife. The problem is if you get caught with them you pay a heavy fine. That's the deterrent to me there, not the fact that it would be hurting the dove population.

Only little investment is necessary in producing doves. Unlike the quail, which is said to respond to paternalistic management, mourning doves have taken favorably on their own to the immense fields and new agricultural practices of the New South. Doves build their flimsy nests adjacent to the fields and may bring off several broods of young during a summer. Toward the end of the summer large flocks perch along electrical wires and in trees and feed in the open fields. Their presence around fields is eagerly awaited by sportsmen as a harbinger to a successful shoot. Sites for shooting doves are contingent upon the yearly rotational strategies of farmers and beset by capricious weather conditions and the unpredictable migratory dispositions of the species. These uncertainties provide the structure for a frenzy in competitive marksmanship.

Excessive shooting, together with unsportsmanlike behavior such as failing to look for downed birds, is not condoned on all Labor Day shoots. Some shoots are by invitation only, with postcard invitations presented to a gatekeeper for entry to the feast and afternoon activities. These shoots also pass out sheets listing state regulations and what constitutes sportsmanlike behavior.

After Labor Day, dove shooting becomes a relatively open sport. Once permission is obtained from a landowner, harvested fields generally become open for groups of men or for individuals joining a shoot already in progress. Recently, some farmers have begun to supplement their incomes by charging an access fee of several dollars to shoot over their lands. Despite this recent charge, dove shoots are a relatively inexpensive sport and among the least invested in social structure. For the most part, dove shooting entails cooperative landowners willing to provide access to their lands, a shotgun, plenty of shells, a small-game license, and perhaps a shooting stool and a cooler for drinks.

Even with such easy access, dove shoots are not for everybody. While compiling a list of game hunted among my county sample, I encountered some who were dead set against shooting doves. Their abstinence was expressed with religious fervor and involved images of the incarnation of the Holy Spirit in dove form or the dove's role in finding land for Noah after the flood. The following bit of dialogue with a tenant was typical:

I don't like to hunt doves. I just don't like to.

SAM: *Any particular reasons?*

Well, you know, they always said, you know, you ain't supposed to shoot 'em or somethin' another about, you know, a drop of blood or somethin' come out of your gun barrel when you shoot one of 'em, and they always ever since I was small, they said I wasn't allowed to shoot one of 'em, but I have went. But I have killed a dove.

SAM: *And did you see blood come out of the barrel?*

I ain't seen it. One of them boys up there at the store was tellin' about it. He said he went and he didn't seen no blood.

Sometimes the ideas behind the statements have more immediate and practical consequences. Such seemed the case for a textile worker who was living in the country, caretaking his landowner's coveys of quail. His reasons reflect those of an earlier generation striving to protect songbirds for their role in destroying agricultural pests:

I don't dove hunt, period. If I owned this whole entire United States and I saw a man dove hunting on it, I wouldn't let him dove hunt no more. Because it's I think one of the biggest sins. A dove is the most beautiful and got more common about him than anything there is. You get up in the morning time and hear that mourning dove coo. He'll have the pitifulness and the best sound to him, and he will take care of a farm if you'll let him.

SAM: *What do you mean, he'll take care of a farm?*

He'll go up and down the rows and eat all the bugs and insects there is crawling on the ground and if people will leave him alone. Now nobody don't hunt dove back here. That man better not catch you dove hunting back here. No way, and I don't blame him.

On Dealing with Doves

Although certain business deals are made within the well-bounded haunts of quail hunters, they are more open and widespread within the context of dove shoots. The abundance of doves, the open fields of scattered shooters, and the periodicity of its season mark dove shoots for other social functions. Many may be invited to shoots, but few are chosen as associates within the more intimate circles of power. Invitations to dove shoots provide hosts the opportunity to scrutinize the demeanor and styles of strangers, newcomers, and neighbors, selecting some for more intimate associations. It is also possible to translate invitations into business deals.[22]

Within the limits of his cultural repertoire, an individual says something about himself and his locality through his choice of activities, materials, and behavior. Each person is both a source of judgments and choices and a subject of judgments and choices. His choices are bounded by the discriminatory tastes he is helping to establish or to maintain. And this universe often has an occupational handle.

Contrast the statements made by two brothers, both avid sportsmen. The older brother is in real estate and local politics; the younger one resides on the family farm where they maintain a clubhouse to which they invite friends for meals and fellowship and to an annual dove hunt, an event on Labor Day in honor of their father. They would not confuse the proprietary boundary between quail hunts and dove shoots, even as they do not confuse male and female realms. Status operates within the hunter's realm, gender along the border between hunter and nonhunter. They carefully avoid any conflict between the two realms. Before considering the vocational expressions of their hunting interests, they begin with the importance of land and limits:

We have access to some three thousand acres of land that we hunt and control by hunting it, posting it, and by planting bird feed. I feel that if a person doesn't control it to a certain extent, then there's not going to be any hunting at all. Of course, you've got to have the land. For a lot of land around here, people don't care if you hunt on it. We do care, and we don't let people hunt here except with my brother and myself.

We bought up quail hunting because there's a lot of quail in this area. And a lot of corn, soybeans, a lot of small grain are planted that quail feed on. Mainly Daddy loved to quail hunt and dove hunt, but we like to watch the dogs work and take care of the dogs. Also another thing, on our land when we have somebody to hunt, we abide by the rules and kill just the limit. No more than the limit. Even on the dove hunt, we've had people come out here and kill way over the limit. But they are never invited back when that happens. Because if the limit's twelve, twelve is what you kill. That's it! You get out of the field and somebody else will go in.

SAM: *Does hunting relate to your work in any way?*

I'm glad you asked that question. I tell my brother and all my hunting buddies that I try and farm revolving around hunting rather than trying to make the almighty dollar. There's a lot of land I should be clearing up that would be good land to put under cultivation, but I don't do it because that's a good bird-hunting area. I've gotten entirely out of the cotton business primarily for the reason that birds don't eat cotton, and you have to spray the cotton too, and you're killing the birds and rabbits. So mainly, I grow soybeans and corn and various legumes. Of course, I'm on the farm with my truck all the time and I enjoy seeing the quail and the rabbit, and a lot of time I keep a dog with me in case I want to hunt some quail. Keep my gun with me, you know, so it does directly relate to my farming.

SAM: *You're saying that economic circumstances were not your motives for giving up cotton farming. It was more in terms of trying to establish a culture more amenable to bird hunting that you and your father enjoyed.*

Yeah.

SAM: *What about your brother?*

I'm in a different business, but I also like to be fair and honest with everybody. I think that in hunting you abide by the rules. You don't kill more game than you're supposed to kill. I think this directly relates to the way you want to be in your life. I just feel like that if you're gonna play the game fair, you're gonna play it with business and recreation and other ways.

SAM: *Let me pick up and play with those ideas and I hope you won't mind the intent of my question. Most of us look upon realtors and politicians as a hustle game. You're not only out to make a buck, you've also got to be in on information that makes your living possible. You've got to have sources of information that's not available to most people. Have you followed me?*

Yeah.

SAM: *Now, how does that relate to hunting? Do you use hunting to further those objectives?*

That's a terrible question! I'm not gonna take advantage of people, and I have opportunities to take advantage of people. I probably do more free work than I should do in my business. I do things for older people in this town and this kind of stuff. And maybe I don't make as much money as some of the other realtors or even in insurance business. But this is not the main thing with me. Daddy always said if you work hard and you're honest with people that you can get along all right. But if you start trying to make the quick buck and try to be dishonest with people—and I have seen this happen over and over again—that they might have a rise at one time, but they're gonna fall sooner or later.

SAM: *You're saying that, for you, hunting is not a means to those ends. It seems to me that a hunting cabin, like this one, lends itself to a lot of possibilities for politics and trading in information.*

Well now, like I have some friends who carry their insurance with me and I may sell a house. When I have the big dove hunt, I like to invite people that I do business with, but I'll tell you one thing. I wouldn't invite them unless I like them. Just to get their business, no. But if you have the business and you like the fellow and this might influence him if he was going to buy some insurance or something anyway to come and see me about it. If he doesn't, it's all right too, but it sort of helps, you know.

You might say a lot of politicians do come out here, particularly on the first day of the dove hunt, whether they're in office now or want to be in office. It's really a good political—I don't know the word—but they get to know a lot of fine people when they come out here. We've had Luther Hodges and Bob Jordan. Terry Sanford's come here hunting with us, numerous senators and representatives. Daddy was in the state House of Representatives for four years and we got to know a lot of them that way.

SAM: *I've heard that hunting is a good way to get to know another person. Has that been your experience?*

I think so. I think you can learn a lot about a man by going hunting with him. You can learn if he's a game hog. You can learn whether a man, if he likes to hunt, is willing to sacrifice. Maybe helping us to post the farm, or maybe helping us plant some feed patches. And you can stay in a duck blind with a fellow all day, and if the ducks are not flying too good and you start talking, you can learn a whole lot about that person, about their philosophy of life. I tell you from experience, there's nothing more miserable than being on a duck stand with a fellow that you didn't hit it off with too well!

SAM: *Do you ever go hunting with women, or when women are along?*

Well, personally speaking, I really don't see women hunting. We don't particularly like to see them out here, but occasionally they come out here to dove hunt.

SAM: *If I follow, your preference is for hunting to be exclusively masculine?*

Absolutely. I feel like that they're kinda like out of place here, for the simple reason that when we get through hunting, we like to come in and clean birds, tell jokes, tell a bunch of jokes, have a drink, play some cards, something like that, and that's no place for a woman.

I don't believe I would have a good hunting buddy whose wife liked to hunt, because I wouldn't want her going hunting with us. It's as simple as that. If he felt like every time he went out hunting his wife needed to go along, we wouldn't do much hunting together.

A more coherent connection between hunting and business was expressed by an insurance salesman in his thirties. He was reared on a county farm where his father and uncles still provide him access to hunting opportunities for his clients. I begin by asking him if hunting is better for gaining clients than golfing.

That would depend entirely on the client. I'm not a golfer because I spend my spare time during hunting season hunting. And for clients that do hunt, hunting is much more effective, they enjoy it more. I can't entertain as many clients hunting as I could golfing because there are more golfers than there are hunters, I think. So I'm sure that if I were using it just as a business promotion that I would be better off to play golf. I can't take very many hunting and it is more time consuming than golf if you really go at it. So I can't say that I'm doing it just for the business even if it is effective when I do it.

SAM: *Does hunting provide a way for a newcomer to break into a community, or for building relations among businessmen?*

Right. I'm in the insurance business and my wife's into real estate. I do meet just about all the new people that come to town. We will go out to eat with someone when they first move to town. I'll find out if they're interested in hunting and I'll tell them about it and then I'll invite them to go if they like it. We get along fine and we'll do it again occasionally. I've done a lot of insurance business with a car dealer and his group. I'm not sure this would have come about without the hunting aspect. The first time I met them I realized they were hunters and I invited them to go hunting. We went hunting with a group of relatives. Of course, all of them drive pickup trucks and one sells pickup trucks, so it's a kind of reciprocating thing.

It gets a newcomer into a group with the same sort of values that he has. I think most hunters that I know have similar values. I can tell you that most hunters very seldom are heavy drinkers, almost never. Most of them are fairly religious. They may not be the pillars of the church, but they're usually churchgoers. They're usually married. They usually have a strong-knit family. They learned hunting from their fathers that they pass onto their children and they have a strong sense of fair play. I don't know the opinion of single people.

Mor to der P'int

The capacity of quail to retain the luminary of people and place is a cultural artifact built upon the perceived biological characteristics of the species. As the chosen vehicle for sending and receiving finely tuned messages, the tastes associated with quail are recognized by those within and without the enclaves of county power. The broad sets of agreement concerning what is desirable, who is permitted to join and under what conditions, constitute a sign registry of social values and evaluations marking the boundaries around some groups and differentiating them from all others. In the process, quail has become metonymic of a whole system of power, property, and status—a bastion of aristocratic and agrarian values. Yet such bastions are never secure for long. The art of creating them in the public mind becomes a Trojan horse of change—a monument built upon the tensions and paradoxes arising from the wishes of those in power to create a closed universe, and from those aspiring to greater influence to challenge these pretensions and to gain entry. No wonder then that Mr. Bob, once he is recognized as a standard-bearer, has to change his habits and appearance in order to survive.

On another symbolic branch sits the mourning dove, whose numbers flourish in the broad swaths of modern agriculture. The perception of such prodigality enhances the cultural currency of inflated inclusion and competitive conclusions. Moreover, dove shoots provide occasions for landowners to reciprocate, thereby incorporating others into their tasks of building community bonds and, perhaps, making deals in other fields.

Eight

Small Game for Large Numbers: Stalking Squirrels and Running Rabbits

Now I really enjoyed rabbit hunting because I had my pack of dogs. I had about eight or ten beagles. I'd go and turn 'em loose in the woods. They all was after a rabbit, everyone of 'em was doing their part. And they was making all kinds of music, you know, and I'd just stand. Seemed like the cap just went right off my head when I'd hear 'em run like that and I'd have to keep pulling my cap down. You know how it is whenever you get rejoiced over anything and it sounds so good. That's just like getting up in church, hearing a choir get up in a choir and singing. Everybody's trying to do their part, and whenever they try to do their part, it sounds good to the auditorium. You see what I mean? And so that's just the way it is with every dog that's in there after that rabbit and every one of 'em's trying to do their part. That's pretty music. Some people say they don't care nothing about hearing 'em dogs bark, but I do. I enjoy it. So that's what I like about hunting. And there's nothing no better, a sport for me, than to hunt.

(A retired mill worker)

SQUIRRELS AND RABBITS are popular game species and have provided food and sport for many generations of rural residents. These small mammals may be taken through a variety of techniques—with traps, with throwing sticks, with gun or rifle, and with or without dogs. "Rabbit hunters like instant results" is how one man identified his sport. The predictable habits and habitats of squirrels render them popular targets for initiates. Two varieties of squirrels (the gray and the fox) and of rabbits (the cottontail and marsh) are found within Scotland County. Their numbers, particularly that of rabbits, fluctuate widely, for few apparent reasons.[1]

The characteristics and dispositions of small game, together with their association as food for the masses, contribute to the mundane manner in which they are discussed and pursued. Yet through listening carefully to the stories of small-game hunters, we learn about the experiences and exposures of their lives and life-styles. Reflecting their local status, hunters of small game are generalists, often opportunists, pursuing a broad spectrum of game as their chances and networks allow. We begin by seeking advice from an old codger, whose insights were lovingly passed on through his grandson.

Advice from an Old Man

Robert Ruark's Old Man was annoyed by people who stumbled through life, not seeing much and not venturing outside of their inherited cultural bounds.[2] These convictions led the Old Man to make sure that his grandson's inclinations were different. As a consequence, they devoted a summer to learning lessons from nature. Learning about nature was merely a mirror for reflecting the Old Man's thoughts on his experiences in the human world. What observation of things "out there" taught was discernment in one's personal life.

A superb teacher, the Old Man begins on his grandson's level, with observations on squirrels. Appropriately, the lesson is about love. Two squirrels chasing each other brings out the hidden meaning of acting obliviously in the presence of other beings. The lesson of "losing your head over a lady, . . . is fatal whether you're a squirrel or a boy."[3] But from here, the lesson deepens into puzzlement.

"I try to figure out what God had in mind," the Old Man continues, "when He made all the different kind of things, and I can't for the life of me decide why He made so many different kinds of squirrels. It seems to me that if you were just going to make squirrels you'd cut 'em all to the same mold and forget the whole business." And with that comment, the Old Man's puzzlement shifts back to human nature for a similar comment and a standing resolution. "But he made a lot of little people and big people and people of all sorts of colors and languages; so I guess He just had to balance off with squirrels."[4] Even squirrels had strong defenses against threats to their identities. That note became the object and subject of the next lesson.

It was a new experience even for the Old Man, but not one to leave him without explication. The observation was the appearance of an albino squirrel, an occurrence that brought out a streak of meanness in all other squirrels. The reception began with a snarl, mediated with a bite from the largest male, and ended with a scamper through the treetops. The Old Man concluded the lesson by asking and answering his own question as to why the other squirrels found the albino's behavior so distasteful. "It was because he was different," was the Old Man's answer, and that difference made the white squirrel "a curiosity," "a foreigner" in his homeland.[5]

And with that lecture on conformity, the boy's attention span had lapsed. He was not only tired of squirrels, he needed some action to focus his attention. The attentive Old Man quietly folded his philosopher's tent for the day and they took off for the beach. The observations had begun with differences, centered on squirrels, and ended with tactics for keeping differences different. Some Old Men, like the biggest squirrels around, knew how to keep everything in its place!

The lessons were to continue on other days and would be concerned with other ways of seeing and being. Every type of game and its pursuit had a lesson to teach. Watching squirrels and rabbits provided the Old Man with some germane lesson plans. With so many around, it was hard for the Old Man to know exactly what to make of them. Yet what he made of them depended on what he had experienced of them—which for the Old Man was never as profound as for the other more celebrated species.

I used the Old Man's conventional wisdom many times in listening to and learning from squirrel and rabbit hunters. The Old Man told the boy more about squirrels than he did about rabbits. Rabbits were one thing he didn't know much about. Something got in the way of the Old Man's learning about rabbits: his quail and his dogs—or his way of thinking what his dogs should be about. And basic to the Old Man's thinking was the learned difference between business and pleasure. "There never was a good bird dog that didn't like to chase rabbits. Rabbits are fun for him, where quail are just hard work." You could tell when a bird dog pointed a rabbit, for he looked like "the village idiot." This idiotic behavior had to be discouraged and disciplined early in those destined for higher things.[6]

To listen to squirrel and rabbit hunters in Scotland County is to tune into a diverse world. For elderly men in particular, their tales reveal a life different in many respects from the one familiar to most urban dwellers today.

About Life in the County and Hunting

Most county teenagers began to hunt by seeking squirrels. The initial kill of any animal is a significant event in the life of a young boy and most men vividly recall that feeling of accomplishment. Subsequent to these first kills, few individuals confine their exploits exclusively to squirrels; rather, they pursue other species as opportunities allow. As adults, they remain generalists, generally hunting a little of every game as its season comes in.

For the most part, their hunting histories merge from prolonged country living and farming. Their stories and distinctions flow from seasonal rounds of activities on familiar landscapes. Missing from these stories are the specialized boundaries posted by competitive lives in the cities.

My first conversation was with Malcolm Chavis, a farmer in his sixties. With his sons, he farms about seven hundred acres of soybeans, corn, and vegetables. He lives with his family on the farm, surrounded by other kin with whom he "swaps time" putting in tobacco and with other seasonal chores. Here he informs us of a "coming of age" ritual and something about his values:

When my father was living, me and him used to go hunting, and at that time it was mostly possums and coons. And after I got married and got out, I got interested in rabbit hunting, which I have a trove of beagles. And me and the Reverend Locklear and Mr. Billard, we had us a kind of club together. We had approximately fifteen to twenty head of beagles and we'd put them together and they ran mighty good. So we hunted I reckon ten to twelve years like that, and then the Reverend he died and then I go kindly aged now and I don't hunt like I did and I got shed of my dogs.

SAM: *Do you remember the first animal you killed and what it was like?*

Well, I remember the first one, like it was a squirrel. I was a boy then at home with my father. I was about fourteen. I slipped the gun off and went into the swamp and I was standing on a stump when I fired at the squirrel. It was a single-barrel old gun he had, and when it kicked me I fell off the log. And I had killed the squirrel, so I had a time finding the place where he was at. Well, I taken it home and dressed it, and told my father about it then, you know, because I realized that I had something to talk about. Anyway, he was thrilled about me having that luck. He praised me for it. He said it was mighty good that I had killed the squirrel.

SAM: *Is there anything about hunting as it relates to farming life generally that you would like to talk about?*

I think it's something that people when they get off ahunting they just kindly in a relaxed mood and they forget their troubles and everything else and have something to look forward to kindly relax their minds.

You take my children, they're all married now, but the boys, they'd rather have the rabbit meat than to have barbecue, a hog. They just enjoy it so. We take and boil the rabbit and then take it off the bone and put the barbecue sauce on it. I've had people come and have a meal with me and they'd think they was eating hog meat.

Yeah, we feed the wildlife, you know. You have something for them to feed on and everything to help them survive. Then it's like a crop that you growed. That's the main object there, just as you would have a peach orchard or something, you're looking for something to harvest.

SAM: *As you look back on your times hunting and farming, has hunting enabled you to do anything that you wouldn't have done or accomplished otherwise?*

I think it has and it's been something that I could enjoy and relax my mind. I'd be sitting at home worrying a lot of times. If I was hunting, I was enjoying life more.

SAM: *What about meeting people?*

Well, that's another thing in hunting. You meets lots of friends and make lots of friends. It's something that just can't be hardly expressed. It's just something about a person that loves to hunt. You can sense real quick, you know, whether or not he is really a friend. His personality, he shows it right quick.

SAM: *How is that? In terms of whether he's a game hog, or whether he lives by the rules, or?*

Yeah. Now you take I was in that deer hunt club with those boys. We had rules, you know, that you didn't shoot a doe and try and slip it by and hide it. Because any time you get to killing the does, you're killing out your crop.

I knowed a few years ago another club, they would come and get my trailer and haul their tractors to go and plant the grain for their deer, laying out the land. They got on me to go with them to hunt. It come a rain and I couldn't harvest my beans, so I got up with one of them guys and he told me they were going the next morning and I went. It was raining and we were out there and had on my raincoat. We walked out to our stands and some went off with the dogs and they got in there just about, I reckon, ten minutes or something, and I never heard such shooting in my life. So they gave the whistle—that was the signal to come together. We went back together and this one guy raised his hands and fingers, and had done killed three, and two of them was does. Well, that wasn't good, and of course, they hid them and got by with it. I think they put them under the trunk of a little Volkswagon or something. Something like that is not good, because you know, a few years back they'd set doe days and just leave maybe one or two at a season.

Justin McLaughlin is an elderly worker born in the county, but now living in town. He tells a slightly different story: about growing up fatherless, about learning how to master the shotgun, about hunting before the law came to enforce the seasons, about laying off of the Old Man's quail, about the mysteries of how dogs learn, and finally a story reminiscent of slaves' tales of "trickin' Ole Massa" by culling game from under the landlord's supervisory nose.

Well, I was always interested in hunting from a kid. I like the dogs, and facts about it was I started hunting with a slingshot or jewembas. I wasn't old enough to carry no gun, so I go over there for my mother. I saw a rabbit one day sitting in a bed and I asked her to let me take the gun and go down there and kill him.

SAM: *Was it your father's gun?*

My mother's gun. I was without a father because he died when I was about four years old. She lets me do it. Lets me take the gun and go down there. So I killed the rabbit and I reckon she just figured I was old enough. I'd say I was about twelve then. So from then on I started going with other men, boys and things like that, so that's where I took it up from. My uncle, when I was living around him, I wasn't old enough to hunt then. I wasn't but a kid boy. But he loved to hunt possum and rabbits.

Back then you ate possum. You don't mess with them now. You hardly ever find anybody now that will eat it. If I be hunting now and my dogs maybe find them in a hole and when I find out what it is, I just catch him and take him away from him because I don't eat them.

SAM: *When you shot your first rabbit, did your mother give you unrestricted use of the shotgun?*

No, she just said you'd better be careful now and don't shoot yourself. You'd better hold it tight, it might kick you. I had shot a gun before on Christmas, I believe it was. Mama let us all shoot the gun and the first time I shot the gun, I didn't realize how to hold it. I just had it up under my arm and when I shot it, it went up and busted my lip. So from then on, she said you'd better hold it tight now so it don't kick you. But I had already learned how to hold a gun then, and after that gun kicked me this guy told me that's the way I did it. I had it under my arm when I should have put it up and braced it, you see, and it went up and hit me.

My mother farmed on the farm. It was all on the farm as a tenant farmer, sharecropper. She moved about 1927 in Scotland County. Well, my mother never did move off the farm until she got sick and had a stroke. All of us were married then. Me and ma wife was living in the house with her because then rest of them had done moved away. There wasn't anybody but me and a wife and the kids and we just stayed on there till after she had a stroke and couldn't contract the business, so I had to take over. We moved around a bit. Just like you farm here and that man over there probably had a better outlet for better deal over there. That's why they change places, trying to better theirselves. That was back in the days when they'd have mules. There wasn't no tractors.

SAM: *Any things, or values, that are associated with hunting?*

Well, I just love it. That's about all I can say. I just love hunting. I just love the dogs for one thing. I just love to hear them run. I enjoy going out there hunting and hearing the dogs running. Maybe I don't even get nuthing, no game at all, but I just love the sport and I get a kick out of hearing the dogs. I go coon hunting. If you coon hunt, everybody in the crowd don't have no gun, you know that? They'll have a rifle. I just go along with them to hear the dog's voice, that what I do.

SAM: *Is hunting related to landownership?*

Mostly, if it's a strange place, and you don't know those people, you always go ask them if it would be all right. Now you take a whole lot of people who like to hunt birds. They don't want you to hunt the birds. I know several years ago down here beyond John's Station where all them big fellows they've got a place. There's a big field that's laid out with woods around it, and they had put a bunch of birds in there. So we were down there hunting and the dogs were running rabbits, and the owner came and he said, well, I'm sorry, you all are going to have to move out from here. He said now I know what sport you're hunting because I know you wouldn't be hunting birds with beagles. He said, now there's two or three guys that I hunt with, and we come here and we know about where them birds range and you all come in here walking through and the dogs running, they get them birds scattered and we can't get them together. He said now, anywhere else in this community you're welcome to hunt, but we just don't want you to hunt in here because we've got some birds here.

SAM: *What changes have you seen in hunting in your life?*

It's not changed with me! Yeah, I can start from way back. I used to hunt when you didn't even have to have no license. Anytime you caught a rabbit or anything you were about to eat, you hunted. September, well, that's mostly when people start hunting squirrels and rabbits any time it would turn cold. Now rabbit season, squirrel season, dove season, quail season, all them got a date now, you see. You'd better not be out there hunting rabbits until somewhere after Thanksgiving.

I never will forget it. I had three beagles. I give twenty dollars for one of them and I raised two puppies. Nobody didn't know who they belonged to. So I raised them up and I had this old dog and I took them down in the woods and I had an old tree I'd bent down to sit on and the old dog would be running. So one day, I got quiet and I could hear them running and I said, they're running behind Old Sam down there. And I looked, there's a path that come by the tree that I was sitting on, and boy, they were coming too. The rabbit came hopping on down. He didn't see me. He came so close I could have kicked him. When he saw me, he just went on out like that, and when them puppies came to where that rabbit come out and went across that path, they swirled around and come back and got on it and here they come toward me, and boy they run that rabbit! I said good gracious alive!

I come on here to the house. I left them down there, and the guy that lives in that house down there, I said if I tell you them puppies was running, you wouldn't believe it. He said, no man, them puppies ain't running. I said come here and walked around my backyard there. He said I'll be doggoned if them things ain't running. And I'm gonna tell you the truth, them things would naturally run a rabbit until somebody killed it.

The day after Christmas, I couldn't go. I was working and I couldn't go with them. So they wanted to use the dogs and I told them, yeah. There was two carloads of them and they went. When they came back and parked their car, I went around the back of the darn thing and they had killed thirty-five rabbits and laid them out on the back of the car that day with my dogs. They'd run it till somebody killed it. That's all there was to it.

I only hunt rabbits and we hunt just about anywhere. I can't hunt them around here now because they've done moved the city limits. Last year, we didn't get a chance to do no hunting worth nuthing because you couldn't find none.

I used to tend an old farm now where the college is at. You remember that hill where all the pecan trees and water trees are at? That's where the big house was and the white one, that's where my boss man lived. My house, they done tore it down, but I lived right down there from where the L.A. building is. That's where my house sat. I had these push windows and I could sit right in that window and see them squirrels coming from down the bank. And they had to come to the ground to get to that hickory tree. I'd wait until about three or four get in there and I'd go through the cornfield and come up down beside the woods to get to that hickory tree. And then I'd shoot them.

Well, the man didn't want you to kill no squirrels. He didn't mind me hunting rabbits but he didn't want me to kill no squirrels and them quails. Well, I'd wait for them squirrels to get to that tree and I'd go down and around and my cornfield was right in front of the door. You see, I'd get between them and the woods. And my boss's coming now. He gonna come down there, thought somebody would be hunting down there, you know. Well, by the time he'd get down there I'd done got four squirrels or however many I got and gone got in the house with them. He asked me, Justin, did you see who that was shooting down there. No, I ain't seen them!

I'd knowed some white boys and they'se been squirrel hunting. But the boss man wouldn't allow nobody to kill them. But boy, one of those days, them boys were ashooting. And he slipped in there on them. I was picking cotton in my field there and he come down and said he's caught them. And I said no, I ain't gonna tell nobody. He caught a man one morning shooting squirrels and took his gun. But there were squirrels down there, but he didn't allow no hunting. Now I got all I wanted. To tell the truth, I stopped hunting squirrels ever since I left the farm out there. See, I lived right in the woods then.

The stories told by Hubert Gaines, one of the few remaining farm caretakers, have a different flavor. Gaines is caught in the role of protecting his land-owner's land against trespass and his own squirrels from the bag limits of others. His idioms capture a local wisdom, a wisdom which city folk confuse with "leg pulling" since it appears more provincial than their own. Like his own methods of protecting his terrain, they only "work" if one is in the game or resides in the community. Hubert Gaines is not a farmer. He supports his family by working in the mills.

I just felt like I wanted to be a sportsman and I took it up on my own. My gun that I first started hunting with was one of the first Columbias dey ever made. It's about 145 years old now. Dat first Columbia was made with a birch handle to it. My grandfather's daddy give it to 'im when he was a boy. It's a 36 inch bore choke and he went to a turkey shoot and he was drunk and I reckon dat's where I got mine from.

SAM: *Your father wasn't a hunter?*

No. My father he was in the army all my life. I stayed with my uncle most all the time and he'd hunt. And he said to me one day, you want to go with me squirrel hunting? I said yeah. And he said I'm gonna let you shoot 'im if you see one. I said, dat's all right. He said you see dat one dere? I said yeah, let me slip up on 'im. And he said, well, dat's what you've got to learn to do. You've got to slip up on 'em and all. I snuck up on 'im and crack! and I killed it. Oh, I was about fourteen when I killed dat one.

SAM: *And your uncle?*

He watched and den he said, well, now dat's all right. And den ma first cousin he come out of the army and he was down in the woods with me one day and dis here squirrel went across. I said just watch me hit dat squirrel. I was down on ma knees crawling among dem briars and all. He looked up dere and said, you know one thing? I said, what's dat Jake? He said you make me think of an old timey Indian crawling around hunting. I said dat's right, I knowed how to hunt now. I got the squirrel. He said dat squirrel didn't even move. How in the world did you go in dem bushes without making a sound? I said well, I learned something, hold your breath and crawl or walk and you don't make as much a sound as you do breathing. Now you don't believe dat, do you? Well, it's the truth.

SAM: *What things are associated in your mind with hunting?*

Well, I got the idea of hunting is the best sport dere is. You can concentrate. You can take a squirrel or rabbit and watch it and the dogs can be ready, and the rabbit will get away in front of the dogs and you can whistle and he'll stop. The rabbit will stop and he'll look. If he don't hear nothing, he's gone again. He concentrates with the dogs and concentrates with the hunters if he can hear anything. And a squirrel, you can go in the woods ahunting, and he can tell the sound of you and you've got a scent. Dey go by smell.

SAM: *Squirrels do?*

Yeah, you can shoot one right now and you see another one. He's gonna get behind a tree and hide somewhere because he smells dat gunpowder and he knows you're around. And if he can sneak down, he'll come down the tree, and his best point is to come down on the back side and dat way he'll be off. He won't go off in a flash, he'll go off so you can't hear 'im. A squirrel is a sensible little fellow, he'll get on the ground and go. At the first of the hunting season if he goes by the trees he knows dat he's got a better chance to getting dere without you seeing 'im. And later on in the fall of the year, dey'll get on the ground and go back.[7]

Dere's more game back here in this place dan dere is any place else because dere isn't nobody hunting back here. It's private property and it's posted. This here land belongs to Leroy Mercy. It's his sister's land and dey call it the Mercy Farm, and dere's plenty of rabbit back here and coon. Dere's everything back here besides deer. Dere's possums and foxes.

SAM: *Is that where you get a lot of your meat during the winter?*

Well, I go down dere squirrel hunting a lot wif my boys. Dat one dere [his son is thirteen years old], he killed his first one this fall. I told 'im, now you've got to be mighty, mighty quiet. When I put 'im on a stand, I said now, nobody else is around you. I didn't want dat gun to shoot, you know, without hurting anybody. I put another on the stand and I said, whatever you do, don't shoot toward one another, shoot in the opposite way, behind you, but don't shoot across. And I say, don't move dat place. Just stay dere until the one's dat's with 'im comes back and gives you a whistle. I learns 'em a certain kind of whistle. And I found out dat a hunter, if he don't want nobody to know he's in the woods, he ought to be just as smart as smart can be, whistle like a quail or either have another code whistle to go by and learn dat whistle and the other ones will know it. Dere are a lot of times a person just don't buy a license to go in the woods and try to outsmart the game warden. Dey got a code too.

SAM: *You're fifty years old; has hunting changed in your life?*

Dere ain't as many game now as dere was twenty-five years ago because all this here dust [insecticides] and dat here mess has killed dem out. You take dese airplanes, dey're flying around here and dese little ole quails and rabbits dis here spray kills dem.[8]

I believe dat dey have learned to be smarter. Dere's a lot of old stray dogs comes drough the woods and right young teenagers dat goes drough the woods ahunting, a bunch of dem. Dey ain't got no more business in the woods dan dere is in trying to fly because he ain't old enough to get a license. He's just old enough to shoot somebody. Oh, I didn't see nobody. I said the bush shakes, and you got to know how to hunt without shaking a bush.

My boy called me from Detroit a while ago, said dat man come over yet, Daddy? Said tell 'im about me. I can't hardly wait till I get home so we can go hunting. And I was thinking the other day where I'm moving to now. I'm going back to my old hunting territory, where I first got married, and I knowed dem woods just like I knowed the back of my hand. Sometimes you think about it, you just can't hardly wait for the time to come for hunting. It's a release because you can be tired. I sometime come in from work and I say I just got to get my gun and I'll sit behind a little tree and rest and relax and sit dere. Hunting is a good thing. It's the best sport dere is. Dere's a lot of people now, dey love to play basketball, football, and tennis and all such as dat and I wouldn't give you two cents for it. I'd rather get me a box of shells and my gun and go down in the woods and listen even if I don't do a thing. Before the season comes in, I goes down in the woods and sit and listen at 'em chattering. I listen to 'em chatter and chatter back at 'em.

I got a little nephew, he's young. He told me back in the summer, he said, Uncle, I want you to learn me how to hunt. He said, I'll go with you. I learned 'im how to fish and now he wants me to learn 'im how to hunt. He don't worry about dat gun akicking 'im. You watch dat target, den you bring your gun up. Dat very gun dere kicked my boy off a stump, knocked 'im half crazy. He didn't hardly know where he was at.

Most of the time you get in dere and you shoot. Other one will get in dere and say, get any? Naw, boy dat squirrel is de smartest thing I've ever seen in ma life. Well, you laugh about it, so he's got 'im fooled and he goes in dere, he'll probably run up on a yellow jacket's nest in dere and you know about where it's at, and he gets in dere and he stirs dem up. When he stirs dem up, he's had 'im 'cause dey bit 'im, about you know what, and he ain't going in dere again. But you want to shoot a time or two to make people think dem squirrels is in dere and dere ain't nothing in dere. You just go somewhere else and say, yeah boy, dere was something down in dere.

People get out dere and get to hunting and acting greedy. Dere's a limit to game, but if he wants to act greedy and wants to act smart, I don't think he should be allowed to hunt. Now when dey limit dis stuff, dey gonna be strict. When I go in de woods, I probably kill one or two squirrels. Dat's enough because dat's about what I think people can eat and I just let it do. I've seen people just go in dere and somebody say how many you got? I got nine. Somebody says I've got six. Well, what you gonna do with dem? I don't know, I might make a stew out of 'em, and I come to find out dat he just gave 'em to the dogs or threw 'em away. I don't think a person oughta hunt if dey ain't gonna eat 'em.

Like Hubert Gaines, most county hunters eat what they shoot and have little empathy for those who do not. Even Ruark's Old Man shot more squirrels on occasion than he should have. When he did, he was careful to deliver the squirrels to Abner McCoy, a black farmer with a large family. McCoy could use the meat. More importantly, the poor man's noblesse oblige secured the Old Man's lease on McCoy's quail for the season.[9] Squirrels sometimes enter the rural economy in that way. The expendable nature of squirrel in the sporting economy of the affluent is shown in the remarks of a landowner's son, himself of sufficient age to know the difference:

I've shot in squirrel nests before, but I don't think the squirrel's as valuable a creature in some sense of the word like a quail is. A quail is, you know, part of our heritage. He's a very valuable little fellow and I think we love him. There's nothing more beautiful than seeing a pair of quail or just the mama walking with all the little hickorynuts running behind.

For whatever reason they hunted, hunters thought it important to consume what was killed. Nothing brought out stronger sentiments from the heart of the Old Man than those who reputedly wasted their game. It is this trait that Hubert Gaines despised also.

On Remaining Close to the Land

Some county residents have remained close to the land, and the land provides. However, staying close to the land is getting harder to do with all the recent changes in thinking and work. Tony and Leroy McLean, two brothers in their early thirties, explain. The McLean brothers inform us of county life not so long ago. They tell us of the hardships of growing up on a farm, about poor schooling for blacks, about training and friendship with the landowner's son, about the tragedy of transition from farm to mill life, and about how they have remained true to their father while avoiding his "recreations." Hunting out of necessity takes many skills and knowledge, especially for those possessing only a modicum of means—combining bird traps and work, knowing how to place oneself when rabbits emerge from their "beds" and how to throw and lead their targets, and knowing where to find the game. These brothers speak with a certain bitterness about their past, which, together with their marriages and conversions to a charismatic Christain cult and perhaps a more stable life in the town, has led them to reject hunting. Unlike their parents, who worked in the mill and were tenant farmers, they both work in the contract carpet business. They were interviewed while working a job:

Ma first kill was a robin with a trap. I roasted it over the fire while they was shuckin' corn afta school. Shuck corn and exchange it for flour, meal, and stuff like dat. The robin bird would be alookin' for corn around the barn out there and we had somethin' like an old milk crate. Prop it up wid a stick and tie string to it and when the bird ago unda dat thin', we'se pulled the stick out, kill 'im, wash 'im, and eat 'im, and keep on shunkin' corn. We had a fireplace, ya know, wid an open fire, and we would take turns washin' and pluckin' the bird and throw 'im on de fire and cook 'im and would sit and eat corn, killed birds all dey. It was easy to do and we needed the meat more so than we do now, don't ya see, and we made a change, ya see. I don't eat wild animals like I used to. Don't go huntin' any more either. I don't need meat that bad. To me the animals wanna live. Now I see it differently than what I saw it den.

SAM: *Did you ever hunt with a gun? Did your father own a gun?*

Yes, but he wouldn't let us hunt wif it. Not unless we was wif 'im because he was afraid we'd get hurt wif it. Afta we moved out, every Thanksgiving he'd let us shoot a gun. Most of the odders wouldn't hold it right to shoot it. But I love to shoot.

He didn't hunt no quails and he didn't hunt squirrels as much as he did rabbits. But he just as well have hunted, for I used to go huntin' wif 'im. Too much walkin' was involved for quail. When I was twelve years old he lost his legs and he had artificial legs. He didn't do much huntin' with walkin' involved. He worked in a mill in town and my older brodder stayed home and did the farmin'. And he didn't get much education and I didn't get to go to high school but for two or three months because I got tired to the ways the kids treated me, so I quit. I never did graduate. We worked hard on the farm. We went to school bout onced or twiced a week. On Mondays and Fridays when you went they'd start a subject and when you go back they'd endin' it and we just didn't want to go.

They didn't care, man. 'Cause all the blacks had to stay home so the whites went to school. They educated their kids so the blacks didn't get any. Ever time they'd get anodder new kid, your mofver had to go up and take care of dat kid, and when they got inside they would end up callin' us niggers and stuff like dat. Your mofver raised dem too! They didn't care if ya made it or not. Ah, most of dem have died out now, but there's some left. Ya still see 'em around now and den. This generation of kids sure do has it whole lots easier than we did.

SAM: *How did you get into squirrel hunting?*

Well, the man who owned the farm where we worked at, Mr. McCurdy, he had a son. Called 'im gentleman. He had a single-shot rifle, and we used to slip down in 'em woods wif 'im. We taught 'im how to drive, how to smoke, everythin', how to curse. Yep, ever where he visits he's always glad to see us. He used to come and eat wif us. Just like one of us, ya know. We called 'im frog man.

We went frog huntin' a lot at night, but we wouldn't eat anything like that. The frog's a bugga man. They'd say, well, now don't kill dat frog, the devil gonna get ya and we thought that was the devil itself 'cause it looked so different. So we'd be soft-brained, so when guy come to go to bed everybody be sleepin' but us. Nothin' gonna stop us from killin' dem frogs. We used to be so mean, we did.

SAM: *Anything about squirrels?*

Unhun, 'cause I've never haf to hunt 'em, ya know. I'd go into da woods almost anytime of the day wif ma gun on ma shoulder alookin' for squirrels in da trees. I'd didn't know you haf to sit and wait. Man, I was alookin' for me one. I happened to see a man who was huntin' and said was lookin' for squirrels and he told me ya had to sit and wait and be quiet. So I was out there adoin' pretty good. I'd get me behind an old tree and get me a stick, prop it up against a tree and see if I see one. I step on the stick and break it and a squirrel will stand up and look to see where the sound come from and then you have a good chance to shoot. Ya know, we'd rake the leaves out from unda the tree. We'd hunt in the afternoon before it get dark. Wouldn't shoot but one or three and then I'd go back home. This was back in the '50s 'cause about '57 we was messing wid those cars.

SAM: *Do you remember hunting anything else?*

We'd hunt rabbits just walkin' through the woods with a stick. Somethin' we'd do with someone else. I don't think I ever killed a rabbit. We used to catch 'em in a rabbit box. They're too fast for me. It's a moving target. We weren't allowed to shoot a gun nohow then, and then, too, shootin' at a rabbit wouldn't be safe.

SAM: *You mentioned earlier that you had given up hunting. Any particular reason?*

Well, ma wife is a Jehovah's Witness and I studied wif her for a year. And I read in the part of Genesis where it tells ya that this meat I give ya if you need it. Eat the meat, but do not eat the blood. And we do eat meat, but we didn't go out and kill it like most people do for sports. I feel like the animals want ta live just like we do, ya know. I'd wanta kill 'em while we was akillin' 'em. We just did it. We didn't need to eat 'em den, 'cause we had plenty hard meat and stuff. We gonna change the menu a little bit, I guess.

Now I don't do it for no reason at all. But my uncle might want me to go with him for a little. I bought ma license last year, but didn't use it at all. I likes to fish. But I don't like to hunt no more. It's too dangerous too. Too many people in da woods, and some don't even know the safety of a shotgun and a gun go off can hurt a lot of people.

When we was kids, we could catch anythin' and tear up anythin' too. Me and ma brodder used to go rabbit huntin' wif a long stick and a pair of pliers.

You see the pliers would turn and you throw 'em and they were about this long and they would spin like dis here man and would hit a rabbit. Like when there's snow on da ground. We'd used to track 'em outta beds and would get the rabbit started and run 'im down and catch 'im and kill 'im. Kill 'im before we catched 'im.

SAM: *Would you bring it home for your mother to cook?*

Sometimes we wouldn't get home wid it. We'd cook it in tha woods. We could take care of ourselves now. We can survive, we can cook, we can sew anythin' we need to do. I can. When it was too cold to be in the cornfields apullin' corn, we would be in the woods huntin', and when we get hungry we would go and find us a rabbit and kill it and cook it and keep cuttin' wood.

SAM: *Tony, I take it you're not as much a hunter or a talker as your brother?*

Right. Well every time I used to go rabbit huntin' with 'em, they were always too fast for me. So I said we just ground feet, just ruined our feet. Another reason might be the answer to the whole thin'. Well, when I was about twelve, ma mother shot ma father's legs off with a shotgun.

He had trained a dog with a shotgun just before the one with which he got shot wif. And he gave it to me, and I let his wife use it 'cause he had two jobs workin' at night and during the day and she shot 'im with the same gun.

SAM: *Was it an accident?*

That was what they say, but I don't know. She can answer dat for herself. She didn't want to shoot 'im, she was ascared of the gun. He was mad about arunnin' around, womanin', and drinkin'. There was eight of us in the family so she asked 'im to come home wid 'er. He cussed 'er out and said he wasn't goin' no way. We went back home and she got the gun. On 'er way out, dis lady next door said, you're gonna get 'im dis time, ain't ya honey? Mother said, Yeah, he's gonna acome wif me.

She got three shells and put one in dey gun and put the other two on the side here. When she got there, she said for 'im to come on out or she was gonna shoot the door down. He said that if he get dat gun, he was gonna kill ya. So he come out de door, she had the gun apointed at 'im like dis, ova his head and she kept abackin' up. The more he come out, the more she backed up. She was gonna throw it in de bushes right dhar and he grabbed the barrel. She kept jerkin' it and jerkin' it and evidently it musta cocked. And he jerked the last time and it went right off in his legs. Broke it all the way off. Only thing that was holdin' it on to 'im was the front skin. He fell, she took her skirt off and tied it to 'im to keep 'im from bleedin' to death. And cut up a new tube that we were gonna put in a car tire. She stripped it up into little strips and tied the other leg and called the marshall to come get 'im 'cause back then we didn't have no rescue squad. He came wide open, man, and laid 'im out on the stretcher. I ran a mile and haf alongside the ambulance. We weren't doin' but 20–25 mph so weren't doin' that far. The doctor wanted 'im to bleed to death. We never did like 'im.

My father did the best with what he had, but there was too many of us. The worse time of the year was when my father wasn't workin'. He used to try to borrow some money from someone and he wouldn't let 'im have it 'cause it was no way that he could pay it back. And we grew up wif dat on our minds too. I've always wanted to grow up and take care of my mother and father too in the future.

There are a lot of circumstances at work that circumscribe the occupational and hunting opportunities of those on the lower end of the economic profile. More of these circumstances are suggested by Willie Thomas, in his twenties, who works the swing shift at a local mill. He tells me that last year he hunted rabbits and deer once, "but I didn't call that deer hunting." I ask him to explain:

I wasn't deer hunting, I was bootlegging. I didn't have no license. I was sitting out there with the gun in a lot of bushes and all of a sudden a deer just leapt out. I fired and the gun just left me. Yeah, I was scared. All of a sudden this thing come through the woods banging his head. And there I was. I threw the gun down to protect him, I guess. If I hadn't been the youngest person there and my first time, my buddies would have eated me up. Because they really hollered at me and really gave me a fit. If I'd abeen a little older or something they'd really cut me up, clotheswise. I don't think they killed a deer that day, that was the best shot they had and I blew it.

SAM: *What part of hunting do you like the best?*

Well, I would have to say the kill. Just the kill. I did it mostly for sport, like I said, and to keep from cleaning the rabbit, I give it away. Give it to somebody that'll clean it, somebody who wants it, because nobody here in my family don't eat rabbit.

SAM: *Any major problems with your hunting?*

Well, my time is one. I work the swing shift. Like today, I could hunt today, but I just got outta bed not too long ago and by the time I get out there and get to hunting, it'll be time for me to come in and go to work. You're out there hunting with work on your mind.

Right now I don't have no dogs. I've got one dog, but my dog is starving and I'm getting ready to get shed of him. The price of dog food is so high you can't hardly raise dogs no more. Course, that's the same thing with food. You can't hardly raise chilluns no more.

On Time and Work

As Willie Thomas above and Eviatar Zerubavel elsewhere remind us, time and work are central dimensions of one's social world.[10] By providing the world with structure, the scheduling of our work orders our lives in certain ways. Moreover, this order has consequences for our identity and standing in the communities wherein we make a living. A swing-shift worker, whose schedule diverges from that of most others, is conscious of how time operates both as a unifier and as a separator. Although the late night shift emphasizes the temporal dimension he shares with others in the identical schedule category, his engagement in night work makes it difficult to mesh his activities with others with more normal schedules.

The meaning of social acts, such as hunting, is largely dependent upon their "temporal" context. If hunting is done when most other people are working, it may be evaluated negatively or regarded suspiciously. Consequently, individuals working the swing shift and hunting during the week may find it difficult for many reasons to sustain these recreational activities.

Wilmer Leviner, a mill worker, tells us about hunting time. He lives with his wife in a trailer park surrounded by fields. He informs us of more varieties of rabbits than we knew about before:

Well, it's food for one thing. It's a good sport and it's a lot of fun. And it gets us together. We usually hunt every Saturday if we can get off. Some of them go when the others can't. Some of us have to work Saturdays and stuff like that. But it's usually on a Saturday that we go. We used to go every evening, when I was on second shift, me and my cousin. He was on second shift too.

Last year, I didn't do no hunting. I didn't even get a license because I had other things to do. I was working on some cars so I didn't have much time last year and couldn't really afford it. But I'm gonna do a whole lot more hunting this year than what I done.

SAM: *When you mention hunting as a sport, what do you mean?*

Well, it's getting to know how to kill things. A lot of thrill in killing a rabbit or something and him moving like that. You show your skill and all. A deer's complicated, but like I said, I haven't been going very much deer hunting. They're hard to kill. And then you've got to know what you're shooting at, too. You can't shoot a doe. You've got to make sure it's a buck. I've always wanted to bring a deer head home.

SAM: *When you're out hunting, you mention that you generally talk more than you kill.*

Yeah, a lot of times it's like that. Especially when you're not killing anything anyway. If you walk all day and maybe see two or three rabbits and you hadn't killed any, all you've got to do is stand around and talk or walk through the woods and talk. If your dogs get to running, then you get more interested in hunting then.

SAM: *Does your wife understand that?*

I don't know. She knows that mostly whenever I go hunting if I don't bring nothing home, she knows that we've just been talking. But we be hunting at the same time. Usually if you're out there in the woods and your dogs are not running, all you've got to do is stand around and wait. But when the dogs start running, then you've got to be ready for the rabbit. Rabbits are about as smart as a deer. They will hide and they'll run a dog to death, especially is he's a swamp rabbit. He'll run in the swamp and backtrack itself and all.

SAM: *So there are swamp rabbits and what else? Cottontails?*

Cottontails and what we call a graveyard rabbit. It's just a regular rabbit, but he stays in a graveyard. It's just a legend that they're hard to kill, but there's nothing to it. We had a little chicken dog at my uncle's house and he was talking about that today. My uncle said this man told him he couldn't kill no graveyard rabbit and he said he shot him and killed him and held him up and told that man, said, look, I killed one. So I guess it's just a tradition.

Willie McQueen is the son of a sharecropper. He is employed in a mill, having recently returned to Scotland County from working in the North. He explains his reasons, and how his father's sense of station, timing, and hunting differs from his own. For one, his father lived on a farm, surrounded by game, which was taken occasionally as time allowed. His son's spaces for work, home, and sport are all separate:

My father was one of the old-timey hunters and he used to take me out when I was a kid. We were brought up on a farm and when there was nothing to do on the farm, we would always go hunting, fishing, and the like. And I just loved it to death. My father hunted rabbits and squirrels.

My first animal was a rabbit. I was about fifteen. Well, actually that rabbit I killed, I wasn't supposed to went hunting unless I was really with my father. But he and my mother went to town that Saturday and I stole the gun out of the house and went hunting, me and my friends. When I killed that rabbit, I was afraid to take it home, so I gave it to my friend 'cause I knowed I woulda got a beating, 'cause he always said like don't play with guns. He would take us out hunting at twelve or thirteen, teach us about it but going in the house and taking the gun out, no. I did it on my own.

I was from a big family. There was ten in our family and there was so much to do. We lived on a big farm and we'd get together and play ball. I liked the country life, I really did. Like here now, the kids don't like it.

My father was a sharecropper and he could only hunt at certain times, like Thanksgiving. Him and his buddies would get together and go rabbit hunting and things like that. You had to gather the crops in. You didn't have time to go out there and hunt whatever you wanted to hunt. Take me now. I'm off work. If I wanted to go hunting I could. It wasn't that many mills back in those days, and like there was something to do on the farm about all the time and you weren't just going to drop that because you wanted to go hunting and go. Seem like to me, the less you went hunting the more fun you would get out of it. Like if you jumped up and went hunting two or three times a week, it would take a lot of the fun out of it. It would be right boring, you know, hunting all the time. Say once a week, seems like you get more fun out of it. Didn't make a kill today. Say, hey, next week maybe I'll have better luck. That's the way I feel about it.

My father, he always went squirrel hunting early in the morning. But he was back in time to get in that field when daybreak. You wait for the squirrels to come in and in forty-five minutes' time they done come in to feed and you have to leave them anyway and that's the way he used to do it. And after we started getting up where we could handle the farm and everything ourselves, he would have more time to go hunting. And he didn't just jump up. He'd go once in a while, like on Saturdays. Saturday afternoon we would go hunting. We would work a half day Saturday and that afternoon we would go hunting.

My father, he made a man out of me. He really did. He taught me the points about life, and like I said, he didn't have that much to offer me but from what I learned from him. He was a good man and I tried to follow in his footsteps.

On Staying in One's Place

Rabbit and squirrel hunting ritualize propinquity. It solemnizes thinking close to the soil. It's about close associations with relatives and neighbors, about rural life even if the hunter no longer lives there. It takes for granted that one knows the land and that one is known to the landlord, especially if the hunter does not own the land. Spatially its participants may live in the town; culturally they are still folk.

By their own confession, the commitments of some small-game hunters remain close to the ethos of their fathers. Many country families believe in mutuality and the ideal of self-sufficiency. The persistence of familiar ways of doing things have helped them cope with changes. They continue to live close to where they were reared and try to meet as many of their needs as possible.

Rabbit and squirrel hunting in Scotland County are rituals about territory and subsistence. One family unit or group of relatives is set up against another. People try to best their contemporaries in the game of survival, if not in harvesting the bounties of squirrels and rabbits. These well-known boundaries of country living lend themselves readily to exploitation and manipulation by others. These others often live in cities, or at a distance—a distance that is cultural and social as well as spatial. Among city dwellers, the operative boundaries are more diffuse and the major social groupings are defined by many factors, among them economic class, occupational category, regional origin, religious preference, political affiliation, residential placement, plus age and sex.

In the South, these postbellum urbanites have interacted with rural dwellers, not in terms of some abstract political or economic theory, but in terms of the activities and values that were already in place. In the Old Man's terms, it was keeping access to the quail while letting the squirrels, and especially the rabbits, go. Even if one worked through surrogates, as the Old Man did, keeping his dog's mind on the valuable quail and off the mundane rabbits was a constant struggle. Some dogs (read people) were more into the business of survival than into the grandiose designs and restraints of the business culture. Quail hunting was about the latter—about "watching the dogs work, and taking it easy, and shooting just enough, and walking slow, and enjoying the day."[11] Operating within the constraints of his cultural system took most of the Old Man's time and energies—and is probably the reason he didn't waste his breath telling us about the rabbits. Or was it a more subtle way in which the landlords, now displaced in the cities, contributed toward the maintenance of social relations in the countryside and toward strengthening the cultural significance of the types of rural solidarity already in place?

Willie McNair is a mill worker. He has been unable so far to turn opportunities to his advantage:

Well, I use to live beside a doctor. He was one of the old black doctors here in Scotland County and he used to hunt a lot. He got me interested in hunting by going with him and just watching and taking care of the dogs and this sort of thing. My father did not hunt.

My father and mother broke up when I was real young. So the only contact I had was with my mother. My mother was from Scotland County and my father was from somewhere around Charleston. I was born in New York and came here when I was sixteen years old. This was home for me. I grew up with my first cousins and I kind of liked getting away from New York. I didn't have any insight, I don't think, then for the city being different because that's all I knew. I'd come here for the summer and wow, lots of freedom and space and this sort of thing so I started leaning this way. I came back and she finally let me come back.

I went to college on a football scholarship. I was injured and had a series of operations and I stayed out so long I lost the incentive to continue. I guess I thought football was everything along then. That was one of the biggest mistakes of my life, not having the right insight, being optimistic about things at that age. Then I went into the service and to Vietnam. But then, they say, experience is the best teacher.

SAM: *Are you saying that you wished you had stayed in college?*

Yeah, my wife finished. She works in the Social Services Department and we get involved with a lot of people. I don't feel inferior. I tell you, when I'm on third shift, when I have to get out of that bed and go to work, I say what the hell. It's no fun. I make a good living. I make a pretty good salary, but then if I had finished school, it would have been different. It would have been a lot more enjoyable.

SAM: *What did the doctor that lived next door hunt?*

He was a deer and bird man. I went deer hunting with him, and I didn't like deer hunting. Deer hunting requires a lot of patience and there's a lot of intrigue. I just didn't have that. You know the waiting and the anxiety. Somebody on a stand down there and here come a deer and everybody gets excited. I said, what's to get excited about? You've been here five hours and here comes a deer, so what! I never killed a deer. I guess that's kind of against my grain or something. Just to shoot one in flight, you know, boom.

SAM: *I find that blacks around here don't generally hunt deer. Do you think that past history and race relations have anything to do with why blacks are not into deer hunting?*

It does. When I went deer hunting a couple of times and the guy—early in the morning——they always liked to begin with a big breakfast. The wife could fix the breakfast. So when the guy found out that I was coming along he got kind of nervous. So I figured, well, I won't eat any breakfast. I'd eat when I got home. So his wife came and said, why don't you come in. So I told her, I said, well look, I won't come in because I know you're not used to a black guy in your kitchen and around your home. I said, I'm sure it's something maybe you don't want right now. I said, you might not ever want it, but I don't want to infringe on your feelings. So I just sat out here in the truck. I've been to this guy's house a couple of more times. You see her husband on the job and you go to the Christmas plant party. Without saying anything, things just seem to get better. Nobody ever apologized. Nobody said, well, hey, I was wrong. The guys get more involved now because there's more contact. A guy say, hey, come on, let's go hunting, when before they wouldn't ask you.

SAM: *You used to hunt birds with the doctor. Tell me about that.*

The doctor had a dog that came all the way from Ireland and that was the first dog I'd ever seen imported. The thing came in on the train to Hamlet and we went and picked him up. I used to feed his dogs for him next door and take care of his dogs. Then he asked me did I want to go hunting? And then he brought me a gun for my birthday. It was single barrel, .20 gauge, I think, and he said that would probably be good for me to just start learning on. And I used to go around and take a potshot at the birds when you've got twenty-five to thirty birds to a covey where I could get a shot. Well, maybe when it's about five or ten, you've got to be good. And then they had an automatic shotgun.

I like rabbits. Well, a rabbit don't offer too much challenge. When a rabbit jumps up in your range, you can hit it. I guess rabbit hunters is those kind of hunters who like instant results. You go out there and most time you'll get one or two rabbits, this sort of thing. You're gonna bring back something.

And one thing about hunting small game, if your license covers that particular game, you can hunt it. If you're out there, even though you're hunting rabbits and birds fly up, you can shoot birds. In deer hunting, you're out there and you've got a rifle and you've got a shotgun with double ought buckshot in it. If you shoot a rabbit with that, boy you'd blow him to a million pieces.

Another thing about hunting, who you're hunting with is a lot of time how successful you're gonna be. Like Quick, he's a good rabbit hunter, so I've learned a lot from him just by being around him and watching him, and he'll tell me about different things. One thing about rabbits, a rabbit's habits are predictable. Rabbits travel in circles. He can come up here and the dogs chase him. He'll come right back. I really like to eat rabbits. I love them. My wife won't cook them.

SAM: *Your wife won't cook them?*

Yeah, but I think it was my mama's sister. I got in the habit of calling her mom, too, when I was coming back down here, so she fixes them. She likes rabbits too. Course my uncle, he likes rabbit, so she fixes them and I love them. Yeah, you boil them down and put a little sage in and then you fry them just like chicken and they are delicious.

SAM: *Do you get any satisfaction from demonstrating skill in rabbit hunting?*

Well, with an automatic shotgun, what chance does a rabbit have? I mean, like if you had to chase them with a stick or something like that, then maybe there'll be a little skill or maybe a little intrigue in it. When a rabbit jumps up and you have three shots, really the rabbit don't stand too much a chance.

SAM: *Has being a hunter had any effect on your life?*

If I wasn't a hunter, I don't think I could have the friends I have now. I know a lot of people that hunt and the friendships with them. Like last week, I needed a chainsaw and I didn't have one. This guy, he hunts, and had a chainsaw and he let me borrow it.

I get a county hunting license. It's very seldom I venture out of the county. A lot of guys buy a sportsman's license with the stamp on it and everything. Some of them say get your sportsman's license and you can cover everything. I'm just a small-game hunter. I don't know too much about big-game hunting, just what I've heard the guys talk about, you know.

For Willie McNair, the insights seemed to come too late. The potential advantages of growing up in New York, of association with a quail- and deer-hunting doctor, of an athletic scholarship were dissipated. His story reminds us that the lure of quail hunting as a professional emblem transcended racial lines. He lacked the stamina and fiber to take a stand for deer, and he eventually settled into rabbit hunting among kith and kin. His friendships and interests overlap and intertwine, enhancing his group's distinctiveness through borrowing, etiquette, language, and proximity. His evaluations of skills for rabbit hunting, as in his job, are not eloquent. For the moment, he seems safe within the confines and boundaries of his group. To step outside is to become vulnerable and that is painful.

Antonio Love, a thirty-two-year-old bachelor working for the railroad, is a confessed nonconformist. Some of his values come through conversations about his types of hunting. In them we gain a glimpse of the expenses involved with so many modes of hunting. He belongs to one of the county's lower-ranked deer clubs, notorious for not confining their kills to bucks. He is also a hunter of rabbits and has just taken to coon hunting:

My father, he used to buy rabbits from the fellows and my mother would cook 'em and I enjoyed the food so much. It seemed like we never had it often enough. So I just said, well, when I get old enough to kill some rabbits, I can kill as many as I want to. And I started doing that and I found out that I liked the sport more than I do the food. I don't care all that much for the food now. Of course once in a while, two or three times a year, I eat rabbit.

SAM: *Tell me, how did you get started in deer hunting?*

Well, like I said, you really have to love it because I wouldn't dare sit down and tell you how much money I've spent to do it. If I told somebody this, they'd say well, you're crazy. But I've always figured, if it makes sense to me and I'm doing it and it's not costing them anything and I'm not doing any harm to anybody, well, why should they feel like that?

I know it's real expensive and most of the guys I hunt with, they don't really want to invest as much as you have to enjoy it. So that's one reason. You have a lot of fellows that I feel like they use you. You know what I mean? But it costs like the devil.

I have four dogs I run on deer. I mean I now have three. I had four, but somebody left the wildlife management lands before I got off that day. They picked up my dog from what I've been told, because the fellow who had him said that somebody came and claimed him and got the dog and went on. I've never seen the dog since.

And that truck of mine. I mean it's a hog on gas. It burns a lot and it destroys a twenty-dollar bill when you fill it up. And when I go deer hunting, sometimes I burn a tank of gas. It's fun, but there's so much that's so expensive and aggrevating about it.

The hunt club is mostly whites. I was invited. Anyway, how I got started? Well, I haven't always been a member of that club. That club is three years old and I was a member last year. I don't knock a thing unless I try it. I've always felt like a lazy man wouldn't like to hunt because you have to move around.

I had some friends that I rabbit hunted with before I went in the service and I've known all my life, and when I got back I really did a lot of it. And we'd get together, and maybe I'd bump into them sometime and we'd talk about what we had done for that year and how our hunting had been, and one or two of them deer hunted. As far as the black guy that's done it, very few of them do it, and more of them would do it, but they have to be asked. And sometimes you don't know who wants to go. You know what I mean? The older fellows won't go, fellows that have been rabbit hunting that are forty, fifty, sixty years old, that have never been deer hunting. Most of them have tried it once or twice, but they didn't do it long enough.

You got a bunch of slick guys when you deer hunt. Things that you hear about you just can't put your finger on what happened. They hear about it and they feel like they've been had. You hear somebody shooting way down in the woods. BAM! And nobody shot! Seems like it was the man next to you and nobody shot! Nobody killed anything! So they're out there for a good mess of deer meat, and then when they get in and they don't have anything and they felt like something was killed and that somebody run off with it. Then they don't go back because they feel like the hunters were a bunch of bad sportsmen.

SAM: *How did you start hunting?*

Certain things be in people that never come out until a certain event happens. After I started hunting, my great aunt use to tell me, the way I do and the way I love to hunt, she said, well, you're just like your grandaddy, talking about her daddy. Back down in the family, there was a lot of hunters.

In our house, we didn't have no shotgun. I've heard my mother say when we were small kids that she didn't want a gun in the house. So when I first went hunting, I borrowed my cousin's gun, a single-barrel .12-gauge shotgun. I always think independently because I'm a last-minute person. When I'm ready to do something, I'm ready to do it then, and if you rely on what another fellow has, you have to do it when he want to do it. I borrowed his gun and went squirrel hunting with it and I got a few. I brought them both home and I dressed those squirrels and my mother cooked them for me. Oh yes, she knew how to cook squirrels and rabbits, but she never cooked any deer. Well, she can cook anything by recipe. There's so many recipes for deer until I don't know the right one. Sooner or later I'm gonna keep sampling here and there and when I find one I like I'll ask some of the ladies how do they fix it.

SAM: *What kinds of hunting do you currently do?*

Well, I did some raccoon hunting. I've just started and you usually have to have a first-class dog. You mostly have to raise them. If you're out hunting with somebody, they keep the best. If I'd sell one I wouldn't sell the best. I have dogs I can catch a coon with. I don't have anything special because I'm just starting doing it. But I like it and before I stop I'll have as good as anybody in town.

SAM: *Do you enter your dogs into competitions, field trials?*

I never have been to one. I used to rabbit hunt and I never did do it because when I rabbit hunted, just about everybody I hunted with, I use to kill more rabbits than they did. I'd kill more rabbits myself. That's what I am, really a rabbit hunter, but I deer hunt and I like it and I get by and I'm learning. I'm still learning to catch a coon. I can kill a deer, but rabbit hunting, I feel like I'm just at the top of the list.

I guess I've killed more rabbits than some hunting parties in a season. I mean I've killed a bunch of them, and I'd had dogs that were just as good as any I've ever seen hunt. Talking about rabbit dogs, I've got just as good as they come. And before I started deer hunting, splitting my time, I had four or five, and really when I went hunting and didn't get any rabbits it wouldn't be the dog's fault. It would be mine and I didn't have many times like that.

I've never cared about the competition because I've always mastered that, and I notice that you have a young hunter comes out there and you've been doing it for eight or ten years and he watches the way you do it and he's ashamed of his results. And so I don't say too much about it. I've gone hunting with a couple of fellows and I've killed more than four rabbits than I'm supposed to. I've killed more than the bag limit when somebody else kills one or two. If I brag about it that person won't hunt with me again and he just might quit. So I don't bring it up. But I'll compete with anybody because when it comes to rabbit hunting, I tell the fellows, if we go and we come back and we start counting the game up to see who has this and who has that, I say, if you don't be careful, I'll still be piling them up when you count it out. But I don't needle a person about a thing.

SAM: *It's nice to come out ahead, isn't it?*

It always is. But you know, I compete with my brother and with people who don't mind it and people who don't get angry and people who don't get greedy. People get greedy. I mean I just tell the fellows I try and get what's coming my way and don't take no wild shots. I don't want my dogs shot, I don't want nobody shot. I want to get them the safe way and compete with people who try and do it right.

My brother, we'd go hunting sometimes and he'd kill six and I'd kill two and he'd come in and tell my mother, well, I shot him out. He didn't let me get hardly anything. I'd say, OK buddy, you got what came your way. I said the next time they'll be running my way. The next day I'd do him the same way. We use to compete against each other. I didn't compete against just anybody. Some people are poor losers.

SAM: *Do you say it's skill or just luck, or does it depend on who you're saying you got more rabbits to?*

Well, it's skill. I mean with him, my brother, it is. It's just the way hunting is. I mean sometimes you find game, sometimes you don't. With him, it's not luck, it's skill, because usually when I kill more rabbits than he does, it's because I had more opportunity than he does. You make the best of them. When you kill eight rabbits, you kill them because you know how to kill them. You can make a lucky shot, but you don't make ten lucky shots.

Although Antonio is a bachelor, he reminds us, along with Willie McNair, that black women control the recipes for game. As an inversion of "assumed" male dominance in white households, black men generally turn their game over to their women. Access to good food for blacks comes through the recipes controlled by women. He finds the same clandestine maneuvers among the lower-ranking deer hunt clubs as other blacks, but decides to stick with it. Eventually there may come a time when his hunting expenditures conflict with other goals. His perceived choices at that point would be instructive. Does he give up hunting then? Does he carry on with deer, coon, or drop back to rabbit?

Although in one sense, Antonio Love misunderstands my question about formal competition, he shows clearly something equally important, viz., the boundaries of informal rivalry. To claim skill as the reason for success among familial rivals adds energy to the furnace of informal contests; to claim skill outside of these bounds ends the game!

On Transcendence

The meaning of one's activities changes in relation to where the teller stands (or sits) in relation to his life cycle. The need in youth for immediate, physical feedback that produces pleasure often shifts in older age toward the problems of relatedness and the maintenance of networks of enduring relationships.

Elder hunters are often concerned with providing opportunities for youngsters and for ensuring the survival of their sport, including the roles of hunters, dogs, and the hunted. These concerns were as familar to the Old Man as they are to Calvin Lowery. Calvin Lowery is a retired Lumbee professor, who sought to make the most of his life. He begins by telling us of his first kills, always vivid memories of accomplishment. Recalled in later life, these events are told and recast as stories capturing sentiments of affectionate bonds within families. Such stories are part of the lessons told successive generations to interest them in proper techniques and behavior. His reminiscences are as revealing as are his enjoyments of his beagles:

I learned a lot of tricks of the trade. My daddy was a great squirrel hunter and he'd carry me along. I was a little boy of about six years old and we're walking along and we were in the swamp under some big oak trees. He was looking up in those oaks. Finally, he just come to a dead stop and said, you keep walking. I didn't know what was happening. Directly, I heard the gun, Pow! Thump! and I turned around and there was a squirrel on the ground. I said, Daddy, what happened? He said, well I saw a squirrel up there in the tree and when he saw me, he turned to the other side of the tree and I know if you kept walking and the noise got beyond the tree he'd turn on my side. That's the reason I wanted you to keep walking. And I said, well, that answers that and from then on I'll walk. Yeah, we had lots of fun.

SAM: *So part of the value of hunting for you is the relationship you enjoyed with your father.*

Very much. My daddy loved children. He loved human beings. He was a man that enjoyed life and there was nothing that suited him better than having some big watermelons at home and getting his nieces and nephews, and he'd invite them all over and we'd have a watermelon cutting and we'd visit. We all lived right in the same community.

Well, now I'll tell you the thing I get out of hunting in my old age. It's been years since I've fired my gun unless it's a predator, something like a fox or possum, trying to get into my rabbit hutch. To me today, wildlife is part of luxury. I don't like to see people come around and kill squirrels because I like to see them playing up and down trees. I haven't killed a rabbit in I can't remember when. I use rabbits now, and dogs, as a sport rather than as meat.

SAM: *So you have come through a transition in your attitudes toward wildlife.*

Right. Squirrels, oh man, you go out and have six or eight squirrels, man that was something. Have you doves and birds, bird pie, that's something to look forward to. That was what it was all about. That was a fancy meal. That was eating high on the hog. Well, it still is. I know people today that raise quail by the dozens and the hundred. Then they deep freeze them. It's in order to have a group over for a quail dinner.

SAM: *Those dinners have a lot of intimacy attached to them. It's not something you feed to everybody.*

Right. That's something extra. Just like I say, well, let's go out to my cabin and we'll have a fish fry. That's just an excuse to get together and socialize. That's a chance to visit like the good old days.

SAM: *What are the other reasons hunting is special for you?*

It's been for meat and kindly a family affair. Boys away from home. They come home Thanksgiving, they come home Christmas. My oldest brother would bring a couple of good bird dogs and they'd get out with Daddy and they'd bring all the birds, and the next day at lunch they'd expect a whole bunch of quail you know. And we had to have something special because we were reared to hunt. They knew what it was to have a bird pie and have some squirrels cooked and squirrel hash and things like that. As far as we were concerned, Christmas wouldn't have been Christmas nor Thanksgiving Thanksgiving unless we could have had some quail on the table and some squirrel.

It was a tradition in the family. My daddy always at Christmas holidays would say, we gonna kill a hog. We'd get up in the morning and go out and build a fire around the pot. At sunup, the water'd be boiling. They'd get up and yell, yeah, and go out. One of my older brothers, he'd take the rifle and go down, I want to do the killing today, and then we'd drag the hog out. And it was just a celebration. Come on and throw the hog in that boiling water and get the hair off of him and hang him up and dissect him and get all the intestines and liver and lungs and heart and all those things and let him hang there. After breakfast, the hog's hanging out there, it's cool and everything, getting our hunting clothes on, gone to the woods, and old dad would be right along with them. Boy, there were things, just hilarious, just the top of the totem pole. And they'd get off there and you'd hear, Pow! Pow! Pow! just in time to get out into the fields. Come back in about one o'clock and maybe we'd have the quail killed or something. Maybe we'd just have a regular meal or something. Some good old chicken cooked and pastry and sweet potatoes baked, and some peaches and apples opened, and pies cooked and cakes and things like that. The girls, they knew how to get it right.

Then come back in the afternoon about one thirty or two o'clock. It'd be cold and we'd have a big table. They'd pull those hogs down and cut them up, hams and middlings and shoulders, and all that sort of thing. They would separate the fat from the lean, throw the fat into the pot and stir it up. They had some of those cracklins. They go out and they'd stir that with a stick they got in the woods and pour that into a stand and let it freeze up. That was what you seasoned biscuits with. So it was a kind of celebration and it was a lot of fun reliving.

The boys would get around there tusseling with each other, seeing who could outwrestle and who could outrun the others. They'd get to tusseling and my dad he'd have to yell out, cut it out in there now or you'll tear the bedstead down. We'd sweep the yards and put sand in the low places and paint things up, and it was a homecoming in the full sense of that word.

SAM: *What activities do you currently do that involve wildlife?*

Now I belong to two beagle clubs. You've got sanction trials and fun trials and on the other side, at the bottom, you've got the license trial, which we draw people from all over this part of the United States. See, if I had a dog that I thought would be field trial material, I'd get a person who would take my dog and campaign him. They come down here with their dogs and start these field trials in the early part of the year, right after Christmas. A dog's got to make 180 points to become a field champion. Then I'd have to pay the handler ten dollars every time he enters the dog in the field trials and then he gets half the win money. If you've got thirty dogs that you're handling, you'll go to a field trial every week. You get ten dollars for every entry, that's three hundred dollars and you're making a living. And we've got handlers that's doing that.

It's a sport. The dogs never see the rabbit. They are judged on their ability to trail. I'm chief marshall. We sit down and tell jokes and talk while the judges are running those two dogs. And the two people that own the dogs are right along there with the judges. When they make the decision, they say, pick them up, and the owners they go pick up their dogs. They say, next race. I say, let's go fellows. We get up on our sticks and we go out across the bushes and there goes a rabbit. Tally ho!

I just hunt rabbits with beagles. Now, they don't catch the rabbits. I turn my dog, go jump my rabbit, and then I come back and get my dog, and put him on the trail. I don't want my dog to catch him. I don't want him to go in a hole in the ground either. I just want him to be smart. I want him to have a lot of fun fooling my dog. A rabbit's smart. I've seen them make their checks, run logs. I've seen a rabbit make a circle. He'll stop and lick his feet and cut across.

SAM: *Any adjectives to describe a rabbit?*

Well, he's very prolific. He's beautiful. There's nothing any more beautiful than a little rabbit strutting around in the backyard. He's so graceful when he runs and shows that old powder puff. And I just get a thrill out of seeing a rabbit. I see a rabbit in relation to my beagles. I just kind of enjoy seeing any rabbit that's outside of my rabbit range. I come over here with my field glasses and I'll sit in here and watch a rabbit out there chewing and nibbling the grass.

To me, it's become a form of entertainment to just stalk a rabbit and look at it through my binoculars and see how fast it chews and all that. And I see him in relation to my beagles and then he's a beautiful thing.

SAM: *So part of your enjoyment comes from finding a rabbit and observing it?*

No, it comes from the ability of my dog to trail a rabbit.

SAM: *So your dog is a stand-in for yourself in his ability to outsmart a rabbit and to figure him out. And you get pleasure from watching the dog figure through those rabbit tricks?*

Right, it's amazing. You can jump a rabbit and there he goes. You can bring that dog down there and put him on the trail. You know which way the rabbit was going and it's amazing how that dog can sniff and tell you which way that rabbit went.

SAM: *How do they do that?*

I don't know, but one of the greatest indictments you can put on a dog is let him backtrail. No sir, if a dog backtrails, you've got his number then. But it's amazing that a beagle, a field champion dog, he'll come to check and he'll sit there and sniff that scent and he won't move until he decides which way that rabbit went. He has to decide whether he went straight ahead, or turned right or left. And I'll tell you, when that dog does that and the judges come along and your dog is in the winning bunch, when you go out there and pet that dog, that dog'll eat you up, like a child!

In his lifetime, Calvin Lowery went from perceiving game as meat and a special commodity marking seasonal rituals to an idealized rabbit running tracks for his competing beagles. In his transformation, Lowery has taken the country out of the boy and sustained his ideals in a way only possible by those making a living in ways generated by city living. He remains true to his roots and the rabbits don't suffer. It's a transformation the Old Man was hoping for his grandson.[12]

A Concluding Resolution

Hunters of small game are generally generalists and frequently opportunists in their pursuits, as in their lives. In tuning into their stories, we garner ideas about their life and work. If the poignancy of their plights is revealed in the details of their stories, their themes are rarely unique. Similar texts may be found among most other groups. The more elaborately orchestrated rituals of the socially prominent offer us a clear declaration of how the nature of things is intended. Not so among these rural residents of more humble bearings.

Their more mundane dramas present more of the recalcitrant and competing complexities of life, not so readily compartmentalized and unraveled. The meek may inherit the earth because their stories are more real and compelling than those we often tell ourselves.

Nine

Up a Tree: Of Honorable Hounds and Crafty Creatures

Well, I like the chase, you know, listening for the hounds. Listen to them as they pursue it and feeling like that it's a good animal they're after, and a good big one, and that he's got him in a good swamp, and it's gonna be a good chase, and they gotta be on their toes if they get it, you know, come out a winner. It's a teamwork between a dog and his master. The handling of a dog and the way that he has his dog under his control, the dog in a way has his master under his control. He's out there doing things to please him and for his own pleasure and for his master's pleasure. It's teamwork.

(President, Rockfish Coon Club, 1980)

I consider the biggest thing that has changed is a man that hunts. It used to be a poor man's hunt, a country man's hunt. But now you find people from all walks of life, living uptown, keeping the dog in his back yard. The dogs have changed. The competition hunting has changed the style of dogs. You want a quick dog. If he goes to the tree and if he lies, you want him to stay there. Because in competition, he gets points where he stays there. Before when you had a dog that went to a tree, you wanted meat to be there. If you wanted any meat, you wanted him to leave it before you had to walk all the way in there. Costs has changed tremendously.

(Master of Hounds, Rockfish Coon Club, 1979)

THE RACCOON is strictly a New World creature, and chasing it is a Southern tradition. Unlike fox hunting, a daytime spectacle wherein the gentry could put on elaborate displays of emotion, color, and power, the raccoon chase takes place at night, when such displays have minimal effects. Chasing the 'coon,' or ringtail, became the domain of slaves, freedmen, and the poorer whites who were into the practicalities of feeding themselves rather than impressing their neighbors. Today, the sport continues to attract rural residents of all races, not so much out of a need to feed themselves as a re-creation of what they are about. According to local accounts, the *pretext* to coon hunt has also served some as a cover for illegal whiskey distillation, womanizing, and perpetuating nocturnal violence. There remains a dimension of racial stigma in the activity, in that rural blacks make up a large segment of the producers and consumers of raccoons.[1] With such a detracting association, coon hunters are often berated and their ways stigmatized. Yet stigma and suspicion originate in the eyes of the beholder. Consequently, in this chapter we will take several sightings with and on coon hunters.

Coon hunters are mostly of the shy and retiring sort—"not much on atellin' ya much"—until you make the time to know them. There are wisdom and insight in their provincial experiences and rituals. To learn their wisdom, I joined a coon club, attended their monthly meetings for five years, participated and performed in their "nite"[2] hunts, and helped with the cooking and preparations for their infrequent barbeques and other club functions. Although there are many ways one might go about telling their stories, I decided to focus on their negotiations about standings and on the rationalizing processes that increasingly attempt to reshape their worlds.

"Something I Done as a Boy Agrowing Up"

As with the pursuit of other creatures, coon hunting is learned early, usually from one's father or from close neighbors. Such youthful learning and its memorable associations become structured in the activities and are perpetuated in the identities and stories of many adults who have invested their lives in rural environments. Here, a farmer recalls the relative poverty of his childhood, the hard work of early married life, and the difficulties of keeping abreast of outside events. In his role as a deputy sheriff, he realizes the heavy price paid for keeping up with outside demands and for confronting the tragedies of neighbors. Perhaps for these reasons, he remains ambivalent about "the news," and his escapes into coon hunting take on a transcendental quality. The lives of rural men are filled with stresses that are different from those living in urban settings. Coon hunting provides a retreat into the tranquility of a world of one's own making while remaining mentally removed from the larger worlds within which men struggle to make ends meet. The conversation begins with his initial interests in chasing coons:

Well, something I done as a boy agrowing up. My father took me coon hunting and I loved it and it was about all there was to do long, cold, winter nights.
Wasn't no TV and there wasn't even no radio back then. Somewhere they had
it, but we didn't have it, not in the early days. We got a radio somewhere in
the '30s, but I started hunting as a boy in the late '20s. I moved into this area
during World War II, married and stayed here. And I took up hunting again
when I moved to my present address, which was about 1965. I started hunting
with Mr. Brown and then I got me a dog, and another one. I've got a yard full.

SAM: *So there was a long interval in which you did no hunting?*

Yes it was. Them busy years araising a family. When my family was
young, I had to work long hours—part-time farming and part-time public
work. And then for the last ten years before I started back hunting, I was a
deputy sheriff and that took day and night, and it took up 365 days out of the
year just about it. All except vacation time.

And when I moved to my present address, Mr. Brown was there and had a
pen full of dogs and I started hunting with him pretty regular and then I got me
a dog. It's something to do. You get tired of looking at TV all the time and you
read the newspapers and listen to the newscasters. There ain't nothing but bad
news just about all the time.

When you get out in the woods listening to your dog and you know him,
you know when he's trailing a coon, the progress he's making, and you give
him your full attention. You even get aggravated when a helicopter or airplane
comes over and disturbs you, or house dogs barking. But the best part about
it is when you wait and listen to see if your dog's gonna be able to—well, it's
one animal pitted against another. The coon is very crafty. A fox is crafty too,
but I think a coon's got the most sense. And if he's ever been run two or three
or maybe half a dozen times, he gets what I call dog-wise. He knows how to
handle the dog, and the dog's got to be a mighty smart one if he handles the
coon. But it's getting out and I'll come home real tired, just tension all over,
and get out in the woods and get relaxed and there in the quiet of the night,
everything's quiet. And just that hound, he's in there on that track and if he
puts it on the coon, well it's soon over with the coon if he's not in a hole. But
if he's smart, he'll get in a hole and you have to walk off and leave him there
to run him again. But if you knock him out, the kill is quick and by the time
you shoot him out, the dog finishes him off right quick. I like to catch maybe
one or two coons a night and not go out and just knock them all out of the tree.

SAM: *You don't act or look like the typical deputy sheriff to me. You're milder
tempered than the other sheriffs I know.*

Well, I tried to be meek and mild even when I was doing the job, and I think
maybe it might of helped out. I tried to be compromising and get the job done
so I wouldn't provoke them. To try and do what you had to do and not let it
grow none, because I've never seen a man in my life that I wasn't sorry for

when he was in trouble. I've arrested many times and took them in when they had done the most heinous crimes you ever saw in your life. I was still sorry for them. But I don't mean that I would lighten up on them in any way. But what a waste, what a wrong doing! Seeing one human being doing something to another one like that. You just ask yourself, why did he do it? Of course, sometimes it would be crimes of passion, sometimes it would be just overt meanness, just lowdown, just shooting.

I reckon the worst crime I ever had anything to do with was with an Indian couple. They were young, and it was on a Sunday afternoon. And he had took an axe and knocked her down first with the axe handle, and then he turned it, turned the blade while she was up against a large oak tree where the roots was real big. He changed hands too and chopped her again in the head with that axe. She was a small thing, about seventeen or eighteen years old, and already had two small babies. Just a crime of passion. Well, her sister had killed his brother, stabbed him, also one Sunday afternoon, and I made that arrest.

SAM: *Where you glad to give up your job as deputy?*

Well, yeah, in a way. It goes both ways. You miss being in the know. If a law enforcement officer is alert, he knows just about everything that's going on. Because he works out of the courthouse, and that being the center of the county and the government, and anything the government has to do up above comes down. You stay pretty well up on things because you consort with other officers and the judge when he comes.

SAM: *How many coon dogs have you had? Good ones?*

Good ones? Well, my dad owned them back when I was a boy. We had two that I remember that was unusually good, Old Spot and Jim. We had ordered one of them, Jim, from Arkansas, and he was a Blue Tick, and Beaver, but it was awful! He had the beautifulest voice on him you ever saw. He was a short, stocky built dog. And Spot raised him off a litter—I think now she was English gyp. She was red and white, and mated with a Blue Tick, and he come out Red Tick. Just as soon as he got up big enough, my dad took him to the woods and he treed his first coon the first night he was ever in the woods. Treed him and never stopped. We sold him for seventy-five dollars in 1933, and then that seventy-five dollars was equivalent to about seven hundred dollars today. Ever bit of it. In this country I don't think there was nobody here who had that much money. Well, you know what the new owner wanted to do with him? He wanted to run cat with him!

"Coon" is regional derogatory slang for blacks. It was used by whites of an earlier era, struggling to survive and suspicious of any liaison between blacks and outsiders that might overturn the tables of white supremacy. The post-Depression years were hard on rural blacks as well as on whites and Lumbees living in the country. Survival was hard work; it was hard to find someone who could pay for labor, and there were hardly any opportunities to enhance one's lot, besides emigration.[3]

Since then circumstances have changed for some, as an entrepreneur reminds us. One of these changes is that Southern bankers are willing now to loan money regardless of the color of an applicant's skin. Deek Jones's story is tied together from a day I spent helping him and others prepare a barbeque for club members. The barbecue is dished out free to families of the club members, whereby the proceeds from a successful nite hunt are redistributed and provide an occasion for socializing:

I was born and raised around here. My father was a farmer and there were nine boys and five girls, all of them living. Ain't but three of us left around here. Rest of them's up in New York. My daddy didn't do a thing but work. I don't give a damn how cold it got or how hard it rained. He had something for you to do. If it was raining where you couldn't get on the outside, he'd put you in the barn shoveling corn, cleaning out stables. He half cropped, but he owned his own mules and stuff, kept five head of mules all the time.

SAM: *Those days have gone, haven't they?*

Yeah, but a lot of places are still here, still using mules right on. But it got so to where the little farmer couldn't make a living. The landlord, he expects the little fellow takes too much, in other words, he weren't getting but half of what he paid for everything. That's the way it was when we farmed. My grandmama farmed tobacco. Then she took it back out of the field and put it in the barn, tied it and dried it, graded it, after that, that's when the landowner came to take half the crop. So he took our half and we never accomplished nothing. He didn't expect half, he got half of everything. You wind up with nothing. You couldn't buy clothes for your younguns to wear to school and he could buy more big farms out of his half, and here you couldn't see how he done what he did.

My first job was as a well digger with Mr. Edwards. He lived close to us. Raised up there with his children together. As soon as I got big enough to work, he put me to work with the pumps and I worked with him right up until I got married and went into business for myself. See, his son took over the business when the old man died. His son wasn't use to all that money. He just turned out to be an alcoholic. Now he's got all that equipment his daddy left him and it can't be sold or nothing.

SAM: *So the big break came when the old man died and you were able to float a loan from the bank. So how'd you do that?*

Let me tell you what I done. I got married and I had six sets of younguns. I built me a house, and that's all I accomplished out of work. Yeah, and fourteen acres of land. This man I was working for, he was working for hisself, and I was working for him by the day. He would pay $20,000 to

$30,000, go to Tennessee and buy him a horse, two or three of them, and bring them back here. On Saturday and Sunday, when I won't digging wells, I had to be working on his horses. I knew damn well the money was going somewhere. He'd keep buying equipment and stuff and he said he won't making no money. He was putting it in them horses and having a big time. We'd get out there where all them people were. Big shots and hell, he'd be a big shot too when he'd get out there. He'd have a big time and when we'd come back home, I'd be working like hell again. So I got tired of it. If you're gonna be a big shot one time, be him all the time.

SAM: *Did you ever confront him with how you felt?*

No, I didn't know no better. It's like an old mule. You never pick up a trick. You plow him so hard, he gets where he don't give a damn. Well, actually, a man who tries something, you ain't got nothing to lose. You work harder then than you have ever worked because you ain't got nothing. But if you've got plenty of money, you don't give a damn whether you lose it or not. But if you ain't got it, you'll scratch like hell to stay in.

If I had been a rich man, then I'd have something to lose. But see, I ain't never had nothing. I been a poor boy all my life. And still ain't never accumulated no money trying to get this equipment and stuff. If the bottom falls now, the bank'll just get their stuff back and I'll go back over here and get me a job and go back to work. Doing something.

If I hadn't got that first loan, I couldn't have made it. See, the bank people, we done the work for the bank. See, everybody knows me, even when I worked for Mr. Edwards, I was the one that done the work. They knowed I done the work and that was a good chance for them to make money off that thing, see. I was dealing with homefolks. My rig was my collateral.

SAM: *Your first loan was for $85,000. How long did it take to pay that off?*

Eighteen months. I took everything I could rake and scrape. I didn't know how long the bottom was going to stay good. I took everything and put it in until I got it paid off. And when I paid it off, they didn't bat an eyelash when I told them I wanted another one for $100,000!

It's hard to believe that I work that many years and then come to get on my own. I don't know still how I done it. Everybody ain't got brains enough. See, now what some people would have done, if they'd ever get the first one paid, they would have stopped right there and never tried to do nothing else. They would have took all the money they was making and blow it, and the first thing they knowed they'd be another alcoholic like Mr. Edwards did. And what I want to do is get just as much as I can and keep going and get bigger and bigger. I'm gonna keep buying equipment. If I clear enough money this year above expenses, what I've got to pay the government, I'll use to improve my equipment to keep from paying them. Government don't need it.

SAM: *Let me ask you about coon hunting. How long have you been a member of the club and how did you join?*

I was one of the original members that got the club together. I joined in 1960 something or other. I knowed about everybody to start with. I was digging some wells out on a golf course development and met a member while there. He talked to me about coming here and joining. I was getting some dogs from him too. That's how a lot of members join. A lot of it is a member here and he knows a fellow over yonder coon hunting. He knows he's got dogs and things. He knows something about the reputation of the man. He'll ask him to come up and meet with the club and ask him about joining maybe. A lot of time, they come up to these dog shows you have at the club and then they want to join.

I've been hunting now about twelve years, I reckon. There's some white boys right next door to me. They've been hunting since they was big enough and they had a little beagle down there. Best coon dog I ever seen in my life. They'd rabbit hunt him all day and coon hunt him at night. Same dog. If he ever barked at night, you get your boots and gun because he's treed it. Didn't have but that one dog, but they caught more game than anybody in this county.

Them boys, they depended on that for a living. They cut pulpwood when cutting season was on, and when hunting season come in, they dropped everything. They didn't hit another lick or nothing until hunting season was over. I seen that long, tall boy down there, I seen him pull his clothes off and go in the mill pond and get a coon in there with ice spew out of the ground.

Whenever I got married, I had a dog that if that scoundrel treed, I went to him. I like to got drowned one night like that. Some boys supposed to go with me and I was anxious to go hunting that night. They never did show up so I said I'm going hunting and told my wife. She said, you'd better not go by yourself. I put on my hip boots and went on to the woods. Walking through a little water, all of a sudden, I stepped off in a deep hole and got plum near drowned. Couldn't get out, boots done filled up with water. I bet you I stayed in that water about an hour and half. That Indian boy that lives down there was the one who came in and got me out. He turned in where I went to go hunting that night and found me there. If he hadn't, I'd froze to death there in that pond. When you get hip boots on and get 'em full of water, you can't move.

Just coon hunting is all I do, just for fun. Ever since I fell in that hole I ain't been back to the dogs. I sit on the back of the tailgate, that's all I do. Now, if it's close by where there's no water and mud and stuff, I'll go.

Through the metaphor of the Old South mule, Deek Jones reminds us of his transitions in thought and in standing. Whereas his means may greatly exceed that of his contemporary neighbors, his style of life is similar to theirs, and he remains immersed in a dense network of family and friends. In his story of getting mired in mud, he indicates some of the tragic consequences of "going it alone."

"What Is Best Is What Ya Do fer Yerself"

Proximity and interests in dogs brings neighbors together, and in the process of doing things, some men and dogs build up enviable reputations. These reputations are built upon sustained performance, not upon heredity or upon the laurels of past accomplishments. Specialized dogs, like men, are products of their environments and distinctive training.

In many ways, dogs are the means of acquiring information about the environment and of gathering stories. Beyond these roles, dogs reflect the ideal states of their backers. Dogs are vehicles conceived, manipulated, supported, and vetted by their owners. Coon hunting is not just for "getting way from it all"; it may become serious business. With a little luck and talent the sport might even pay for itself. Making the sport pay for itself, learning from nature, and escaping to the "frontier" are topics on the mind of a thirty-one-year-old man, who works at odd jobs for the state.

I started out, I guess, as a boy, when I was small I just came to hunt with my grandfather. They were all big hunters and I guess it just passed down through the generations and they got me started in it and I kept on going.

My father wasn't a hunter. My mother's side of the family that's where it come from. My grandfather for years he run a hunting club and he hunted all his life. Of course, back in those days, hunting was dependent for food. You're talking back during Depression times, like that. I can remember back when Grandpa used to give his sons one shell and send them out hunting. And if they missed what they shot at, they got a whipping. All types of hunting they did. Where we do it as a sport now, they did it to eat.

Myself, I really enjoy hunting. I probably do as much of it or more than the average person does. I'm hunting anywhere from two to five nights a week. Coon hunting. Because I train dogs for profit, and raise them for myself to sell and own puppies. I'm just now beginning to get in a position to where I can show the profits. It's a long hard struggle to get the type of dog I've got now and to really notice to where the money's coming from. You see, like in training a dog, I'm just now getting in a position that I can take a dog and train it for profit and I can guarantee that person results on the dog provided the dog's got the blood in him and the nature to make a dog.

SAM: *Would you say that, for you, coon hunting is a business?*

Well, yes in one sense and in another, no. I think that for me it is a hobby. I hold down a job, a forty-hour-week job and I do this at night, and my wife, she's involved with it too. And we really enjoy, it and yet we can make a little money on it. Nothing to really get extravagant about or brag about, but just enough that kind of helps us with the feed bill and different things. And it's something that we can enjoy and it doesn't come all that out of our pocket like a beach trip that pulls your pockets down.

SAM: *So this is a hobby that pays its way?*

Right. In the winter when you're catching coons, the fur that you sell buys dog feed and if you have any distance to drive, it helps you out on gas.

I love the outdoors. I love the nature. I love dogs, hear and see them work, and it's a kind of different feeling. I can take those dogs and get away from everything. I'm out there on my own. I don't have anybody out there bothering me. I know some people who might go out to the beer joint and drink beer and get drunk and wind up in trouble and everything. I've felt like that I liked it a lot better out there, because I'm not somewhere I shouldn't be, in the wrong environment or something. And really you're out there, you and the dogs and the Good Lord above. I've always felt like the more a person's in nature out there, he'll see more than a person that's not hunting. You see it all and learn a lot about nature.

SAM: *Can you tell me something that you've learned recently?*

To respect rattlesnakes. We went a couple of weeks ago and we turned the dogs out on top of a rattlesnake and the snake struck at me and missed me, but the dog got bit twice; once in the head and once in the back. When we turned the dogs loose, they hit a hot coon track and just came out the box onto him. My friend had went around the snake; he didn't see it either. And I went to try and catch up with him. I went by and brushed the bush and the snake was lying under the bush, about three inches from my foot. And when he struck at me, I heard the racket and looked behind me and he started singing and he was probably two feet from me.

I'm out in the woods all the time. A lot of people say, well don't you get tired of seeing that day in and day out, but I don't. I never get tired of being out there. If I had my way, I'd just be way back, and if it hadn't been for the family, I might be moving way back in the woods. But with a family, you can't go to a remote area. You can go there and visit, hunting, but as far as going and staying, there's not much way you can do it with a family.

These initial interviews reveal that among coon hunters, as among their more pretentious fox-pursuing brethren, women are tolerated. The wives of coon hunters often work full time, and, if in the mills, they work at comparable jobs. Some wives help the club by cooking food and baking cakes for the nite hunts and by helping the club raise money through its raffles. Women may even "be involved with it too" (translation: feed and train the dogs), as the young man said, but he realizes the constraints placed by marriage on his masculine zest for "moving way back in."

Frontier experiences today are vicarious. Joining together with others in a club becomes an expedient way to escape from the tyrannies of work and homeplace. The coon club serves both as a place for escaping mundane concerns and as a space for sorting out masculine suppositions.

Locally, coon hunters were one of the last sportsmen's groups to organize. The local clubs that began in the late 1960s were the product of earlier economic transitions. In the words of one man who changed from chasing fox to coon during the 1950s, "Me and my father couldn't afford to keep a large pack of dogs no longer. Feed was so expensive, and coon hunting doesn't require a lot of dogs." These men downscaled their recreational modes in keeping with their economic prospects for rural living.

If one listens carefully, coon hunters often compare themselves to fox hunters. These comparisons recognize the wealth and organizational power of fox hunters as well as a common interest in dogs and in the force of New World circumstances. Their recognition of affinity is with the Forks of the Creek field trialer rather than with the bench-show variety. The six recognized breeds competing with the numerous "grade" (homegrown or unregistered) dogs contrast with the relative stability of single-breed competitions among fox hunters. Performanace counts, for through their self-made dogs owners seek to win approval for their newly created and self-defined categories. Many cooners disdain the venerability of pedigree and its empowering vested interest to manipulate and to purchase. In their nite competitions, unregistered dogs owned by "blue collars" often compete against the "blue-blooded" registered dogs of those more economically prominent.

While the structure of coon-dog daytime bench shows are similar for most dog shows, the nighttime competitions are inversions of those of the fox field trials. In the "nite" hunt, one judges dogs by sound rather than by sight (as for the fox), and the scoring of the four dogs in each "cast" (each group of four dogs) is by peer agreement rather than by a cadre of "impartial" judges. Furthermore, coon hunting has a reputation of being consumptive, in that the coon is frequently taken for its valuable skin, and its carcass is served up as human or dog food, in contrast to the nonconsumptive rhetoric of fox hunting. Unlike fox hunters who flaunt class, coon hunters tend to accept others' statements about themselves while hoping for a hearing about their other values.

The local club is a stockholders' association whose vested interests remain informal despite the subsequent turnovers and decreases in membership. Despite an egalitarian ethos, fiscal and other important decisions remain in the hands of a small group, which has constituted its center from the outset.

The club owns a house, a pond, and an open shed on its twenty-one acres of land. After several experiences of having to vacate other temporary quarters, the club bought the land from a widow. The clubhouse provides a place for monthly meetings and is headquarters for competitive events and for informal "buddy" hunts. The pond provides the watery medium for the contest in which ranks of dogs swim in pursuit of a "coon on a log," while the open shed is for the daytime bench show and for shelter from rain. Neighboring farms, creeks, and forests provide the arenas for the important nite competitions. Through formal competitions, raffles, informal hunts, and sales from its kitchen, the club raises money to pay for its mortgage and essential expenses. Proceeds beyond those necessary for expenses are plowed back into barbeques and "feeds" for members.

Along with the church (mainly Baptist and charismatic Protestant) and work (mainly blue-collar, part-time farm, and mill workers) the club is an important identity marker for its members. For members, coon hunting perpetuates a rural tradition in which a man molds and masters his environment through his implement and proxy, his dog. As a consequence, much of the time and energies of members outside of their work are spent in rearing, caring for, talking about, and following their dogs. The only sure way of knowing your dog is "to raise him from tittie to the tree," as one club member put it.

"The Only Way to Get a Good Dawg Is to Make It Yerself"

Dogs are the basic currency among coon hunters. Through the mediums of established breeds and unregistered dogs, men compete for the higher stuff of status and standing. Verbally at least, cooners champion the unregistered grade dogs for their ability to whip the certified class (the recognized breeds) in finding and bringing to tree the wily raccoon. Furthermore, between men, dogs are often a part of the social cement bonding the relationship. As gifts among new friends or old, the loyalty and performance of dogs remain constant, unlike the ups and downs of most social relations. Relationships are mostly egalitarian, for rarely does either a man or dog consistently best his peers in what they are about.

Dogs are cared for and discussed with more emotion than most other relations. Their performance becomes the stock-in-trade of conversations through which lore of lineages and landscapes is generated. Through these stories, the teller reveals himself, his relationships with others, and interprets the contest between his dog and its adversary. These themes are tied together in the following account:

I went out coon hunting one night and went to this fellow's house and he couldn't go. He said, I'll tell you somebody who will go wif you, said Andy McBride. Well, I knew 'im when I seen 'im, but I didn't knowed 'im. I went over to Andy's house. He said let me get ma britches on. Me and him went out

and caught some. I just give dem to 'im. I had one good dog, but he was old.
Andy had an old bulldog, he was solid. Dat old dog o'mine, he'd open good.
He'd quick tree dem and let dat dog o' Andy's, he'd be in dere, he'd tree wif
'im. He was a young dog. Andy said, you know, I ain't never had enough
coon meat. He said I like it. One night we caught four dat he brought in. Just
a few nights after dat we caught four more. Went back to Andy's, said, Andy
you done eat all dem coon? He said no, I done salted dem down in barrels. I
was about to get more coon dan I could eat. He had salted dem back in the
barrel now!

   Andy's dog got run over during some time or another dere. Well, I happened to be up at ma uncle's. He had an old trick dog up dere, you know, trick
fox dog. Dey said she's quit running fox and has gone to running coon; she's
not all dat good. She's just as good or as sorry as datever you put 'er wif. I
asked for how much he wanted for 'er. Weren't so very much he wanted for
'er. I come back 'ere. I see Andy in a few days and told 'im about 'er. He said,
well, I'd like to have the dog, but I tell you, I just ain't in shape to go buy one.
I said, Andy, me and you been hunting together. I said, now, if you're interested in the dog, I said, we'll ride up dere one of dem nights and look at the
dog. I said if you want the dog, the only thing you've got to tell me is dat you
like the dog. I said, I'll buy 'im and you can take 'im to your house and you
can pay me whenever you can. My uncle will sell me the dog cheaper dan he
will to you or somebody else. We got up ere and looked at the dog. Andy liked
the looks of 'er so we put 'er in the truck and we brought 'er home. We went
hunting. Sure enough, she tracked right with dat dog o'mine. I think she treed
wif 'im.

   One night I went by Andy's house. Andy said, I just can't go tonight, but
go on out dere and get the dog. Dem dogs struck. Dey went near about out
o'here, with me trying my best, in other words, to get dem to stay in 'ere.
Directly dey turned and came back acrost the hill, started coming crostways
to dem branches. Sure enough, dat last branch dat dey hit dey finally treed
dem on. Dey come right on down through the swamp. You could hear dem in
dere, but dey won't saying nothing, because dey was scorching—putting out
everything dey could put. Dey were putting it out.

   Dey turned around and went back up dere and I heard dat dog o'mine tree.
And I heard Andy's dog tree. We walked in the swamp dere and got to mine
first and Andy's dog was sitting over yonder. Mine was on a great big old
poplar. I throwed the light up dere, coon come around the top. Stuck his head
and shoulders down in the hole up dere and backed out. Made another circle
around the tree and he come back on my side of the tree. I dropped him. Here
come anodder one around dat tree. And I got 'im too. Both o'dem come to the
ground at the one time. The dog got one o'dem and I told the colored fellow,
I told 'im, now you stomp the other one over dere.

   Dat other dog o'Andy's was sitting over dere treeing. All right, now I go
over 'ere and see dat this one over 'ere got. Wasn't too big a tree. I looked up

dere and in a little bit I seen one. I shot dat one out. Looked back up dat tree and in just a little bit, I seen anodder one in dat tree. I shot dat one. I shot two coons out for each one o'dem dogs and I believe dere was one in dat hollow tree. How come dat other one to back out, in other words, up dere in dat dere 'ere my dog was? Dey had run dem coons for ova two hours.

The whole family of dem, dey was all arunning together. But whenever dey treed, dey didn't all go up in the same tree. The dogs run dem so hard dat den dey hit the tree, dey didn't know dat tree dey hit. I'm saying dat dey thought the dead tree my dog was at was the tree dey were making for and the dog was so close on dem and so many coons on dere dat the coon didn't have time to go up dere and had to go on over 'ere and go up anodder tree. Dat's what I'm athinking.

Through their dogs, hunters experience the capriciousness of their adversary, the coon. For the most part, the coon's tactics remain hidden from view, like the shades of night which cover all such maneuvers. Its tricks of survival become visible through reconstructing events through the vocal tracings of the dogs. If there is admiration for the sharpness of the pursued, it is countered by the belief in the skills and persistence of its pursuers:

You take an old coon, we get out there and he's running, that dog be trailing. Put it dis way, he done had a head start. He hears the dog on his track and he knows. He'll run up on the side of a tree and he'll jump off ova yonder. Now what do you call dat? I call dat a cunning animal! Some dogs will just run right up there to that tree and just sit there and say, here he is, come on down here. With another dog, instead of doing dat, he'll go up there and he'll circle around out yonder and he'll pick the track up out yonder and he might let you know, he say, he's been here. One's sittin' up there tellin' you he's here, but that there one is sayin' he's been here and he'll circle off out yonder and he'll pick his track up and go with him again. Well, after a while the dog will be successful, in other words, he will make him go to a tree.

If you hunt 'im enough, you can be over yonder half a mile and by what dat dog's adoing you can read dat track just like you're reading dem questions to us off dat paper. When you understand your dogs and you've hunted dem enough, you can read every move of dem.

Some men search continually for competent and compatible dogs. Sometimes one buys into the illusion of a winner, accepting the evaluations of another rather than trusting one's own judgment. Such lofty ambitions attract disreputable dealers who sell inferior animals to unsuspecting buyers. Anyone is a ready victim of more knowledgeable wheeler-dealers:

I sold him because I just wanted something or other that would get on the tree a little bit faster. See, he was a little slow in locating the tree. He was a good coon dog. He was the best one I've ever owned, as a matter of fact, and he hunts good and trees good, but he's slow on locating. See, in competition, you've got to have something or another to find that tree and get on it and stay there so whenever you get to the tree he's there. And there's a lot of times that these other dogs will tree and he might get about a second or maybe third tree, but usually I got about first track on him. He was finding that tree a whole lot faster than what he had been at whenever I started competition.

SAM: *And you sold him to buy another dog?*

Yeah, this here's one that a man's had that he's had a pretty good while and I'm kind of ashamed to tell you how much I got in him and he's not even ready. I'm in the process of getting him ready, I'll put it that way. They say he's the fastest thing that he's ever hunted and he's been in for about fifteen or twenty years, in business. He said that he's the best dog he's ever owned.

SAM: *Can you believe what other people tell you about their dogs? Did you take him out for a trial run?*

Well, there's a lot of people that's been hunting with him that said he was just like that. Well, the man was wanting my dog so I let him have my dog and he carried him up yonder to Georgia and sold him for me. Sold him for me, about one thousand dollars out of him. Well, I had a gyp there that was out of Hickory Nut Harry and she was ready and everybody had been trying to get that dog off of him and they couldn't. He sold that dog for two thousand dollars one time, one that I got now, so I decided that I'd try and get him. So I had to give him fourteen hundred dollars for that dog and he told me that if I ever got shed of him that he wanted the first chance to buy him back. And he's about three years old now.

SAM: *Well, has he been worth it to you?*

I don't know. Whenever I got him he was et up with the heart worms and I been having to treat him for the heart worms and next week will be the deadline on that. I got to carry him back next week and he's supposed to check him to see if the heart worms are all gone and if they is, we're gonna start him on the preventive. Then he said I could start hunting him.

SAM: *You didn't bring your dog here for competition?*

Oh, no. He's not down here. See, I ain't hunted him none. Matter of fact, I hunted the dog one time and then forgot him. And I treed then but I didn't never seen no coon. I don't even know if the dog'll run or tree a coon or not.

SAM: *So aren't you taking a big risk in getting him?*

Right. I'm gonna end up with about fifteen to sixteen hundred dollars in him by the time I get him ready.

Not all men can afford such patience or postponement of their ambitions. Once a dog's faults are discovered, it may be traded off to others less picky or knowledgeable. However, dogs that do not measure up to their owners' aspirations or show despicable traits are usually sacrificed:

I bought a Redbone. She was about the size of dat dawg dere. Good dawg. She waz a good dawg. She waz a runnin' and treein' her own coon. I went out there one mornin' and dat bitch snapped at me. I didn't do a damn thing. I went right back into the house and got ma gun and shot her. Killed her. I stopped whosoever damn fault it was. I stopped it. I'm feedin' dat thing and she snapped at me.

Stories, both fanciful and real, are but one aspect of the information communicated through the medium of the dogs. The other aspect is in the formal competitions and the sorting of owners according to the outcomes.

"You'll Own Only One Good Dog in Your Lifetime and Judge All the Rest by Him"

We now examine the bench and nite competitions from the viewpoint of several Masters of Hounds, who are paid to officiate at these occasions. They determine which dogs measure up to the standards set for the breeds and sanction their choices by presenting trophies. Their comments and evaluations are a step removed, or a sleight of hand away, from those of the owners.

A Master of Hounds explains the bench show and the many breeds recognized by the sponsoring organization. The important criteria are functional ones, enabling the dog to stand and to pursue. All dogs come from basically the same stock.[4] Permitting unregistered ("grade") dogs in these competitions allows their owners to notch, if not destabilize, the more refined standards of breeds and money:

Well, for the big trophy, you're talking a best registered female of show and best registered male of show. A champion of show and a grand champion of show and you've got some grade dogs and have a best grade female and a best grade male.

SAM: *What does a registered dog have, a breeding certificate?*

A breeding certificate, a certificate of ownership from the United Kennel Club (UKC). There's also another organization, the American Coon Hunters' Association (ACHA). Both of them operate basically the same, but they're two different kennel clubs. Most of your hunts through here are UKC.

You show males and females separate. Never together. They have different standards. Females are supposed to be a certain height, males a certain height, weight and different classifications. You have six breeds. Black and Tan, Blue Tick, English, Plott, Redbone, and Walker. To start with, you show the male Black and Tan first.

Alphabetical order. You show males first. UKC policy. Up until last year, you could show either one first. This year to make everything standard, they specified males first. You have three classes. A puppy class, which is from the time the puppy's born up until he reaches one year of age. From one year of age to two years, he is a junior. Then after two years of age and over, he's a senior. You get a winner out of each class. Then you bring all the male winners back and show for the best male Black and Tan, first class. Then you go to females, same thing, same classes. You get the Black and Tan, and then in alphabetical order, you get the Blue Tick male and female, English male and female, Redbone male and female, Plott male and female, and Walker male and female. I got the Plott and Redbone switched. Then you bring all the male breed winners back and show for best registered male. That dog that wins that has won everything, he can win on the bench that day.

Then you bring the females back, show all six breeds for the best registered female of the show. The female that has won that, has won everything she can for that day. OK, then you move into champion class. This is a dog that has won best of show and has accumulated one hundred points. All champions show together, male and female, Blue Tick, Redbone, etc. You put all the champions on the bench and there's only one winner. Next you go to grand champion. All the dogs show together. A dog that is a grand champion is a dog that has won three champion shows and he becomes a grand champion. After he becomes a grand champion, he's gone as high as he can go in UKC without going through a national hunt. And then you go to your grade dogs. A grade dog is something UKC doesn't even recognize. This is just local club rules for boys and men who are hunting nonregistered dogs. You show all your females together no matter what breeding they are. You show them all and get one grade female and the same thing for males.

These boys know what it takes for a win. People can look at a dog and tell that. I mean I might be judging the dog, but they know what it takes. If I make a bad call, they know it. And you get a reputation for making a lot of bad calls and you won't be asked back.

On any particular day, maybe one dog feels a little better and he's more alert than on the next day. And just because this dog beat one on one given date is no sign that he's going to beat him the next time he shows. But now the most important points on all the dogs is his back. You want a strong back, a slight arch. Don't want a swayback dog. You want good strong straight legs and catfooted (up on its toes).

All the tree dogs at one time were basically one breed. They gradually separated out over the years and the Walker and Blue Tick were all one breed. Walker men pulled out. They were looking for one thing and the Blue Tick men were looking for something else. And the Black and Tan and Redbone. One guy breed for a red dog and the other guy liked Black and Tan. So at one time, both of them were saddlebacks, and all the dogs are basically the same so you're not looking for the same characteristics. Good straight legs, strong characteristics that make a dog hunt good. Good wide lungs make for plenty of air so he's got a lot of endurance and all. And, of course, your hound ears. That's one of the characteristics that don't make them go any better. Long flappy ears protect his ears where they get ticks stuck in them and all. The Black and Tan has the longest ear span. They must touch the end of his nose.

Another Master of Hounds talks of organizational changes and of ambition. The interview begins with my observation that he seems to judge the bench show by eyesight, rather than taking specific measurements on the dogs in each class:

Right, if it'd been a big show, the height might have made a difference and I would have a ruler right there tape recording it. There weren't but one or two that would push the top. This kinda shows that your dogs are close enough that you don't have to worry about it.

Now there are some rule changes made during the year which are placed in *Full Cry* magazine. There're minors of things I should watch for to cut out errors that happened last year. Like the papers you're supposed to have to enter the dogs. You have deadlines to meet. This is getting well organized now. Used to be that you could bring a dog in if you had his number you could hunt, but now you take each as it stands. The president of the association says, if you can't do it right, don't do it. And this has made a change in the people who's willing to hunt. I got cussed out about four times at another club hunt because a judge had taken the crimp off the papers before and I come up there and tell 'em, "Do it by the rules." They get mad because they thinks it's my fault.

SAM: *So the competitions are getting more organized.*

Yeah. You know, the large and small papers that people's been bringing in here. For every dog in the bench show, you must have both papers. The small paper shows who owns the dog, the big paper shows its age. And there are strict classes. All right, they bring in the big paper here, and I don't know who owns the dog. They bring in the little paper and I don't know how old he is. And these guys will swear that this dog is two years old, but I got no way of knowing. But what they was doing at this club was taking the big paper and entering them in a hunt. They're gradually cleaning all that up. And most of the clubs go with the deadline thing.

Now I went to a club about four years ago. To start with, they didn't communicate with me, like not much. Then they was taking entries up to the 7 o'clock deadline and they got it extended to 7:45 P.M. All right, another thing they was doing, all dogs must have an equal chance of draw against each other. When I first started that was the way they did it, you put the numbers in a cap. If you think you are going to have about ten casts, you put ten ones and ten twos and let them draw for the cast. But you can't do that no more. You don't know how many dogs you're going to have so you fill out the quick entry blank. Now everybody draws against each other.

SAM: *Tell me how you got into coon hunting.*

I got into it 'cause I couldn't do a thing else. I was fifteen years old going to school, working in the afternoons after school. The only time I had left to do anything was at night. Another thing I had was eye trouble. I have got that cleared up now but still when I was growing up as a kid I didn't get into rabbit hunting and stuff 'cause I couldn't see well enough. But my brother started and brother-in-law and I started going with them. And night hunts was all I could do 'cause it was the only time I had. I started, dropped out at different times, but I always went back. And I got into judging part of it about three years ago 'cause it got to where every hunt you went to there weren't but about two or three judges, see, and one of them was bad.

SAM: *What do you mean that one of the judges was bad?*

It's technical. In other words, we had one of them that favored a certain breed. We had one who wouldn't go by the rules. Stuff like that.

SAM: *You mean his errors were so visible that even the spectators could tell?*

Right. So I got into it and I have been judging ever since. I also had a friend who was one of the national judges. He judges all the big shows in the country and he said, "If you're worried about it, why don't you be one yourself. You can solve your own problem then!" So I went into it. I've judged the Grand American this year. Made bad calls, but I know it.

SAM: *Tell me about that. You learned from your mistakes, didn't you?*

I did it right. A friend, I judged his dog twenty times, and he never said a word, but when I said that dog is the best-looking dog, he said, "You done made a mistake!" Right, it's too late for that show, but I was at this dog and he was right. Once you make a decision, it's gone, it's already past. I told him the next time I saw him. It don't bother me, I know I can make mistakes. There are some judges that won't admit it. We've got some people now straining about some of the calls out there today. But by the way I read the rules, the right dog won. Just like that guy that just come in here. He showed a dog that's not of the same breed. He got beat by a different breed. He jerked that sucker off, then he brought a female Plott here that was the best dog on the bench. The only trouble I get into sometimes is trying to be too impartial. You judge your friend's dog, your breed, harder than you would just somebody bringing in the dog and putting it up.

The problem is that I'm too impartial. You try and compensate for it. Well, I realize my problem and try and weigh the impartial aspects so I come up right.

I do this judging show more than I've hunted. All my free time at home is spent in getting ready. Like today, I was late today 'cause some fool done called and tole me that he was going to be there where I work this morning and I had to go down and show him what he needed.

I breed English dogs. I've got the best ole girl right now. Brought a young male and got another female, but I've got puppies. I've shipped puppies all over the country.

The first year I had a big volume. I cut back and went for quality. I bred part of the bitches all the time, the ones I didn't like I took 'em out. I just replaced them with a better dog. Trying to improve. Wasn't interested in producing two hundred puppies a year. I'd rather produce one good one. I just found a dog that got the blood line, breeding, and performance.

SAM: *Is making money your motivation?*

I'll tell you what I'm after—producing the best dog in the country. And I'm going to produce the world championship dog whether I own it or someone else owns it. Just so it's got my name on that picture at the top of the ACHA hunt. It's a once-a-year hunt. It is *the* money hunt in the country. It is the biggest hunt, ACHA World Hunt. The ACHA will hunt five hundred dogs. It's a five-night elimination hunt.

SAM: *So your purpose is to get your name on a champion. What will that get you besides your name and picture in the papers?*

I want to produce that dog that will win. Well, notoriety, the money part of it don't bother me. I have never been motivated by money in such things as my work, my dogs, or anything. If I see a dog I like, I will pay for it, but you have to understand that I'm not able to pay the amounts that some people can.

SAM: *One of your objectives is to be able to live off your hunts and dogs?*

Well, I think there's three people in the country that's doing that. I'm not sure I can make a leader. I enjoy working, one of those weirdos that enjoys working. I don't want to get that big, takes too much from you. You have to go and be there at every show 'cause maybe you could sell a dog or something.

Like enforcement officers, Masters of Hounds are at the forefront of change— making sure contestants conform to the lines laid down by more distant organizations. Judges take the guff when locals resist such regimentation. Bad judges, like bad judgment calls, are not peculiar to coon hunters. In any competition where show rankings have equivalents in cash and enhanced reputation, the prospect for fraud is a serious problem.

The position of Master of Hounds is acquired by patronage. Often this includes an apprenticeship coupled with a desire to know why and how things happen. The following Master talks about his nonconsumptive interests, the differences between dogs, and the nature of coons:

To me, I have no particular idea to get out and kill something. I was brought up to believe that if you kill it you're supposed to eat it. If I caught a fish and I brought it home, my mother made me clean it and I eat it, one time or another, and I don't have a desire to kill anything.

SAM: *How would you describe a coon to somebody who didn't know what it was? Say the characteristics that make coon hunting so enjoyable for you?*

His ability to run and climb a tree. You can turn a fox dog loose and he can run all night long and you may never see a fox. Same thing for a deer dog, he can run all day. You don't know whether he's doing anything or not. All you do is get out here and run all day. A bird dog, a retriever, is strictly mechanical. Coon dog, there's nothing in the world mechanical about him. You've got to teach him to have enough sense to do it on his own. Good coon dog, you can turn him loose, you can hear a good chase, might last for one hundred yards, might last for ten miles, but sooner or later, for that dog to accomplish what he started out to do, he's got to tree. And I think an old coon's a fairly smart animal. He's a lot of things the others doesn't do. A deer, he just runs and that old coon can climb up here, run through a fence, he can climb up a tree and jump off, throw the dogs out, and he can go upstream in a creek. He's tried all these things. He must have a little bit of sense, a little bit of this, that, and the other.

I have always been the type that if I'm going to participate in something, I want to be in a position to know what's going on. Acting as a Master of Hounds keeps me in touch with more people who know what's going on, and I'm not one to sit back and keep my mouth shut. If I make a decision on my judgment call, I'm man enough to speak out. I'm the type of guy who's willing to make a decision and stick by it and step out in front of people and say it's got to be this way, where the other guy maybe don't want the responsibility. It's a pleasure and when it gets to where it's not a pleasure, I'll quit.

Still another Master of Hounds talks about dogs and their scoring for the nite hunt. His characterization of coon hunters, in jest for my benefit, shows his familiarity with an outsider's view:

The bench show means a lot, but now 99 percent of men here had rather have a dog that runs and trees a coon than have one that will show. It helps if you got a dog that's a show champion and a nite champion. But if you have a choice, it would be a nite champion.

Most of your people who are breeding dogs will breed to a dual grand champion—that is, grand day and nite champion. A nite champion is one that won in the nite hunts. He's got the looks and also the ability that goes with it.

SAM: *Now what does he get for that?*

Stud fees and recognition. That's what these hunts are about. That's what most of the guys here are wanting, grand nite champions so them breeds can get started.

Stud fees run from seventy-five dollars to one hundred dollars. World champions get four hundred a clip. Puppy's one hundred out of a good dog, but I've seen puppy's high as two hundred fifty dollars or three hundred dollars out of a World Champion. For some people, it's big business. For the average man, it's just a hobby and he will spend money on it. Just like fishing and golfing. People will think you are crazy for putting out. But you go around here and offer a man $500 for a good broke rigid dog. He'll laugh at you, walk off. It takes a thousand or fifteen hundred dollars to buy a decent dog, and this isn't even a championship one, just your average dog. Grand nite or show champion will cost you five to six thousand dollars. You put six thousand dollars in a dog, they will tell you you're crazy.

SAM *Anything else I should know about coon hunting, or shouldn't know?*

Everyone will lie to you, especially if they own a dog. To become a coon hunter, you need to lie and cheat and chew tobacco!

SAM: *Is the relationship between the man and the dog the most important relationship in coon hunting?*

Like in sports, you have good and bad. Coons are eighteen dollars a piece this season. You got men out thar who are after every living coon. You got men out thar who don't care whether you kill them or not. And they are thar for the dogs. I enjoy the dogs, that's what I'm out thar for. I kill my share of the coons. I enjoy a good dog better'n anything else in the world. A man can really go out and buy a dog and have no personal feelings toward him whatsoever. Put him in the pen and take him out into the field and it not mean a thing in the world. But as far as winning the hunt, a man has got to know his dog, know when that dog is cold trailing, know when he's in water, just by his bark. And the scoring system is based upon striking your dog when he first smells a track. The dog is not supposed to bark until he smells a coon.

If he barks, tell the judge to strike my dog. The first dog that strikes gets 100 points, second gets 75, third gets 50 points, and fourth gets 25. And you have got to know your dogs to be able to call it. The dog whose handler calls first tree gets 125 points, second 75 points, third 50 points, and fourth 25 points. You can split treeing points among all dogs in a cast if they decide and each gets 33-⅓ points rather than give them all to one dog. If the dog trees a possum he gets minus points. Deer is just minus points. If he barks on a track and quits and comes back he gets minus points. The only way in the world which he can get plus points is strike and tree a coon.

SAM: *So each hunter has a dog and knows what its bark is like and he can differentiate it from the others. How do you know when a dog lies to you, when he just barks?*

It happens. You got plenty of dogs that are called automatic strike dogs. You turn him loose and yawk, yawk, yawk, right on and on. But now you know he's out there and there's nothing to do about it. What you have to do is prove when he quits and comes back to you and gets his minus points. Now, if he was pulled up and treed on a telephone pole, a slick tree, he definitely gets minus points for lying.

SAM: *So there's a challenge in getting the dog to do what you want him to do?*

Yep, like the man said, you'll own only one good dog in your lifetime. Everybody's looking for him. But you will find one dog in your life that you will judge all the other dogs by as the best. Now don't rush off, you're liable to learn something.

"When the Tailgate Drops, the Bullshit Stops" (Bumper Sticker)

With the dogs, the proof of performance comes not with the tales of its owner, but with getting the jump on other cast members in the nite hunt. That's the jest of the bumper sticker quoted above. Although pedigrees and appearances are important for the discriminations made in the daytime at the bench show, the night performance is what counts. It is then that grade dogs can demonstrate that mere looks are no compensation for performance afield. Coon dogs, like their owners, are workers. Only the Champion and Grand Champion dogs are protected from parvenues. They hunt in casts consisting of canines of similar status.

The following events and conversations are from my field notes for a UKC nite hunt, July 26–27, 1979.

There are 103 dogs registered for the nite hunt by the deadline of 7 P.M. At 7:15 P.M. the Master of Hounds assembles all handlers in front of the clubhouse, assigns them to their respective cast, and appoints a guide and a judge to casts that request them. Guides come from the sponsoring club, know the local terrain and sites habituated by coons, and are generally assigned to casts of novices or handlers who have come from a distance. It is not necessary for a judge to attend each cast, for the handlers may serve as their own judge, provided they all agree on the distribution of points at each call. The Master of Hounds mentions the general rules: coons must be seen to be counted, dogs may hunt for up to three hours, and the score cards much be returned by 3 A.M. to be included in the tabulations for winners. There are twenty-five casts of four dogs each and one championship cast of three dogs. My friend, a sociologist, decides to join the championship cast while I accompany another regular cast. After the hunt is concluded, my friend and I compare notes on our way home.

Each cast leaves the clubhouse and hunts in a different area. The cast I join has a nonhunting judge and a guide in addition to four dog handlers. I travel in a truck with the judge and the guide. The handlers, previously unacquainted, follow our lead in their trucks. On our way to the first casting site the conversation in the lead truck turns to memories of past hunts and poor losers.

JUDGE: Every onced in a while you will run into a man who there's something that's happened between him and that other fella. Something or other, he thought he got gypted.

SAM: *So he doesn't want to hunt with him.*

JUDGE: Well, sometimes with judges too. That's happen especially with a hunting judge.[5] Sometimes, now if a man strikes and knows the rules and while he makes the decision he don't back up and he don't give a little bit, you know. You can get yourself in trouble by not sticking right to the rules. And one man sometimes he will think the man's being too hard on him or something. Thinks the man's taking something away from his dog.

SAM (to the guide): *Do you know where we will hunt first tonight?*

GUIDE: Yep. Well, I put it dis way. First place I'm going into, if someone hasn't beat me to it, we'll hunt. A little place ova here on Wool Creek runs into Drowning Creek. And if nobody's at de place, we'll hunt it and den we will move to Blue Farm right across from Mouse Creek. If things work out for us, we'll hunt a little while in one place and den hunt another. We hunt for three clocked hours. We might not see a coon in dat time. We might see five or six, but I'se alookin' maybe we tree two maybe three. We have got to see it to count it. If it goes in a hollow tree and we can't see 'im or make 'im come out to where we can see it while de dogs point, den we circle de points and dey only count in a tie. We can only have ten minutes on de tree lookin' for de coon.

SAM: *Do the landowners know that we plan to hunt on their land this evening?*

GUIDE: Well, yeah, de biggest part of it. Now, I didn't get written permission. We are supposed to have written permission, but all dese folks on land I'se be ahunting on now have gif me permission to hunt. Put it dis way, allotatimes a man will let you hunt by you going and coming to ask 'im. If you didn't ask 'im and he catches you down thar, he would run you off and never would letcha hunt thar nomo'.

SAM: *Have you hunted these particular lands before during the year?*

GUIDE: Oh, yeah. I don't know how many times I've hunted in heah. I've been in heah on some nite hunts, on some buddy hunts, and I've been in heah just flashing. I've already caught several coons, I don't know how many. And dere's still coon in heah from de last time I run coons but I didn't get nar one o'dem. Treed three times and I knowed we got one slick tree.

We arrive at our first release point and stop along a dirt road bordering a field and woods. The men assemble their dogs around the judge and the guide before turning the dogs loose. The judge asks the handlers to tell him about any particular characteristics their dogs have which might enter into his judgments and scores. Three handlers mention characteristics of their dogs:

Mine won't leave a tree by herself.

Well, I've seen mine one time go back to the tree. Outsida dat, she's just independent.

Mine's independent, I'll put it dat way. Far all that, libel to go one way and she might go annudder. She's running a track, but she just won't break ma track.

The guide asks everyone to synchronize their watches with his. Then he retrieves his compass from his pocket and reminds them that, "anyway we go back up thar we come back west." He leads the handlers and their dogs to the edge of the woods. The dogs are turned loose at the judge's signal and the three-hour competition begins. The dogs wander around close to their handlers at first, sniffing the ground. Then they drift deeper into the woods and are lost to sight. The guide tells the handlers about the nature of the terrain, and the judge mentions handling options for the first three minutes.

Each of the dogs opens as it "strikes" a coon trail and is called by its handler. The judge records points for the dog depending upon whether it is the first, second, third, or last to open on the track. When a coon is treed, the dog's bark changes, and the first handler to call his dog "treed" receives more points than the others in the sequence.

When each of the dogs is "struck" and "treed" by its handlers, we leave the edge of the woods and proceed to the dogs, now about a half mile away. We pick our way through the thick underbrush and arrive at the tree where the dogs are barking. One dog is missing. The handlers catch and tie the other dogs. Then they shine their light beams over the tree and squall like a wounded coon to induce a coon, if present, to open its eyes, thereby reflecting the light. There is a leaf nest in the tree, but no coon shows as a handler jerks on vines leading from the nest to the ground. After ten minutes, with no coon visible, all points on the judge's tally are circled. The outcome of this encounter remains neutral unless later there is a tie; then these points will count. We leave in search of the missing dog trailing in the distance. The other dogs are turned loose. Conversations among handlers continue with frequent pauses to listen for the dogs. The handler with the missing dog attempts an explanation.

HANDLER: See the big part is if mine hadn't barked in ten minutes, they could have still had theirs in hand. I got mine minus points back there because mine left the tree. And she went back on the track. Track was mighty cold.

JUDGE: Twenty-five points is all you'se gonna get.

SAM: *Do you think the dogs will circle back to the same tree we just left?*

GUIDE: Naw, now dey might. Dat's a possibility but I think dey're headed data way. Dey have either stricken another track or dat coon has ripped up another tree. Dey have it or if he won't dey got de track where he laid it. See, we had a nest up dat tree dere and dere was vines and we couldn't swear dat were a coon on up dere although we shook de nest. And I've seem 'em lay silent.

HANDLER (explaining): I tole de judge, judge just remember now if she goes on da trot when one dog's atreed I want ma strike points. Because now that's the only times that would have done me any good if she had been at dat tree. If I had struck it, them strike points would have been struck out, been no good.

SAM: *So you had to make that call before you went down to the tree, didn't you?*

HANDLER: Un huh, but here's what it was. Them other boys were done treed. After a dog trees, then you can be no more dogs struck that goes to that tree. That's the way it is. Now you are supposed to strike your dog if they go to that tree, then you cross 'em out. But if she goes on like my dog did then it still stays open, see. If she had went over there and got anodder tree, it would have been circled, minused or plused, whatever the dog deserved.

JUDGE: Still, when she trees, them udder dogs can't be on strike. So she had to go back in, unless she split trees. Your dog had to go on a separate track because the tree was closed on that track. After all four dogs are declared treed that track is declared closed. She was minus on the tree, open on another track. If the big judge ever comes through and asks any questions, we will have to tell him just what happened.

ANOTHER HANDLER: Now I tell you what, I'd say he's right. That's when it's getting a little bit complicated. But that puts the clock on it for sure.

HANDLER: I was gambling you know, when I called my dog treed. I knowed she wasn't settled like she oughta be. She was giving me some noise and I didn't have but a few seconds to call her, but then again she treed 'em. As long as they are holding the track open, you can go on and on.

JUDGE: That's right. After you get to the tree, the first man who calls the dogs treed gets the most points, 125 points, 75 points for the second one, 50 points for the third, and 25 points for the fourth.

We drift through the woods in the general direction taken by the dogs. Conversation is intermittent. I break a period of silence by asking the judge why men participate in these competitions, and he replies:

Some of them use the club as a sport. They like to coon hunt now, but they find out that they can make a living if they raise the right kind of dogs. A whole lot of dis hyar field trials is to put a man and a dog in competition to make a champion out of him. So it advertizes his dogs and he's using that dar dog to stud and to find out what he's throwing off as offspring. If they comes up anything near like his is, then the man can pay his way with his sport through his dogs. He won't have to take anything outta his job, no money. Just like that school teacher from South Carolina I introduced ya to at the club house. Now he had one dog. He bred him some and was throwing some good offspring 'cause he was from Ohio and he paid $4000 for the dog. He had anodder one right after dat man offered him $5500 for him and he went a hunt one night. That skinny got run over and got killed.

The dogs are trailing along the creek some distance ahead. We return quickly to the trucks and drive to a paved road that transects the creek downstream. We catch the dogs as they cross the highway. Apparently the coons crossed earlier and escaped into dense swamp. When all the dogs are recovered, the judge signals that 64 of our allocated 180 minutes have expired. At this point, all dogs have circled points.

We turn the dogs loose at two other locations. They strike and tree at each place. A coon is seen at the second strike so all dogs now have plus points. Returning to the trucks after seeing the coon, the judge signals that 9 minutes of hunting time remain. Both he and the guide discuss the prospects for finding a coon in the remaining minutes.

JUDGE: Well, while we are riding be thinking of a good place and if we don't strike nothing we won't say nothing. We'll just head on into the clubhouse with everybody got plus points now. If they strike something, they might come in with minuses. We're gonna have to give them dogs a pep talk before we turn 'em loose.

GUIDE: Well, dere's a streak right ova here now. It's up on a hill. It's got good oaks in it, dogwoods in it, got hollars in it, grapevines, but dere could also be a deer in it too. I've got a whole lota places to go, but I'm trying to figure out what's de best. I know where dere's a short swamp at and whenever I've been dere, it's a pretty good little swamp. Dere was a fresh coon track at de upper end of it, and he had been afollowering around dere a bit lately. Now let me back up here and we'll try dat little short swamp.

Dis used to be a big plantation. Dere's 3,400 acres now and I knowed dere's been 1,500 sold off of it. One of de heirs sold all of 'is. Now dere will be two different branches, but you could throw a rock in either one of 'em. But since time's a little on the short side, I'll take de one on the left. Dat's where I seen dat coon track right out yonder on de edge of dat woods.

The dogs are let loose at the edge of the woods. They begin trailing immediately and tree a coon within the time remaining. All cast members spot the coon, exclaiming how big he is. The dogs are recovered and the cast reassembles at the trucks prior to departing for the clubhouse. The time is 2 A.M.

GUIDE I enjoyed being in the woods wif everyone of ya and I hope to be in de woods wif ya again sometime soon.

OTHERS: We enjoyed it I tell ya dat. Excellent job.

JUDGE: Well, I hope you don't think I gypted ya. I judged it all right.

OTHERS: I don't see a thing that went wrong tonight. Boy, I think everything went mighty.

Ya put down what we put on dem dogs.

My dog is hollering now telling me what a stupid idiot I was to call her on that tree off ayonder when she was barking. Rather she was atrying to get through the woods.

Well, I tell ya one thing, there's not many times when you put out four times and run yourself four covers. We done run five tonight.

Yeah, ever time we asked for it in a certain time he would gif it to us. Yeah, he sure did.

I leave for the clubhouse with the judge and the guide. Both are happy about the turn of events and about the fact that all the dogs have plus points. The guide comments:

I felt like we'd get dem tracks pretty quick or none at all. Now dat's how I felt about it. And I knowed like I'd told you acoming down, I knowed where a coon's acoming in from off dat field off up yonder. In the summer time, de plum bushes are planted all up in hyar. Coons range right across into dem grape vines and all. Plenty of feed. And up here around de curve, dere's anodder field, little sprig of swamp. Right down in thar, about two acres of it, you can walk all around it and still stay on the hill. Dis is the only high level at dis place. I didn't tell ya, but we really weren't supposed to turn loose afta midnight. 'Cause it's Sunday morning, ya see. Now if a dog had been arunning just like we put out down dere, any warden could have pulled if he had been across at us. If he awanted to get down dere and got tight on us. But on dis certain place here, I have never seen a game warden on it in de last fifteen years.

He's welcome, ya see, but de fellow back dere he oversees de place and dat's part of 'is job to see dat nobody don't come in here dat aren't supposed to be in here. De people dat owned it, dey're primarily interested in birds—quail. Now dese coons will tur up a quail nest. Now I don't mean dat dey would just go out and tur one up, but if dey run up on a bird's nest, dey will tur it up and dey aren't as bad as some of de other animals in the woods, like foxes.

We return to the clubhouse by the 3 A.M. deadline. Some of the club members, including their spouses, have remained at the house, preparing grits, bacon, toast, and eggs which the returning handlers purchase. The proceeds from these sales, together with the profits from the tickets for the dog events, support the club.

At 3:30 A.M., the Master of Hounds awards the trophies to the dogs having accumulated the highest number of points. One dog in the cast I accompanied wins fourth place with 425 points. Most handlers eat breakfast at the club, for many will spend up to five hours on the road before they arrive home. I return home accompanied by the sociologist who tells me about his experiences with the championship cast:

We had an awful night. It started out very well. We sat down and released the dogs and they had a coon treed in twenty-three minutes! So I thought that was the way things went! And then we took them to another spot and let them loose and we clocked them for an hour and then we were stopped by the game wardens. And so after that we went to another spot and they sprung some cold trails and they went into the swamp and wandered around. And I guess they were on the trail before treeing for an hour and a half. By that time, our time had expired. Some of the trainers made dumb moves. One had some points but he called a tree when it wasn't one, so he was minus 125 points. Apparently a good score for this area is 500 or above. That's only two coons struck and treed by the initial dog without any mistakes.

You asked that I be on the lookout for the application of the rules and their interpretation. I saw an awful lot of interpretation of the rules tonight, kind of bent and squashed! The judge had to do that. We let the dogs go and then we lost track of them and we went looking for them on the road. So after some discussion, the judge decided to call it interference, which means that none of that time which we spent on the road counted. That considerably influences the outcome when you decide that such long stretches of time when nothing was seen counts in the total of three hours. Or the judge warned a fellow that his dog wasn't close enough to the tree and that next time he might consider giving him negative points for it or, at least, not giving any positive points.

It was interesting interaction between all three men. One guy withdrew his dog because another fellow, who's a dog breeder, had insisted that the judge should have taken off points when the former saw his dog run back through where we were all standing and said, oh, that's negative points. And according to the interpretation of the rules, if a dog stopped hunting that would be negative points, but if the dog continued it wouldn't be. What the dog breeder contended was that the owner had to call the dog, and since he said what he did, therefore, it should be negative points. The owner said that he was more or less making an exclamation like, oh, that's negative points! So they had a big debate about it.

None of the people wanted to appear unsportsmanlike. They all insisted that the points be allocated either way. Well, you put a question mark and take it to the Master of Hounds if you can't come to an agreement in the field. But in order to have that question mark resolved by the Master of Hounds, everybody has to go to those involved and ask for his interpretation. And so we were in a bind because we couldn't get our hounds in before the 3 o'clock deadline and the other guy was insisting that it remain a question. And so he could have wiped out the scores from everybody simply by insisting. So one of the parties withdrew his dog as a compromise and then we could send the scores back with another fellow who was just there tagging along. The others could stay and look for the dogs. But it took them about twenty minutes to come to that conclusion.

SAM: *That was an interesting resolution.*

Nothing was really direct. The fellow, who was the dog breeder, he would bring it up and somebody else would bring up another case where the rules were questionable and they decided another thing. Then they would talk about where the dogs were, and then they'd come back to the discussion again. And then they'd walk apart. Then the guide, who was just tagging along as a friend of the judge, would get off and talk about what they should do in this instance. And then they would come back together on it. When we went back to look for the dogs, the judge and I and the dog breeder went and then the other two fellows, who were in competition, went in another direction looking for them. So I think that was a way of separating and of getting rid of the hostility that was there.

It was an interesting situation how they negotiated the rules as they went along. By the judge deciding that when we stopped on the road was an obstruction, he gave us an hour more hunting time. But he wouldn't come out and say it. He would say things like, well, I could call time out here and before he knew it, we'd all decided that it was a time out! The judge was extremely fair. He was doing what you had to do in that situation.

SAM: *The people who must enforce the rules and make judgments are very conscious of what the other people will think of them.*

Yeah, the judge was introduced to the three cast members and people would come over and talk about how fair the judge was. So the night began with that tag on the judge. He's a fair judge; he'll do you right!

SAM: *You picked up some terms?*

Yeah, I got some of them down. Making a lap. It's where the coon keeps backtracking. A more colorful one is pissing on your leg! Ever heard of that one?

SAM: *Is that when the dog does something that he ought not do in front of other people?*

Well, it's when the dogs comes and kind of piddles around or he may be out of sight but he's not going anywhere. Just kind of lollygagging around. They talk about a drifter and a bobbler or a totterer. These may be an individual's terms rather than the group's. A drifter is a dog that will pick up a cold scent and then drift over and catch another scent. A bobbler, or a totterer, is one that will pick up the cold scent and keep going back and forth on the same scent. Not go forward.

SAM: *What would you say about the composition of the groups at the club?*

It was segregated within the clubhouse, I thought. Because all the Indians were in one corner and all the whites in the other corner. But I thought it was remarkable, given that background of people, that there would be such a relatively free mix of people. I would bet that there was just all sorts of different grades of people within the club. The two older men I was hunting with, the dog breeder and the other fellow, were very sophisticated about breeding dogs. They knew an awful lot about it and they knew the laws. They knew the game laws and one of the fellows claimed that he was going to talk to the director of the Wildlife Commission about this midnight curfew.

I got the impression that the executive duties and decision roles weren't exactly desirable, and those were things that were pushed on whoever happened to get roped into it. That reminded me of my mother's family, the men sitting around the house letting the women run around and do things for them. In some ways, it seems that kind of relationship rather than one that was imposed on somebody. Also I was thinking that the occupations most of the men were in conditions them in their other relations in the club. So if you're told what to do all day in your work, maybe you withdraw from formal organization or direct participation. Some of the guys sauntering up there to get the trophies, reminds me of how students are in classes, where they don't come forth as if they like the honor of being chosen for scholarship. They seem to be not only shy but also cynical of any reward!

SAM: *Did you get the feeling that they knew the rules, but they also knew that the rules were not hard and fast? It was rather a chancy exercise to be designated a winner?*

Yeah, I talked to one about that. There's a great deal of chance involved in it. Who you get as a guide is a big chance. What area that guy takes you to is another big chance; even the call that you make for your dog. When you call the tree, there's always the rush to be first because you get the most points then. But that's also an awful lot of luck because the dogs can stop at that tree or go to another one. I asked him about the dog and how he chooses a dog. And there seems in that choice an awful lot of chance. You get a good breeder and yet the dog you buy may not turn out to be very good.

One told a little story. One of them was about a fellow who had accumulated 800 points and eight minutes left in the set hunt. His dog treed a possum and was eliminated. Stories like that illustrate the quirks and chances.

Another way the rules were bent was at the very beginning. The judge said, right before we even left the clubhouse, that if any of the dogs had any peculiarities to tell him right then. That was a way of bending the rules because you could have said, my dog doesn't get close to the tree or whatever and the judge would have to adjust the call to that behavior.

Do you know what running trash is?

SAM: *That's like chasing possum?*

Yeah, I don't know if this is the time to talk about putting the pencil on something, which meant, you scratch your dog and give it negative points. One of the men talked about one dog that he was offered $3,000 for.

You know that fellow who came with me? He said that you've run into him not only in this club but also in a deer-hunting club too!

SAM: *Yeah, some of these men hunt different game and get around in the community. I've learned from seeing them in different roles at different times.*

Let's see. I already told you about the midnight limit and the license thing with the game warden. One of the men told a long game warden story. The only reason I mention it is because it sounds fanciful and maybe it's a folktale. The young game warden had just gotten out of game warden school, drove by and saw our gentleman walking across this field with his gun. It was after sundown in quail season. So he drove up and he stopped him and said he was gonna give him a ticket. And my friend said he wasn't hunting, he was taking his dog back and if he took him out to the road the dog would get killed. And the game warden insisted and eventually he had to let his dog go. His favorite retriever crossed the road and was struck and killed. And he got so mad then, he told the game warden that he wouldn't accept the citation. And so the game warden took it down to the sheriff and asked that the sheriff go up there and pick him up and the sheriff wouldn't do it. Of course, he wouldn't pick up a fine fellow like the one telling the story. Then he went to trial and the judge threw out the case, vindicating him against this young, upstart game warden. Later a retriever puppy showed up at his house, so he was sure that the game warden, feeling badly about what he had done, had brought and delivered it. And now this game warden never asks our gentleman for his license or anything like that.

Another fellow followed that one with a story about how he shot three doe deer, apparently without a doe permit in this area. He boldly drove his car up right to the place where the game warden was getting a coke, talked to the warden, and drove away, getting away with the three dead does and fooling the game warden. Or about another foolish guy, who hid his deer in the bushes and then put them in his trunk. This fellow wasn't bold to simply bluff it. He kept feigning and being fearful and then when he finally did make his move, they caught him and confiscated his truck, his gun, his knife, and sold them all. And he was convicted and got a big fine and sent to the county jail. I'm sure there's a whole catalog with those people and their game warden stories, beating the game warden or having the game warden make false amends.

The Bark from the Bottom (The Bottom Line)

Through their recreational and conversational modes, coon hunters provide a clear message of their social standing within the rural community. Their recreations and the rules they play by enable them to re-create and sustain their egalitarian standings. Created in the hunter's image, the dogs perform out of sight but not without a hearing. They remind us that many of the pedigrees and social conventions within the larger society may not hold sanction under more practiced scrutiny and that resoluteness changes with the times and the circumstances. Rules made at one time may be broken or modified at others, especially if they are a means to keeping everybody at a par. The poor man's "tale" may be just as crafty as that of the rich; the coon may be smarter than the fox. Maybe the Old Man was right to assert that the coon was created so adults could leave their routines and not have to take life so seriously.[6]

Ten

Fowl Play: The Passage from Quail to Quacks

My favorite time of the year has got to be from the middle of October to the middle of November. It's a sad time of the year in a way. The productivity of the year has come to an end, and you can see it, see the leaves falling off the trees. I guess it's sort of symbolic for the end of life. But it's harvest time and wildlife is really at its peak. The days are nice, usually cool, crisp. You get to thinking about the things you're gonna do and the things you've done. It's a pretty good time to be outside. Never in my whole adult life have I ever had any time to enjoy that time of year! Summer is my least favorite time and that's when I have the time.

(A Scotland County Teacher)

HUNTING is not ephemera in a play world of little consequence. It is about life and death, about methods and means, about power and standing, about stories and myths, about buying and selling, about winning and losing, about economics and ecology, about people and the beasts within and without. The hunting cloth originates and connects with most other activities within the sorted continua of cultural behavior. Hunting is inseparable from the wider worlds of social and environmental realities, and its meanings entwine with them. Only by scanning both channels can we appropriately interpret its messages.

Many of the hunting forms in Scotland County and in the rural South have their roots in a predominantly agrarian social world. These rhythms from the past beat through the sentiments of the teacher quoted above, who senses a loss in the shift from the agricultural seasons of his youth to the industrial work cycles of his present livelihood. The close associations of work, neighborhood, and kinship that provided the earlier meanings are eclipsed now by the corporate endeavors of working away from the land and the mass cultural activities of more regional and national groupings.

We begin this chapter with a discussion of some boundaries within and around the hunting fraternity. Those who hunt are not oblivious to shades of behavior within their ranks nor to the impending crisis in sensibilities between those who, like themselves, pursue game and those who do not. This clash of values has deepened as the gulch between urban and rural America has grown. Similar battle lines are replicated in the cultural skirmishes between urban, industrialized societies and agricultural, rural inhabitants of Third World countries.

I was able to decipher some of the cultural codes within a Southern community through descriptions and conversations provided by its inhabitants. These pastimes allow further reflections: wild animals are not only good to pursue and to eat, they also give us distance to reflect upon ourselves. If we can depend on our intuition, then we can draw some tentative conclusions about the forms animal quests may take in the future. That interpretive challenge lies behind the avian symbolism of the chapter's title.

Boundaries Within and Without

There is an underside to hunting, as there is to other human activities. To hunt is to kill, or sometimes to maim, other forms of life. This is a blind spot for most hunters, who in their more reflective moments tend to think about other givens in the relationships between different forms of life.

There are two cultural divides: those within the hunting fraternity, and those marking hunters from nonhunters. The former boundary circumscribes those who are called "slobs," among other things. Included in this category are those who remain oblivious to the tastes, ideals, and erstwhile sensibilities about what the "game" is about. In their pursuits, "slobs" uncaringly transgress upon the terrains of others, exploiting and appropriating a "grossness" in human conduct, which, once witnessed, is not forgotten nor readily forgiven. The definition of "slob" has a social reference, variously explicated. For those who hunt, "slob" forms a category on the far end of a continuum that begins with a self (and with those most like self) called "sportsman." For the quail hunter in the following conversation, the distinctions begin with the generic "hunter," who, though distinguished from "sportsman," does exhibit shades of sporting behavior:

There's a lot of difference between a hunter and a sportsman. As the old doctor always said, a true sportsman is a gentleman that's not gonna cause you any trouble. He's out in the woods finding birds. Anybody can be a hunter. If you're a sportsman, you ought to abide by the game laws, which very few people do that consider themselves sportsmen. If they get a chance to kill over the limit, if they get a chance to shoot after dark, they're gonna do it. If they get a chance to do anything that pleases them to bring in game, they're gonna do it. And I think that separates a lot of sportsmen from what I would do just to bring in the game. I'm not gonna go out and break a law just to bring in the game even though I do enjoy bringing it in.

You've got two types of hunters, not sportsmen. One that kills for the game because he enjoys getting the game and selling it or giving it away. And then you've got the one that likes to kill, to kill, and don't care if they ever quit hunting birds.

The poacher, the slob, and the hunter, all three are not abiding by the game laws. The game laws are written for the sportsman anyway. I'll admit it's hard to kill a duck in the evening before sundown, and I'll admit it's hard to kill a dove without putting a little corn out there. All right, a sportsman might throw corn out there on occasion to bring ducks into a certain area, but when he goes out there he's gonna kill his limit and that's it. He's not going in there and kill all he can kill like some people do.

SAM: *What you've admitted, I wouldn't find many sportsmen outspoken about. Game legislation is basically social legislation. Sportsmen write the laws to protect their interests and these laws discriminate against others who may refuse to recognize the authority of these laws. There must be some laws that you take as more important than others?*

That's right. And going out and shooting deer at night, or shooting twenty doves in an afternoon, or shooting without a plug in your gun on migratory waterfowl. It's where you set your values, your importance of hunting. We know that if we get a duck in this area, we're gonna have to throw a little corn out, and we know that on occasion we might have to shoot five minutes after sundown to get that duck.

SAM: *Do you see conservation as paying the costs for the game you are interested in and as paying for the enforcement of the boundaries between your interests and those of other groups? And that others may be differently inclined?*

Right, realizing that on doves, that 80 percent of them are gonna die anyway. They gonna die from natural causes. Now what a hunter kills is immaterial. If every hunter went out and killed twenty doves every day, it wouldn't

make any difference on the population of doves next year. Still, the laws are
there for the limit of doves and they should be abided by. We do discriminate,
you know. Through every aspect of life we discriminate against people we
don't want to be around. When you're around them you're good to them. As
far as taking John Doe out to go quail hunting with me, I don't want him. I got
my select group.

This conversation ends with a Darwinian perspective on wildlife management, that the deaths of most individuals have little effect on the survival
of a population, and with the assumed right of individuals to choose their
peers.

I was never aware if someone I interviewed was a self-confessed "slob." I
mention "slobs" because hunters are concerned that crudeness within their
ranks hurts their "public image." And "public image" has become an issue in
the Age of the Consumer, when that great cultural chasm between rural and
urban America shows its steep sides whenever the issues of gun control and
animal rights surface. Within the polarized worlds of some gun-control
and animal-rights activists, the attributes of the "slob" are often indiscriminately applied to all hunters and sportsmen.

Most men have no ready answer when asked why they hunt. Recreational
tastes and activities spring from the past and present rhythms of their lives. It
is easier to pinpoint the circumstances under which the learning began than to
sanction the rationalizations by which the processes continue. Nonetheless, it
is part of the landscape of our tribalized knowledge that makes it appropriate
to question the reasons behind the acts.

People hunt for a myriad of motives. Men hunt for the pleasure of being
outdoors, for the enjoyment of accomplishments associated with youth, for
the company of their friends, for the mastery over canine companions, for the
sake of learning, for competition, for diversions, for hearing the dogs run, for
an affirmation of faith in their fathers' teachings, for performing an important
cultural activity, for a sense of achievement, for putting meat on the table, for
a sense of freedom and autonomy, and for the other choices that hunting allows. The reasons are endless.

Following a long discussion about recent incidents of wildlife protector
surveillance, a raccoon hunter summarized his thoughts with: "When I go out
there, I just want to hunt with peace of mind, I don't want to be half scared,
in other words, got to be looking for the game warden with one eye and this
guy with the other." Often the reasons interweave and flow together from
moment to moment while being mutually reinforced in the identity of the
person.

The answer to the question of why men hunt has a long lineage of discriminating ideas. Those enjoying elevated social positions have always considered their reasons more worthy than those given by men of lesser social stature. William Elliott and Alexander Hunter insisted that they hunted for sport

and not out of necessity like the rest of "them." Most people today know that "hunting for sport" is the preferred answer to the posed question. To claim another reason is to risk prolonged discussion, if not outright rejection. Local awareness of these invidious labels sharpens social distinctions as well as develops them over time. Those hunting for "practical reasons" often reverse the direction of normative sentiments, as a mill worker did in response to my inquiry:

I think that people that go out hunting just to be banging something will rank lower on my scale for their values and stuff. If a guy goes out hunting, I can see that, because that was part of what this country is about. When they first came here they had to hunt and they had to fish. So if a guy needs to go hunting for food or something like that, that can always be accepted. If a guy goes hunting and don't kill anything, you rib him. Some guys that hunt now take a camera with them and we have a bulletin board at work and they put up all kinds of pictures up there of hunting. And they stick it up there and say, oh, look at that, and everybody thinks he got a ten-point buck!

Those shooting for the table, or "killing," are making statements that are often symbolic rather than descriptive of economic necessity. In their view, they are reenacting the American frontier tradition, as suggested by Hubert Gaines's first cousin in chapter 8, whereby the hunter returns home carrying the fat of the land over one shoulder and his self-esteem over the other.

This book has not been an account of the life-styles of an alien group or of a deprived or marginal segment of American society. Many of the assumptions about life of Scotland County residents are, if not American, at least Southern ones. If there is an enemy in the quest for a better, if not more sane existence, he is, as the protagonist Pogo put it, in us all. This conundrum of the human condition in a society priding itself on the quantity of its meat consumption was expressed by the same teacher whose reflections opened this chapter:

It's a heck of a lot more humane to kill a quail flying across that field than packing those chickens in a crate at night under soft light. I mean those chickens never had any purpose in life except to be meat on somebody's table. Now I eat chickens. I'm not knocking it or cows, but their main purpose for existence is to be meat. Animals, I'm sure they enjoy life. I mean a quail sitting on a fence post calling is enjoying life. I don't want to shoot a deer, but they'd be better shot than to starve. That's a lot more humane to me than mass producing meat. The only criticisms I care to hear about hunting is that coming from vegetarians.

We live increasingly in an artificial world to which we respond in ways largely predetermined by vested and consuming interests. Most of us live in cities and rarely recognize our increasing dependency upon technology and upon consumerism. Rarely do we take the time, or feel the need, to question the substance of our subsistence or of the sustainability of our life-styles. Furthermore, we have barely begun to understand how our ideas about wild animals have evolved as we have changed from a rural, agricultural society and how these transitions have affected our attitudes toward one another and toward wildlife.[1]

Industrialism and materialism have given birth to a new type of social order, an order that is centrally organized around the domination of nature. The games pursued are no longer "wild," for their existence depends upon human decisions as surely as the context of the dawning ecological order. Our lack of curiosity as to where we might be headed and our uncritical acceptance of our cultural heritage provide lessons for us all. Categories are conventions, not given in the nature of things nor in human nature. Categories are learned and institutionalized in what anthropologists summarily call culture.

Wildlife as Food for Thought

My argument from ethnography is that discourse about wildlife is essentially about human relations. Biologists are on the wrong trail if they confine their scrutiny solely to the biological processes of organisms whose ecology increasingly bear the imprints of human providence. Even behind the loss of critical wildlife habitat lie the imprints of human incentives, conflictive rights, and "benign" traditions. Our profound attempts to make nature useful have made the environment in which most Americans live a reflection of their own materialistic myths. Furthermore, this world has become structured and maintained by professionals, who often are both cultural and political conservatives. One source of the problem may lie in the limited professional and legal definitions of wildlife as resources. Wildlife species are not exclusively "properties."[2]

Today the games played on the Southern hunting fields are usually not about subsistence. Competition is not over calories, although an abundance of kilocalories may be expended in obtaining game and in continuing to have access to it. What is contested are the ways in which wildlife is socially constructed. Deer, quail, rabbits, raccoons are all biological species invested with local cultural evaluations, a litmus test of personal status, identity, and gender.

To keep this perspective, we must synthesize biological knowledge with an understanding of the powerful forces of exclusion that arise when humans seek control of valuables and that continually make new divisions in our society. As Marshall Sahlins observed, "bourgeoisie totemism" is potentially more powerful and elaborate than any "wild" or natural variety because nature itself has become domesticated.[3]

The act of hunting is a representation of "a self" in relationship to some group, a community of others, perhaps predecessors, and to the means, the land, and the techniques making this behavior possible. Observing these dramas and exchanges provides material for synthesizing a host of connections. I have sought to capture some of these connections and divisions through observations and interpretations of hunting scenes, linking them to the upstream discharge of cultural categories and to the bedrocks of social structure and history over which this current of Southern heritage flows.[4]

By their choice of associates, methods of pursuit, and fields, individuals mark their differences from others in gradations that are locally acknowledged and understood. Through their membership in groups and participation in rounds of rituals, hunting men define, defend, enact, and reaffirm their distinctiveness and standing. Each individual is a source and a subject of judgment; each is a member of a scheme of meaning that he and others are helping to establish or to maintain; each strives to leave his mark on the community's space and time. The kinds of worlds these men create are constructed from the equipment brought to bear on the task at hand, the landscape, and the sharing of names, events, and products. In a reflective mood, a raccoon raconteur confessed that he was bored from hearing the same old stories until he started repeating them himself! Traditions are pushed into the future by such conscious acts.

Examined within the long sweep of Southern history, the rhetoric of hunting has not always matched its material realities. During William Elliott's times, cultural attitudes toward wildlife and human life differed from those today. Slaves were his "natural" commodities as surely as the commodities of nature that he pursued on horseback. In this pre-Darwinian era, Elliott's concept of deer and other immutable creatures formed a hierachy of creation similar to the stratified society he was desperately trying to implement and uphold in his social world. Yet the mundane truth of the frontier was that everybody, including Elliott, hunted out of necessity and that their social world was maintained increasingly by force.

In this century the rhetoric of hunting has turned "democratic," the landscape has been transformed from "wilderness," wildlife is legally catalogued, and hunters are effectively restricted in how and what they can take. The Lacey Act passed by Congress in 1900 put out of business those who sought game for enterprise and restricted game taking to those who could afford it for sport. In these post-Darwinian times, the malleability of Alexander Hunter's quail makes sense, for our reflections on nature express our thoughts about the nature of human society. Status and power remain racially, economically, and recreationally encoded, yet it takes a sympathetic ear to hear them and a discerning eye to see them.

Men may continue to hunt, cut shirttails, argue with their neighbors over boundaries, vet their dogs against one another, count coup with slain game, mount forays against poachers, and in the process make cultural distinctions between themselves and others. There are insidious economic and political sides to these recreational forms as men struggle to perpetuate traditions learned in their youth. The variety of these struggles is revealed in the behaviors and biographies of the participants, and the outcomes and meanings may be lifetimes in the making. In my view, wildlife and conservation are about people's lives and the activities they value. The challenge is the building of a cultural consensus that encourages a sensitivity toward all forms of life.

A Bestiary for Development

A proverbial problem of all interpretations is change. Changes occur and will occur with increasing frequency within the industrial order. For the most part, I have argued that the rural South has seen few moments of precipitous change—the loss of the Civil War and the subsequent Reconstruction, with the movement of the lower social ranks into dependency and into the labor force during the early years of industrialization. These new conditions demanded a new marker, a quest different from the pursuit of the deer by William Elliott and his likes. Although the tune for this new quest came from elsewhere and involved a step further removed from humans on the evolutionary scale (a change from fur to feathers), the pursuit of quail was largely still orchestrated indigenously. Prominent individuals, who thought of themselves as Southerners, continued to control change through their selective responses to outside prospects.

Despite change, the cultural envelope remained grounded in Southern soil. The image of quail and its hunters became increasingly refined and celebrated in literature and the arts until progressive environmental and cultural erosion removed their "covers." Synthesized within these media were the love of land and lineage, patronage of place and heirlooms, small exclusive circles of intimates and vetters of outside information, and specialized breeds of dogs sniffing out a constantly changing quarry. A place was left for others—the rabbit, squirrel, and raccoon hunters—in which to carve out their own cultural landscapes, provided they did not trample on a landowner's valuables.

This cultural system also had its detractors and its downside. A parody of the quail hunter is captured in the obnoxious character of Oscar Hubbard in Lillian Hellman's drama, *The Little Foxes*. Set in 1900, this play shows the tensions between blacks and whites during the dark days of Reconstruction, when Lionnet, a plantation, shifts from Birdie's, Oscar's wife's, side of the family to his own. Birdie objects to her husband's hunting on moral grounds, to kill just for the killing: "It's wicked to shoot food just because you like to shoot, when poor people need it so." When her family was the proprietor of Lionnet, it had distributed the spoils of the chase among the slaves and allowed them to supplement their rations with what they could kill for themselves. Later Oscar is approached by Cal, his black servant who pleads for a return to the former noblesse oblige by reminding him that the field hands "ain't had no meat since cotton picking was over" and that he knows that Oscar had "enough bobwhite and squirrel to give every nigger in town a Jesusparty." Oscar replies with the admonishment, "If I catch a nigger in this town going shooting, you know what's going to happen."[5] With the resurrected norms of the Old South, women and blacks (and poor whites) were pushed out of bounds farther from the gaming fields. This cultural reserve still survives in the minds of some, who can afford to perpetuate the past in the present, and in the experiences of some rabbit and coon hunters who have transgressed on "massa's quails."

The emergence of the New South economy and consumerism calls for a new symbol as the mix of change has shifted decision makers from the county's agricultural fields to the banquet banter at the local country club. It was here during the mid-1970s that a new quest emerged in the form of the Ducks Unlimited fund-raising banquet. This spectacle, advertised for "drakes only," featured free booze, seductive young women offering raffle tickets, an auction, a dinner, and an orchestrated evening, for the purchase of a ticket and subscription to the organization's journal. Individuals attending this annual event were mainly local businessmen and professionals. Few (less than 10 percent) had ever hunted ducks and even fewer knew how to steward the fragile ecosystems depicted in the waterfowl prints and paraphernalia, the coveted auction items converted into cash for preserving waterfowl habits and habitats in foreign countries. The "game" sought here were images for the office, the preferred habitat being along the shores and coastlines of distant places belonging to moneyed professionals whose movements and values were less circumscribed than before. My participation in these pageants brought the realization that here was a different quest from the others I had witnessed.

Consumerism has led to new ways by which individuals can make claims about social status. The focus has shifted from the quest to actual possession, the business deal of outbidding local peers in a show of money for prized objects. These changes bring about new materialistic styles and roles for moneyed professionals who find little significance in the older system of hunting stratification. These newer objectives will cull some meanings from previous traditions and undoubtedly encounter similar problems, as witnessed in the reflections of one who had outbid his competitors for a prized shotgun and now was faced with going home and confronting his wife with its cost.

The decisions by communal leaders to move away from the land, to consolidate farms for agribusiness and for corporations, to actively solicit residence by outside managers, to join the cultural, if not the economic, "mainstream" are decisions about future connectedness in community life. These decisions about work and consumption are also about play as it re-creates the practicalities of living. Choices about work, residence, and play cause the chooser to be better hooked up or more cut off from the main channels of change. As small Southern communities become increasingly cosmopolitan, interpreting their rituals will take us beyond their provincial and local habitats. The problem becomes one of increasing scale and of integration of broad knowledge from diverse sources. Deciphering the meaning in the recreational modes of many sportsmen's organizations takes us into the national and international boardrooms of corporate America.

Socializing at country club banquets may not become the style for many Scotland County residents, for undoubtedly they are not for everyone. Many residents will continue to consider their "traditional" haunts as best, for as long as they can. Yet the emergence of new social and environmental phenomena opens the way for new questions that partake of new ecological complexities and uncertainities through the reframing of status. Status is a kind of power within a group consisting of respect, consideration, and envy. A person with status sets the standards and norms by which others act; undoubtedly, these canons will trickle downward into the community. The most potent of all status symbols is money and what it can stand for. That such sentiments regarding change had already begun to percolate downward is shown in the comments of the teacher from whom we have already heard earlier. As a local landowner, he was fascinated with ducks, and I asked him about his interest:

The first thing I think of when I think of a duck is that it may be the very last really free thing that we see. I mean, here's a duck, came from Saskatchewan. He might have come from some wild place where there's nobody. He's flying that same route that a hundred or a thousand generations have flown. Some two thousand years ago some Indian out there on some long-dried-up lake was hunting this same bird.

It's continuity with the past. I think he's free. I think that duck is. But a quail, he's different.

SAM: *Tell me about the quail.*

A quail is a semidomesticated bird. I love to shoot quail, but I don't get quite the same thrill out of quail. The quail's been changed tremendously by man. They've even changed in my lifetime.

SAM: *You've presented me with a dichotomy. One is a bird that just stays around and has changed a lot. The other is a bird that moves around, is free, and is timeless. How do you put these two together? Are they a part of you?*

I would probably say that they are. I don't think I've ever really given thought to that. But they are both birds and they're as different as they can be. They're the extremes of the bird kingdom.

Maybe the duck is doing something that I've never done and that fascinates me and I've thought about that. You see, I've never been a whole lot of places. I keep thinking I am, but I'll probably die without going anywhere. I want to go to California to see those big trees, and I hope to get to see them. Duck hunting represents that epitome. There's nothing more graceful to me than a duck. Ducks have always fascinated me. I've thought about this too, I could really never justify shooting another duck. I think to be a real sportsman, you have to have a tinge of regret about killing.

I think if we ever get to where we can explain our own feelings, we might as well give up and go away. You know, for me, that's part of human nature, not to ever completely understand your relationships.

My hope is for the conversations to continue.

Appendix A

Questionnaire about Wild Animals and Hunting

Agreement with statement includes the responses "strongly agree" and "agree."

(B = Black, $n = 17$;   L = Lumbee, $n = 15$;   W = White, $n = 46$)

ATTITUDES TOWARD WILD ANIMALS

It is proper to feel affection for other people, but to have the same kinds of feelings for wild animals is silly.
      B 59%, L 20%, W 17% agree

The practice of killing or trapping wild animals for their fur should be abandoned (or at least stopped) now that we have so many other materials for making clothes.
      B 47%, L 40%, W 35% agree

Animals do not have feelings or feel pain, to the same extent as humans do.
      B 41%, L 7%, W 22% agree

When faced with a problem they have never been up against before, most wild animals can use reason (use their heads, think about) to figure out a solution.
      B 53%, L 67%, W 61% agree

Man is vastly superior to all animals in almost every conceivable way.
      B 53%, L 53%, W 54% agree

Some wild animals kill simply for the joy of killing.
      B 24%, L 20%, W 33% agree

GENDER AND HUNTING

It is difficult for women to understand and appreciate the world of hunting.
      B 59%, L 67%, W 54% agree

Hunting is one of the few things you can do these days that will get you away from women.
      B 47%, L 60%, W 43% agree

Although men welcome the participation of women on hunts, her other preoccupations with home chores and loss of face among her own sex conspire to limit woman's participation in hunting. (Most men would like women to come along on hunts, but other women prevent them from participation.)
      B 82%, L 60%, W 57% agree

Whether or not a man is a real hunter comes when he marries. If he continues with the same zeal as before marriage, he is a true hunter.
B 65%, L 73%, W 74% agree

SOCIALIZATION IN HUNTING

Through hunting, youngsters learn fair play, patience, and unselfishness, and develop a keen sense of observation and self-reliance, which are all a part of sportsmanship.
B 88%, L 87%, W 91% agree

Hunting provides an opportunity for a boy to identify with the masculine world (world of men), which is the most important influence of hunting on a boy.
B 100%, L 100%, W 85% agree

SATISFACTION IN HUNTING

For me, the enjoyment of nature is an important part of hunting.
B 53%, L 100%, W 98% agree

Hunting for me is important primarily as a means of reaffirming and strengthening my already established social bonds with my buddies.
B 71%, L 67%, W 59% agree

Hunting is good for what ails a man.
B 12%, L 60%, W 70% agree

Hunting is one means by which I publicly demonstrate my ownership or power of control over (the productivity of) the land.
B 18%, L 53%, W 46% agree

Hunting is just like any other sport such as baseball and football.
B 41%, L 53%, W 35% agree

SPORTSMANSHIP AND WILD ANIMALS

Chemical and mechanical devices that attract wild animals and birds to a hunter take unfair advantage of the animal and should be unlawful.
B 82%, L 87%, W 76% agree

Wild animals that I hunt and kill are symbols indicating a successful pursuit or are targets that allow me to display particular skills and capabilities.
B 76%, L 47%, W 70% agree

For me, competition and challenges are important aspects of hunting.
B 71%, L 73%, W 87% agree

Fox hunting, duck hunting, deer stalking, bullfighting and other varieties of so-called sport all represent the destructive and cruel energies of man directed toward the pursuit of more helpless creatures.

    B 35%, L 20%, W 20% agree

I get a thrill from just seeing wild animals in their natural habitat even if I come back home without killing anything.

    B 100%, L 100%, W 96% agree

CHARACTERISTICS OF THE HUNTER

What do you think of Teddy Rossevelt's remark that "the hunter must be sound of body and firm of mind, and must possess energy, resolution, manliness, self-reliance . . . (characteristics) without which no race can do its life-work well?"

    B 82%, L 67%, W 93% agree

Skill in hunting is related to the number of participants on a hunt. The fewer the hunters, the higher the skill required.

    B 76%, L 67%, W 67% agree

Prestige rating (status) of the game depends upon the purpose of the social class pursuing it; the wild animals of those who hunt for food and to escape from the drudgery of their lives rate lower than of those who hunt for sport and pleasure.

    B 76%, L 67%, W 65% agree

Unsportsmanlike conduct, which includes illegal acts, should not be reported to authorities but the individual should be disciplined by future exclusion from the group.

    B 82%, L 67%, W 41% agree

Hunting organizations fulfill the needs of individuals (such as providing hunting grounds, sufficient dogs, good friends) that individuals alone do not have.

    B 47%, L 60%, W 83% agree

If it were not for sport hunters, there would still be plenty of wildlife.

    B 59%, L 33%, W 28% agree

Hunting and guns are a definite part of my identity (how I see myself).

    B 35%, L 47%, W 74% agree

Hunting reflects the human past in which people depended upon what men obtained through hunting and what women gathered. The satisfaction I get from hunting comes from these basic behavioral feelings and instincts.

    B 71%, L 80%, W 70% agree

DOGS AND HUNTING

A dog is the extended self of its owner and it gains or loses prestige (favor) for its owner by its performance.
B 94%, L 100%, W 87% agree

Obedience and respect for authority are the most important virtues a dog can learn.
B 100%, L 100%, W 85% agree

HUNTING AND ITS MANAGEMENT

Predator control is generally a very effective way for increasing populations of game animals.
B 88%, L 80%, W 65% agree

It is legitimate (okay) for poor families living in rural areas to hunt or trap squirrels, rabbits, possums, and coons for food outside the declared open season.
B 18%, L 20%, W 20% agree

Wild animals are a harvestable crop like any other natural resource.
B 76%, L 67%, W 91% agree

Species like the black bear and turkey, which can be hunted now, should have their hunting stopped until the state wildlife agency determines that these species are no longer endangered.
B 65%, L 87%, W 91% agree

In some cases, hunting female (doe) deer will actually benefit deer populations in addition to increasing the number of deer taken within a given year.
B 53%, L 73%, W 85% agree

Every sportsman should have equal opportunity and access to hunting privileges for all species of wildlife.
B 88%, L 93%, W 59% agree

Without any game laws and their effective enforcement, there would not be any game left today.
B 82%, L 100%, W 89% agree

Appendix B ⸻⸻⸻⸻⸻⸻⸻⸻⸻

Questionnaire about Individuals, Family, Community,
and Society

(B = Black, n = 17; L = Lumbee, n = 15; W = White, n = 46)

INDIVIDUALS

Competition and struggle generally tend to weed out the weak and inferior
and to reward the strong and intelligent.
> B 94%, L 93%, W 93% agree

Too many people today are weak and dependent; we need to return to our
pioneering values of self-reliance and independence.
> B 88%, L 93%, W 85% agree

If possible a man should try and own land and preserve it for his family.
> B 88%, L 100%, W 83% agree

In any work, it is important that the job is interesting, that I have lots of
freedom of choice, a chance to help people, and to use my God-given
abilities.
> B 82%, L 87%, W 96% agree

Equality, hard work, improvement, and hope gain meaning and worth through
one's work.
> B 76%, L 87%, W 100% agree

A man should strive to be economically and politically independent. It is
important for a man, by age forty, to have achieved a significant degree of
financial security.
> B 94%, L 73%, W 78% agree

War and aggression are inherent in human nature.
> B 71%, L 80%, W 78% agree

As a religious person, I feel that it is necessary for individuals to become born
again and for the community to witness that individual's conversion.
> B 76%, L 53%, W 56% agree

My most important friends are either related to me or go to the same church
as I do.
> B 35%, L 40%, W 39% agree

It usually pays to turn the other cheek rather than get into a fight.
> B 47%, L 67%, W 61% agree

I am generally more interested in beauty than in useful values.
   B 35%, L 47%, W 39% agree

FAMILY

Obedience and respect for authority are essential values for children to learn.
   B 94%, L 100%, W 98% agree

If possible, a man should try and own land and preserve it for his family.
   B 88%, L 100%, W 83% agree

It is important to have sons in order for them to associate with the father and to carry on the family name.
   B 82%, L 66%, W 72% agree

The man of the family should have the final authority in discussions within the family and at work.
   B 59%, L 53%, W 39% agree

COMMUNITY

A person should generally seek to avoid direct confrontation. Conflicts should be resolved without fighting through the church, among kin, and in the workplace or neighborhood.
   B 100%, L 100%, W 93% agree

Differences in social classes tend to encourage hostility and distrust as well as unfairly concentrate power in the hands of a few individuals.
   B 88%, L 87%, W 72% agree

The welfare of the community is more important than that of certain individuals within it.
   B 76%, L 67%, W 89% agree

All things considered, would you say Scotland County is the best county in which to live and work?
   B 59%, L 80%, W 63% agree

Change in society is inevitable. Scotland County should keep in touch with other happenings in the state and the nation.
   B 65%, L 73%, W 93% agree

Change in society is accidental and often comes about when communities lose control of their own destinies. Communities such as Scotland County should strive to maintain control over their own stability.
   B 35%, L 27%, W 20% agree

We've got to accept the fact that building homes and factories is usually more important than protecting a few wild animals.

    B 59%, L 17%, W 39% agree

SOCIETY

Our society needs more activities that combine traditions and feelings of togetherness.

    B 100%, L 100%, W 91% agree

It is important for our modern society to restore its faith in religion and in God.

    B 100%, L 93%, W 96% agree

Too many people today are weak and dependent. We need to return to our pioneering values of self-reliance and independence.

    B 88%, L 93%, W 85% agree

The nationalization of big business leads to bureaucracy, inefficiency, and stagnation.

    B 35%, L 73%, W 67% agree

Production and trade should be as free as possible from government interference.

    B 23%, L 67%, W 70% agree

A trouble with America today is that too many people are engaged in occupations that do not contribute to the production of goods.

    B 83%, L 93%, W 59% agree

Baseball in many ways symbolizes for me the American dream in which hard work, savings, and individual initiative earn their reward. Accountability remains clear and rules prescribe the individual's responsibility.

    B 71%, L 60%, W 70% agree

Football in many ways symbolizes the American dream, with a flashy quarterback who is totally dependent upon the behavior of his teammates, all of whom fulfill highly routine tasks.

    B 41%, L 47%, W 50% agree

Notes to the Chapters ———————————————

Chapter One
On Metaphors and Models

1. For cultural goods as symbols of self and community, see Mihaly Csikszentmihalyi and Eugene Rochberg-Halton, *The Meaning of Things: Domestic Symbols and the Self* (New York: Cambridge University Press, 1981).

2. Victor Turner, *The Forest of Symbols* (Ithaca, N.Y.: Cornell University Press, 1967); E. E. Evans-Pritchard, *Nuer Religion* (New York: Oxford University Press, 1956).

3. The figured-knots metaphor is from Rhys Isaac, *The Transformation of Virgina, 1740–1790* (Chapel Hill, N.C.: University of North Carolina Press, 1982), p. 332. For an ethnography of the adjacent Lumbees, see Karen I. Blu, *The Lumbee Problem: The Making of an American Indian People* (Cambridge, Eng.: Cambridge University Press, 1980); for the ethnographic problems of working in Southern communities, see John Dollard, *Caste and Class in a Southern Town* (Garden City, N.Y.: Doubleday Anchor, 1937).

4. For a discussion of metaphors and models, see Greg Dening, *Islands and Beaches: Discourse on a Silent Land, Marquesas 1774–1880* (Honolulu: University Press of Hawaii, 1980), and Isaac, *The Transformation of Virginia.*

5. The rapprochement between history and anthropology is a rather recent one. For examples, see Dening, *Islands and Beaches;* Marshall Sahlins, *Islands of History* (Chicago: University of Chicago Press, 1985); and Arjun Appadurai, ed., *The Social Life of Things: Commodities in Cultural Perspective* (Cambridge, Eng.: Cambridge University Press, 1986).

6. Hunters feel the sentimental view of wildlife fails to recognize the utility of humans as predators within an ecosystem. See Paul Shepard, *The Tender Carnivore and the Sacred Game* (New York: Viking Press, 1973); John G. Mitchell *The Hunt* (New York: Knopf, 1980); C.H.D. Clarke, "Autumn Thoughts of a Hunter," *Journal of Wildlife Management* 22, no. 4 (October 1958):420–27.

7. Nelson W. Polsby, *Community Power and Political Theory* (New Haven: Yale University Press, 1963); Paul Tillett, *Doe Day: The Antlerless Deer Controversy in New Jersey* (New Brunswick, N.J.: Rutgers University Press, 1963); G. William Domhoff, *The Bohemian Grove and Other Retreats: A Study of Ruling Class Cohesiveness* (New York: Harper Colophon Books, 1974); Lionel Tiger, *Men in Groups* (New York: Vintage Books, 1970). For an explication of economics and consumerism, see Thorstein Veblen, *The Theory of the Leisure Class: An Economic Study of Institutions* (New York: Modern Library, 1934); Chandra Mukerji, *From Graven Images: Patterns of Modern Materialism* (New York: Columbia University Press, 1983); Appadurai, "Introduction: Commodities and the Politics of Value," in *The Social Life of Things*, pp. 3–63. As a focus of economic activities, hunting pumps money into and within rural communities. National and state conservation agencies monitor this economic pulse at

intervals. See, for example, the pamphlet by Howard J. Stains and Frederick S. Barka-
low, Jr., *The Value of North Carolina's Game and Fish* (Raleigh, N.C.: Wildlife Resources Commission, Game Division, 1951); and U.S. Department of the Interior, Fish
and Wildlife Service, and U.S. Department of Commerce, Bureau of the Census, *1980
National Survey of Fishing, Hunting, and Wildlife-Associated Recreation* (Washington, D.C.: Government Printing Office, 1982).

8. Robert Ruark, *The Old Man and the Boy* (London: Hamish Hamilton, 1957), p.
255. See also Mary Hufford, *One Space, Many Places* (Washington, D.C.: Library of
Congress, American Folklife Center, 1986); Angus K. Gillespie and Jay Mechling,
eds., *American Wildlife in Symbol and Story* (Knoxville: University of Tennessee
Press, 1987); Richard Bauman, "Verbal Art as Performance," *American Anthropologist*
77 (1975):290–312.

9. Greg Dening, *Islands and Beaches*; Isaac, *The Transformation of Virginia*; Clifford Geertz, "Deep Play: Notes on the Balinese Cockfight," *Daedalus* 101 (1972):1–37;
James Howe, "Fox Hunting as Ritual," *American Ethnologist* 8 (1981):278–300; Har-
riet Ritvo, *The Animal Estate: The English and Other Creatures in the Victorian Age*
(Cambridge, Mass.: Harvard University Press, 1987). Another text of this genre is
Elizabeth Lawrence, *Rodeo: An Anthropologist Looks at the Wild and the Tame* (Knoxville: University of Tennessee Press, 1982).

10. Clifford Geertz, *The Interpretation of Culture* (New York: Random House,
1973). The interpretive school also includes J. David Sapir and J. Christopher Crocker,
eds., *The Social Use of Metaphor: Essays on the Anthropology of Rhetoric* (Philadelphia: University of Pennsylvania Press, 1977); James W. Fernanadez, *Persuasions and
Performances: The Play of Tropes in Culture* (Bloomington: Indiana University Press,
1986); Dening, *Islands and Beaches*; and Isaac, *The Transformation of Virginia*.

11. For example, read Isaac, *The Transformation of Virginia*, his discourse on
method, pp. 223–357. For William Faulkner's use of the past in the present, see F. Gar-
vin Davenport, Jr., *The Myth of Southern History: Historical Consciousness in Twenti-
eth-Century Southern Literature* (Nashville: Vanderbilt University Press, 1970), particularly chapter 3. The Faulkner quote is from Noel Polk, ed., *Requiem for a Nun: A
Concordance to the Novel by William Faulkner*, vol. 3 (West Point, N.Y.: U.S. Military Academy, 1979), p. 317.

12. Yi-Fu Tuan, *Space and Place: The Perspective of Experience* (Minneapolis:
University of Minnesota Press, 1977); Leonard Lutwack, *The Role of Place in Literature* (Syracuse, N.Y.: Syracuse University Press, 1984); and Edward M. Bruner, ed.,
Text, Play, and Story: The Construction and Reconstruction of Self and Society (Washington, D.C.: American Ethnological Society, 1984).

13. Despite this communal pride in education, Scotland County rates among the
worst in the South in formal illiteracy. The Census Bureau measures illiteracy by educational attainment. The conservative standard is the attainment of at least a fifth-grade
education by adults aged twenty-five years or older. The official reading for Scotland
County, published in the 1980 census, was 10.8 percent. The comparable figure for the
state was 1.4 percent. Only 47.8 percent of the men and women of Scotland County
over twenty-five years of age had finished the fourth year of high school; see U.S.
Department of Commerce, Bureau of the Census, *Characteristics of the Population*,
1980, vol. 1, pt. 35, chapter C, North Carolina, table 175, p. 415. I thank Jack Roper
for showing me these paradoxical statistics.

14. One absorbs a lot of lore about place through living there for many years. Therefore, it is difficult for me to pinpoint the exact source of ideas and events, or to remember exactly when and why they coalesced into meaningful stories. A few of these county stories are to be found in "Scotland County," *The State* 10 (November 21, 1942):1–2, 20–24; in Betty P. Myers, "Scotland County," eleven pages mimeo on file in Scotland County Memorial Library, 1977; and in Dick Brown, "Scotland County," *News and Observer*, Raleigh, N.C., March 11, 1956.

15. Jim Dumbell, "Strange Indentations Cover Coastal Plain," *Charlotte Observer*, April 12, 1981, pp. 1–2D; "Scotland: A County Profile," *Laurinburg Exchange*, Annual Business and Industrial Review, June 21, 1982, p. 5D.

16. "Editorial Comment: Only in Scotland County," *Laurinburg Exchange*, May 16, 1980. In 1980 the county's per capita income of $6,707 ranked it sixty-second in the state's one hundred counties. The average state per capita income of $7,832 compared with the national average of $9,511. The county's unemployment rate was 9.4 percent in 1975, 9.1 percent in 1980, and 12.0 percent in 1982. A labor-management relations circular, supplied by the Chamber of Commerce, shows three union elections, zero union wins, zero days of work stoppages, and zero man-days lost for the forty non-unionized manufacturing and 362 nonmanufacturing firms between 1970 and 1977. Information from North Carolina Department of Commerce, Business Assistance Division, Raleigh, and 1980 Census.

17. Between 1950 and 1970, the number of blacks in the county declined 19.7 percent, while the numbers of whites and "other races" increased 22.4 percent. See "Scotland County: Sketch Development Plan, 1971–1991."

Chapter Two
Propriety and Property

1. William Elliott, *Carolina Sports by Land and Water; including Incidents of Devil-Fishing, Wild-Cat, Deer and Bear Hunting, Etc*. (New York: Derby and Jackson, 1859). The page citations throughout this section are to this edition and are given parenthetically. In 1846 William Elliott published in Charleston a collection of sporting episodes originally printed as separate pieces in journals under the pen names of "Venator" and "Piscator." The first section of this published collection consists of narratives on the author's adventures with fishing, among which he chronicles the harpooning of large rays in the bays and sounds of his native South Carolina. In the second half of the volume he describes field sports in the swamps and forests along the Carolina coast. In these hunting adventures we glimpse the planters' role in antebellum society and their attitudes toward other social groups and toward wildlife.

2. Jay B. Hubbell, *The South as American Literature 1607–1900* (Durham, N.C.: Duke University Press, 1954), pp. 564–68, contains a short biographical sketch of William Elliott.

3. Lewis P. Jones, "William Elliott, South Carolina Nonconformist," *Journal of Southern History* 17 (1951):361–81.

4. Dickson D. Bruce, Jr., *Violence and Culture in the Antebellum South* (Austin: University of Texas Press, 1979), chapter 9.

5. P. B. Munsche, in *Gentlemen and Poachers: The English Game Laws, 1671–1831* (Cambridge, Eng.: Cambridge University Press, 1981), discusses how the sale of

game undercut the aristocratic privileges in England. Daniel R. Hundley, *Social Relations in Our Southern States* (New York: Henry B. Price, 1860), defines "driving" as "a right royal sport" as it "engages the attention of the Southern Gentleman" in comparison with other types (p. 39).

6. For an exposition of William Elliott's deer-hunting episodes, see Louis D. Rubin, Jr., *William Elliott Shoots a Bear: Essays on the Southern Literary Imagination* (Baton Rouge: Louisiana State University Press, 1975). William Elliott was a very perceptive observer of his social world, and his writings interpret many of the meanings and symbols implicit in plantation styles of hunting. Horsemanship was a particularly valued ritual of the chase. "H" of Chatham County, North Carolina, wrote that "in the part of the county in which I reside, deer are not killed with the view of wholly to venison, nor that the lucky huntsman should add to his count, but we are only emulous in superior horsemanship in heading the deer oftenest before he is run into by the dogs, or in dexterity in shooting." See "Deer Hunting," *American Turf Register and Sporting Magazine* 2, no. 2 (1830):86.

7. Guion G. Johnson, in "Social Conditions in North Carolina, 1800–1860" (Ph.D. diss., The University of North Carolina at Chapel Hill, 1927), p. 124, mentions that "the fox chase was a popular diversion in which the ladies not infrequently took part." Henry William Harrington, Jr.'s, entry for October 23, 1861, reads: "Fox chase—Col. B. F. Pegues—his daughters rode out the whole chase and were joined just as the fox was killed by their cousin Caroline Pegues"(Henry William Harrington, Jr., Papers, no. 314, manuscript in Southern Historical Collection, The University of North Carolina at Chapel Hill). Sometimes women inadvertently witnessed the kill; see, for example, the account of Hawkeye in "Buck Hunt," *American Turf Register and Sporting Magazine* 3 (1832):290–95. Yet Hundley, *Social Relations in Our Southern States*, p. 35, confesses not knowing of Southern ladies who participate in fox hunting.

8. 'Juliana Rosebud,' "Miseries of a Sportman's Wife," *American Turf Register and Sporting Magazine* 2 (1831):339–40.

9. F. H. Whitaker Papers, Manuscript Department, William R. Perkins Library, Duke University, Durham, N.C., letter from L. J. D'Berry dated September 21, 1859.

10. Ibid., October 19, 1859.

11. Clarence Gohdes, *Hunting in the Old South: Original Narratives of the Hunters* (Baton Rouge: Louisiana State University Press, 1967).

12. Bertram Wyatt-Brown, *Southern Honor: Ethics and Behavior in the Old South* (New York: Oxford University Press, 1982), chapter 7; William Faulkner, "The Bear," in *Go Down Moses* (New York: Modern Library, 1940). Hundley, *Social Relations in Our Southern States*, provides a sketch for the male life cycle of hunting types expected of Southern gentlemen.

13. William Faulkner, "The Bear," in *Bear, Man and God: Eight Approaches to William Faulkner's "The Bear"*, 2d ed., Francis L. Utley, Lynn Z. Bloom, and Arthur F. Kenney, eds. (New York: Random House, 1971), p. 6.

14. Wyatt-Brown, *Southern Honor*.

15. Hunting was an affirmation of masculinity and the male role in Southern society. Its displays occurred away from the household, which remained the domain of women. In the home, the wife had an important role in managing the everyday life of the plantation. A study of the structural relations of male/female, place/space, nature/nur-

ture would reveal the symbolic potency of hunting as a masculine activity. See Hundley, *Social Relations in Our Southern States*, pp. 72–75, 98–99.

16. George Anderson Mercer Diary, no. 503, Southern Historical Collection, The University of North Carolina at Chapel Hill, written May 9, 1855.

17. Ibid., written in New York, October 31, 1850.

18. Ibid.

19. Ibid.

20. Describing a deer hunt near Raleigh in 1830, Hawkeye wrote:

> I rose, uncased my famous gun, Chester, and in a moment was mounted—blew a loud call, which brought out the only remaining dogs of our pack; to wit, Mr. J. H.'s Jolly, Carolina Bell, and my old dog Potliquor—all in fine spirits. The latter, the only dog I ever saw, could really laugh; and it may be said with truth, a better Jack Falstaff was never made in the shape of a brute. I made a short speech, told them, that was to be their master's day, for good or for evil. Old Pot jumped and capered, laughed and nodded his head most significantly, giving me distinctly to understand, there was nothing I could require would not be done by *him*. Jolly was serious, as is his manner, but ready. Caroline seemed more amused and delighted with the antics of old Jack than any thing else.

American Turf Register and Sporting Magazine 1, no. 1 (1830):349–51. See also Ringwood's account of "Deer Hunting," *American Turf Register and Sporting Magazine* 1, no. 4 (1929):194–96.

21. Wyatt-Brown, *Southern Honor*, chapter 13. For blacks as storytellers, see Carl L. Carmer, *Stars Fell on Alabama* (New York: Farrar & Rinehart, 1934), chapter 7.

22. F. H. Whitaker Papers, Manuscript Department, William R. Perkins Library, Duke University, letter from L. J. D'Berry dated December 10, 1859 to F. H. Lousasah (?).

23. The notes are excerpted from the intermittent diary in the Henry William Harrington, Jr., Papers, no. 314, Southern Historical Collection, The University of North Carolina at Chapel Hill. For a depiction of the cultural and symbolic context of hunting and violence in the prewar South, see Bruce, *Violence and Culture in the Antebellum South*, and Wyatt-Brown, *Southern Honor*.

24. Jeffrey J. Crow, *The Black Experience in Revolutionary North Carolina* (Raleigh, N.C.: Department of Cultural Resources, 1977); Eugene D. Genovese, *Roll, Jordan, Roll: The World the Slaves Made* (New York: Pantheon, 1974); Charles Joyner, *Down by the Riverside: A South Carolina Slave Community* (Champaign: University of Illinois Press, 1984).

25. Elliott, *Carolina Sports by Land and Water*, in identifying game in South Carolina, mentions only the black bear, deer, wildcat, and fox among mammals (p. 261) and the wild turkey, partridge, dove, golden plover, woodcock, and snipe as the principal birds (p. 270). Henry William Harrington, Jr. (Papers, no. 314, Southern Historical Collection), of Richmond County was primarily a deer and fox hunter who occasionally took squirrels and geese, and sometimes attended a rabbit hunt in his old age. Frederick Law Olmstead, *A Journey in the Seaboard Slave States* (New York: G. P. Putnam's Sons, 1904 reprint), pp. 388–89, described the whites inhabiting the "turpentine forest" near Fayetteville in 1853 as mostly "uneducated, poverty-stricken vagabonds" without

definite occupation or reliable means of livelihood. They cultivated few crops, possessed some hogs that lived off the land, and owned a rifle and a pack of dogs. The men
spent most of their time hunting and sold game or meal to purchase other things. See
also Hundley, *Social Relations in Our Southern States*, and his accounts of various
social groupings and their recreations.

26. Even the contemptuous, demagogic Southern politician Benjamin Ryan Tillman
in his youth participated in possum hunting with blacks; see Francis Butler Simkins,
Pitchfork Ben Tillman: South Carolinian (Baton Rouge: Louisiana State University
Press, 1944).

27. Quoted in Guion G. Johnson, *Ante-Bellum North Carolina: A Social History*
(Chapel Hill: University of North Carolina Press, 1937), p. 556.

28. Blacks also set a variety of deadfalls, traps, and pens for wildlife See Hundley,
Social Relations in Our Southern States, pp. 342–43; Johnson, "Social Conditions in
North Carolina," p. 123. Many similar traps are used to snare wildlife in central Africa
today. For examples, see citations in Stuart A. Marks, *Large Mammals and a Brave
People: Subsistence Hunters in Zambia* (Seattle: University of Washington Press,
1976).

29. George P. Rawick, ed., *The American Slave: A Composite Autobiography*,
North Carolina Narratives, vol. 14 (Westport, Conn.: Greenwood Press, 1972), p. 202.

30. Ibid., pp. 144–46. Slaves sometimes used their hunting episodes as metaphors
to explain and evaluate their condition in slavery. When asked to evaluate slavery,
Stephan McCray of Alabama replied: "Every time I think of slavery and if it done the
race any good, I think of the story of the coon and the dog who met. The coon said to
the dog, 'Why is it you're so fat and I am so poor, and we both is animals?' The dog
said: 'I lay round Master's house and let him kick me and he gives me a piece of bread
right on.' Said the coon to the dog: 'Better then that I stay poor.' Them's my sentiment.
I'm lak the coon, I don't believe in 'buse." See idem, Oklahoma Narratives, vol. 7, p.
209, quoted in Bruce, *Violence and Culture in the Antebellum South*, p. 160.

31. For an English example of the multiple meanings of game legislation, see
Douglas Hay, "Poaching and the Game Laws on Cannock Chase," in *Albion's Fatal
Tree*, Douglas Hay, Peter Linebaugh, John G. Rule, E. P. Thompson, and Cal Wins-
low, eds. (New York: Pantheon Books, 1975), pp. 189–253. See also Munsche, *Gentlemen and Poachers*.

32. Thomas A. Lund, *American Wildlife Law* (Berkeley: University of California
Press, 1980), chapter 5 on State Wildlife Law.

33. John Lawson, *The History of Carolina, Containing the Exact Description and
Natural History of that Country, etc.* (Raleigh, N.C.: Strother and Marcom, 1714;
reprint, 1860), p. 29.

34. Verner W. Crane, *The Southern Frontier, 1670–1732* (Durham, N.C.: Duke
University Press, 1929).

35. A concise summary of English and early American wildlife laws is in Lund,
American Wildlife Law.

36. Ibid., chapter 3. See also James A. Tober, *Who Owns Wildlife? The Political
Economy of Conservation in Nineteenth-Century America* (Westport, Conn.: Greenwood Press, 1981).

37. John D. Cushing, ed., *The Earliest Printed Laws of North Carolina, 1669–
1751*, 2 vols. (Wilmington, Del.: Michael Glazier, 1977).

38. Claims by servants, slaves, or Indians were redeemable by their masters or by another recognized claimant. The magistrates received 10 percent of the award, and were expected to destroy the scalps and raise the funds for bounty payments by assessing all taxables within the county. See Cushing, *The Earliest Printed Laws*, vol. 1, pp. 261–62.

39. The surviving records of Richmond County, North Carolina, for 1798 and 1802 show nine grown, nineteen juveniles (including six younger than six months of age), and nine wolves of unspecified ages and two bears bountied. In addition, bounties were delivered on two adult wolves in 1809 and on eight young wolves with no date specified; Richmond County records on file at North Carolina Division of Archives and History, Raleigh, filed under Miscellaneous—Bounty on Wild Animals, 1798–1812. Similar schemes were prevalent in other states; see Tober, *Who Owns Wildlife?*, pp. 23–24; Lund, *American Wildlife Law*, pp. 32–34.

40. Lawson, *The History of Carolina*, pp. 25, 44, contains descriptions of Indian methods of ring firing and stalking. See also Tom Taylor, "How the Indians Hunted and Fished," *Wildlife in North Carolina* 45, no.2 (1981):6–11.

41. E. Lawrence Lee, *Indian Wars in North Carolina, 1663–1763* (Raleigh: Carolina Tercentenary Commission, 1963), p. 49.

42. Robert Beverley, *The History and Present State of Virginia*, Louis D. Wright, ed. (Chapel Hill: University of North Carolina Press, 1947), p. 155.

43. John Bricknell noted that wolves

follow the Indians in great droves through the Woods, who only kill the Deer and other Beasts for their Skins and generally leave most part of the dead Carcass behind them, on which the Wolves feed, this being what induces them to follow the Indians after that manner. Formerly, there was a Reward (in this Province) for all those that kill'd them, which made the Indians so active, that they brought in such vast quantities of their Heads, that in a short time it became too burthensome to the County, so that it is now laid quite aside, and the Indians will not kill them.

John Bricknell, *The National History of North Carolina with an Account of the Trade, Manners, and Customs of the Christian and Indian Inhabitants* (Dublin, Ireland: James Carson, 1737), pp. 119–20. An injunction against leaving deer carcasses in the woods to encourage the predator population became law in 1745 and was subject to a fine of forty shillings. In addition to having a reputation for destroying property, Indians were accused of killing the settlers' cattle. Witnesses to such acts of destruction or theft were empowered to apprehend the offenders and take them to one of the commissioners for appeal and restitution. See Cushing, *The Earliest Printed Laws*, vol. 1, pp. 38, 189.

44. The hunter-naturalist C. W. Webber ("The Viviparous Quadrupeds of North America," *Southern Quarterly Review* 12 [1847]:273–306; and *Wild Scenes and Wild Hunters of the World* [Philadelphia: J. W. Bradley, 1852]) believed one could construct a historical model relating advances in the code of the hunt with progress in human society. The wild hunter was relegated to the bottom rung of the ladder of human development. The hunter was a necessary trailblazer, acting as an agent for the inevitable domination of nature by the settled husbandman and by civilization. In this typology, if the rustic frontier hunter was in the vanguard of civilization in the New World, the planter with his sense of refinement was its epitome. Such sequential schemes were commonly used in antebellum times to explain the sequence of settlements and developments in North Carolina. See, for example, A. R. Newsome, "Twelve North Caro-

lina Counties in 1810–1811, Moore County," *North Carolina Historical Review* 6 (1929):281–94.

45. In 1738, the General Assembly made it unlawful to "kill or destroy any Deer, running wild with a gun or other means between February 15th and July 15th each year." Any person caught in violation and convicted was subject to a fine for each deer in possession. All slaves and servants caught acting on their own, if convicted by the oath of credible witnesses, were sentenced to thirty lashes unless someone agreed to pay a fee to be split between the informer and the church wardens; see Cushing, *The Earliest Printed Laws*, vol. 1, pp. 91–92.

46. An additional provision was directed toward the "many idle Persons, who spend their chief Time in Hunting Deer" and who were following the tactics ascribed earlier to the Indians. Such persons, upon conviction, were to forfeit forty shillings. See Cushing, *The Earliest Printed Laws*, vol. 1, pp. 188–89.

47. Johnson, *Ante-Bellum North Carolina*, p. 85.

48. Johnson, *Ante-Bellum North Carolina*. Some Southern localities were relatively barren of large game before the Civil War. See Gohdes, *Hunting in the Old South*, pp. xiv–xxi.

49. In his diary for December 9, 1833, Harrington wrote: "Booth and I go fire hunting tonight South of the road and I have 3 shots in the course of a few minutes at a deer but did not succede in killing it." On December 12, after hearing wolves: "I seized my gun and fire pan and went in pursuit of them." Excerpts from the journal of Henry William Harrington, Jr., Papers, no. 314, Southern Historical Collection, The University of North Carolina at Chapel Hill. See also Wah-o-pe-kah's "Deer Hunting on the Water by Lamp Light," *American Turf Register and Sporting Magazine* 3, no. 6 (1832):296–97.

50. Johnson, "Social Conditions in North Carolina," p. 167, mentions threats of alleged insurrection in 1802, 1808, 1821, and 1831. For whites' fear of insurrections, see also Wyatt-Brown, *Southern Honor*, and Bruce, *Violence and Culture in the Antebellum South*.

51. John S. Bassett, *Slavery in the State of North Carolina*, Johns Hopkins University Studies in Historical and Political Science, Series 17 (7–8), 1899. Chapter 1 of Bassett's volume provides a review of the legal status of slaves in North Carolina including their right to hunt. A paper in the Scotland County Library, Laurinburg, North Carolina, shows that the local patrol whipped twenty-eight blacks (Negroes) between March 11, 1843, and January 13, 1844. A law restricting slave movements from the premises of the master without written permission was in effect as early as 1715. In 1741 another law sought to prohibit slaves from hunting with guns and dogs, yet this edict allowed each owner a single license permitting a slave to hunt for the plantation. Despite these and subsequent laws, slaves continued to hunt, trap, and run wild game with the means at their disposal; see Johnson, *Social Conditions in North Carolina*, p. 167. Other evidence of slaves consuming game is found from recent archaeological excavations; see Tyson Gibbs, Kathleen Cargill, Leslie Sue Lieberman, and Elizabeth Reitz, "Nutrition in a Slave Population: An Anthropological Investigation," *Medical Anthropology* 4, no. 2 (1980):175–262, and Joyner, *Down by the Riverside*, pp. 100–101.

52. In 1831 the legislature made it unlawful for a slave to possess a "gun, sword, club, or other weapon" or to hunt with a gun under penalty of receiving twenty lashes.

Furthermore, this law made the master of the offending slave subject to a fine and made it illegal to sell or provide firearms or accessories to slaves. See Johnson, *Ante-Bellum North Carolina*, p. 555.

53. A statute restricted the possession and carrying of firearms to free blacks who satisfied authorities that they could handle weapons with propriety. The licensing of guns in the hands of free blacks failed to placate some whites, who continued to seek further restrictions. In 1856 the citizens of Robeson County petitioned the General Assembly to permit a free black to possess a gun only if "he is a free holder and gives bond with good security and then not be allowed to carry it off the land." These same citizens sought regulation on the rights of blacks to possess dogs. Finally, in 1861 a law was passed making it a misdemeanor for any black to possess a firearm. See John Hope Franklin, *The Free Negro in North Carolina, 1790–1860* (New York: Russell and Russell, 1969), pp. 76, 78.

54. See E. P. Thompson, *Whigs and Hunters: The Origin of the Black Act* (New York: Pantheon Books, 1975).

55. Lund, *American Wildlife Law*, chapter 5.

56. Steven Hahn, "Hunting, Fishing, and Foraging: Common Rights and Class Relations in the Postbellum South," *Radical History Review* 26 (1982):37–64. Also see Forrest McDonald and Grady McWhiney, "The Antebellum Southern Herdsman: A Reinterpretation," *The Journal of Southern History* 41, no. 2:(1975):147–66.

57. Elliott, *Carolina Sports by Land and Water*, pp. 285–86.

58. Ibid., pp. 289–90.

59. Ibid., pp. 291–92.

60. For a description of some effects wrought by subsistence farmers on their surrounding habitats and on wild mammal populations, see Marks, *Large Mammals and a Brave People*, especially chapters 8–10. For the changes in landscapes brought on by European colonization in the New World, see Albert E. Cowdrey, *This Land, This South: An Environmental History* (Lexington: University Press of Kentucky, 1983), and William Cronon, *Changes in the Land: Indians, Colonists, and the Ecology of New England* (New York: Hill and Wang, 1983).

61. Bricknell, *The Natural History of North Carolina*, pp. 107–29. Both the elk and bison were hunted for their meat by Indians and early European settlers. The elk was gone from the state by 1750 while the bison lasted until 1760. The larger carnivores, the cougar and wolf, held on longer. As their natural prey declined, these carnivores increasingly preyed on livestock on the open range. John B. Funderburg and David S. Lee, "Where the Buffalos Roamed," *Wildlife in North Carolina* 42, no. 7 (1978):11–13, give the dates of the last occurrences of wildlife species extirpated from North Carolina.

The causal linkages between human activities and wildlife abundance did not escape the perceptive observation of some, such as William Elliott, who wrote: "If my observation serves me faithfully, I should say, that unlike all or nearly all other game, [quail] have increased instead of diminishing with the clearing of the country. The extensive grain fields furnish them with ample subsistence; and it may be, that while man has increased *his* means of annoyance, *that* from birds and beasts of prey has, in greater proportion, decreased." *Carolina Sports by Land and Water*, pp. 271–72.

62. Quotations from Alexander S. Salley, Jr., ed., *Narratives of Early Carolina* (New York: Charles Scribner's Sons, 1911), p. 47.

63. John Lawson described the Indian techniques for killing deer, including the firing of cane swamps and decoy stalking. The latter tactic, by which stalking hunters disguised themselves in deerskin and antlers, was so clever in "counterfeiting" the exact motions and behavior of deer that several stalkers were mistaken for deer and killed by other stalkers; see Lawson, *The History of Carolina*, p. 68.

64. John Lawson scores the Indians for their practice of "starving and beating" their semidomesticated "wolves." For their horses, he notes, the Indians "continually cram and feed with Maiz, and what the Horse will eat, till he is as fat as a Hog; never making any further use of him than to fetch a Deer home, that is killed somewhere near the Indian's plantation." See Lawson, *A New Voyage to Carolina*, reprint, Huge Talmage Lefler, ed. (Chapel Hill: University of North Carolina Press, 1967), p. 44.

65. William S. Powell, in James W. Clay, Douglas M. Orr, Jr., and Alfred W. Stuart, eds., *North Carolina Atlas: Portrait of a Changing Southern State* (Chapel Hill: University of North Carolina Press, 1975), part 2, "History," pp. 12–31.

66. Crow, *The Black Experience in Revolutionary North Carolina*; Powell, *North Carolina Atlas*, part 2, "History," p. 26.

67. Lawrence Lee identified the Indians of North Carolina as belonging to three groups. The Cherokees of the mountains were the most numerous, followed by the Catawbas of the Piedmont and the Tuscaroras of the Coastal Plain. A century after the first permanent white settlements, the Tuscaroras were in a dismal state of rapid population decline. The Catawbas of the Piedmont fared little better. They were decimated by a smallpox epidemic in 1759–60 and the survivors fled to South Carolina, where a reservation was created for them. E. Lawrence Lee, *Indian Wars in North Carolina 1663–1763* (Raleigh, N.C.: State Department of Archives and History, 1963; reprint, 1968); Ruth Y. Wetmore, "The Role of the Indian in North Carolina History," *North Carolina Historical Review* 56, no. 2 (1979):162–76; Blu, *The Lumbee Problem*.

68. North Carolina was considered the most democratic of the British colonies and the one in which the "leveling spirit" was well advanced. See Alan D. Watson, *Society in Colonial North Carolina* (Raleigh, N.C.: Division of Archives and History, 1975), p. 10.

69. Franklin, *The Free Negro in North Carolina*; Genovese, *Roll, Jordan, Roll*; Crow, *The Black Experience in Revolutionary North Carolina*; Joyner, *Down by the Riverside*.

70. Harry R. Merrens, *Colonial North Carolina in the Eighteenth Century* (Chapel Hill: University of North Carolina Press, 1964).

71. Sam Bowers Hilliard, *Hog Meat and Hoecake: Food Supply in the Old South, 1840–1860* (Carbondale: Southern Illinois University Press, 1972); Cornelius O. Cathey, *Agricultural Development in North Carolina, 1783–1860* (Chapel Hill: University of North Carolina Press, 1956). Chapter 9 of the latter volume is on the care and maintenance of livestock.

72. Angus Wilton McLean, *A History of the Scotch in North Carolina*, 2 vols., bound in the North Carolina Collection, The University of North Carolina at Chapel Hill, n.d., see p. 83. As governor, Angus McLeon helped institutionalize the first State Game Commission in 1926. See next chapter.

73. Merrens, *Colonial North Carolina*.

74. John B. Funderburg and David S. Lee, "Where the Buffalos Roamed," *Wildlife in North Carolina* 42, no. 7 (1978):11–13.

75. Familiarity formed the basis for the classification of mammals proposed in 1731 by Mark Catesby, a British-trained naturalist. Catesby described the Carolina mammals and catalogued them into four groups. In the first group were fourteen species whose types were also found in Europe. In this group were deer, squirrels, foxes, polecats, and porcupines. A second category included species such as the beaver and the house rat, which Catesby considered the same as those found in Europe. Domesticated mammals that Europeans brought with them and introduced into the New World made up his third category and included the horse, donkey, cow, sheep, as well as other domesticated mammals. His final category included the opossum, raccoon, and wolverine—species not found in the Old World. See Mark Catesby, *The Natural History of Carolina, Florida, and the Bahama Islands*, 2 vols. (London: Benjamin White, 1771).

76. For South Carolina, see Olmsted, *Journey in the Seaboard Slave States*, p. 411. See also Hilliard, *Hog Meat and Hoecake*, pp. 47–49, 70–83. Hilliard reviews the literature on the diet of antebellum Southerners. For a later postbellum period, see W. McKee Evans, *Ballots and Fence Rails: Reconstruction in the Lower Cape Fear* (Chapel Hill: University of North Carolina Press, 1966), p. 103, for a depiction of venison and possum in Wilmington markets.

77. Hilliard, *Hog Meat and Hoecake*.

78. Henry William Harrington, Jr., Papers, no. 314, Southern Historical Collection, The University of North Carolina at Chapel Hill. In his diary Harrington reports killing squirrels on November 15, 1849, and on May 19, 1851; geese on November 28, 1849; and rabbits on March 18, 1961.

79. See C. W. Webber, *Wild Scenes and Wild Hunters of the World*, 1852, pp. 34–77.

80. Elliott, *Carolina Sports by Land and Water*, p. 273, devotes only four lines to the passenger pigeon, noting its "occasional visits." The date of last sighting of wild pigeons in North Carolina was 1894; see Funderburg and Lee, "Where the Buffalos Roamed," p. 12.

81. The reminiscences of Kemp Plummer Battle reveal the tension, impatience, and competition one feels when growing up in the shadow of an older brother, who always got to carry the gun: "It was my privilege to walk behind and carry any birds which might be the victims of his prowess. As a reward I was allowed to shoot a sparrow or snowbird toward the close of the hunt. Such was my devotion to him that I was proud of this companionship. If the game had been more plentiful, I should have had more frequent chances. He was afraid to trust me to shoot a large bird and besides it would have detracted from his glory" (*Memories of an Old-Time Tar Heel* [Chapel Hill: University of North Carolina Press, 1945], p. 61).

82. Rawick, *The American Slave*, vol. 14, pp. 199–200.

Chapter Three
Progress and Poverty

1. Like William Elliott, Alexander Hunter was born in the Old South, the son of a planter, and wrote about his sporting life. Yet their worlds were very different. Hunter's sporting life embraced the traumatic transitions of the Old South, Reconstruction, and the beginning of industrialization. Planters often tried to disguise, if not deny, these major discontinuities in political and economic life. See Alexander Hunter, *The*

Huntsman in the South, vol. 1, *Virginia and North Carolina* (New York: The Neale Publishing Co., 1908). The page citations in this chapter are to this edition and are given parenthetically. Alexander Hunter also published a book of his combat adventures during the Civil War and wrote sporting articles. See, for example, his "The Club Houses of Currituck Sound," *Harper's Weekly* 36 (March 12, 1892):253–55. The George Anderson Mercer diary, no. 503, is in the Southern Historical Collection, The University of North Carolina at Chapel Hill.

2. The phrase is from Gavin Wright, *Old South, New South: Revolutions in the Southern Economy Since the Civil War* (New York: Basic Books, 1986).

3. Thomas Gilbert Pearson makes a similar point on the amounts of money brought into North Carolina at the turn of the century by Northern quail shooters. The extensive quail preserves in the state at that time kept large kennels of pointers and setters: "Many hundreds, if not thousands, of guards, dog-trainers, stablemen, servants, and assistants were employed. Railroad fares, hotel bills, guns, ammunition, hunting equipment, hunting licenses, payments for leases, and other expenses ran into very large sums. Similar conditions obtained also in sections of other Southern states where the quail naturally is abundant" (*Adventures in Bird Protection* [New York: D. Appleton-Century Co., 1937] pp. 106–107.

4. Elsewhere Hunter depicts the great difference in character between setters and pointers. After a year's absence, his pointers did not recognize him, yet in obeying his commands their memories were gradually regained. Setters are different for "their faithful, loyal hearts never forget" (*The Hunstman in the South*, pp. 120–21).

5. My summary treatment of these late nineteenth-century issues and political maneuverings owe much to Tober, *Who Owns Wildlife?*; Lund, *American Wildlife Law*; and to the other authors cited in this section.

6. Theodore Whaley Cart, "The Struggle for Wildlife Protection in the United States, 1870–1900: Attitudes and Events Leading to the Lacey Act" (Ph.D. diss., The University of North Carolina at Chapel Hill, 1971). Also Tober, *Who Owns Wildlife?*, chapter 2.

7. Since all hunters ended up killing what they pursued, the distinguishing characteristics separating sportsmen from other hunters were at first not readily apparent. Some sporting associations marketed their bags of game, primarily waterfowl, until the line between sports and market hunting became more sharply drawn through intensified political debate in the last quarter of the nineteeth century; George T. Nichols, "Notes on Dogs and Hunting, 1875–1880," notebook in Manuscript Department, William R. Perkins Library, Duke University. See his Letter to Editor, *Rod and Gun*, dated March 13, 1877.

8. Nichols, "Notes on Dogs and Hunting," January 1875, manuscript in Perkins Library, Duke University.

9. Ibid., August 9, 1876.

10. An example of an individual market hunter was Ward Allen, who lived in the shadow of Savannah, Georgia, and supplied game to local merchants; John Eugene Cay, Jr., *Ward Allen: Savannah River Market Hunter* (Savannah, Georgia: The Pigeonhole Press, 1958). For other references to market hunters and their methods see H. Clay Merritt, *The Shadow of a Gun* (Chicago: F. T. Peterson Co., 1904); David and Jim Kimball, *The Market Hunter* (Minneapolis: Dillon Press, 1969).

11. Frederick C. Havenmeyer II, "Currituck Sound" (pp. 189–201), and Edgar Berke, "Pamlico Sound" (pp. 202–22), in *Duck Shooting along the Atlantic Tidewater*, Eugene V. Connett, ed. (New York: William Morrow, 1947).

12. In South Carolina, market hunters were initially licensed in 1883, and non-residents in North Carolina, by county option, beginning in 1895; T. S. Palmer, U.S. Department of Agriculture, Bureau of Biological Survey, Circular 54, "Statistics of Hunting Licenses" (Washington, D.C.: Government Printing Office, October 1906).

13. Lund, *American Wildlife Law*.

14. James Lee Love Papers #4139, Southern Historical Collection, The University of North Carolina at Chapel Hill; W. E. Stone, *Walton Stone* (New York, J. J. Little & Ives, 1931).

15. John B. Alexander, *Reminiscences of the Past Sixty Years* (Charlotte, N.C.: Ray Printing Co., 1908), p. 425.

16. In an agricultural society, use rights in land underlie basic social relationships. Steven Hahn suggests that the motives for landowner behavior and disposition toward the inevitable postbellum skirmishes over trespass, enclosure, stock, and game laws are to be found in the larger context of the transition from slavery and the reorganization of agricultural labor. See Hahn, "Hunting, Fishing, and Foraging," pp. 37–64; also Harold D. Woodman, "Sequel to Slavery: The New History Views the Postbellum South," *Journal of Southern History* 43 (1977):523–54. One of the first petitions to the General Assemby of North Carolina submitted by the citizens of newly created Scotland County was for a law "requiring written permission from the landowner for hunting on all kinds on [*sic*] lands in the county." It was signed by Maxey S. John and forty landowners. North Carolina State Archives, Legislative Papers and Petitions, 1901 (Box 46, Wildlife and Hunting).

17. John F. Stover, *The Railroads of the South 1865-1900: A Study of Finances and Control* (Chapel Hill: University of North Carolina Press, 1955).

18. The railroad expansion in the South after the Civil War facilitated the spread of field sports and made regional and national competitions possible. Horses, dogs, as well as baseball teams moved about the country. Owners also moved their breeding stock and contracted for stud fees over greater distances. The potential for movement and travel demanded standardization and the creation of mutually agreeable rules and regulations in formal competitions. These new practices eclipsed local traditions, for money and reputations could be staked out at larger field trials. See John Richards Betts, *America's Sporting Heritage 1850–1950* (Reading, Mass.: Addison-Wesley, 1974), and Richard D. Mandell, *Sport: A Cultural History* (New York: Columbia University Press, 1984).

19. Quote is from William Bruce Leffingwell, *The Happy Hunting Grounds, also Fishing in the South* (Chicago: Donohue and Henneberry, 1895), booklet in the North Carolina Collection, The University of North Carolina at Chapel Hill. By the beginning of the twentieth century, sporting-goods manufacturers and marketing agents could provide field sportsmen with standardized equipment and mass-produced accessories. The perfection of weapons and cartridges after 1875 made hunting affordable and accessible to many urban men. The processes of participation in sports, sports business, and the integration of sporting myths into American culture were swift and perhaps more pervasive than elsewhere in the world. The very wealthy displayed their affluence

to outsiders and to each other by conspicuously expensive sports-yacht races, by exclusive memberships in country clubs, and by plantation-style battues. The integration of sport into the life-style of the working class was aided by better and cheaper transportation and communication, by their greater disposable incomes, and by shorter working hours. See Tober, *Who Owns Wildlife?* For comparable changes in life-styles and the enthusiasm for sport in the Old World, see Richard Holt, *Sport and Society in Modern France* (Hamden, Conn.: Archon Books, 1981).

20. Southern Railway Company, *Shooting and Fishing in the South* (New York: Frank Presbrey, 1897), promotional booklet in the North Carolina Collection, The University of North Carolina at Chapel Hill.

21. Ibid., p. 25.

22. Ibid. See also Atlantic and North Carolina Railroad, *Hunting and Fishing in Eastern North Carolina, Time Tables of Passenger Trains and Thorough Schedules*, 1905, promotional booklet in the North Carolina Collection, The University of North Carolina at Chapel Hill.

23. Field trials at Pinehurst and elsewhere in piedmont North Carolina were becoming "traditions" by this time. See Southern Railway Company, *Hunting and Fishing in the South* (Washington, D.C., 1904), pp. 15–16; copy in the Sterling Library, Yale University. Seaboard Air Line Railway, *Seaboard Game Trails*, 1921, promotional booklet in the North Carolina Collection, The University of North Carolina at Chapel Hill.

24. Quail preserves in North Carolina were large and numerous at this time. See Lawrence S. Earley, "Quail Paradise in the Piedmont," *Wildlife in North Carolina* 50, no. 12 (1986):18–23; Hugh T. Lefler, ed., *North Carolina History: Told by Contemporaries* (Chapel Hill: University of North Carolina Press, 1965), p. 561; Pearson, *Adventures in Bird Protection*, p. 105; Herbert Job, "The Story of a Game Preserve," *Field and Stream*, September 1909, pp. 441–46; *Prospectus*, Shocco Game Association, 1894, promotional copy in North Carolina Collection, The University of North Carolina at Chapel Hill.

25. Southern Railway Company, *Hunting and Fishing in the South*, p. 18.

26. Atlantic and North Carolina Railroad, *Hunting and Fishing in Eastern North Carolina*, p. 8.

27. The quote is from Pearson, *Adventures in Bird Protection*, pp. 83–84. Pearson was a professor of biology at the State Normal College in Greensboro and secretary of the state's Audubon Society. Ernest Ingersoll, "A History of the Audubon Movement," *Forest and Stream* 82 (March 14 and 28, 1914):339–40, 405–407. Pearson's autobiography is *Adventures in Bird Protection*.

28. W. W. Greener, *The Gun and Its Development* (New York: Bonanza Books, 1910); Richard Akehurst, *Sporting Guns* (London: Octopus Books, 1972). For one of the many debates among sportsmen on the qualities of different weapons, see "Breech vs. Muzzle Loaders," *Forest and Stream*, March 2, 1882.

29. Roger Longrigg, *The English Squire and His Sport* (New York: St. Martin's Press, 1977).

30. Ibid.; Keith Thomas, *Man and the Natural World: A History of the Modern Sensibility* (New York: Pantheon, 1983).

31. Elliott, *Carolina Sports by Land and Water*, pp. 191–92.

32. Lawrence Rawstorne, Esq., *Gamonia: Or the Act of Preserving Game; and an*

Improved Method of Making Plantation and Covers, Explained and Illustrated (London: Rudolph Ackermann, 1837), copy in Beinecke Rare Book and Manuscript Library, Yale University.

33. Anthony Vandervell and Charles Coles, *Game and the English Landscape: The Influence of the Chase on Sporting Art and Scenery* (New York: Viking Press, 1980).

34. Using British models and examples, some well-placed groups of Northern sportsmen sought to achieve their objectives through the private expedient of game preserves, an idea and instrument long used by English sportsmen. The first large-scale demonstration of integrated resource planning for recreational purposes was the Blooming Grove Park Association, incorporated in 1871. This park, some 4-½ hours by rail from New York City, contained over 12,000 acres in northeastern Pennsylvania. See John F. Reiger, *American Sportsmen and the Origin of Conservation* (New York: Winchester Press, 1975), p. 57; Tober, *Who Owns Wildlife?*, pp. 126–27. The Blooming Grove Park Association led sportsmen elsewhere to imitate its organizational structure. The recently subdued South offered potential as preserve land to wealthy, well-organized Northern entrepreneurs. See Pearson, *Adventures in Bird Protection*, p. 105; Clifton Paisley, *From Cotton to Quail* (Tallahassee: University Presses of Florida, 1981).

35. The publishers of sporting magazines were operating in a rapidly changing field. An expanding human population together with available capital and a dynamic technology provided the basis for the development of American territory and resources. In the process, society's forms of entertainment and sport were transformed. Betts, *America's Sporting Heritage*.

36. Reiger, *American Sportsmen*.

37. Among the most influential organizations was the Boone and Crocket Club founded in New York in 1887 by Theodore Roosevelt. The club was a "veritable clearinghouse of conservation ideas and personages," which included among its membership criteria that "members must have shot an adult male of at least three American big-game species of fair chase methods or still hunting." See Thomas L. Altherr, "The American Hunter-Naturalist and the Development of the Code of Sportsmanship," *Journal of Sport History* 5, no. 1 (1978):7–22; also Reiger, *American Sportsmen*.

38. George T. Nichols, "Notes on Dogs and Hunting," for February 8 and 16, 1875, Manuscript Department, Perkins Library, Duke University.

39. Cart, "The Struggle for Wildlife Protection."

40. Such differences underscored the enforcement problems of regulating the interstate commmerce in game. The Lacey Act passed by Congress in 1900 was designed to remedy these problems. It sought to regulate the marketing of wildlife by placing Congress's constitutional power over interstate commerce at the service of the states. Although the Lacey Act had the effect of immediately broadening state power in regulating wildlife harvests, its ultimate effect was to make that power narrower, since the federal government was introduced as a competing regulator. See Lund, *American Wildlife Law*; Tober, *Who Owns Wildlife?*; and Theodore W. Cart, "The Lacey Act: America's First Nationwide Wildlife Statute," *Forest History* 17 (October 1973):4–13.

41. An extreme example of local legislation is a statute passed in 1897 "to allow N. W. Craft to collect birds on his premises at any time of the year." Cited in U.S. Department of Agriculture, Division of Biological Survey, Bulletin No. 41, "Chronol-

ogy and Index of the More Important Events in American Game Protection, 1776–1911," by T. S. Palmer (Washington, D.C.: Government Printing Office, 1912), under North Carolina. North Carolina, with 316 game laws passed between 1901 and 1910, was well ahead of all other states with such laws, though they applied only to specified counties. Petitions by citizens to the state's General Assembly are referred to a committee in either the House or the Senate. If a petition is approved by the committee, it becomes a bill and is read three times before the chamber before a vote is taken. If it passes, the bill is routed to the other chamber for a similar process of actions and readings. If both House and Senate approve the bill, it becomes a law.

42. A petition dated February 12, 1909, bearing the signatures of 149 citizens of Rowan and Davidson counties, protested the closing of the quail season because "we believe that the passage of this law would be to the great injury of our own citizens, in that no person would be allowed to kill a quail for his own use or in case of sickness, for the use of members of his family." Petitions are filed in the North Carolina Division of Archives and History, Raleigh, under Legislative Papers beginning in 1901. For a listing of North Carolina laws relative to the transportation and sale of game, see U.S. Department of Agriculture, Division of Biological Survey, Bulletin No. 14, "Laws Regulating the Transportation and Sale of Game," by T. S. Palmer and W. H. Olds (Washington, D.C.: Government Printing Office, 1900).

43. N.C. Reports, vol. 126, pp. 979–84. In 1896 the United States Supreme Court, in *Geer* vs. *Connecticut*, decided that the country's game belonged not to the landowner but to the state, which held it in trust for all citizens; see John B. Burnham, "The Old Era—and the New," *Bulletin of the American Game Protective Association* 14 (January 1925):13.

44. U.S. Department of Agriculture, Division of Biological Survey, Circular No. 54, "Statistics on Hunting Licenses," by T. S. Palmer (Washington, D.C.: Government Printing Office, 1906). Within North Carolina, Dare County had a nonresident hunting license for $25 in 1895. In 1903 the General Assembly passed a law requiring a statewide nonresident hunting license costing $10.25. The proceeds from license sales were to support the work of the state Audubon Society. In 1927 a new state law required licenses from residents as well as nonresidents. North Carolina, Department of Conservation and Development, Bulletin No. 36, "Hunting in North Carolina" (Raleigh, N.C., issued June 1928). A legacy of watchful resistance toward preference by legislators given to wealthy individuals ensured that the cost of resident licenses remained low in comparison to charges for outsiders, and that landowners hunting on their own land in season were exempt. The problem of preventing funds solicited from sportsmen for the support of state wildlife agencies from being used as general state revenue was tackled later by federal policy. The Pittman-Robertson Act of 1937 stipulated that proceeds from federal taxes on hunting equipment were to be redistributed to the states on the condition that hunting-license sales in those states were earmarked exclusively for their respective wildlife agencies. See Lund, *American Wildlife Law*, pp. 85–86.

45. Thomas Gilbert Pearson, the secretary of the state Audubon Society, was aware of the revolution he was instigating by implementing the game laws in North Carolina. In a few choice paragraphs he mentions the disparate county laws that govern the take of the same species, the shipment of game birds to Northern markets, the selling of live songbirds, and the frequency of game for sale throughout the state. For example, "Country men and boys, both white and colored, shot and trapped game-birds every-

where, and traded them at the 'cash and barter' stores for food, ammunition, chewing tobacco, overalls or cloth for their women's dresses" (*Adventures in Bird Protection*, pp. 82–83). For the law establishing the Audubon Society in North Carolina, see Private Laws of the State Of North Carolina at its Session of 1903, c. 337, s. 1, 8, 10. Chapter 40 of Thomas B. Womach, Needham Y. Gulley, and William B. Rodma, *Revisal of North Carolina Code* (Raleigh, N.C.: E. M. Uzzell & Co, 1905), contains the charges of the Audubon Society, its wardens, support by nonresident license fees, and county laws on the taking of game mammals and birds.

46. Local laws proved the bane of the Audubon Society. According to Pearson, *Adventures in Bird Protection*, some in the state looked upon the idea of bird protection and the Audubon Society as a "Yankee idea" and opposed it for that reason (p. 108). Opposition also came from the quail and waterfowl hunting interests in the state. Eventually the "killers of birds" organized for political action and influenced a state senator to work a "trick" by introducing a bill for the better enforcement of game laws in Bertie and Currituck (p. 168). The bone of contention was local rather than state control of enforcement and license money. A majority of counties subscribed to the bill and withdrew from the Audubon Society. See Pearson, ibid., pp. 167–73. For the content of the law and a list of counties affected by the 1909 law, see "An Act for the Better Enforcement of the Game Law in Certain Counties," *Public Laws of North Carolina*, Session of 1909, c. 840, pp. 1230–1232.

47. Robins were legally taken in North Carolina from October 15 to April 1 until 1903. Before their northward migration, robins concentrated in the state and were killed by the thousands. In the spring of 1897, some 2,700 robins were killed; their carcasses were shipped north, where their sale was prevented within the District of Columbia. See U.S. Department of Agriculture, Division of Biological Survey, Bulletin No. 12, "Legislation for the Protection of Birds Other Than Game Birds," by T. S. Palmer (Washington, D.C.: Government Printing Office, 1900). Bobolinks (reed or rice birds) were killed in enormous numbers for the market and for sport when they descended on the rice fields of the Carolinas each autumn. On the lower Cape Fear River in the late nineteenth century, the arrival of these birds marked a festive occasion. The rice fields were thrown open to all hunters—blacks, whites, men, boys, and even women. See W. McKee Evans, *Ballots and Fence Rails: Reconstruction on the Lower Cape Fear* (Chapel Hill: University of North Carolina Press, 1966), p. 245; also Archibald Rutledge, *Old Plantation Days* (New York: Frederick A. Stokes, 1921), pp. 271–81. After the passage of the "model bill," bobolinks continued to be shot as pests. Their numbers diminished when the rice plantation and its economy collapsed.

48. Four groups of birds—the Anatidae, Rallidae, Limicolae, and Gallinae—included most of the species commonly hunted for food and sport in the United States. This ornithological classification by family and genera was the basis used in the model bill. An exception was the mourning dove, a species rare in many Northern states but plentiful in most Southern states, where it remains a major game species today. Other species not belonging to these four groups, including the flicker, meadowlark, bluebird, and robin, were deemed by legislators as more valuable to the farmer as insectivores than to hunters as a few mouthfuls of meat. See U.S. Department of Agriculture, Division of Biological Survey, Bulletin No. 12, "Legislation for the Protection of Birds Other Than Game Birds," by T. S. Palmer (Washington, D.C.: Government Printing Office, 1900).

49. Administratively, this structure linked wildlife closely with forestry, fisheries, and other conservation programs. It had the same governing board of twelve appointed members, with the governor as chairman ex officio. *Public Laws of North Carolina*, 1927, c. 51 and 60.

50. North Carolina Department of Conservation and Development, Bulletin No. 36, "Hunting in North Carolina" (Raleigh, June 1928), p. 14.

51. The annual fee for residents hunting their respective counties was $1.25; for those hunting throughout the state it was $5.25. Nonresidents were charged $15.25. Residents under twenty-one years of age and seeking game on their own land in open season and parties hunting on leased farm land needed no license. The possession of a hunting license did not give its possessor the right to hunt on another's land without the landowner's permission. Hunting licenses provided the Game Commission with its first estimates of hunters and their kills. During the 1927–28 season, 26,035 resident county, 11,686 resident state, and 878 nonresident hunting licenses were sold. In Scotland County, 584 county and 50 state resident licenses were sold. With two-thirds of these license purchasers responding, Scotland Countyans reported killing 2,638 rabbits, 2,307 squirrels, 1 deer, 27 raccoons, 398 opossums, 19 minks or skunks, 39 muskrats, 3,370 quails, 6 turkeys, 94 pheasants, 45 snipes, 53 woodcocks, 537 doves, 1 goose, and 74 ducks. See North Carolina Department of Conservation and Development, Bulletin No. 36, "Hunting in North Carolina" (Raleigh, N.C., June 1928), pp. 43, 45.

52. Ibid., p. 39: "The different status of the fox made it a most difficult proposition for any kind of State-wide regulation. In some localities, Reynard is looked upon as a fur-bearing animal entitled to proportionate protection in the same class with other game; in others, he is considered an outlaw and is hunted unremittingly; while in still others, the wily animal is stocked at considerable expense and fox hunting is considered one of the major sports. The fox hunter is assured of ample provisions for following the hounds in counties where the animal is protected."

53. Dense concentrations of wildlife, such as overwintering waterfowl in Currituck Sound, were the first to receive state protection and experimentation in the form of new laws and enforcement, which were then applied elsewhere in the state. It would be worthwhile excursion into regional history to determine whether the promoters of these laws were local groups seeking to preserve remaining waterfowl or market hunters formalizing their agreements to discourage competition from outside groups. For a chronology of state statutes, see U.S. Department of Agriculture, Division of Biological Survey, Bulletin No. 41, "Chronology and Index of the More Important Events in American Game Protection, 1776–1911," by T. S. Palmer (Washington, D.C.: Government Printing Office, 1912).

54. North Carolina Division of Archives and History, under Wildlife Resources Commission, General Correspondence.

55. North Carolina Division of Archives and History, under Wildlife Resources Commission, Report of Game Division for June 30–December 31, 1943, Hinton James, Commissioner. Hinton James was a former resident of Scotland County.

56. The passage of this law was an attempt by sportsmen to take wildlife "out of politics" and away from the influence of forestry and other interest groups. The law provided for nine districts in the state, each represented by a commissioner, elected by sportsmen but appointed by the governor. Additional commissioners are appointed by

the General Assembly. The Wildlife Commission has authority to set and enforce game regulations, hire and fire the executive officer, and manage the use of funds. The Wildlife Commission staff formulates tentative regulations for each district, holds public hearings in each district, and adjusts regulations on the basis of biological and political contingencies. *North Carolina Laws and Resolutions*, 1947, c. 263, s. 3, 4. In 1971 the State Government Reorganization Act placed the Wildlife Commission in the Department of Natural and Economic Resources. *General Statutes of North Carolina*, 1971, 147–247, v. 3C, p. 133.

57. North Carolina Wildlife Resources Commission, "Hunting in North Carolina," by Frank B. Barick (Raleigh, N.C., 1973).

58. The Wildlife Commission operates politically at all levels. By virtue of their organizational skills, wealth, and social network, some sportsmen's groups are better situated to influence the decisions made in the state's regulatory commissions and thereby structure the norms by which others are expected to conform publicly. Political influences are also evident in the appointment of wildlife commissioners by the governor and in the ranking members of each chamber in the General Assembly. Beyond their sporting interests, these appointees have valuable assets such as appropriate political affiliation, wealth, desirable networks, and other attributes considered important by those who make the appointments. Within the commission itself, political dimensions are visible in the decisions it makes, such as how, when, and where to spend money; in the identity of its major benefactors (game vs. nongame interests); in the selection of information on which to base decisions; in the choice of biologists and specialists; and in the setting of time and place for hearings. Prosecutions and convictions fall disproportionately on poorer groups and those less informed of the commission's activities. As with public institutions generally, the Wildlife Commission is most responsive to groups that are politically connected, generally resourceful and wealthy, and organized for lobbying.

59. Wright, *Old South, New South*.

60. The nature, extent, and interpretation of the transformation and relationships between whites and nonwhites, between the city and countryside, and between labor and management are subjects of current debates among historians of the postbellum South. I summarize the major events as they affected eastern North Carolina. In addition to the references cited in this section, I found the following volumes particularly helpful in my attempts to summarize this period of Tarheel history: Hugh Talmage Lefler and Albert Ray Newsome, *The History of a Southern State: North Carolina* (Chapel Hill: University of North Carolina Press, 1973); Dwight B. Billings, Jr., *Planters and the Making of the New South: Class, Politics, and Development in North Carolina, 1865–1900*, (Chapel Hill: University of North Carolina Press, 1979); Paul D. Escott, *Many Excellent People: Power and Privilege in North Carolina, 1850–1900* (Chapel Hill: University of North Carolina Press, 1985); and Paul M. Gaston, *The New South Creed: A Study in Southern Mythmaking* (New York: Alfred A. Knopf, 1970).

61. Harold D. Woodman, "Sequel to Slavery: The New History Views the Postbellum South," *Journal of Southern History* 43 (1977):523–54, and Hahn, "Hunting, Fishing, and Foraging," pp. 37–64, provide a perspective for land closures throughout the South as well as their implications. For North Carolina, see Escott, *Many Excellent People*, chapters 5 and 6.

62. Woodman, "Sequel to Slavery."

63. Ibid., p. 553. Also I. A. Newby, *The South: A History* (New York: Holt, Rinehart and Winston, 1978), chapter 10; Lacy K. Ford, "Rednecks and Merchants: Economic Development and Social Tensions in the South Carolina Upcountry, 1865–1900," *Journal of American History* 71 (September 1984):294–318. Eric Foner, *Reconstruction: America's Unfinished Revolution, 1863–1877* (New York: Harper and Row, 1988).

64. Throughout the 1870s and 1880s petitions to the General Assembly for and against the stock laws were common in North Carolina. For the importance of the struggle for the open range in the state, see Escott, *Many Excellent People*, chapter 7. Also J. Crawford King, Jr., "The Closing of the Southern Range: An Exploratory Study," *Journal of Southern History* 48 (February 1982):53–70.

65. Donald B. Dodd and Wynelle S. Dodd, *Historical Statistics of the South* (Tuscaloosa: University of Alabama Press, 1973), provide information on changes in demography and agriculture in North Carolina. See aslo Billings, *Planters and the Making of the New South*; Escott, *Many Excellent People*; and Jacquelyn D. Hall, James Leloudis, Robert Korstad, Mary Murphy, LuAnn Jones, and Christopher B. Daly, *Like a Family: The Making of a Southern Cotton Mill World* (Chapel Hill: University of North Carolina Press, 1987).

66. James L. Hunt, "The Making of a Populist: Marion Butler, 1863–1895," *North Carolina Historical Review* 62 (January 1985):53–77. The *News and Observor*, North Carolina Quadricentennial Commemorative Edition (Raleigh, N.C., July 1985), section 4, contains articles on these tumultuous times.

67. In the closing days before the 1898 election, "Red Shirts" (white men wearing flaming red shirts, riding horses, carrying rifles) paraded in black neighborhoods, appeared at political rallies, and were particularly active in the southeastern counties. See Lefler and Newsome, *The History of a Southern State*. For a description of black-white relations after the Civil War, see Joel Williamson, *The Crucible of Race: Black-White Relations in the American South since Emancipation* (New York: Oxford University Press, 1984).

The Democrats won the 1898 election. It was followed almost immediately by race riots in Wilmington, where blacks were killed, their property was destroyed, and black officials were forced to flee; see H. Leon Prather, Sr., *We Have Taken a City: Wilmington Racial Massacre and Coup of 1898* (Cranbury, N.J.: Associated University Presses, 1984). Having won control of the General Assembly, the Democrats moved quickly to complete their political conquest and to eliminate blacks as a factor in politics. They reasserted legislative control over county government and proposed a constitutional amendment to disfranchise blacks.

This constitutional amendment required that any applicant to vote must have paid his poll tax and be able to read and write any section of the Constitution. A grandfather clause stipulated that no person who was entitled to vote on January 1867 or his lineal descendants were denied registration because of his inability to read, provided he register by December 1, 1908; see Lefler and Newsome, *The History of a Southern State*, pp. 559–60.

With white supremacy and Negro disfranchisement as the major issues, the Democrats won another sweeping victory in 1900. The adoption of the suffrage amendment deprived the Republicans of large numbers of potential voters, confirmed Democratic dominance in state politics, and strengthened the one-party system. It was not until

1973 and 1984 that a Republican was elected governor. Although blacks did not vote in large numbers again until the late 1960s, the race issue has surfaced at intervals. Earl Black and Merle Black, *Politics and Society in the South* (Cambridge, Mass.: Harvard University Press, 1987), discuss recent developments in Southern politics.

68. The first unit of the Alliance was formed at Ashpole in Robeson County, and the State Alliance was organized in Rockingham in 1887. Lefler and Newsome, *The History of the Southern State*, p. 528. The New County of Scotland, petition to Members of the General Assembly; petition on file, Collection of North Carolina, The University of North Carolina at Chapel Hill (Cp 971.83; R 53n).

69. White supremacy in the 1898 campaign was the topic of a poem written by Scotland County's own poet, John Charles McNeill:

> I cannot see, if you are dead,
>   Mr. Nigger,
> How orators could earn their bread,
>   Mr. Nigger,
> For they could never hold a crowd,
> Save they abused you long and loud
> As being a dark and threatening cloud,
>   Mr. Nigger.

Quoted in ibid., pp 558–59.

70. A brief account of John F. McNair's accomplishments is in "Scotland County," *The State* 10, No. 25 (November 25, 1942):22–23. Additional information is derived from my interviews with people who knew him.

71. For a sketch of Mark Morgan's life, see Samuel A. Ashe, Stephen B. Weeks, and Charles Van Noppen, eds., *Biographical History of North Carolina*, vol. 2 (Greensboro, N.C.: Charles L. Van Noppen, 1905).

72. The county was following a well-documented mainstream phenomenon in American development. Publicity was crucial for the economic success of the developing town and county. The *Laurinburg Exchange* became the vehicle for the rhetoric of "boosterism" with the community treated as a collective enterprise in which everyone was expected to benefit. The operative metaphor of the day was borrowed from baseball: everyone was expected to be a team player. Yet it was the community of property holders who gained most from increased land values and the increased volume of commerce. See Thorstein Veblen, *Absentee Ownership and Business Enterprise in Recent Times* (New York: B.W. Huebsch, 1923), as quoted in Wright, *Old South, New South*, p. 43. *Laurinburg Exchange*, May 15, 1924. Subsequent quotes are from this edition.

73. The railroads connected farmers and merchants to national markets. The county also had a hard-surfaced road that passed through Laurinburg and a highway on the drawing board to connect the road to South Carolina. As the twentieth century progressed, highways became more important than railways. The automobile removed the farmer from isolation and helped destroy some of his provincialism. Investment in an automobile may have kept many farmers poor, but it also gave them contacts. In 1927 Scotland County ranked thirty-sixth in the state with 2,195 cars, or one car per 7.5 inhabitants. *University of North Carolina Newsletter* 14, no. 2 (November 10, 1927), published by UNC Press.

74. All quotes from the *Laurinburg Exchange*, May 15, 1924.

75. Fred Hobson, *Tell About the South* (Baton Rouge: Louisiana State University Press, 1983).

76. How else does one explain the symbolic rivalry between Northern and Southern sportsmen? See, for example, Frederick Arthur, "How I 'made good'. A tale of rivalry on North Carolina quail between a local champion and a 'Yankee' who could shoot," *Field and Stream*, November 1906, pp. 659–61, and instances in Havilah Babcock, *Jaybirds Go to Hell on Fridays, and Other Stories* (New York: Holt, Rinehart and Winston, 1965), among others.

77. Dr. Hall was described as "a most eloquent and charming speaker" by the *Laurinburg Exchange*, May 15, 1924. Among other things, this religious idealism meant that Appomattox had not really settled the issue of Southern distinctiveness. Hobson, *Tell About the South*, and Williamson, *The Crucible of Race*.

78. In 1930 the farm agent sponsored a "Live at Home" program emphasizing the importance of home gardens to meet family food needs. Although he reported good results among "Negroes and the tenant class of white people," the agent found that tenants were not getting support and encouragement from their landlords. After holding a meeting with the large landowners and merchants, he reported increased interest by both landlords and tenants, with merchants, in some cases, refusing to extend credit to tenants without gardens. See North Carolina Agricultural Extension Service, North Carolina State College of Agriculture and Engineering, and United States Department of Agriculture Cooperating, Narrative Reports of S. E. Evans, County Agent, Scotland County, for years 1923–32 inclusive.

79. In 1928 North Carolina ranked sixth in the nation with 387,000 horses and mules, 90.4 percent of the number recorded for 1920. As the number of horses decreased and their function on the road and field was replaced by the automobile, the number of mules increased. In 1928 there were 25,000 more mules than in 1920. *University of North Carolina Newsletter* 14, no. 20 (March 28, 1928).

80. Agricultural Experiment Station of North Carolina State College of Agriculture and Engineering and North Carolina Department of Agriculture, Cooperating, Bulletin No. 309 (May 1937), "Recent Changes in the Social and Economic Status of Farm Families in North Carolina," by C. Horace Hamilton. His table (p. 26) shows an 8.4 and 10.2 percent decrease in white and black (colored) farm populations, respectively, between 1930 and 1935. Between 1900 and 1935 there were considerable shifts in the categories of farm owners, tenants, croppers, and laborers for both blacks and whites, as individuals either improved their economic status by moving up the "agricultural ladder" or as unfavorable conditions brought a trend in the opposite direction.

81. *Public Laws of North Carolina*, 1935, ch 226. The General Assembly authorized the Department of Conservation and Development to accept the land purchased by the Resettlement Administration as a game refuge and management area; see K. B. Pomeroy and James G. Yoko, *North Carolina Land: Ownership, Use and Management of Forest and Related Lands* (Washington, D.C.: American Forestry Association, 1964).

82. Wright, *Old South, New South*.

83. Gunnar Myrdal, *An American Dilemma* (New York: Harper and Brothers, 1944).

84. North Carolina Agricultural Extension Service, Annual Narrative Reports for Scotland County, 1957–1964, mimeographed on file, Scotland County Farm Extension Service.

85. In 1961 the county agricultural agent summarized his observations for the previous two years in these terms: the number of farms and farm operators had decreased, allowing for larger and more productive units; tenant-operated farms continued to dwindle and cash land rental became common; the harvesting of row crops was mechanized; and farm families were demanding more economic information both for agricultural production and for home management. The mechanization of cotton harvesting had become the concern of the Laurinburg Chamber of Commerce; see Laurinburg Chamber of Commerce, Agriculture Development Committee, "Here's What You Did in '60," report dated January 24, 1961. By 1963 the number of mechanical cotton harvesters rose to eighty-two, and the two-row machines increased from eighteen to thirty-three. In the same year, the agent believed that 85 percent of the cotton crop was harvested by machine, giving the county its highest yield per acre. See North Carolina Agricultural Extension Service, Annual Narrative Report for Scotland County, 1963.

86. U.S. Department of Commerce, Bureau of the Census, 1982 Census of Agriculture, Preliminary Report, Scotland County, North Carolina. Also U.S. Department of Agriculture Agricultural Stabilization and Conservation Service, Annual Reports, 1970–1976, Scotland County.

87. The complex of events and circumstances that led Scotland County to industrialize in the 1950s and 1960s goes beyond the popular explanations. The observations that the mechanization of agriculture was forcing people off the land, that young people with no local work prospects were leaving the community and that business had stagnant horizons, were true, but do not explain why Scotland County was more successful than its neighbors in attracting industry. Neighboring counties had similar conditions and offered the same advantages of inexpensive labor, land, location, and low taxes to entice industries. It is true that Scotland County's success can be attributed partly to its civic-minded, far-sighted leadership, but this influence does not account for the whole success story.

88. See the editorials in the *Laurinburg Exchange* for November 30, 1956 ("When Industry Takes a Look at Scotland County"), and December 7, 1956 ("Another Mill Closing" and "What's Good for Business Is Good for North Carolina"). On January 11, 1957, the *Laurinburg Exchange* carried the headline, "Organization for Industry Started—14 Man Group Acts."

89. *Laurinburg Exchange*, January 26, 1951.

90. If unchecked or poorly managed, industrialization by outsider interests has the dynamic of destroying any sense of local "community." Those in decision-making positions must be able to sustain, manage, and control the rate of industrialization and the forms it takes. See James C. Cobb, *The Selling of the South* (Baton Rouge: Louisiana State University Press, 1982).

91. Wright, *Old South, New South*, p. 273.

Chapter Four
Pursuits and Provincialism

1. Notes from a lecture by Robert B. Hazel, Chief, Division of Wildlife Protection, N.C. Wildlife Commission, before a class at N.C. State University, March 1961.

2. Mark Taylor, "Meet Norm L. Hunter," *Wildlife in North Carolina* 48 (March 1984):18–21; Terry Sharpe, "Wildlife by the Numbers," *Wildlife in North Carolina* 50 (February 1986):26–27.

3. Sharpe, "Wildlife by the Numbers," pp. 26–27.

4. It is possible to fish without a license in North Carolina, provided the person fishes in his county of residence and uses natural bait.

5. Demographics for Scotland County from North Carolina Office of State Budget and Management, Demographic Research Population Note No. 5, February 1980. Throughout the South until rather recently, whites have used a variety of complementary strategies to sustain black subservience and dependency. Blacks' education was limited to acquiring those skills useful in manual and farm labor. They were constantly reminded of their "inferior status" in a segregated society by prompt and severe force if they violated or defied expected behavior. Those not bending to the accepted mores were encouraged to head North. See the biography of Benjamin E. Mays, *Born to Rebel* (New York: Charles Scribner's Sons, 1971), p. 33–34. Also see Black and Black, *Politics and Society in the South*, p. 79.

6. Some of these state and county statistics may be compared to those collected nationally. Since 1955 these national surveys have been conducted every five years. In 1980, 17.4 million persons participated in some form of hunting, spent 330.2 million days hunting and $8.5 billion on licenses and equipment. Big-game hunting (deer, elk, bear, etc.) accounted for 11.8 million hunters, 112.8 million hunting days and $2.8 billion. Hunting for small game (squirrels, rabbits) occupied 12.4 million hunters, who spent 151.2 million hunting days, and $1.7 billion. Hunting for other types of animals (fox and raccoon) accounted for 2.6 million hunters, 38.4 million days afield, and $251 million. Men were much more likely to hunt than women: 92 percent of all hunters nationwide were men. Towns and rural areas, where 16 percent of the inhabitants hunted, were also home to 69 percent of all hunters. The 1980 survey found that 88 percent of all hunters hunt only in their states of residence. Big-game hunters averaged 8 trips and 10 days per hunter and spent an average of $236 per hunter and $25 per day of hunting each season. Small-game hunters spent an average of 12 days afield, $135 per hunter, and $11 per day. Hunters of other animals, including raccoons and foxes, averaged 15 days afield per hunter, who spent $95 during the season, or $7 per day. See U.S. Department of the Interior, Fish and Wildlife Service, and U.S. Department of Commerce, Bureau of the Census, *1980 National Survey of Fishing, Hunting, and Wildlife-Associated Recreation* (Washington, D.C.: Government Printing Office, 1982).

7. This high percentage is part of the continuing legacy of the region's underinvestment in public education. The majority of Southerners sampled in 1968 ended their formal education without obtaining a high school diploma; in North Carolina the figure was 61 percent. See Black and Black, *Politics and Society in the South*, p. 226.

8. Stephen R. Kellert, "Perceptions of Animals in American Society," *Transactions of the North American Wildlife and Natural Resources Conference* 41 (1976): 533–45.

9. Gwen K. Neville uses the anthropological concepts of kinship, community and socialization to explain persistence among Southern Presbyterians; see her "Kinfolds and the Covenant: Ethnic Community among Southern Presbyterians," in *The New Identity*, John Bennett, ed. (St. Paul, Minn.: West Publishing Company, 1975).

10. Trailers or mobile homes are associated with mobility, lower economic standing, and newness within a community. Trailers are relatively inexpensive and are left when the occupant is able to afford more permanent accommodations. Wooden frame

dwellings, often refurbished farmhouses and tenant shacks, are usually old, while houses made of cinder blocks are more recent in construction. Houses made of brick are the more substantial and durable types found today, although many newer dwellings combine wood with the sturdier materials. These housing types provide some general guidelines to the relative economic status of respondents within Scotland County.

The 1970 census listed 7,842 housing units in Scotland County: 4,320 owner occupied, 3,067 tenant occupied, and 265 vacant. Many of the vacant units were used seasonally. Of the occupied housing units, 5,677 had piped water, toilets and baths. The median value of owner-occupied houses was $10,500.

11. When the Democrats effectively established a one-party system in 1900 they transformed elections into a meaningless ritual. Scotland County continues this tradition and remains heavily Democratic. Fewer than 24 percent of eligible blacks voted in the 1960 election; see Figure 5.1 in Black and Black, *Politics and Society in the South*, p. 114. In 1982 the number of blacks in elected positions was four or less in both Scotland and Richmond counties; see Figure 6.2 in ibid., p. 149. In the May 1972 primary, 4,651 people voted out of 9,752 of those eligible; see Provisional League of Women Voters of Scotland County, "Know Your County," dated October 1973, 109 pp.

12. Kellert, "Perceptions of Animals in American Society," pp. 533–45.

13. These statements came from a variety of sources. Some of the ones about attitudes toward hunting and animals were taken from Stephen Kellert's study commissioned by the U.S. Fish and Wildlife Service, "From Kinship to Mastery," a copy of which I obtained in mimeographed form. Some statements about individuals and society were taken from Colin Bell and Howard Newby, *Community Studies: An Introduction to the Sociology of the Local Community* (New York: Praeger, 1973), and from Carole E. Hill, "Anthropological Studies in the American South: A Review and Directions," *Current Anthropology* 18 (June 1977):309–26.

14. Kellert, "Perceptions of Animals in American Society," p. 539.

15. For whites' attachment to their guns, see John Shelton Reed, *The Enduring South: Subcultural Persistence in Mass Society* (Chapel Hill: University of North Carolina Press, 1974), chapter 5; idem, *One South: An Ethnic Approach to Regional Culture* (Baton Rouge: Louisiana State University Press, 1982), chapter 11; and for a popular account, see Geoffrey Norman, "Why Southerners Love Guns," *Southern Magazine*, December 1986, pp. 59–62.

16. "The dog held a high place of esteem among domestic animals. Like the horse, he was believed to have hereditary qualities which were passed on for generations like those of the family to which he belonged. . . . A man who would strike he dog would beat his wife" (Ivey F. Grigg, *Man of the Piedmont: A Profile* [Lenoir, N.C.: Crabtree Press, 1976], p. 24). See also James William Jordan, "An Ambivalent Relationship: Dog and Human in the Folk Culture of the Rural South," *Appalachian Journal* 2 (1975):238–48. Ritvo, *The Animal Estate*, chapter 2, provides the background for understanding the evolution of the many dog breeds in Britain during the past two centuries.

17. This statement came from Karl A. Menninger, "Totemic Aspects of Contemporary Attitudes toward Animals," in George B. Wilbur and Warner Muensterberger, eds., *Psychoanalysis and Culture: Essays in Honor of Geza Roheim* (New York: International Universities Press, 1951), p. 45.

18. "Localism, violence, and a conservative religion are all plausible responses for a minority group, surrounded by a culture which is viewed as powerful, hostile, and unresponsive; all can be seen as adaptive reactions to the situation in which Southerners have, time and again, found themselves. I am suggesting that these defenses, mobilized in the antebellum sectional crisis, have been sustained by the chronic crisis which has been Southern history since" (Reed, *The Enduring South*, p. 89, reprinted with permission). Reed writes good prose and is a scholar of Southern persistence. Hill, "Anthropological Studies in the American South," pp. 309–26, provides a review of earlier studies in and of the South.

19. Reed, *One South*, p. 136, reprinted with permission.

20. Reed, *The Enduring South*, p. 35, reprinted with permission.

21. Reed, *One South*, pp. 159–60, reprinted with permission.

22. Ibid., chapter 12, and summarized in Black and Black, *Politics and Society in the South*, p. 226.

23. Reed, *One South*, p. 160–61, reprinted with permission.

24. This ideology on the part of Southern elites has been labeled the "traditionalistic political culture" by Daniel J. Elazar, *American Federalism*, 2d ed. (New York: Thomas Y. Crowell, 1972), pp. 99–102.

25. Reed, *One South*, p. 136.

26. See, for example, Wright, *Old South, New South*, and Black and Black, *Politics and Society in the South*.

27. Identified by Hill, "Anthropological Studies in the American South," p. 313.

28. Reed, *One South*, pp. 139–53; the quote is from p. 141.

29. Hill, *Anthropological Studies in the American South*, p. 313.

30. Blu, *The Lumbee Problem*.

31. Gwen Kennedy Neville, *Kinship and Pilgrimage: Rituals of Reunions in American Protestant Culture* (New York: Oxford University Press, 1987).

32. Samuel S. Hill, Jr., *Southern Churches in Crisis* (New York: Holt, Rinehart and Winston, 1966).

33. Charles Reagan Wilson and William Ferris, eds., *Encyclopedia of Southern Culture* (Chapel Hill: University of North Carolina Press, 1989).

Chapter Five
Fox Field Trials

1. D. R. Hundley, *Social Relations in Our Southern States* (New York: Henry B. Price, 1860), p. 35, and George W.P. Curtis, "Washington a Sportsman," *American Turf Register and Sporting Magazine* 1 (September 1829):6–9.

2. Hundley, *Social Relations in Our Southern States*, p. 342 for slaves, pp. 260–63 for poor whites.

3. For remarks on breeding foxhounds for color and quality, see "Don Juan," "Fox Hounds," *American Turf Register and Sporting Magazine* 1 (November 1829):127–30.

4. "The unspeakable in full pursuit of the uneatable" is what Oscar Wilde called hunters in *A Woman of No Importance*, Act 1.

5. Roger Longrigg, *The History of Foxhunting* (New York: Clarkson N. Potter, 1975).

6. Woods Walker, *Walker Hounds: Their Origin and Development* (Cynthiana, Ky.: Hobson Book Press, 1945), pp. 2, 3.

7. Walker, *Walker Hounds* and Longrigg, *The History of Foxhunting*, p. 194.

8. For a cross-cultural approach to metaphors, see James W. Fernandez, "Persuasions and Performances: Of the Beast in Everybody and the Metaphor of Everyman," in *Persuasions and Performances: The Play of Tropes in Culture* (Bloomington: Indiana University Press, 1986), pp. 3–27.

9. Edmund Leach, "Anthropological Aspects of Language: Animal Categories and Verbal Abuse," in *New Directions in the Study of Language*, Eric Lenneberg, ed. (Cambridge, Mass.: MIT Press, 1964), p. 54.

10. J. David Sapir, "The Anatomy of Metaphor," in *The Social Use of Metaphor: Essays on the Anthropology of Rhetoric*, J. David Sapir and J. Christopher Crocker, eds. (Philadelphia: University of Pennsylvannia Press, 1977), pp. 3–33; James Howe, "Fox Hunting as Ritual," *American Ethnologist* 8 (2):278–300.

11. The formal rules for the competitions are in National Foxhunters' Association (NFHA), "By-Laws, Running Rules and Regulations" (Lexington, Ky.: Chase Publishing Company, 1978).

12. "Swinging" or "skirting" dogs have long been selected against. Yet their "smartness" continues to find expression in current breeds. See 'Don Juan,' "Fox Hounds," p. 129.

13. Various cultural images of the fox are discussed by Mary Hufford, "The Fox," in *American Wildlife in Symbols and Story*, Angus K. Gillespie and Jay Mechling, eds. (Knoxville: University of Tennessee Press, 1987), 163–202. For an antebellum characterization of the fox, see "Natural History—Fox," *American Turf Register and Sporting Magazine* 1 (November 1829):141–45.

14. These laws were subsequently amended because of pressure from the trappers' association and from other sportsmen. This also led the Wildlife Commission to propose a process by which foxes in certain counties could be taken legally. This process begins with a petition to the Wildlife Commission signed by 15 percent of all license purchasers within a county. The commission then undertakes a study of the fox population and holds a public hearing. If all of these steps are followed, the commission may set a season for trapping and taking foxes under controlled conditions, whereby all pelts must bear tags and only a certain number may be taken. In many North Carolina counties, local laws continue to have precedent over statewide regulations.

15. Some fox hunters see a natural progression in hunting that culminates in fox hunting. This final stage, with its nonconsumptive associations and empathy for the fox, is achieved by a few. An elderly fox hunter told me:

It's the nature of man. A young man has to prove things to hisself, and after he proves it to him, then he moves on to something else. I used to tail them, you know, catch them and hunt most everything. But this hunting sort of peaks when you get on this fox hunting thing cause its something you can enjoy on two walking sticks. If you're young, you can see which one's the fastest, you or the dogs or the fox and try and outsmart them. Now I still like to outsmart them, the hounds and the fox, and try and see the fox while driving my pickup truck. I'll drive like a fool just to outfigure which way the fox will go, just to see the fox. I still love to catch them and for the hounds to take them, you know, but I'll be just as happy if I see him sitting up there in the tree or he goes into the ground.

16. The red fox apparently was introduced into the New World in a number of places and at various times. 'O,' "The Red Fox," *American Turf Register and Sporting Magazine* 1 (October 1829):74–75. For an early account of its appearance and spread in

Virginia, see 'P,' "The Red Fox," *American Turf Register and Sporting Magazine* 1 (December 1829):197–99.

17. For a discussion of the ascribed differences between the two species of foxes, see Hufford, "The Fox," pp. 164–72.

18. An inveterate field trialer, who purchased a few acres near the casting grounds in Scotland County, expressed his views on exclusion this way:

> Some of them might have called me selfish, but if I bring in a neighbor, the next thing I knowed when I went to trigger, they'd already been there. And so I won't ask nobody. I started it one time back yonder and had a few down, but now I don't ask nobody to come and I've been here a long time.
>
> If enough of them will come in here, then somebody better have a place for the association to go. For you can't rub it, rub it, rub it, and then a pile of us come in and rub it again. We gonna rub it out. You can't have a field trial without a lot of foxes.

19. Woods Walker mentions that the National Foxhunters' Association was organized in Waverly, Mississippi, in 1893; see *Walker Hounds*, pp. 5, 6. See also NFHA, "By-Laws, Running Rules and Regulations," 1978, p. 1.

20. NFHA, "By-Laws, Running Rules and Regulations," 1978, p. 3.

21. Although the NFHA began in an era when members rode to the hounds on horseback, the association has become a pastime mainly for hound owners. The time, cost, and skill one must invest in caring for hounds, horses, and horsepower (the current way of keeping abreast of the hounds) have taken their toll, for few individuals can keep up all three forms of identity and ego expression. While participation in the mounted tradition has declined over the years, the symbol remains a potent one for the association.

22. "One Gallus" refers to poor farmers who had only one suspender to keep up their trousers. Remember Sam in chapter 3? (p. 41)

23. In 1829 Don Juan's concern was "too much regard has been paid to speed, and dashing qualities; with too little respect to the *music that dwell upon the tongue* of the hound of 'olden times' " ("Fox Hounds," *American Turf Register and Sporting Magazine* 1 [November 1829]:127–28).

24. A reference to the hound boxes carried in the back of field trialers' trucks.

25. It is noteworthy that my informant left out the bench-show bunch as a distinctive group. Bench showers are a comparatively small but powerful group within the NFHA. A small clique held power for several years until my informant, in alliance with groups of field trialers, was elected president. He might have forgotten to mention bench showers, or blocked them out, since their earlier dominance was resented by the groups they had rebuffed.

26. Bench standards and rules are provided in the NFHA's "By-Laws, Running Rules and Regulations," 1978, pp. 47–51.

27. Hounds placing on the bench but not entering the field trials are listed as "Failed to Answer," and their names and those of their owners are not listed in *The Chase*. See NFHA, "By-Laws, Running Rules and Regulations," 1978, pp. 45–46.

28. Roles and rules for field-trial judges are stated in NFHA, "By-Laws, Running Rules and Regulations," 1978, pp. 20–25, 27–40.

29. Rules governing horse shows are given in NFHA, "By-Laws, Running Rules and Regulations," 1978, pp. 41–42.

30. This definition is from Munsche, *Gentlemen and Poachers*, p. 32.

31. Marshall Sahlins, *Culture and Practical Reason* (Chicago: University of Chicago Press, 1976), chapter 4.

32. NFHA, "By-Laws, Running Rules and Regulations," 1978, pp. 54–57, contains Chase Futurity Rules.

33. Howe, "Fox Hunting as Ritual," pp. 278–300.

34. Ibid., esp. pp. 291–93.

35. Michael Thompson illustrates the applicability of geometric expressions and catastrophe theory to anthropology; Michael Thompson, *Rubbish Theory: The Creation and Destruction of Value* (Oxford: Oxford University Press, 1979).

36. "Hill topping" isn't just found in the mountains. See Mary Hufford, "Foxhunting in the Pine Barrens," in *History, Culture and Archeology of the New Jersey Pine Barrens*, John Sinton, ed. (Pomona, N.J.: Stockton State College, 1982), pp. 222–34. See also David Lyne, "What Are They Saying? A Study of the Jargon of Hilltopping" (M.A. thesis, University of Kentucky at Bowling Green, 1976).

37. Marcel Mauss discusses "total social phenomena" in reference to the study of whole social systems and the importance certain rituals play when members take "emotional stock of themselves and their situation as regards others"; see *The Gift: Forms and Functions of Exchange in Archaic Societies* (Glencoe, Ill.: The Free Press, 1954).

Chapter Six
Horned Heads and Twitching Tails

1. Archibald Rutledge, "The Whitehorn Buck," in *Old Plantation Days*, pp. 46–59.

2. Robert Ruark, "Dixie Deer Hunt," *Saturday Evening Post* 219 (October 26, 1946):25.

3. Herds may become depleted of bucks, and the surviving bucks may not be of the best genetic stock. This problem is exacerbated when deer populations reach certain densities, and illnesses and disease occur in the absence of natural predation. A review of deer problems from the standpoint of the Wildlife Resources Commission's biologists is found in Tim Hergenrader and Curtis Wooten, "North Carolina Deer Roundup," *Wildlife in North Carolina* 42, no. 10 (October 1978):2–12.

4. "Deer hunting" is here used pejoratively, in opposition to "buck hunting," for those failing to discriminate between legal and illegal targets.

5. Deer season opened one month later on game-management lands than it did on private lands. For the difference in deer harvests caused by this later opening day, see table 6.2.

6. See "Ten Face Possible Conviction, Deer Hunting Brings Numerous Changes," *Laurinburg Exchange*, January 7, 1976, p. 2; "Fines, Sentences Given for Hunting Violations," *Laurinburg Exchange*, February 11, 1976; Mark Taylor, "Busting the Great Wildlife Conspiracy," *Wildlife in North Carolina* 42, no. 4 (April 1978):16–19; "Night Deer Hunting Arrests Reach All-Time High," *Laurinburg Exchange*, May 7, 1979; "Wildlife Violations," *Laurinburg Exchange*, August 29, 1979; "Night Deer Hunting Arrests Continue to Rise," *Wildlife in North Carolina* 44, no. 6 (June 1980):23; "Law's Long Arm Reaches Hunters," *Laurinburg Exchange*, December 10, 1980; "Firelighting Nears Seasonal Peak," *Wildlife Newsletter*, September 30, 1981, pp. 1–3.

7. James Fernandez, "The Mission of Metaphor in Expressive Culture," *Current Anthropology* 15, no. 2 (June 1974):119–45.

8. William Faulkner, "Delta Autumn," in *The Portable Faulkner*, 7th printing, Malcolm Cowley, ed. (New York: Viking Press, 1969), pp. 635–61.

9. According to Ruark's Old Man, "Women are natural-born preverse"; see Robert Ruark, *The Old Man and the Boy* (London: Hamish Hamilton, 1958), p. 259.

10. Money (time) in the household may be programmed as follows:

	"Domain of contestation"	
Wife's money	Husband's income	Husband's private fund
Money within household		Money outside household, not always present

11. Any surplus cash has to be spent in socially approved ways and follow strict rules of reciprocity. A situation similar to the one described here is among miners in the West Yorkshire coalfields. See Mary Douglas and Baron Isherwood, *The World of Goods: Towards an Anthropology of Consumption* (New York: W. W. Norton, 1982), pp. 167–70.

12. Robert Ruark's Old Man had made "a lifelong study of women, under all climatic conditions." For his conclusion, see Ruark, *The Old Man and the Boy*, p. 258.

13. For an analysis and description of the rise and fall of cultural boundaries in anthropology, see Thompson, *Rubbish Theory*. For a depiction of the creation and use of "tradition," see Eric Hobsbawn and Terance Ranger, eds., *The Invention of Tradition* (Cambridge, Eng.: Cambridge University Press, 1983).

14. Hergenrader and Wooten, "North Carolina Deer Roundup," pp. 2–12.

Chapter Seven
A Bird in Hand

1. John Charles McNeil was born in 1874 near what is now the Scotland County town of Wagram. He attended Wake Forest College and was granted a license to practice law. He opened law offices in Lumberton and later in Laurinburg. For McNeil, law was not an absorbing profession and he was often said to close his office to go fishing or to take a walk in the woods. In 1904 he joined the staff of the *Charlotte Observer*, providing him with the time to write poetry. He died in 1907 and is buried in the Old Spring Hill Cemetery in Scotland County. See Richard Walser and Mary Reynolds Peacock, *Young Readers' Picturebook of Tar Heel Authors* (Raleigh, N.C.: Department of Cultural Resources, 1981), p. 19.

2. Horace Lytle, *How to Win Field Trials* (New York: D. Van Nostrand Company, 1950), p. 134. H. F. Coleman, *The Amateur Sportsman: A Practical Treatise on the Art of Quail Shooting and the Training of the Dogs for Usefulness Afield* (Rogersville, Tenn.: Herald Book and Job Office, 1900), pp. 17–21, depicts the norms and terminology of a successful bird hunt at the turn of the century. Charlie Summerson ("Quail Hunting with a Tar Heel," *Sportsman's Digest*, March 1924, pp. 17, 93–94) hunted around Carthage. Virginius ("A Week in North Carolina," *Field and Stream*, August 1921, pp. 389–90) hunted along the Lumber River.

3. Paisley, *From Cotton to Quail*; William R. Brueckheimer, "The Quail Plantations of the Thomasville-Tallahassee-Albany Regions," in *Proceedings of the Tall Timbers Ecology and Management Conference* 16 (1979):141–65. For plantations

somewhat closer to Scotland County, see Charles F. Kovacik, "South Carolina Rice Coast Landscape Changes," in *Proceedings of the Tall Timbers Ecology and Management Conference* 16 (1979):47–65.

4. Pearson, *Adventures in Bird Protection*, pp. 105–107.

5. Alexander Hunter, *The Huntsman in the South*, vol. 1 (New York: Neale Publishing Co., 1908), p. 135.

6. Henry Wack writes of his exploits near Hamlin (Hamlet?) with a Southern gentleman from Maryland, who entertains his field friends, trains his dogs, plays a smart game of poker, and reminisces all winter on his 6,000-acre estate. Quail became a subtle advertisement for the South, attracting Northern men of means, who, when not pursuing quail, could pursue vast opportunities for their investments. See Henry Wellington Wack, "Bob White, 'Coon, and 'Possum," *Field and Stream*, February 1909, pp. 865–71; Arthur Frederick, "How I 'Made good'. A Tale of Rivalry on North Carolina Quail between a Local Champion and a 'Yankee' Who Could Shoot," *Field and Stream*, November 1906, pp. 659–61; Babcock, *Jaybirds Go to Hell*, chapters 11 and 13.

7. Ruark, *The Old Man and the Boy*, p.5.

8. Some quail-hunting tracts are full of paternalistic references to blacks. See, for example, Virginius, "A Week in North Carolina," pp. 389–90, and Ray P. Holland, *Scattergunning* (New York: Alfred A. Knopf, 1951), p. 14.

9. Ruark, *The Old Man and the Boy*, p. 170.

10. These insidious influences are chronicled in Babcock, *Jaybirds Go to Hell*.

11. Ibid., p. 115.

12. Havilah Babcock, *Tales of Quails 'n Such* (New York: Greenberg, 1961), pp. 123–29.

13. John D. Chalk, "What to Do about Quail," and L. E. Smith, "And Here's What Others Say," *The State* 5, no. 35 (January 29, 1938):1–3.

14. Rich Estes, "No Longer a Gentleman," *Wildlife in North Carolina* 44, no. 2 (December 1980):25–28. "Wildlife Agency Seeks to Stem Decline among Rabbits, Quail," *News and Observer*, Raleigh, N.C., February 24, 1985, p. 12B, and "NCSU Scientists Study Bob White Quail Decline," *News and Observer*, November 15, 1987, p. 14.

15. John Davis, "Dove Clubs: Recipe for Tradition," *South Carolina Wildlife* 28, no. 5 (September–October 1981):43–45.

16. Ruark, *The Old Man and the Boy*, p. 143.

17. "Hunters Beware," *Laurinburg Exchange*, August 31, 1979, p. 1; "Dove Season Opens for Area Hunters," *Laurinburg Exchange*, August 29, 1979, p. 12A; "Dove Hunting—Fields Are Full of Eager Hunters"; and "County's Dove Population in Good Shape," *Laurinburg Exchange*, September 12, 1979, pp. 1B, 11B.

18. The federal government has modified its regulations several times concerning what constitutes "baiting doves." Currently any normal agricultural practice is a legal way of providing food for doves and of attracting them. Recent changes allow the farmer to mow or cut his grain crops into the ground rather than to harvest them. However, once removed from a field, grain may not be redistributed legally to attract doves. See Fred Bonner, "Successful Dove Hunts Require Some Planning," *News and Observer*, August 31, 1986, p. 12B.

19. Cliff Turner, "Dove Hunting: Make a Mistake and Friends Will Swoosh Down," *News and Observer*, August 26, 1979, p. 12–II; Tom Higgins, "Dove Season's Open-

ing Day: Ah, Those 'Great' Memories!" *Charlotte Observer*, September 2, 1979, p. 13C.

20. Ruark, *The Old Man and the Boy*, p. 142.

21. During the 1979 dove season, the Scotland County Wildlife Protector was quoted as saying that in the previous hunting season, thirty-one North Carolina hunters "accidentally shot themselves, with seven dying as a result." None of these statistics occurred in Scotland County during that year, but it is significant that the article appeared near the opening of the dove season. See Coble, "Dove Hunting: Fields Are Full of Eager Hunters."

22. On One Southerner's acceptance through dove shooting, see Hodding Carter, *Southern Legacy* (Baton Rouge: Louisiana State University Press, 1950), p. 15.

Chapter Eight
Small Game for Large Numbers

1. Among the articles on squirrel and rabbit hunters in North Carolina, see: Frank B. Barick, "Hunting in North Carolina" (Raleigh, N.C.: North Carolina Wildlife Resources Commission, August 1973); Tom Higgins, "Rabbit Hunting Isn't Good in Good Weather," *Charlotte Observer*, February 29, 1976, p. 11C; idem, "Tales of a Rabbit Hunter," *Charlotte Observer*, January 2, 1977, pp. 1B, 10B; Ron Swain, "He's a Real Rabbit Hunter—and That's No Bull," *Durham Morning Herald*, November 25, 1979, p. 10B; Rick Estes, "A Trio of Bushytails," *Wildlife in North Carolina* 45 (September 1981):3–4. The differences between Raleigh bureaucrats and local hunters over regulations have a long history; see James Smith, "Should the Squirrel Season be Curtailed?" *Atlantic Sportsman* 1 (November 1931):3.

Habitat improvements for quail often help rabbits as well. Biologists have become aware only recently of the connection between the decline of small farms and small game populations throughout the state. Many erstwhile hunters of small game have subsequently taken after deer, which have become the most popular target of hunters in North Carolina. See Mark Taylor, "Future for Small Game," *Wildlife in North Carolina* 44 (November 1980):10–14; Terry Shankle, "Bonus Bushytails," *Wildlife in North Carolina* 50 (October 1986):4–7; North Carolina Wildlife Resources Commission, Special Report, *Friend of Wildlife* 34 (December 1987):6; Terry Sharpe, "Small Game as a Crop," *Wildlife in North Carolina* 52 (December 1988):16–21.

2. These initial lessons are from Ruark, "A Walk in the Woods," in *The Old Man and the Boy*, pp. 15–18. Other references to this volume are given as they occur in the text.

3. Ibid., p. 16.

4. Ibid., pp. 16–17.

5. Ibid., p. 17.

6. Ibid., p. 105. With rabbits and quail encountered in similar habitats, exhibiting similar histories of booms and busts in their population cycles, and with new genetic strains introduced into local populations by state game agencies, the Old Man was fighting simultaneously to maintain cultural, biological, and environmental boundaries. Whereas changes in quail were visible very early (viz. Alexander Hunter), changes in rabbits have become noticeable only more recently. See, for example, Taylor, "Future for Small Game"; Carl Betsill, "Are We Hunting a New Breed of Bunny?" *Wildlife in North Carolina* 49 (August 1985):10–14.

7. For more local wisdom on bagging squirrels, see "Squirrel, Wet Leaves Give Hunter the Slip," *Laurinburg Exchange*, November 15, 1976, p. 6.

8. The reference is to aerial applications of pesticides, a practice on which most of the county's agribusinesses depended during the 1970s and 1980s.

9. Most game enters the pot, but not necessarily that of its slayer. Ruark, *The Old Man and the Boy*, pp. 153–59.

10. Eviatar Zerubavel, *Hidden Rhythms: Schedules and Calendars in Social Life* (Chicago: University of Chicago Press, 1981). See also Emile Durkheim, *The Division of Labor in Society*, George Simpson, trans. (New York: Free Press, 1964 [1893]).

11. Ruark, *The Old Man and the Boy*, p. 149.

12. Ibid., p. 151.

Chapter Nine
Up a Tree

1. For the association between blacks and coons and possums, see chapter 2. Also see: F. A. Olds, "A Christmas Morning" and "A North Carolina 'Possum Hunt," *Outing* 35 (1899):383–84, 36 (1900):32–35; Hunter, *The Huntsman in the South*, chapter 2; Henry Wellington Wach, "Bob White, 'Coon and 'Possum with Something about the Beautiful Carolina Country Where the Sportsman Can Find All Three," *Field And Stream*, February 1909, pp. 865–71; James Smith, " 'Possum Hunting as Is," *Atlantic Sportsman* 1, no. 7 (March 1932):87, 88, 90. In the rural South, the possum is considered a lower-status creature than the coon, as seen in the following stanzas from a poem by Scotland County's own John Charles McNeill.

The Possum and the Coon

Ef yuh has seed de possum, boss,
    Yuh sho' won't trust 'im far:
He looks es gentle es Sister Sal
    When de pahson's a-leadin' in pra'r:
En all of er sudden he's up en turnt
    (When yuh's totin' 'im desso)
En fastened 'is jaws to de calf er yo' leg—
    Den, Sadie, bar de do'!
    Den, Sadie, bar de do', my gal!
    O Sadie, bar de do'!

'S fer me, I'd rather hab de coon,
    'Ca'se he's jis wut he is:
He don't hab no dog nosin' his ribs
    Whilst he lay still, lik dis;
But all de time, lak Sister Sal
    When de preachin' is over en gone,
He's es sassy en mean es a hongry cur
    A-gwineter bury his bone.

From John Charles McNeill, *Possums and Persimmons* (Wendell, N.C.: Broadfoot's Bookmark, 1977), p. 30.

2. Coon hunters, including the United Kennel Club, Inc., Official Nite Hunt Honor Rules, spell "night" as "nite." I have retained that spelling throughout this chapter. Befitting their lower social standing, coon hunts did not feature prominently in the local or regional press. A few references are Tom Higgins, "On Track of 'Treeing' Title," *Charlotte Observer*, December 3, 1972, p. 14C; idem, "Johnson Takes Pride in His Coon Dogs," *Charlotte Observer*, October 5, 1975, p. 13F; Joe Holley, "A 'City Boy' Discovers Coon Hunting," *Charlotte Observer*, March 13, 1977, p. 15D; David Zucchino, "Bluetick Days," *News and Observer*, September 25, 1977, pp. 1, 2; "Gibson Coon Hunter—Blackwell's Blue Ticks Keep Him Up All Night," *Laurinburg Exchange*, April 25, 1984, p. 9A.

3. The *Laurinburg Exchange* featured a picture of a black standing behind an albino raccoon, which he had captured and mounted. The ironic caption under the photograph discloses that "the raccoon died of a broken neck when Davis cut down a tree he was hiding in. Davis said he was trying to capture the raccoon, not kill it. At first, Davis said, he didn't know what it was. A game warden told him he'd found an albino raccoon. The animal, which has white fur highlighted with an orange tint, has been preserved and mounted." Such raccoons are rare. See *Laurinburg Exchange*, April 6, 1984, p. 5A.

4. There are relatively few sporting books on coon dogs and coon hunting. On coon-hunting competitions and breeds of dogs, see Oliver Hartley, *Hunting Dogs* (Columbus, Ohio: A. R. Harding, 1909); Leon F. Whitney and A. B. Underwood, *The Coon Hunter's Handbook* (New York: Henry Holt, 1952).

5. A hunting judge is one who judges and runs a dog in the same cast.

6. Ruark, *The Old Man and the Boy*, p. 253.

Chapter Ten
Fowl Play

1. For the beginnings of this understanding see Thomas, *Man and the Natural World*; Ritvo, *The Animal Estate*; and Thomas R. Dunlap, *Saving America's Wildlife* (Princeton, N.J.: Princeton University Press, 1988).

2. For example, the new sources of value for wild species in transforming human values proposed by Bryan G. Norton, *Why Preserve Natural Variety?* (Princeton, N.J.: Princeton University Press, 1987).

3. Sahlins, *Culture and Practical Reason*, especially chapter 4.

4. For cultural goods as symbols of self and community, see Czikszentmihalyi and Rochberg-Halton, *The Meaning of Things*. The rapprochement between history and anthropology is a rather recent one. For example, see Dening, *Islands and Beaches*; Sahlins, *Islands of History*. It is also new to combine perspectives from economics and anthropology. For examples, Douglas and Isherwood, *The World of Goods*; and Appadurai, *The Social Life of Things*.

5. Lillian Hellman, *The Little Foxes* and *Another Part of the Forest* (New York: Viking Press, 1966).

Index